STUDIES IN PUBLIC COMMUNICATION

KEEPING THE FLAME

Media and Government in Latin America

STUDIES IN PUBLIC COMMUNICATION

KEEPING

THE FLAME

Media and Government in Latin America

by

ROBERT N. PIERCE

University of Florida

with the collaboration of
John Spicer Nichols
Pennsylvania State University

COMMUNICATION ARTS BOOKS

Hastings House, Publishers · New York 10016

For Guido Fernández, Robert Cox,
Enrique Zileri, the Mesquita family,
the late Alberto Gainza Paz, Julio
Scherer García and all the others who
have kept the flame.

Library of Congress Cataloging in Publication Data

Pierce, Robert N
    Keeping the flame.

    (Studies in public communication) (Communication
arts books)
    Includes bibliographical references and index.
    1. Mass media policy—Latin America.　I. Nichols,
John Spicer.　II. Title.
P95.82.L29P5　　　301.16′1　　　79-16775
ISBN 0-8038-3950-2
ISBN 0-8038-3951-0 pbk

Published simultaneously in Canada by Copp Clark, Ltd.
Printed in the United States of America
Designed by Al Lichtenberg

CONTENTS

PREFACE

THE HAITIAN DIPLOMAT and his North American guest were picking their way through one of the seedier areas of downtown Port-au-Prince, hurrying to a business engagement. Throngs of poor people milled on the broken sidewalks and streets, their clothes and status setting them off from the elegantly dressed diplomat, his bearing molded by a classical education and years of service in the world's sophisticated capitals.

Abruptly the two men came upon a huge pile of rotting, reeking garbage in the street; it obviously had been there a long time. The diplomat, without once commenting or glancing at the pile, drew out a snowy handkerchief and clapped it to his nose. He sailed past the garbage as if it did not exist. The visitor glared poisonously at it, carefully sidestepped it, mused on who was responsible and calculated what should be done to get rid of it.

Although Haiti is Latin America's poorest country and most of the streets in the region are clean enough, the two men's different reactions symbolize the relationship between Latin America and the European-North American cultural region. Both have garbage problems and the smell is offensive to both, but the two cope with it in different ways, both as communities and individuals. To the North American visitor, muffling his nose would have been cowardly; to the Haitian diplomat, it was a rational expedient. Nothing he could do had any relevance to garbage collection, so why should he carry on about it?

The North American, facing a similar problem at home, would demand action from the mayor, badger the local editor to print a picture, organize neighborhood action—in short, make himself miserable until the problem were overcome. The Haitian knew these options were not open to him, and he could avoid the misery besides.

So careful analysis reveals both men's actions as part of a larger complex. This book is written in hope that such analysis will help everyone, perhaps even Latin Americans, understand why the region's mass media are so similar to but so different from those in the rest of the Western world.

Why should such an understanding be important?

The writer does not intend to justify this work on either of two grounds which have been *de rigueur* for all books dealing with Latin America in recent years. The first of these is the "sky-is-falling" appeal. Quite fashionable in the decade following Fidel Castro's victory in Cuba, this argument held out the possibility that leftist revolution might result in isolating the United States as the only capitalist country in this hemisphere, except for a somewhat unreliable Canada. Of course, it didn't happen, and the authors of all the alarmist books scarcely can take the credit.

Nor is the second rationale offered. This is the cry that "the silence is ominous." Ever since Castro's attempts to interfere in the rest of Latin America turned sour, the only substantial fears of damage to United States interests by Latin Americans have concerned the price of coffee and sabotage of the Panama Canal. This scare tactic is more useful than the other, because silence can remain ominous indefinitely.

This book does not rest on these bases because it is not written for United States citizens alone; thus it would be in bad grace to speak to only part of the audience. Furthermore, a book which offers a cork to plug the leak of the moment would be valuable a very short time, and it is hoped that this book gives some insights that may have some lasting utility.

Rather, it is proposed that anyone who pretends to being educated ought to know about all the forces at work on the minds of nearly one-tenth of the world's population, occupying an eighth of its land area. We also should understand the governments of these people—something the rest of the world talks about frequently but with vast ignorance. To get this understanding, one must look at how the governors and the governed tell each other their desires—the glue that holds all governments together. Oddly enough, even scholars specializing in Latin American government often ignore the need to study mass communication, like deaf persons offering themselves as music critics.

If more practical reasons are sought, one should look at the economic possibilities. That is what the phalanxes of Japanese and German salesmen jamming the region's airports are doing. Despite the vastness of poverty still to be found, the region has generally been making economic progress since the mid-1960s. This portends not only the world's most underdeveloped market for consumer goods but also potential competition from Latin American producers selling elsewhere in the world. Their capacity as suppliers of manufactured goods, foodstuffs and mineral products has by no means reached its limit.

PURPOSES

Since no one previously has published a book on these subjects, its readers have no precedent to tell them what to expect. Some guidelines which the author imposed on himself are these:

1. The primary goal was to isolate traits of the media-government relationship which seemed to have some permanence, either in individual countries or in Latin America as a whole or in both. Events are cited only as evidence of these traits, and no pretense at a complete chronology—particularly before the

1970s—is made. Some highly newsworthy events are given short shrift because the author felt they were mostly of passing interest; on the other hand, some episodes such as a proposed law which did not pass are emphasized because they illuminate some deep-running characteristic.

Thus, those who seek either a conventional history or a highly topical work will be disappointed.

2. Working with a highly controversial subject, the author tried earnestly to be dispassionate. True believers of various camps will find much to be hostile toward. The only relevant biases to which the author admits are predilections for honesty in what is uttered publicly, for professionalism in journalism and against brutality and waste of human resources. Enemies of these ideals can be found on the left and the right, in government and in the media.

Furthermore, the author has not subscribed to that most pernicious of journalistic myths—that giving "both sides" is the way to the truth. If the two sides being heard in a dispute happen to be putting out nonsense, then truth is poorly served by perpetuating this nonsense. Anyone who would make an honest attempt at inductive logic is obligated to seek *all* the relevant evidence—not just that evidence offered by the most vocal combatants; to examine that evidence with the greatest possible intelligence and impartiality; to select the valid evidence from among the spurious; and to fit the valid evidence together into simple but meaningful statements. This is what is attempted here, with the full realization that others may do it differently.

3. Conceding the use of jargon peculiar to some group—journalists, political scientists, communication specialists, etc.—is the quickest way to win superficial acceptance in that circle, the author has rejected this approach. Much of the background study for this work was in such cloistered areas, but the guiding concept here is that plain language is not necessarily obscene.

4. Comparative analysis is the main objective. This comparison operates on two dimensions—within the Latin American area and between this region and the rest of the Western world.

"Latin America" is defined here as the 20 independent nations of the Western Hemisphere which have been molded primarily by the Latin cultural traditions of Europe. This includes all the land mass between the Rio Grande of the North and Tierra del Fuego, except for the Guianas and Belize. Also included are the Caribbean nations of Cuba, Dominican Republic and Haiti. I fully realize that other political units in the Caribbean basin—even Puerto Rico—are rapidly building links with Latin America, but the time does not seem ripe to lump them together.

Working within this 20-nation community, I have sought to isolate some characteristics widely found throughout the region, while taking account of variations among the countries and even within each one. Aware of such a set of patterns, the observer can understand future events not as freakish accidents but rather as expectable outgrowths of the Latin American dynamics. This is not intended to denigrate those heroic individuals who struggle against the gags which others would put on them; in fact, it is hoped that a better understanding of the forces arrayed against them will make their task less painful. They are the true agents of change—the hardy souls who drag boulders into the river to divert its course.

METHOD OF ANALYSIS

Preparation for this book has been more or less continuous since, at the age of eight, I was taken on a trip to Mexico in 1940. Since then I have accumulated many file drawers and bookshelves filled with notes, documents, books, magazines and newspapers from or about Latin America. The early avocation has turned into a professional commitment, pursued through the doctoral level of academic studies and in numerous visits to the region, extending to all 20 countries.

The present analysis thus began with my own survey of relevant background material in history, political science, economics, sociology, literature and anthropology, in addition to the scattering of available communication studies. The next step was to form a model of communication not only as a set of commercial companies, as a recorder of events or as a platform for political protest, but rather as an institution which is both the cause and the effect of what occurs in all the other institutions of society—government, commerce, schools, church, arts, entertainment, etc.

Ideally, to understand the mass media one would define all these linkages, and this is what I set out to do. However, dealing with the media-government relations proved to be so extensive a task I decided to concentrate on them, with hopes of making the matrix more complete in later studies. I fully confess that this one-dimensional view is by no means a complete sculpture.

Basically the three procedures most relied upon in gathering data were (1) to develop a set of categories or a typology of media-government relations, (2) to determine the extent to which phenomena in each country fell into each of these categories, and (3) to observe these phenomena over a decade or more—actually, in the retrospect of all recorded history—so as to discover their tendencies, whether rising, falling or stable.

These kinds of data were gathered in all 20 countries, with the assistance of Dr. John S. Nichols for Cuba. However, in the effort to reduce a mountain of data to surmountable heaps, it was found that only those countries whose experience was most distinctive could be fitted into separate chapters because of space limitations. These happened to be the larger countries, plus one of the smaller ones, Costa Rica. I assure all those kind and learned informants who helped me in the other countries that their evidence was carefully considered in the writing of the summary chapters.

Sources for the data included interviews, articles, news reports, books, documents, observation and content analysis of the media. Interviews, now numbering nearly a thousand, were mostly of the structured type, with respondents answering the same questions as everyone else, even though random input was allowed for. The purpose in this was not only to look for a consensus on a topic, but also to check for inaccuracies in factual assertions. Even a source's testimony about his own work was not fully accepted without enough confirmation.

Interview subjects were persons such as publishers, editors, reporters, correspondents in foreign and domestic bureaus, advertising executives, distributors, academic specialists, commercial researchers, and government officials, including foreign diplomats. Personnel of all types of media, from newspapers to billboards, were included, and they ranged from general-audience to specialized and protest functions. Although the major efforts were made in the largest cities, care was taken to extend the study to interior locations as well. Any relevant subgroups of professionals such as women and racial minorities also were checked. Beyond all these, I spent considerable time in gathering evidence from the most important link in the process—the consumer of media material; this material was drawn from field surveys done by others and from interviews of my own.

Articles and books used consisted of publications issued in the United States, Latin America and, to some extent, Europe. Aside from my own reading and use of printed bibliographies, these were located through a variety of computerized abstracting services. Documents mostly were gathered at the source, such as government agencies and private research operations.

All news reports dealing with Latin American media dating back to approximately 1970 have been copied from 10 U.S., British and French newspapers, plus incomplete files before then. Utilization of *Information Services on Latin America* has helped in this greatly. In addition, I have scanned and done content analysis on many Latin American newspapers over the last decade.

Observation, that favorite tool of the anthropologist, also has been valuable. Thanks to generous hosts in my visits to media, I have seen the inner operations of countless places of work. I have learned to look past the gleam of the presses and note more telling things such as bulletin boards, working conditions and the attitudes of workers.

The book consists of two parts. The first includes seven chapters examining specific countries (the last one combining three democratic countries). The casual reader may confine himself to one or more of these because of some special interest. This would be regrettable, because the first part is raw material for the second, which summarizes the previous evidence and analyzes it in a way which I hope will be of long-term usefulness, whereas Part One will become outdated. Chapter 8 and 9 are companion units which present forms of analysis somewhat similar to conventional types, whereas Chapter 10 is a type not done before.

ACKNOWLEDGMENTS

In gathering material for this book, I have on the whole been accorded generosity and cooperation which is truly humbling. The prototype of all the persons who have helped me would be one who has diverted hours from a busy day answering my questions, plying me with cups of coffee and handfuls of valuable documents, perhaps inviting me to lunch afterward and driving me to my next appointment. Later I would receive further material from him by mail, at staggering postage rates. Since I usually have been treated this way while I was still a stranger who merited suspicion, I must conclude that my hosts were motivated not only by hospitability but also by a concern that vital truths be known. I fervently hope this book at least partially justifies their confidence in me.

The above is particularly true of persons in Latin America. In certain knowledge that I would commit inexcusable omissions if I tried to list all, I shall name none, except for those who assisted directly with comments about material in the book. These are Guido Fernández, Robert Cox, Ruy P. Barbosa, Charles H. Green, Pedro Penzini, Antonio Pimenta Neves, June Erlick, Alejandro Miró Quesada and Terry L. McCoy.

Among those in the United States for whose assistance I am particularly grateful are Dean Ralph L. Lowenstein for support and encouragement, to the University of Florida for a sabbatical leave, to Ray Jones and to the Staff of the Latin American Collection at the University of Florida libraries, to the University of Florida Center for Latin American Studies for clerical assistance, to the U.S. Department of State and the Office of Education for two Fulbright-Hays grants, to Sofia Kohli for manuscript help, and to Orville L. Freeman for helping to make possible the research on Cuba done by my collaborator, John S. Nichols. And, getting to basics, I want to thank Raymond B. Nixon, Roy E. Carter, Jr., Robert L. Jones, DeWitt C. Reddick and L. W. Plunkett for my academic groundwork.

ROBERT N. PIERCE
Gainesville, Florida

FOREWORD

DOCUMENTARY film writers almost invariably reach into their worn bag of clichés when describing a city, country or continent that they are too ethnocentric or stupid to understand. "A land (city, country, etc.), of contradictions," they say, as they begin juxtaposing newsreel shots of slums against mansions, starving beggars against fat industrialists, oxcarts against Concordes.

Contradiction and its ironies are, however, all conditions of civilization. We are as likely to find them in remote near-feudal principalities hidden in the foothills of the Himalayas as in Los Angeles, California.

Students of revolution like Hannah Arendt and Chalmers Johnson seem to posit a sort of tensile strength that measures the number and nature of contradictions that a stable society can withstand. Beyond this or that intensity of stress, the state's cohesiveness is destroyed, and one of many types of revolution or rebellion is the result. For many reasons, we cannot be certain whether or not this process is inevitable (as Marxists claim), mainly because we always define intolerable contradiction as a major cause of revolution. We end up, therefore, in a cloud of cause-effect redundancy.

Certain cultures in history have achieved to our eyes considerable stability for long periods of time despite what appear to be intolerable societal contradictions in matters of economy, politics, ethics and moral life-styles. The cohesive social strand apparently snaps in various times and places at different cultural temperatures, depending, I suppose, mostly upon national temperament (whatever *that* is) and tradition as much as anything else.

Conventional wisdom has limned a picture of Latin America as a vast, relatively homogeneous territory that suffers from socio-political high blood pressure. In the United States, we have come to think of our southern neighbors as comprising highly volatile publics, forever in ferment, on the brink of revolution and/or alternating between political styles of excess, either on the authoritarian or libertarian ends of the political spectrum, not too scrupulously avoiding moderation. At the same time, Spanish traditions of aristocracy and privilege, as well as peonage, continue along unchanged as they have for centuries.

If power is measured by the scratches it makes on the minds of men and women, it is the Catholic Church that remains in Latin America the dominant psychological institution—a force that, on one hand, contradicts the indigenous urge towards radicalisms *both* of the right and left, just as it, on the other, enforces sexual and family ideals that result in gluts of population and exacerbates starvation and poverty. And, from the multitudes of children (the continent's most fertile crop) gathered in the *barrios,* one hears the rumble of further contradiction and mumbled threats of future revolutions, when today's younsters grow old enough to be tomorrow's guerrillas.

The chief rabbi of one of the more "progressive" Latin American nations was a guest at my office not long ago, a stop on his way to Rome for an audience with the new Pope, not so curious a curiosity, either then or now. "We are saved," he said of his adopted country (having been born in Europe and raised in the United States), "by our talent for identifying and rewarding the mediocre. Mediocrity in all things prevents us from destroying an unbelievably delicate economy and social fabric. And the mediocrity of our radio, newspapers and television remains the great insular force that prevents us from facing up to how mediocre the best we have to offer really is." (I squelched the desire to comment on the mass media in the United States!)

"We have achieved something like freedom and democracy, I suppose," he continued. "But, because one is free, one does not necessarily choose excellence when one has other choices. In my country, we choose the type of classical incompetence that we are used to—that will disturb us and frighten us least."

For good reason, I suddenly recalled William Randolph Hearst's avid —almost hysterical—support of the Spanish American War and his sincere conviction that Cuba's rebellion against Spain was an authentic reprise of the North American Spirit of '76. True, he also knew that a war sells newspapers, but his major conviction (and I think that of Joseph Pulitzer, too) was that our hemisphere was witnessing the repetition on a Caribbean island of a groundswell of political idealism identical with that experienced by America's thirteen British colonies more than one hundred years before.

Hearst was wrong! Cuba achieved her independence and a lot more besides, all of which was uniquely Latin American and set firmly in the matrix of twentieth century politics and commerce: North American economic imperialism largely centered on sugar, rum and cigars, an intransigent United States naval base, various abusive dictatorships of the right and a still-to-be-tested experiment in Russo-Communism, salted along the way with obnoxious American tourists, the world's raunchiest live pornographic theatre (so they say) and Ernest Hemingway. Neither a Jefferson nor a Madison nor even a Hamilton was waiting to pick up from Spain the strands of her destiny. Cuba was independent, as many Latin American nations are or were, to face what are to date the seemingly insoluble problems of so-called "underdeveloped nations" suddenly hurled into an age of mass technology, all the worse because of a strategic military vulnerability which has increased as years have passed.

The mistake Hearst made was much the same mistake we all make when we look at "the other America" and try to find reflections of our own growth and culture in her manifold experiences. Too many of us admire uncritically Santayana's encomium to historical studies and forget for practical purposes the wisdom of Hegel's equally trenchant warning that history only teaches us that history teaches us nothing. The history of the United States during the seventeenth and eighteenth centuries teaches us, I am afraid, *almost* nothing about the history of Latin America in the twentieth, whether we like it or not.

I started to read the original manuscript of Professor Pierce's *Keeping the Flame* too much in the spirit of William Randolph Hearst (or Santayana or, for that matter, Henry Luce) and not enough in the spirit of Hegel! What I ultimately received from it was, first, a new respect and deeper understandings of the way that the inquiring spirit of the social sciences is able to clarify immensely complex issues relating to how the information conduits of nations are involved in their social, economic and political processes.

Second, I gained a better understanding of how and why facile, simplistic interpretations of matters like "press freedom," when directed at countries like Latin American nations, are not only foolhardy but potentially dangerous. Indeed, there exists a "flame" to be "kept" where and whenever men and women undertake to enlighten others by journalistic enterprises. But the way in which press freedom is won, nurtured and sustained poses complex problems that resonate within all the organ pipes of culture, creating a melody different each time it is played and everywhere it is heard—if I may mix my own metaphor with Professor Pierce's.

Third, I felt that at all costs the manuscript should be published, so that its fascinating and, at times, frightening stories might become part of our own free literary record in the United States.

Whether *Keeping the Flame* justifies the inductive-empirical scientific aspirations of its author, more knowledgeable readers than I am will have to judge as time rolls on. Professor Pierce's observations and analyses are obviously and sometimes painfully honest, always correctly suspicious, as he has noted, of the comic gods of "objectivity," who, when all is said and done, may eventually turn out to be our most destructive current enemies both of the art of journalism and the science of social investigation. For all his methodological restraint and austerity, Professor Pierce has, to my eyes, given us a powerful and at times chillingly realistic insight into the two dozen nations to our south whose futures, I think, will be more closely related to the short and long term destiny of the United States than their pasts.

Alienated as we have been in the past from our hemispheric neighbors by languages, traditions, religions, the manipulations of commerce, the caprices of politics and the frightfulness of revolutions—to say nothing of the CIA's peculiar implementations of what various diplomats and bureaucrats have regarded as foreign policy imperatives—I fail to see how *Keeping the Flame* in the hands of the right readers can accomplish anything less than two vital ends: It will, I hope, help journalists and journalism students to quiet their insistent and dangerous professional enemy—parochialism. It will also, I think, clarify many of the snap misjudgments into which we have been led about political and intellectual life in the "banana republics" and "emerging nations" that share

this part of the globe with us as well as our common (and misleading) nickname "America."

In truth, of course, the United States of America, as Daniel Boorstin has
recently pointed out, *has no name*. The multitude of countries to our south *all*
do. The careful reader will certainly find an explanation for this often ignored
enigma, if he or she gives *Keeping the Flame* a complete and sensitive reading.

GEORGE N. GORDON
Muhlenberg and Cedar Crest Colleges

PART ONE

CASE STUDIES

CHAPTER 1

The Argentine Way

A FAVORITE JOKE among the hemisphere's diplomats is that, at meetings of Latin American national representatives, the Argentine delegates feel like teenagers at a children's party.

Observers may not agree on the exact nature of the differences, but most will agree that Argentina is different. It shares many qualities with its neighbors, but just as its wine, steaks and clothing are different so do its communication institutions have some distinctive traits.

As in so many Latin American countries, the worldwide recession of the 1930s put an end to the flirtation with reformist democracy in Argentina, where it had lasted only 14 years, even though the elected conservative governments had not been overthrown since the 1853 constitution took effect. In the 46 years after the democratic period, the presidency changed hands 21 times, often in periods as short as 48 hours.

Although freely elected presidents' terms interlaced with periods of military usurpation and accounted for about half of the time span, these labels meant little for the stability of free expression. Gen. Juan Perón, who served longer legitimately than anyone else, clearly did the most to reduce the media's independence, trampling constitutional norms through his demagogic control of congress.

For mass media that had grown rich and cocksure in the country's eight decades of constitutional security, the worst effect of the post-1930 period was that editors lost any ability to predict what the next day would bring for them. One by one, new ways to control and manipulate the media were devised by governments and political factions.

True, one government's repressive measures might be dismantled by its successor, but the controls had an uncanny way of recurring, once introduced. Editors learned the wearying pattern: The new president would forswear all press restrictions of his predecessor; then, when the press took him seriously

3

and spoke out, the old weapons and some new ones would be brought to bear.

Even more agonizing, Argentina's endemic terrorism led it into a true civil war in the 1970s, and this meant that the media faced pressures and threats not only from the governmental authorities operating openly but also from various guerrilla forces and even from competing factions within the government.

What also distinguishes the Argentine media experience is that the controls there have never been sweeping and draconian, as in Chile, Peru and other countries where democracy has faded. No president—not even Perón—has aspired to total thought control, and only part of the media have suffered at any one time. This may explain why a strong, concerted defense of press freedom rarely if ever occurs in Argentina.

The controls then must be examined not as peculiar to each regime's period but rather as viruses that have entered the bloodstream of Argentine public life. There is little indication that they will be permanently eradicated.

TERROR AS A CONTROL

A listing of journalistic travails in the 1970s clearly shows that the most frequent ones did not come as a result of overt governmental action. They were the kinds of troubles that came out of the darkness of night, their identity masked, their motives confused. Sometimes the victims of their families guessed that they came from some insurgent group of the left or right; sometimes policemen or soldiers out of uniform were the phantoms; sometimes they were common criminals.

Furthermore, the violence struck with the caprice of lightning. Often the victims were not the enemies of the terrorists; they were chosen randomly to frighten all journalists or simply to prove the culprits' power.

Although kidnappings and shootings had happened before 1973, that year saw terrorism become a fixture in Argentina. Small, dedicated groups of extreme leftists who had supported Perón's return to power that year soon found themselves unwelcome in his regime; they decided to go underground and harass it. This sparked the upsurge of a rival group of rightists called the Argentine Anti-Communist Alliance (AAA).

As one journalist who lived through the early days wrote:

> Apparently, the mechanism which they use is simple, but terribly effective. There exists a precise game of reprisals according to which the victims in one band must be avenged by liquidating at least as many in the opposite band. And the operation is carried out with the same criterion with which hostages are chosen in open warfare; that is, practically no one is exempt from involuntarily taking part in the game.[1]*

Clarin's Dilemma

No case could have illustrated the media's dilemma better than one of the earliest cases of terrorism. It involved *Clarín,* a successful middle-class tabloid without strong political pretensions.

---

* Reference notes are in a separate section at the end of this book, arranged chapter by chapter.

In September 1973, four months after his stand-in had become president, Perón was preparing for his own election to that post. The Peronist government had already barred media from disseminating the messages of underground groups, even if paid or intimidated.

A *Clarín* executive was kidnapped on Sunday, September 9, by the country's most militant guerrilla group, the People's Revolutionary Army (ERP). Within hours the newspaper had received a letter from ERP enclosing orders for political advertisements to occupy half the front page and all of two inside pages. Publish them to get back the kidnap victim, the letter said; it apologized for not paying for the space but noted that that had been outlawed.

In tight secrecy to prevent the police from stopping the publication, *Clarín* ran the ads Tuesday morning, and the executive was quickly released. He called a press conference to tell of his captivity, and at that moment, in broad daylight, right-wingers infuriated by the paper's deal with ERP raided the *Clarín* plant. Shouting "Where is the ERP, where are the famous revolutionaries?" the 30-odd attackers sprayed the entrance hall with submachinegun fire, wounding two persons, one of them a 10-year-old girl. They set furniture afire, bombed equipment and beat up personnel.

Although sympathy for *Clarín* and outrage against the terrorists came from many quarters, the government threatened to take court action against any journalistic medium that let it happen again. Perón said *Clarín* should have reported the ERP demand to the police, and he shrugged off the rightists' attack on *Clarín* by saying, "Those who act wrongly often are later hit by their own acts."[2]

Violent Attacks

Before the year was out, journalists had learned two forms of terrorism that became standard—bombing raids on offices and personal attacks on individual newsmen.

In one day, local newspaper offices in Rosario and Mar del Plata, major cities 400 miles apart, were struck. The three raiders in Mar del Plata threatened the workers and set afire the printing area, causing $100,000 damage. In Rosario, the bomb was secretly planted and caused minor damage.[3]

Only four days later, a political and labor news reporter for a daily in San Nicolás near Buenos Aires, José Domingo Colombo, became the first victim in a series of individual attacks. Colombo's editor had received threats from an extreme right-wing Peronist youth group that unless he got rid of "leftwingers, communists and Trotskyites" on the staff, the group would do it for him. Leaflets with the same message were thrown outside the newspaper office, raising workers' fears, but the editor ignored them.

Then, as the staff was busy putting out an edition, two gunmen invaded the office. One marched over to Colombo at his desk and killed him with a shotgun while the second attacker held off the other journalists.[4]

Another notable incident involved Jorge Money, the 29-year-old financial writer for *La Opinión,* an intellectually-oriented newspaper that tended toward mild leftism. He disappeared in May 1975, and a few days later his corpse, riddled with bullets, was found in an area favored by rightist guerrillas for dumping victims' bodies. As usual, friends searched their memories for something that would explain the atrocity; they could remember that Money had briefly been affiliated with a tiny political group years before.[5]

Common criminals have learned to imitate the political terrorists, and it often is difficult to tell which type committed any given atrocity. This intermingling brought repeated tragedy to one newspaper family in the case of the two David Kraiselburds. One of them was the 62-year-old publisher of a provincial daily in La Plata, 35 miles from Buenos Aires; he was a respected leader in national and international press groups but had little political role. Leftist guerrillas kidnapped him, then apparently executed him when besieged by police; they had shot him through his hands shielding his face.[6]

The publisher's son, Raul, took his wife to the United States where they had a baby, but they decided to return. Shortly afterward, the baby, also named David, was kidnapped from the family home. Following a year of uncertainty over ransom demands and over whether the crime was political, five suspects were arrested, including the family bodyguard. They confessed to killing the child just after the kidnapping. Police then announced that four of them were killed trying to escape from jail.[7]

At any given time, the typical Argentine newsman knows that one or two of his colleagues may be in the hands of kidnappers and that he might just as well be the next victim. If he is in doubt, he may get a threatening note. Then he may join the score or more of journalists who fled the country in the year after Perón's return to power in 1953, or he may stay and learn to avoid writing anything offensive. Usually it takes only one note to send foreign correspondents flying home.[8]

This happened in the case of correspondents for *The Times* of London and Paris' *Le Monde,* along with two Bolivian reporters. The *Times* correspondent said three men carrying police-type submachine guns forced him into their car, questioned him, said they didn't like what he was writing and ordered him to leave Argentina within two weeks or risk death.[9]

Perhaps no medium has had such persistent trouble as the strident leftist newspaper *El Mundo.* Its assaults from terrorists have been interlaced with problems with the government. In one two-month period in early 1974 its plant was bombed, police seized and burned an edition, the family of one of its editors was threatened with death, its offices were blasted by submachine gun fire from unidentified attackers, and a mob stormed the offices, after which police arrested 18 of the paper's employees.

Generally the two prestige newspapers of Argentina, *La Nación* and *La Prensa,* remained unscathed by the terrorism through the 1970s. Small bombs were left in doors, and once shots were fired through the window of Alberto Gainza Paz, the famous editor of *La Prensa.*[10] Terrorists seemed to prefer to strike at provincial branch offices, more secluded than the main offices in downtown Buenos Aires.[11]

Various scorekeepers have tried to keep running tallies of the attacks against the press, but in Argentina it is difficult to say who is a journalist, since most professionals hold several jobs. One list showed three journalists killed in 1974 and five in 1975.[12] Some of the pressure seemed to ease in July 1975, when José López Rega, President Isabel Perón's chief assistant, was forced to leave the country. An arrogant conservative, López Rega had infuriated the leftist guerrillas and served as a focal point for their violent protests. In turn, he was believed to be the major manipulator of the AAA, most feared of the rightist terror groups. With the two sides' deadly game slowing after his departure, there was less demand for journalists to serve as pawns.[13] This coincided somewhat with the abandon with which the press felt free to cover the Isabel Perón regime in its last months. However, the military takeover in March 1976, led to a resumption of left-right hostilities and thus to new perils for the media.

A sidelight to the political warfare was the anti-Semitism, never absent in Argentina and showing a slow but steady growth in the 1970s. Among various outrages against Jews were several involving the media. A rightist terror group was blamed for the firebombing of a set where a film about early Jewish immigrants to Argentina was being made.[14] A movie theater where the pro-Israeli film "Victory at Entebbe" was to be shown also was bombed, with heavy damage.[15]

Mainstream political leaders no longer endorse Naziism in public, but its gradual resurgence met with only fitful governmental measures against it. Usually, the inflammatory literature returns after the clampdown is forgotten.[16] The 1977 jailing of *La Opinión* director Jacobo Timerman, connected with the Graiver financial scandal and guerrilla funds, was seen by many to have anti-Semitic overtones.

A grisly reminder of the role news media have played in the Argentine civil war came when the body of honorary consul John P. Egan, murdered by leftists in Córdoba, was found on a country road. Laid upon it was a newspaper telling about the deaths of two guerrillas killed in a shootout with police.[17]

CLOSURE AND SUSPENSION

By far the most frequent official action taken against Argentine media in the 1970s was temporary closure or suspension. It took little effort on the part of the government—merely a closure order issued under some decree law vague enough to cover any need—and it preserved the appearance of legality, since the dispute usually was argued later in court. Most cases resulted in the eventual reappearance of the offending newspaper, either through action of a judge or simply the cooling of official tempers.

The stage was set for the closures of the 1970s when Juan Carlos Onganía, one of the military dictators who preceded the Perón election, shut down the country's best-known news magazine, *Primera Plana*. Its fatal offense was intelligent depth reporting of the kind that later distinguished the newspaper *La Opinión*, and the immediate cause of its closure was its revelations on a subject which always outrages uniformed presidents—feuding within the army's ranks.[18] The action against *Primera Plana* was the most severe press restriction since the first Perón regime, and it served as a useful precedent for the upcoming rulers.

Victims in the succeeding decade tended to be the "little press"—political scandal sheets, magazines or minor provincial papers. The largest number were leftist, during both the second Peronist period and the subsequent military regime, although a few extreme rightist publications also felt the blow.

The raucous political tabloids had descended like a snowstorm on Buenos Aires when Perón's 1973 return was interpreted by many as a license for sedition. Because the papers were so offensive, the troubles they soon encountered raised little concern among the middle and upper classes. They usually focused on internal Peronist squabbles and were rash to the point of inviting retaliation, so the average newsstand customer saw nothing amiss if one disappeared from the shelves. Even the establishment press paid little attention and, although the Association of Argentine Newspaper Entities (ADEPA) often protested the steady erosion of press freedom, it rarely mentioned a closure victim by name. For example, in June 1975, it declared that "for many reasons the conditions required for the normal fulfillment of journalistic functions have been put in grave danger." It only indirectly referred to the 11 publications that had been closed during the first two years of the Perón regime.

Some of the papers that were shut down were the leftist *El Mundo, El Peronista, Noticias, La Causa Peronista* and *La Calle;* and the rightist *La Marcha* and *Primicia Argentina.* Provincial papers suffering closures usually had no political role but simply irritated a local commander.

The most bizarre such case involved *Crónica,* a sensational tabloid with circulation often passing a half-million, thus making it Argentina's largest newspaper. Steering clear of the current political controversies, it adhered to a cause dear to the heart of nearly every Argentine—the century-old effort to reclaim from Britain the barren Falkland Islands in the South Atlantic. (Argentina calls them the Malvinas.)

The 2,000 residents of the islands are British citizens and have voted decisively to stay that way, despite some comic-opera attempts by Argentine vigilantes to seize the islands. Mention of the Malvinas issue is always an easy way for an Argentine politician to get applause, but diplomats from Buenos Aires have been trying in recent years to win over the islands' residents by persuasion, not threats.

This did not deter Hector Ricardo García, flamboyant publisher of *Crónica,* from mounting a serious campaign just before Christmas 1974 to launch a "people's invasion" of the islands. He had long referred to the British as "pirates" in his publications, but this time he set out to get results. In glaring front-page headlines, he invited red-blooded Argentines to volunteer their services not to the army but to *Crónica,* which also was advertising for airplanes to carry the assault force.

Although he drew laughs, he also attracted 20,000 signups from recruits. Even prominent businessmen sent telegrams and support, and workers submitted pledges such as "Ready to die for my country. I await your call."

The government wanted the islands even more than previously because of hopes for offshore oil, but it felt that García was ruining its efforts to subvert the islanders' loyalty. So on December 20, it closed the paper, although it did nothing to stop *Crónica* from returning in stages to the newsstands three months later under an assumed name. García showed no inclination to organize another invasion.[19]

SEIZURE OF MEDIA CONTENT

Although less frequent than closure of the plant, seizure of a newspaper's issues often accompanies the padlocking, and usually they are destroyed. And like the closures, the destruction is carefully cloaked with legality. Authorities became more careful after the unfavorable publicity abroad stirred by news of bookburning under a military government in 1971. Mexican publishers threatened to cut off trade with Argentina if the latter's customs and postal officials did not stop covertly removing from the mails books to which they objected.[20]

The most frequent target of seizures in the 1970s was the leftist daily *El Mundo*. When it sought to evade a closure order in 1971 by appearing under a different name, *Respuesta Popular,* its editions were confiscated.

As in the matter of closures, edition seizures usually fell on the weak and the radical. An exception was seen when the Videla military government seized all copies of *La Opinión,* a major independent daily, because of an article dealing with abuses of human rights. The paper also was closed for two days.[21]

The Argentine government traditionally has utilized one message-interception device which is almost unique in the hemisphere. This is the jamming of Radio Colonia, an Argentine-owned station across the river from Buenos Aires in Uruguay; it has long existed simply to beam its news, music and advertisements toward Argentina without complying with that country's regulations. Whenever rumors of a crisis are flying in Buenos Aires, listeners tune in to Colonia to get the true report. However, the Perón regime set about cutting off this last resort by jamming its signal during critical periods. At least the Argentines were left with the knowledge that when Colonia's signal was masked with a loud buzz, a crisis really existed.[22]

REGULATION AND CENSORSHIP

The Argentine constitution prohibits congress from enacting laws restricting the freedom of the press. In another article, it guarantees citizens the right to ''publish their ideas through the press without censorship.'' But the same article contains the fatal proviso that enjoyment of this right must conform to ''regulations governing their practice.''[23]

Such regulations, whether wearing the face of presidential decrees or of statutes passed by complaint congresses, built up steadily in the 1970s. They did not reflect any general credo about mass communication but rather responded to specific complaints by various leaders toward some perceived journalistic sin. Nor has Argentina developed the systematic, predictable censorship that Brazil adopted.

Regulations generally clustered under two headings as the Peróns and then the generals ran Argentina. One was a spate of laws intended to encourage a euphoria of nationalism—''I am Argentine or I am nothing!'' Isabel Perón would scream at crowds. The other grouping had to do with suppression of information about guerrilla warfare, or, as the rulers would say, publicity for the terrorists.

The nationalistic drive was based generally on the concept, often voiced in

UNESCO, that Third World countries are cultural and informational slaves of the great powers; adding special flavor to this was Juan Perón's sensitivity to what American news media said about him.

Nationalism

When the Peronists took power, Argentina had the rare advantage of several domestic news agencies, including those run as subsidiaries of Associated Press and United Press International. The latter would gather news within the country and, applying to a large extent the objectivity for which the parent agencies are known, would sell it to Argentine print and broadcast subscribers. Included in the service was the international report of each agency. It was an extraordinary benefit for provincial media which could not maintain correspondents away from home base but it provided little if any profit for AP and UPI. The larger one had been operated for 35 years by UPI; it had 20 Argentines working for it and reached 75 subscribers. With only 10 years behind it, the AP's service employed 15 Argentines and served 35 media. The only alternatives for a would-be news consumer were a government news agency or several smaller services.

Just three months into the Peronist regime, a decree law was handed down saying that the foreign-owned agencies could no longer supply Argentine news to Argentine media. This destroyed the UPI and AP subsidiaries' main reason for existence, although the parent agencies could continue to supply foreign news. The agencies quickly planned to disband the subsidiaries and find jobs for their 35 workers.[24] The English-language *Buenos Aires Herald* editorialized:

> The decree will virtually place all but a handful of newspapers, television and radio stations under government control, for only the official government agency . . . will be supplying news. And even the appearance of other Argentine agencies will be received with some suspicion because there is a history of them being used by the state intelligence services. The decree is an outright threat to press freedom.[25]

In response to this fear, the Argentine press set about organizing a cooperative which exchanged domestic news and distributed some foreign news.

Other provisions of the law, although never enforced, further revealed the governmental mentality. They required that:

1. Material about Argentina must occupy at least 50 per cent of the news space. A priority list for news stipulated that Argentina would be given first preference, Latin America second and the rest of the world third.

2. Foreign words must be purged from news reports. Argentina, like much of the world, has been rapidly adopting English words, particularly in regard to technology and fashions.

3. The source of all news, whether domestic or foreign, had to be specified. This apparently was aimed at UPI, which had reported some gossip about rivalries among Peronist leaders.[26]

No clear justification for the new law was given by the government, aside from a phrase in the ruling that said freedom of the press must be guaranteed "in harmony with the aims of the state" and that news agencies' field of action had to be defined to assure competition.

Nearly two years later the Perón government reinforced the news agency decree. It put the responsibility on news media themselves for rejecting Argentine news provided by foreign agencies. This measure was a response to the common Latin American news medium practice of trying to escape punishment by attributing offensive domestic news to foreign agencies. Coming under the ban would be Argentine news gathered in Buenos Aires and put on worldwide wires, or news concerning Argentina and originating from some foreign source. The decree also required that news agency personnel and foreign correspondents register with the government and that agencies must fully inform the government about all contracts with Argentine media.[27]

Licensing

Another indication of the suspicion the political elites hold toward the media, particularly foreign ones, was a decree by the Perón government which would have required licensing of all newsmen by the Ministry of Press and Broadcasting. The purported aim was to improve professional standards through creation of better journalism schools.

The same decree sought to build a ''press palace'' where all news agencies and Buenos Aires broadcast stations would be forced to have quarters. It also contained provisions to put the government news agency on an international footing, to increase the power of broadcast stations on the national borders, and to create new stations there. Even though the Perón regime still had two years before its downfall, none of these provisions was ever implemented.[28]

Nationalism also has found expression in rules requiring favoritism in fine arts and entertainment. In the Perón period, broadcasters were ordered to devote 75 per cent of their musical fare to Argentine music, including 25 per cent to folk tunes and 25 per cent to the traditional tango and milonga dances.[29] Unlike many smaller Latin American countries, Argentina has a substantial music industry, but Argentines also are cosmopolitan in their tastes, and stations never fully abided by the decree.

Roots of Censorship

Authoritarian governments, which Argentina has had much of the time since 1930, have always been nervous about the forces working for their downfall, and they have operated on the assumption that if these forces get no publicity they will wither away. When Juan Perón was overthrown in 1955 and fled into exile, it was forbidden even to mention his name or that of his party in print or on the air. (Some editors got around this by substituting the decree law number for the banned words.) For many years after the law was repealed, journalists played it safe by continuing the ban voluntarily. For 16 years with one exception, the face of Juan Perón, the most talked-about man in Argentina, did not appear on television there.[30]

With the rise of armed terrorism and civil war in the early 1970s and the wane of traditional political parties, the government's blotting out of media content about opponents became steadily more severe.

In the second Perón period (1973–76) the government's main thrust in regulation had to do with efforts of guerrillas to get newspaper space for their long, libelous manifestoes; these efforts usually were backed up by demands

made after widely publicized kidnappings. Again, media were forbidden from
mentioning the insurgent group's name, and this led to more code-word subterfuges. Except for the *Clarín* incident noted earlier, the guerrillas' pressure
usually fell on the smaller papers, particularly those of the Peronist left, which
sometimes would print the ads and face up to the closings that eventually swept
away all of them.

Not content to ban the publication of offensive material, the Perón government even passed a law which prohibited possession of material about terrorists. This made a criminal of every editor who received a letter from subversive
groups even if he did not publish it.[31]

The rare phenomenon of direct censorship for the print media appeared for
only one day after the 1976 military coup. After that, editors were left on their
own to interpret regulations that told them to avoid sensationalism, obscenity
and violence. They should, according to the order, "induce the restoration of
the values of order, work, dedication, honesty and responsibility in the context
of moral Christianity . . . and avoid the propagation of the opinion of unqualified persons who are without authority to express themselves on matters of
public interest."[32]

The military regime instituted its own ban on news of subversives and extended this to unauthorized reporting of the increasingly open signs of civil
war, such as the discovery of up to 23 persons killed through police or terrorist
violence. With bombings, shootings and dumping of corpses becoming steadily
more frequent and public, news media found it difficult to keep their credibility. One editor observed:

> More than a thousand people were killed in political violence last year. . . .
> The press reports little of this because it is prohibited from publishing anything
> apart from official communiques, which are limited to brief reports of some of the
> clashes between security forces and guerrillas. The continuing assassinations of po-
> licemen and armed services officers are also recorded.[33]

To aid journalists in their task of self-censorship, the government maintains "analysts" who can be asked for counsel on whether an article will get
the reporter in trouble. Of one thing they are sure: The generals have no taste
for humor, and for a year or more after the 1976 coup the press could not run
cartoons of President Jorge Videla, whose angular frame gave rise to the nickname "The Pink Panther."

Motion Pictures

No aspect of Argentine media regulations is as hazy and unpredictable as
those governing movie presentations. Films have always been subject to having
scenes clipped by censors but not until 1969 was banning of complete films
permitted by law. A law adopted by a military government then forbade the
showing of adultery; anything that is against marriage or the family; "las-
civiousness" or "morally repugnant" events; the justification of abortion, pros-
titution, crime, antipatriotism or resistance to authority; or scenes that "compromise national security." In 1974 the Perón government added bans on
guerrillas and terrorism to the list, and the military regime that followed called
for "optimism" and "exhaltation of spiritual values, morality, Christianity and
nationality."

Since the 1960s, the state has subsidized the making of Argentine films which exemplify the dogma held by the regime of the moment, and this subsidy has come to be counted on for about 40 per cent of a movie's support. "It's the self-censorship that's licking us," according to Juan Carlos Fisner, a film producer. "Nobody wants to risk investing in anything controversial. . . . These days anything could happen."[34]

Film restrictions eased in the 1973–76 Perón period for both local and imported productions. The showing of an uncut "Last Tango in Paris" in October 1973 shocked the public more for the decision's political significance than for the film's sexual audacity.[35] Even so, the run was halted after two days and the official who had allowed it was harassed in the courts for years afterward.

Nothing illustrates the capriciousness of Argentine press regulation better than incidents in which newspapers are ordered not to halt their presses but to start them rolling. Labor laws set 10 holidays a year when newspapers cannot publish but twice during the Peronist return in 1973 they were ordered to publish on such days—once to celebrate Perón's return from exile and again when he was inaugurated as president.[36] (The military junta later cut such holidays to four.)

STATE OWNERSHIP AND OPERATION

The various rulers of Argentina since the military ousted Perón the first time in 1955 have shown a notable forbearance from setting up some newspaper as the government voice. They have had no need for one, since, through fairness or servility, the media have consistently covered the president's actions and words to lengths that foreigners often consider absurd.

Even ownership of a news agency and a majority of broadcast stations has been little exploited for propaganda purposes, except during part of the second Perón regime. These state media do, however, supplement the private media for quick distribution of government messages.

Capture of La Prensa

Still hanging over Argentina is the awareness of the worldwide disgrace Perón suffered when he confiscated the famous daily, *La Prensa,* in 1951. The newspaper, then at the height of its influence, remained a stumbling block to Perón as he consolidated his power, since it was the only major voice of open opposition remaining. The dictator did not dare seize such a national institution by frontal assault but rather contented himself with the indirect means that eventually won out.

First came a barrage of harassment. The Peronists hired street thugs to attack the stately old newspaper building repeatedly. The owners had installed double steel doors to hold off assaults, but the gangs broke windows and twice started fires. Noise also became a weapon; the tormentors rented an office across the street and kept up a stream of insults through loudspeakers aimed at the newspaper office.

Government-controlled publications and radio stations churned out continual tirades against *La Prensa,* charging it with treason and colonialism. Posters in the street, signed by the Peronist party, demanded that advertisers withdraw from the paper.

In the courts, *La Prensa* director Alberto Gainza Paz often had to appear to answer criminal charges growing out of his editorials, which actually were fairly cautious. Accusations against Gainza Paz included disrespect (*desacato*) toward the president, incitement to disobey laws, or failure to pay taxes; once he was taken to prison without charges' being revealed. Police would prevent trucks from carrying copies of the paper by badgering the drivers with traffic tickets.

On the economic front, *La Prensa* and *La Nación* were ordered to pay nine years of import duties on newsprint that had been suddenly discovered. In a separate action, the government expropriated the newspapers' stock of newsprint and then cut their allocations of it to the point where they were running a small fraction of their usual number of pages.

Finally the news vendors' union, manipulated by the government, demanded that *La Prensa* abandon its circulation system and turn it over to the vendors, plus giving them 20 per cent of the classified advertising income. Even though the owners agreed to a compromise version of this, the vendors demanded complete surrender.

The vendors, acting through hired toughs, prevented the printers from entering the printing plant, several blocks from the main office. Finally, the staff members mobilized a peaceful march to go to work but were attacked by armed gangs, who killed one printer and injured 14. The police then showed up and arrested the printers.

The situation became hopeless. The Peronist majority in congress passed an expropriation bill, the newspaper was turned over to the labor federation, and Gainza Paz went into exile. When he resumed control four years later after Perón's overthrow, he ignored the issues put out during the paper's captivity, resuming the serial numbering from the day of the takeover. But the disrepute Perón brought to Argentina no doubt inhibited similar actions during later presidencies, including his own second administration in the 1970s.[37]

Broadcasting Ownership

Another consequence of the first Perón period is Argentina's triple radio system—88 private commercial stations, 36 state commercial ones and 24 state noncommercial ones. During the earlier period, radio fell into such a propaganda war among political factions that, when Perón was overthrown in 1955, the military government took over many commercial licenses and invited new applications for them. It ended up handing back only three to the private sector, and ever since then the poor quality and money-losing tendency of the state commercial stations has been an embarrassment to various governments. The chain of state noncommercial stations—Radio Nacional—makes some efforts to be cultural media, playing considerable classical music, but the great majority of citizens ignores them.

Shortly before the second Perón regime, the military government had thrown open the state commercial stations to bidding for reassignment of the licenses and rental of the properties to private companies. But Perón quickly reversed this action.

The Perón heritage also shows up in the confused television situation, which somewhat parallels the radio structure except for the lack of noncommercial stations. The state's seizure of television properties came in two stages. The first Perón government, spanning the postwar years when television was born, assigned one channel (in Buenos Aires) to itself and refused to grant commercial licenses. The succeeding military government opened television to private licensees and awarded 22 franchises between 1960 and 1965, fairly well saturating the urban markets and including three in Buenos Aires, which became the heads of de facto networks in the provinces. After 1965, only a few licenses to universities and city governments were granted, although a right-wing military dictatorship has been in power ever since except for the three Perón years.[38]

The most punishing blow to private television's development was the three Buenos Aires flagship stations' loss of their licenses in 1973, soon after Juan Perón became president. They had been given 15-year permits in 1958, and they argued that the period should be counted from the time they went on the air in 1960 and 1961, but Perón was unmoved. Government trustees took over management of the three stations, along with two others in provincial cities, Mar del Plata and Mendoza, whose licenses also had lapsed.[39]

The private stations had never shown much journalistic independence, and a groundswell of defense for them failed to materialize. The government called for a national debate on what the future of television should be, and even anti-Peronists dwelled on European rather than North American models.

The debate ended nearly a year later when the government decided to buy the physical properties and operate the five stations itself. Other private stations in the interior were left untouched, at least until their licenses would expire.[40] The military government which overthrew Perón talked of selling the stations back to private owners, but the stations proved attractive to military officers in search of government jobs.

News Agencies

Aside from broadcasting, news agencies have been the main arena of state ownership of media. The object is to assure the maximum preference to news that is filtered through the government's criteria—even foreign news, as the government agency Telam distributes selected stories it buys from the international agencies.

A government has never tried legally to force media to run its agency's version of the news. Rather, it uses the carrot instead of the stick and combines its news service with an advertising agency. The generally-accepted maxim is that the more an editor chooses Telam stories, the faster government advertising will come.

This advertising includes not just announcements by state offices but also the commercial messages of all the industries the government owns. So the state's share of the total advertising outlay in the country amounts to about 25 per cent.

Right-wing militarists, not Perón, initiated the Telam concept by buying a minor private agency in 1969. Its professed goals were to promote efficiency by "centralizing" ad placements which had been made by countless state agencies and ''to have the means to transmit overseas the image of a nation dedicated equally to . . . spiritual and material values.'' The purpose as to advertising was served, but Telam has never seriously entered global news competition.[41]

Larger, wealthier newspapers have been able to ignore Telam's economic threat to some extent, although *La Prensa* was severely handicapped by Perón's cutoff of government advertisements to it in 1973. Not only was this income lost, but the government intimidated many private businessmen into withdrawing their advertising from *La Prensa*.[42] These problems combined with others put *La Prensa* in serious financial jeopardy before the Perón regime's overthrow.

The government actually did assume control of a major newspaper in May 1977, but only by default. This occurred after the director of *La Opinión* was jailed in a financial scandal and the paper was at the point of collapse. The government appointed a trustee, supposedly to serve only until the company's affairs were untangled.[43]

OFFICIAL PENALTIES

Argentine governments, no matter how illegally they came to power, have traditionally paid great heed to legality once they are established (the laws, of course, often resulting from their own decree-making). Furthermore, courts have retained some measure of independence and sometimes have freed persons harassed by the government under flimsy charges.

Reports of torture have leaked out, particularly under military governments, as early as 1972.[44] Generally, though, when some journalist or other troublemaker falls into official disfavor, he is dealt with in a way that allows the government to disclaim responsibility. This has led to the fearsome legend of the Ford Falcons, the model of car favored by police and those masquerading as police. When one of these, with neither official markings nor license plates, carries off a victim in the dead of night, he often does not return. If he does, he bears the physical or psychological scars of torture. Since the abductors do not identify themselves and they usually blindfold the victim, the press can only describe them as terrorists. Even when uniformed police take away the prisoner, official spokesmen will often deny knowledge of the incident when questioned by reporters.

Those few journalists who are arrested publicly on formal charges usually go free after a jailing of days or weeks, through either dropping of the charges or favorable action by a judge. Such incidents have occurred with little distinction between Peronist and military governments. Most often they have grown out of tensions over the war against guerrillas.

Toils of the Herald

Editors of the *Buenos Aires Herald,* much more forthright in its news and editorials than its Spanish-language rivals, ran into trouble twice in the mid-1970s. Director Robert Cox had managed to avoid incidents until a Wednesday night in October 1975. Cox had always mused over who would be the first invader to burst through his newsroom door, and when seven plain-clothesmen carrying automatic weapons did so, he still was uncertain. They refused to identify themselves, although it soon became clear they were police.

It had been a bad night for the officers, because they had first swooped down on another building across town which had been abandoned by the *Herald* when it moved into new quarters. There they captured only a night watchman, who gave them the same address as was appearing in the paper every day.

The second frustration of the police was that they had organized the raid primarily to arrest the paper's managing editor, Andrew Graham-Yooll, and then discovered it was his day off.

Still another surprise came when the *Herald* staff offered no resistance, although the officers had come primed for a pitched battle, since according to their information the *Herald* was a hotbed of gun-toting guerrillas. In fact, the staff showed more fear of deadlines than of guns and ignored the invaders. (Any local reporter could have told the police that the *Herald* staff was known for being notably apolitical.)

As the police searched the office, Cox phoned Graham-Yooll at home. When the officer in charge noticed this, he became angry because he thought the managing editor would flee; instead Graham-Yooll caught a commuter train and came into the office. By that time the raiders had found files of terrorist propaganda with which Graham-Yooll, like other newsmen, had been flooded. Being a historian, he kept the mailings for scholarly articles.

Graham-Yooll and Cox were led to an unmarked, plateless Falcon; they refused to ride in it until a well-marked car from the neighborhood precinct was summoned to escort them to the police station. There Graham-Yooll was kept in a bullpen with common criminals, questioned about the origin of the guerrilla papers and freed the next morning without explanation or apology.[45]

Eighteen months later, it was Cox's turn. Much less dramatically, he was arrested in his office by two detectives who took him off to jail. He was charged with violating antisubversion and security laws because he had taken note of a Reuters dispatch about some Argentine guerrillas' activity in Italy; ironically the reference was intended as a tribute to the government's success in defeating the insurgents. After Cox spent a day in jail a judge released him without bail and he was acquitted five months later.[46]

La Opinión's Trouble

But the most bizarre instance of official action caught up Jacobo Timerman, director of the intellectual tabloid *La Opinión*. This resulted in Timerman's imprisonment and the near-bankruptcy of the paper.

Timerman was caught up in an international scandal that revolved around the banking empire of 35-year-old David Graiver, a Polish Jew who had emigrated to Argentina. He supposedly was killed in a plane crash in 1976, but rumors persisted that the body found was that of another man and that Graiver had gone into hiding to escape police. The charge was that he had covertly invested $17 million for the Montoneros, one of the two main terrorist groups in Argentina. Presumably the money had come from kidnap ransoms.

Argentine police announced the first of 29 arrests in April 1977. Two were of Timerman and his chief assistant, Enrique Jara. Each was picked up at his home by men in civilian clothes identifying themselves as members of the army. The police, two days after the arrests, said only that Jara was "missing," then admitted holding him the next day. After seven days' captivity he was released.

Timerman waited in vain to be told the charges against him. But Jara told fellow staff members that Timerman had admitted to him that Graiver controlled 55 per cent of the *La Opinión* stock when the paper was founded in 1971; Timerman had claimed then that he held 90 per cent of the stock. Another editor confirmed Jara's report.

Police also were leaking reports that Timerman had received kickbacks from politicians to promote Peronism and had put the money in numbered Swiss accounts.

Regardless of how true the various reports were, they sufficed to alienate a large part of the paper's advertisers, readers and staff members. The management fell into disarray, and the government put the paper in trusteeship.

Since Timerman personally—though not the newspaper—had been closely identified with Jewish community leaders, the case gave rise to much debate over how much anti-Semitism had to do with the jailing and disgrace of the publisher. It at least added to the worries of the Jews, who had become the object of a growing wave of threats and assaults after the military takeover.[47]

Other Cases

Although all governments try to maintain an appearance of civility in regard to judicial processes, unabashed shows of power can result in moments of anger. When Ana Guzzetti, a reporter for the leftist tabloid *El Mundo,* irritated President Juan Perón with a question during a news conference, he told his aides to start a "judicial action" against her. She remained at liberty two weeks, then was arrested along with 17 fellow employees after an attack on their building and was held for two days after the others were released.[48]

It has been fairly common for leading editorial staff members to go to jail when their newspaper or magazine is shut down and its editions seized. This occurred for Hector García, director of *Crónica,* when he tried to organize the Falklands invasion; for two editors of *Marcha,* a right-wing Peronist magazine; and for the director and six journalists of a Córdoba daily when it criticized military spending. García was released on bond, however.[49]

Scattered repressions against journalists and media occurred in the weeks following the 1976 military overthrow of Isabel Perón but not nearly on the scale of what happened in Chile after Allende's downfall. There were rumors that 10 newsmen were arrested, and police raided the offices of the Communist Party's weekly called *Nuestra Palabra.*

ECONOMIC RESTRICTIONS

Despite the fact that Argentina has been run by supposedly right-wing governments during most of the years since 1930, it has taken on a very socialistic shading. The militarists who followed each of the two Perón periods took some steps to sell off Perón acquisitions, but many remained in state hands. By 1975, 60 per cent of the means of production were estimated as being in the hands of the state.[50]

Furthermore, economic regulation has gone deep into the sphere of decision normally reserved for private owners. Argentine news media have developed none of the special privileges familiar in many Western countries, and the fiscal handicaps have hit them particularly hard because of their weakening under other types of blows.

An example was the advertising law passed by the newly-elected Peronist regime in 1973 as part of a general program to control inflation. Among its provisions were those that (1) put a price ceiling on advertisements, which often were already underpriced; (2) decreed that businessmen could not include the cost of advertising in prices of some consumer goods, which discouraged many ad orders; and (3) banned the advertising of new models on the theory that this would drive their cost up.

The government's manipulation of its own advertisement as an enticement to media has been noted earlier, but at times a cutoff in such ads has been a blessing in disguise because the state has fallen far behind in paying its accounts. When Telam stopped placing its ads with *La Prensa* in 1973, it left unpaid a debt of $50,000. Three years later, after the Peronists' fall, the government was even farther behind in ad space payments to *La Prensa*'s rival, *La Nación*. Furthermore, when the government did pay it did so in pesos that were worth 4 per cent of their 1973 value.[51]

However, when the tables were turned and a medium was behind in its payments to the government, the owner was the one to suffer. Tax delinquencies were among the grounds for the license cancellation of the three private television stations in Buenos Aires. They also were accused of evading their duty to pay "social charges" such as pension premiums by holding their staff members under individual contracts rather than wages.

Labor laws dating back to the first Perón regime give workers a wide range of benefits which invited abuses, particularly in the second Perón period. An executive of *La Nación* ranked this as his paper's greatest problem at that time. An employee gets six months' paid sick leave, and his job is kept open for him a year after that. Medical excuses are easy to get; one *La Prensa* employee brought in a note from his psychiatrist saying he was allergic to his desk.[52]

Importing supplies also could lead to problems imposed by the state until the military regime removed restrictions in this field. An importer seeking foreign currency for debt payment was required to deposit his pesos in the government bank in such a way that he was penalized. Imported equipment was taxed 200 per cent, and imports had to come by Argentine ships, resulting in delays and thus production crises.[53]

Although Argentines are hungry consumers of foreign books and magazines, distributors of these items sometimes have faced near-disaster when the government has stepped in to even up the foreign balance of payments. In June 1975 the government of President Isabel Perón left millions of foreign publications rotting in customs warehouses, the importers barred from taking delivery of them. Even when shipments had been received, the importers were prohibited from sending money abroad to pay for them, thus ending their credit and resulting in court suits abroad. "We are becoming virtually isolated from the world's science, literature, thought, and art," an editorial in *La Nación* remarked at the time.[54]

INDIRECT PRESSURES

The government can bring to bear on the media several types of influence which, while not being obvious efforts at control, nevertheless have an effect on the directors' strategy.

Favors to reporters, less blatant than in some countries, do limit these workers' independence and prestige. All Argentine governments try to get reporters on their payrolls as "consultants" or the like; in fact, some editors encourage this because it can give them an advantage in learning official news. Although governments usually do not bribe reporters outright, businesses do it in the form of gifts at year's end.

"Argentine journalists are modest and don't expect much in payoffs," one editor observed. "Besides, few of them are more than hacks who don't get bylines, and who wants to bribe them?"[55]

The old-fashioned perquisites for reporters, now largely discarded in modern countries, still are observed in Argentina. Through custom rather than law, reporters get a 50 per cent discount on airline and train tickets, reduced prices on cars and free admission to theaters. This draws little criticism in view of the reporters' pitiful salaries.

Pressure exerted on media through government-influenced unions has been a frequent threat in Argentina, particularly during the Perón regimes. As has been noted, it was the principal mechanism for the takeover of *La Prensa* in 1951.

Another union that strikes fear and anger into the heart of most publishers is the association of newsstand owners, who do nearly all the distribution of printed products in Argentina and are often accused of being affiliated with the Mafia. The union has collaborated with governments of the left and right; its president once had an office in a government building, acting as adviser to the president. If the government does not like what a newspaper or magazine is publishing, it can simply pass the word to the dealers—called *canillitas.* They can refuse to handle a publication or, as happened once to *La Prensa,* threaten to dump all its copies in the river. These methods were effective in bringing *La Opinión* into line under the military regime of the early 1970s. Even beyond the half of the publication's purchase price that they get, the *canillitas* often pressure publishers into contributing to selected charities.

Though secrecy has long been a way of life in official circles, reporters try to pry loose extra information by playing on the rivalries of government leaders in their separate news conferences. This system was constricted severely when the second Perón regime instituted an information department to coordinate all such releases. Its relative efficiency appealed to the militarists who followed, and they kept it on.

Argentine journalists have learned that if they are set upon by a mob which is serving the government's purposes, they cannot expect police protection, at least not promptly. This was especially true in the Perón periods, such as during the 1951 harassment of *La Prensa* and the first year of the second period. Newsmen covering an assault by gun-toting toughs on striking bus drivers suddenly found they were being beaten and their cameras smashed.[56] When a mob attacked the leftist paper *El Mundo,* policemen contented themselves with arresting staff members of the paper.[57]

PROPAGANDA

Argentina's relatively high degree of education and political cynicism means that in the media where the serious journalism takes place—newspapers and magazines—little overt propaganda has been attempted. The government sends out written press releases, but editors take pride in treating them like other publicity. However, as has been noted, the government has means to assure that reporters covering official sources usually transmit these handouts as their own copy. Also, the releases most often take the form of stories offered by Telam, which has the semblance of being a legitimate news agency.

The mass-circulation newspaper *Clarín* gained the status of favored newspaper if not spokesman for the Videla military government, which succeeded the Peronists in 1976. Readers learned to look to *Clarín* as the purest expression of whatever dogma the generals possessed. The cooperation developed because *Clarín*'s owners were supporters of former president Arturo Frondizi, whose faction was allied with the military. *Clarín* later broke the bond and opposed the government's economic policy.

Television, however, has been the favorite medium for political propaganda and was heavily exploited in the second Perón regime. Tying up the entire video system for an hour or two at a time, the persuaders would thereby force any viewer to watch films, speeches and spots touting the kind of frenzied unity that had brought Perón to power. "All together we shall save Argentina or no one will save her" was one of the slogans repeated endlessly.

The Peronist campaign had begun to cool even before its overthrow, and the succeeding regime heeded the boredom the campaign had caused. The militarists continued their message-spreading in the form of spots and talk shows, but they refrained from blanketing the system, thereby giving the viewer a choice. Themes of the new approach were the more traditional ones—family, church, society.

The Videla government has introduced a relatively new dimension to Argentine propaganda—the foreign campaign. Worried about its rapid fall in world public esteem because of civil rights abuses and an upsurge of Nazism, it set out in 1976 to persuade journalists abroad that the truth about Argentina had not been told. To do this, it hired a New York public relations firm, Burson-Marsteller, to stimulate trade and tourism from the United States, Canada, Japan, Belgium, the Netherlands, Britain, Mexico and Colombia.

The publicists persuaded the American and Canadian chambers of commerce in Buenos Aires to invite journalists from their home countries for expenses-paid tours of Argentina. Coming in several waves, the journalists found their schedule filled with appointments with officials or friends of the government, no time remaining to seek out dissidents.

Although the junkets resulted in friendly coverage in the U.S. and Canada, they also had the curious effect of creating discussion of the human rights issue in the local press. Buenos Aires newspapers which had been afraid to touch the subject took the chance to reprint texts of the interviews. In them, President Videla admitted that abuses had occurred but said they were not customary.

Besides distributing money for the tours, Burson-Marsteller also paid Buenos Aires journalists $35–$75 if they got favorable stories printed abroad.

The world image problem remained large for the Videla government. A respected news magazine in Venezuela ran a cover showing a South American map with swastikas on Argentina, Bolivia, Brazil, Chile, Paraguay and Uruguay. Jewish voters in the United States were growing restive over the surge of anti-Semitism in Argentina. And so intense was the negative coverage in France that the Argentine government complained to the French ambassador that terrorist groups, "through the excessive advantage of free expression" in France, were urging public support there for their goals through "hostile actions against the Argentine people and government."[58]

CHAPTER 2

Brazil:

Where Force Fails

BRAZIL—and all of Latin America, for that matter—had never seen anything like it. Here was a military dictatorship that not only pledged itself to unselfish, sober reform of the nation but set about doing it with a minimum of fanfare. So anxious were the generals and admirals to avert personality cults that they changed presidents every four years with little noticeable rupture in policy.

In one aspect, the Brazilian military reverted to type after it overthrew democracy in 1964: It would not tolerate criticism or embarrassing disclosures about itself. But the fact remains that, after a decade of the most thoroughgoing media controls the hemisphere has seen in modern times outside Cuba, the public and its journalists still refuse to stop thinking, talking and writing in ways that disturb the authorities. Because of ferment produced by this force and counter-force, Brazil remains a laboratory of media-government relations that constantly adds to the global understanding of this subject.

A PECULIAR HERITAGE

Although the scope of media controls that started in 1964 was unprecedented, in many ways they reflected traits of Brazilian national life which had been present from the earliest days of colonization.

For example, the government's disdain for public enlightenment finds its roots in Portuguese colonial policy. Because European settlers of Brazil tended at first to scatter themselves on large plantations, an urban middle class that would have been the natural setting for newspapers was slow to start. Furthermore, when a few coastal towns did develop, they had little sense of community with each other, and their appetite for news could be satisfied by gossip and journals brought by ships from the mother country. Thus, although Portugal's mastery of its colony was relatively weak as compared with the

23

Spanish-area control, the royal prohibition of printing found little challenge from the settlers. They were too busy seeking their fortunes as exporters or as exploiters of mineral wealth.[1]

Only when the ideas of the French and American revolutions began exciting some urban sophisticates in Brazil did the pressure for mass communication begin to build. In defiance of the colonial law, they circulated clandestine publications, often through secret societies such as the Freemasons. One after another, the cities gave rise to protests manifested in pamphlets furtively posted in public places. A typical message was "Cheer up, people of Bahía, the happy moment of our liberty is near, the time when all will be brothers, the time when all will be equal."

But the Brazilians' rhetoric lacked the force of will that developed in Spanish America, and instead of separating themselves from the crown of Portugal, they gained independence when the crown came to them. This occurred in 1808 as the Portuguese royal family and 10,000 supporters fled to the colony to escape the Napoleonic invasion.

Determined to enjoy all the trappings they had known in Europe, the aristocratic refugees set up Brazil's first newspaper, a thoroughly sanitized court gazette giving news of other royal courts in the old world, official announcements, birthdays and obituaries of the nobility, and paeans of praise for the crowned publishers. Called *A Gazeta do Rio de Janeiro,* it was printed on a press brought over by the Portuguese minister of war. The same year, an opposition journal known as the *Correio Braziliense* began appearing, having been printed in England and smuggled into Brazil. It came out monthly and included up to 100 pages.

Several aspects of these first three centuries had a strong bearing on present-day political realities of Brazilian journalism:

1. When journalism did appear, the government took a patronizing role, confident that it knew what was best for the reading public.

2. Partly because of the unusually thin layer of literacy at the top of society, development of newspapers came about a century later than in British America, where the first effort was in 1690, and in the Spanish colonies, where it started in 1722.

3. Cross-currents of liberalism and authoritarianism were felt in the media.

Although printed journalism began to spread across Brazil immediately after the court gazette's founding, censorship also was there from the start. The minister of the interior had the task of preventing publications which offended against religion, government and good manners.[2]

During a 23-year political conflict with Portugal, the press emerged as a strong force for fanning the flames of independence among the Brazilian elite, especially after it was freed from censorship in 1821. Newspapers sprang up almost overnight, growing from 12 in 1827 to 54 in 1831, 16 of them in Rio de Janeiro. In the latter year, the final ties with Portugal were cut and the 58-year regime of the benign, progressive Emperor Pedro II began. Ironically, while journalists in former Spanish colonies suffered widespread repression under republican forms of government, the Brazilian press basked in liberty thanks to a constitutional emperor. He even allowed it to become a vehicle of agitation for his overthrow and the founding of a republic.

The empire came to an end in 1889, but the respect for free expression continued almost unbroken (except for closure of German newspapers in World War I) until 1930. At that time the 15-year dictatorship of Getulio Vargas started.

Like Pedro II, Vargas had a consuming ambition to modernize Brazil, but unlike the emperor he saw no reason to tolerate diversity of ideas. While instituting strict censorship of all media, he also exercised positive as well as negative control by exploiting mass communication for propaganda. Like other adroit political leaders of his time such as Roosevelt, Mussolini, Hitler and Perón, he saw the opportunity to use radio as a personal channel to the minds of his people. A charismatic orator, he put millions under his spell when he began his broadcasts with the standard greeting: "Workers of Brazil. . . ."

To carry out his controls, he set up a Department of Press and Propaganda (DIP) in 1939, and its duties ranged from the press to theater, cinema and the broadcast media. So efficient was it that the saying grew up: "Don't speak— Getulio will do it for you; don't think—the DIP will do it for you."[3]

But Vargas was bound to the Allied cause in World War II although his sympathies were with the Axis. He had to let the Brazilians read about the horrors of the enemy dictatorships, and the lesson sunk in too deeply. When the war ended, Brazil could not bear the shame of having its own dictator, so it deposed him.

Then followed nearly two decades of what many observers consider to be abuse of press liberty, or at least a failure of the press to exercise responsible self-restraint. Certainly the militarists who overthrew democracy in 1964 lived through this period and saw the havoc wreaked by unbridled political libel and sensationalism.

Perhaps a symbol of this period was Carlos Lacerda, owner of a second-rank Rio de Janeiro newspaper, *Tribuna da Imprensa*. He also was governor of the state and a presidential aspirant. Disregarding libel laws, he feuded bitterly in print with a wide variety of opponents. His prime enemy was Getulio Vargas after the former dictator returned to the presidency through a free election. One night in 1954, assassins believed to be Vargas supporters ambushed Lacerda in front of his house, wounding Lacerda and killing an air force major he was talking with. This led to a scandal which ended with Vargas' suicide.

Lacerda was unfazed by this tragedy and continued lashing out at all opponents. One observer credits him with being instrumental in the overthrow of three presidents—Vargas through suicide, Janio Quadros through resignation in 1961, and João Goulart through military coup in 1964:

> The old tradition of respect for the constituted authorities had certainly broken down: the more influential part of the press detested the populist Presidents who held office during most of the period. The most violent attacks were sometimes met by extra-legal invasion by troops or police of the offender's premises, to seize the issue in question, but no newspaper was ever closed or seriously victimized during those years.[4]

Just as the militarists witnessed the invective rampant in the press, they also could not overlook the personalism that saturated political discussion conducted by the newspapers. Rather than debate rival economic programs, too often editors gave in to arguing over superficial labels and the perceived evils of various men's characters. The militarists' later fetish for keeping their rivalries secret must be viewed in this light.

Politicians were not passive in the face of the threats from the press. This was particularly true in the case of Goulart during the three years leading to his overthrow in 1964. He mobilized a massive government propaganda campaign to promote his leftist projects; he also manipulated government loans to bring to heel opposition newspapers such as the respected *Correio da Manhã* and *Diario de Noticias* and the sensational *Ultima Hora*.[5]

NEW GAME, NEW RULES

The military forces turned out the civilian president in 1964 with the hearty support of some leading news media such as *O Estado de São Paulo* and the Rio newspaper *O Globo*. The editors soon found that they had more stability than they had expected. The generals made it clear that they would not allow any diversity of media content, although the mechanisms for enforcing this were slow in developing.

However, one device implemented shortly after the 1964 coup put an effective if indirect clamp on public discussion. This was the stripping of hundreds of leading Brazilians of their political rights, usually for 10 years. Since no elections were forthcoming anyway, the principal effect of this came through the provision that such persons, called *cassados,* were really non-persons for the media; they could not be quoted in regard to any aspect of public affairs. Some journalists were among the *cassados,* but the greater impact was the indirect one.

After three years of public uncertainty over the extent of media controls, the government initiated another three-year period which brought a dizzying succession of new rules. The process continued in the 1970s with instructions about how to handle specific problems such as the visit of Nelson Rockefeller (use only friendly news) and the advent of streaking (ignore it). But these memos produced little surprise for journalists, so thoroughgoing were the decrees of 1967–70.

All the news regulations were issued as decrees and thus did not go through a legislative process. They mainly consist of the Press Law of 1967, Institutional Act 5 of 1968, and the National Security Law of 1969, all of which were incorporated into a new constitution; a set of so-called "recommendations" phrased as rules given by the minister of justice in 1969; and decree laws in 1969 and 1970 elaborating on the earlier ones.

By the time the blizzard of decrees had subsided, editors could form a somewhat clear picture of how this government would exert its thought controls. (See Appendix.) It differed in important aspects from regimes in some neighboring countries:

1. Private ownership of media would remain undisturbed. Unlike in Peru, the government did not seek to scoop up the media properties, even through "popular" organizations. Nor did it seek an official organ as in Chile.

2. The laws were highly pragmatic, and the rhetoric of revolution, whether leftist or rightist, was avoided. The only attitude displayed toward the

media was a negative one—to keep them from stirring the waters with criticism or exciting news.

3. Provisions of the laws implied that the government took a conflict of interest between state and press for granted, even though it expected the press to submerge its interest. Nor were the workers mobilized to the government's cause through special favors; although the unions were made a vehicle for pension and health benefits, this was simply a convenience for the government.

4. The laws were more preventive than punitive. There was little emphasis on provisions to close media or seize their products. Rather, the thrust seemed to be to define offensive actions and their penalties in such detail that any prudent journalist would avoid committing them. Of course, there were always escape clauses to allow for punishment of unforeseen offenses.

5. A high degree of nationalistic protectionism was in evidence. Surprisingly enough for a government which depended on good relations with Western democratic countries, it maintained and reinforced long-standing barriers against foreign investment in Brazilian media and resolved to prevent imported material from undercutting its domestic controls on expression.

6. Prior censorship as an option was thoroughly provided for. Although the laws dwelled little on censorship, it became the most distinctive aspect of Brazil's media controls. It also is entirely consistent with the preventive approach noted above.

Some of the realities that developed in media controls, such as brutal police interrogations, were not reflected directly in the laws. However, they seemed to be a natural outcome of the indefinite suspension of the right of habeus corpus, provided for in 1971 under a state of siege which has been modified only to a "state of emergency."

CENSORSHIP

Every Thursday night, a federal policeman who moonlighted as a medical student would come around to the offices of a small Catholic weekly newspaper in São Paulo. The editors would hand over to him the page proofs of that week's edition, and he would mark out the stories he disapproved. Then, after enough filler copy was found for the holes, the paper would go to press.[6]

Behind such a casual incident lay the most massive censorship operation in the Western hemisphere and perhaps in the noncommunist world. It also was the center pole holding up the tent of control over the Brazilian media before it was suspended in 1978 for newspapers and magazines dealing in public affairs. However, it remained in effect for other types of media and entertainers.

In all, about 90 censors were maintained by the government. They were responsible for seeing that none of Brazil's welter of media laws was violated in the content of nearly 3,000 newspapers, magazines and broadcast stations, plus more than 6,000 book titles, about 800 films and innumerable songs, plays, concerts and paintings.

There was some indication that the burden was beginning to tell on the 90 inspectors in 1976 when it was revealed that 21 had been notified they would be fired because they had failed a psychological screening test given by government bureaucrats. They were defended by their director, who said they had performed admirably, "faced as they were with hostility from the editors of newspapers and radio and television stations." The complaint had basis, as their ill treatment had ranged from being refused a chair in newspaper offices to being forced to do their work on the sidewalk.[7]

Obviously prior censorship could not be carried out for all the individual editions and programs noted above. At any one time only about a half-dozen of the nearly 1,000 newspapers were read by a censor before publication. Instead of doing a complete job itself, the government relied on the help of journalists, artists and mass communicators to censor themselves, knowing that if they were too incautious they could be chastised with anything from a few days in jail to long imprisonment.

"You never know when you are going to be censored," remarked samba lyricist Paulinho da Viola. "It is such a subjective thing, so you end up practicing self-censorship."[8]

Slow Death

In the newspaper field, the number of publications basically opposed to the government was small from the start, and the constant pressure slowly decreased the total. But the rulers did not conduct a massive shutdown of the opposition as was done in Chile, nor did they capriciously suspend publication of individual papers as has been the case in Argentina and Uruguay. So the more informed elites have been treated to the spectacle of certain leftist or independent organs' slowly dying over several years without a fatal blow in evidence.

When such deaths occurred, it usually was through economic malnutrition indirectly caused by censorship. This came about in three ways:

1. Readers stopped buying the publication because all the interesting material had been cut by censors. "It is the anomaly of an antigovernment publication having nothing against the government," remarked one observer. Apparently with intent, the censors allowed more audacious material to appear in the establishment media than in the opposition press.

2. The management spent itself to death on editorial matter that had to go into the wastebasket. It was common for more than a third of the stories submitted to be killed. In the case of a special edition on the condition of women prepared by *Movimento,* a São Paulo weekly, the losses were 283 of 305 columns of writing, 58 of 69 photos and 10 of 12 statistical tables. Much of the material had come from the United Nations and other global agencies.[9]

3. Advertisers deserted the publication because of fear of losing favor with the government or simply because the decrease of readers made the paper a poor vehicle for marketing.

Aside from about 10 days after the 1964 military coup, no major newspaper except *O Estado de São Paulo* has undergone direct prior censorship; it had such control from 1972 to early 1975. Other domestic print media enduring the treatment at one time or another have been *Opinião, Pasquim* and *Politika,* political weeklies; *Vega* and *Visao,* news weeklies; *Jornal do Brasil, Correio da Manhã, Tribuna da Imprensa,* dailies in Rio and São Paulo; *Jornal de Brasila,* a daily in the federal capital; *Pais e Filhos, Ele e Ela, Homen, Status, Nova* and *Manchete,* entertainment magazines appealing to young adults; *Paralelo,* a monthly political magazine; and *O São Paulo,* a Catholic archdiocesan weekly. Typically, censorship of each publication continued two or three years, after which its editors usually stopped trying to test the censors' patience.

In the case of the dailies and some weeklies, a censor came to the office to read the page proofs just before plates were put on the press. The task was staggering for a paper as large as *O Estado,* which runs 100 pages or more; the censor usually read the editorials, national news and foreign news referring to Brazil; he scanned the rest. The government rotated the censors frequently to keep them from getting too friendly with a publication.

Most weeklies and magazines did not have the convenience of such house calls; they had to send their copy 600 air miles to Brasilia from either Rio or São Paulo. Each week was a crisis in meeting the press deadline and being on the street by Monday.

The routine of *Movimento,* a São Paulo-based political weekly, was fairly typical. Its staff rushed to get all editorial and advertising material ready by Thursday. It was packed in a case and taken to the airport to meet the next shuttle flight to Brasilia. There, *Movimento* staffers grabbed the case off the plane and raced to the national censorship office. Later that day they picked up the results and phoned in the cuts to the São Paulo headquarters, taking extreme care not to miss anything.

In São Paulo, the paper was re-edited by substituting innocuous material for what was deleted or, playing it safer, by reducing the number of printed pages. Meanwhile, the censors in Brasilia had sent their instructions to their branch in São Paulo; it inspected the revised version of the paper Saturday morning. Only then, if approval was given, could the paper start the presses and arrange for nationwide distribution.[10]

All censors had the long list of prohibited expressions at their elbows, and new instructions tailored to meet problems of the moment came to them almost daily from the ministry of justice. These banned subjects ranged from internal political situations, such as speculation over the presidential succession, to external matters, such as the number of Brazilian exiles involved in the Chilean coup. Besides serving as working guides for the censors, both in Brasilia and in media offices, the memoranda usually were sent to all editors to guide them in exerting self-censorship. Directors of *O Estado* and its affiliate *Jornal da Tarde* ordered their staffs to ignore the memoranda.

Erratic Rules

Application of the rules by the censors varied widely both as to intensity and as to the stories and the media affected.

Censorship became much more severe as tension rose or fell in regard to a certain subject, although the news media found it difficult to understand the rationale sometime. They normally reported prominently the crimes of the "death squads" which committed frequent murders of leftists, with covert participation by the police; in fact, some media strongly criticized this activity and the failure of the government to stop it. It embarrassed the military, which felt it had been besmirched by misdeeds of local police. So when a military prosecutor charged 15 São Paulo policemen with murder in such a case, the media expected the action to be fully publicized for the military's benefit. Instead, the justice ministry ordered mass media not to touch it; news of the case came to light only through rumor and coverage in the foreign press.[11]

Different aspects of the same story might get divergent treatment from the censor. Disappearance of a prominent opposition politician was widely reported. But when the army admitted three months later that it had arrested him and claimed that unknown criminals had then kidnapped him, the media were confined to publishing only the official announcement. Neither reports of a debate on the subject in congress nor editorial discussion were allowed.[12]

Editors also endured uneven treatment by censors in various cities, particularly the arch-rivals São Paulo and Rio, although the liberality seemed to shift between them at different periods. The headquarters in Brasilia was generally believed to be tougher than either of the major branch offices.

The economic squeeze put on opposition weeklies by uneven censorship has been noted, but discrimination fell on the larger media also. *O Estado de São Paulo* and its afternoon sister *Jornal da Tarde* were frequent victims during the 1972–75 term of direct censorship. In one day they were banned from running three news stories which appeared in other newspapers.[13] So acute did the favoritism become that *O Estado* and the opposition weekly *Opinião,* in separate actions in 1973, filed suit against the government claiming financial damages because of unconstitutional treatment. They won no awards, but they exposed their complaints to the public.[14]

O Estado's Ordeal

O Estado and *Opinião,* along with the satirical weekly *Pasquim* and the Catholic weekly *O São Paulo,* were among the hardest-hit by censorship.

The hardship for *O Estado* was reminiscent of troubles it had had during the Vargas period. After 10 years of opposition from the paper, Vargas ousted the Mesquita family from control and directed *O Estado* through a trustee.

When the Mesquitas regained control through court action after Vargas' overthrow in 1945, they simply canceled the five years of captivity from the paper's official history, just as Alberto Gainza Paz did later after resuming control of *La Prensa* in Buenos Aires, which Juan Perón had seized.

"We don't count those five years," a member of the family said later. "For us, it is as if they never existed in the life of the newspaper."[15]

After supporting the 1964 coup, even to the extent of discussing it in advance with the plotters in the newspaper offices, the editors of *O Estado* slowly became horrified at what they had helped create. "We thought the military would take over, clean up the situation and then, as they had done throughout their history, hand back control of the country to civilians," recalled Ruy Mesquita, one of the two brothers who inherited the newspaper empire.[16]

Instead, the militarists steadily went about snuffing out not only press freedom but also many other civil rights, even while carrying out economic reforms and controls on terrorism which *O Estado* applauded.

The general who had become president, Humberto Castello Branco, bitterly resented the opposition from *O Estado* and felt personally insulted. But he recognized several aspects of the newspaper that made him reluctant to act against it—its obvious patriotism, its conservative sympathies with the revolution's basic goals, its political power, and—very importantly—the fact that it was an integral part of the Brazilian way of life. Explaining his hesitance to retaliate, he remarked: *"O Estado* is a national institution.''[17]

But by 1967 Castello Branco was gone from the presidency, and the other Mesquita brother, Julio, was protesting the highly restrictive new press law to the Inter-American Press Association. When the military threw out constitutional guarantees late the next year with Institutional Act 5, the break between the Mesquitas and the generals became permanent, and the drumfire of criticism by the paper steadily built up, although it continued to praise many government actions.

Direct censorship of *O Estado* was spasmodic until 1972. A particularly irritating article would bring a crackdown, and the Mesquitas delighted in harassing their censors. Their ousting the censor onto the sidewalk was a 1971 incident which followed what they considered insufferable demands from him—cutting several disputed stories and even seizing pictures made of him doing so; further, they said, he had insulted staff members and caused production delays up to four hours.[18]

Although the government did not retaliate directly for the indignities, it reached an impasse with *O Estado* on Aug. 24, 1971. Earlier in the month the paper had criticized in detail the civil rights abuses which were increasing in national security cases. Then the paper began a series of reports on the competition among the generals to become the country's next president, a forbidden subject. The chief of the federal police told an *O Estado* executive not to run anything more about it, and Julio Mesquita sent back the message: "If you want to censor *O Estado,* come and do it yourself. We will not censor our own newspaper.''[19]

This was taken as a declaration of war. Police with submachine guns took up posts outside the building, and censors moved in. Initially they read only the first copy off the press, but then they began checking page proofs and even the printing plate matrices. The staff got caught up in the spirit of bedeviling the censors. Besides being refused a chair at times, they discovered the stories they had banned were posted on office bulletin boards for any visitor to see.

The Mesquitas decided that the most effective way to combat the censors was to continue flooding them with honest news stories and to try to bring them down by ridicule. *O Estado* and its afternoon sister *Jornal da Tarde* soon were forbidden from telling their readers what had been omitted from each day's editions, so they put such absurdly harmless material in place of the killed stories that the perceptive readers would understand and get a chuckle besides. One early device was the use of letters to the editor in comic over-emphasis. While other papers were extensively reporting events surrounding a cabinet crisis, the censors cut *O Estado's* lead story and picture and three whole pages inside, the main cartoon and other stories, all about the crisis; the paper was restricted to using an official bulletin about it. So the editors substituted, in the lead position, readers' letters discussing the smell of a rose and why there still was no blue rose. When the letters could not be stretched to fill the swath cut by the censors, the editors would republish old letters or simply repeat the same one several times in the same edition.

For *Jornal da Tarde,* the ridicule was even more pixyish. It took to running recipes in the censored holes, even on the front page. Day after day, readers

were reminded of the delights of a favorite, orange pudding, and some days the
recipe ran on several pages.[20]

Later the government called down the papers for such mischief, and they
became more sober. *O Estado* filled its editorial vacuums with the interminable
verses of the Portuguese epic poem *Os Lusiadas* by Luiz Vaz de Camões. *Jornal da Tarde* switched to using pious sketches of angels. Meanwhile, the management filed away the censored stories by the hundreds and vowed it would
someday publish them.

By 1974, Brazil had a new president and a new justice minister, both more
friendly to human rights and both aware of the disrepute that the *O Estado* saga
had brought to Brazil. The justice minister, relying on his friendship with the
Mesquitas, offered them a deal of withdrawal of the censors in exchange for a
pledge of self-censorship. The agreement was turned down, Ruy Mesquita said,
by telling the minister, "You created the problem of censorship; it's up to you
to solve it."[21]

In January 1975, *O Estado* was celebrating the 100th anniversary of its
birth, when it was founded to fight the slavery still legal in Brazil and to
promote a republic. (It acknowledged only 95 years of life, excluding the five
years of Vargas captivity.)

On Jan. 3 the censor telephoned the newsroom to say he would not be
coming that night. The next day, he called to add that his departure was permanent. With that, the most renowned episode of direct censorship in Brazilian
history had ended.[22]

The government gave no hint as to the motive. Various guesses were that
the pullout was part of the new president's more favorable policy toward
human rights, that it was a "birthday gift" for the centennial, and that it was
a test to see how *O Estado* would behave without direct control.

The only overt pressure after the lifting of censorship had been occasional
phone calls from the justice ministry asking for small favors as to deletions. *O
Estado* says it refuses, but it has become more sober if no less forthright in its
reportage and commentary.

Proof that the lifting of censorship had not resulted in self-muzzling came
unmistakably in August 1976 when *O Estado* broke a series of what was
believed to be the most painstaking governmental reporting ever done in Brazil.
It was a series of front-page news stories revealing widespread abuses of government expense accounts among bureaucrats in Brasilia. Printing photographs
of official records, the newspaper showed the awesome luxury that could be obtained through imaginative use of one's office. A typical servant of the state
could increase his already large salary by $70,000 a year through legal use of
perquisites such as automobiles, entertainment expenses, and household upkeep, the stories revealed.[23] The newspaper reportedly received no rebukes
from the government over the stories; in fact, it was rumored that President
Geisel had welcomed the stories because they would give him political support
in carrying out reforms he had already planned.

The End of Opinião

Throughout *O Estado's* difficulties with censors, its staff never showed
fear that the problems would endanger the paper's life, considering the money,
political power and professional resources behind it. But a sharp contrast in the

possible effects of censorship was seen in the experience of *Opinião*, a mildly leftist tabloid weekly published in Rio. Unlike *O Estado*, it had few subscriptions and little advertising so was desperately dependent on being able to produce and sell a provocative product every week.

Opinião was started late in 1972 by Fernando Gasparián, who had achieved national attention before he was 40 in his roles as a manufacturer, businessmen's leader and visiting lecturer in economics at Britain's Oxford University. He decided to launch the publication because, he said, he wanted to give dissident young people an outlet for expression other than terrorism. The purpose was plainly laid out in the weekly's name, which means opinion.

Within two months the paper had fallen under direct censorship, having to send all copy off to Brasilia for checking. In an attempt to avoid too many losses, it retreated from original polemics and bought reprint rights from famous European and U.S. publications. Its staff members were mostly idealistic professional journalists who had formerly worked on leading newspapers and magazines.

Soon the paper was infuriating the censors by evading their orders. It was banned from speculating on the next president by name but got around this by running two seemingly acceptable stories side by side, thus making plain who the staff thought would be chosen as president.

Soon the time came when the censors had failed to return two-thirds of a week's pages by the press deadline. Gasparián ordered the presses to roll, but police quickly raided the plant, seized 17,000 copies of the paper and arrested Gasparián and his chief editor.

They were soon released, but the harsh censorship continued. Half or more of the copy sent to Brasilia often would be killed—sometimes entire editions. Among items omitted by censors were reprints from the *Wall Street Journal*, the *Washington Post* and *Harper's* magazine, plus a discourse by Sigmund Freud analyzing the mentality of military officers. One sentence crossed out came from a reprint of the Manchester *Guardian's* chess column, which read, "The whites have a great material advantage while the blacks have almost no legal opening. . . ."[24]

Finally the censors started demanding not just raw copy but finished dummy editions nearly a week before publication time. They promised to return the proofs, with deletions marked, just before press time.

In desperation, Gasparián tried legal resorts. He asked the courts to relieve him from censorship because it was not clearly authorized by law. Surprisingly, a federal appeals court agreed and ordered the censors withdrawn. But President Emilio Garrastazu Medici overruled the court, saying Institutional Act 5 gave him wide powers in civil liberties.[25]

Doomed by censorship to fluctuate in quality and publication time, *Opinião* continued to lose money at the rate of about $2,000 a week. Finally its best staff members began to resign in frustration. A farewell editorial in the last edition on April 1, 1977, said the publication would not resume until it was entirely free from prior censorship.[26]

Books

As in other areas of censorship, producers of books find it difficult to predict either the philosophy or the tactics that will come to bear on the inspection of any new book. Certainly there appears to be inconsistency; to see this one only has to visit a Brazilian bookstore and see volumes by Marx, Engels and Trotsky on sale, although moderate books by native authors are banned. Such lack of direction often serves to encourage authors and publishers to take chances they would not consider under an airtight authoritarian state.

Adding to the uncertainty is the fact that bans on books may come long after they have been initially approved. This reflects the fact that the censors are shorthanded and often approve works with cursory glances. Any military or civil officer can demand the withdrawal of a work, so in effect the censorship has a second round conducted by tens of thousands of bureaucrats and their families and friends once the book, film or song is on the market.

Some Brasilia-watchers also profess to see a liberalization emerging slowly but surely in the treatment of books and other works. All media suffered most intensely in the late 1960s when political terrorism and its repression were at their peak. Hundreds of intellectuals were jailed without charge—perhaps because of what they wrote, some speculated—but later they were released one by one. Few were brought to trial, and only one was convicted. He was Caio Prado, a renowned Marxist historian who was sentenced to 18 months in prison for a 1967 article calling for "revolution."[27]

It was not just leftists who felt the early lash. Brazil's internationally popular novelists Jorge Amado and Erico Veríssimo protested bitterly. Amado refused to allow his books to be put before the censor, even if this meant no sales in Brazil. Veríssimo tried to reason with the proponents of censorship:

> People tell me that Brazilians don't need liberty, but food, housing, medical assistance and a chance to work. I agree that all these are of major importance. But I don't understand the rationale of those who think these things can be achieved only under an authoritarian regime.[28]

During the course of Veríssimo's arguments he came to realize that, although he was not known as a political writer, he had unintentionally been affected by public affairs. He recalled that someone had asked him whether he considered his novels political:

> I said "No," and then I tried to explain the presence of political facts in my books. The more I thought about it, the more clearly I realized that no man, no matter how insignificant he might be, can flee from history. Political events hit us in the face every day by way of newspapers, television, cinema and other communications media. How can we ignore them?[29]

Another indication of the wide range of the censorship at that period was the banning of a new edition of Adolf Hitler's *Mein Kampf*. The justice minister, Alfredo Buzaid, well-known for his restrictions on Brazilian newspapers, explained that the book "fomented hatred against the Jewish people, stimulated the propaganda of racial discrimination and presented a doctrine that helped launch World War II."[30]

However, the literatarians saw a new dawn in 1972 when a military court unanimously acquitted a leftist who had been arrested four years before for publishing a translation of a Soviet professor's theoretical study of Marxism. The court held that the book was no threat to national security and that the charges never should have been filed.[31]

The literary censors did not desert the field in the 1970s, however. They filed charges against publishers of a book by Ernesto (Che) Guevara, and in 1977 they seized copies of a book accusing multinational companies of monopolizing Brazilian industry, even after 800 of the 4,000 printed copies had been sold.[32] Even so, they allowed another book accusing multinationals of financing Brazilian repression to circulate freely.[33]

Perhaps no act of the Brazilian censors brought home better to North Americans the capriciousness of the craft than deletion of the U.S. Declaration of Independence from the pages of the weekly *Movimento*. After this, *O Estado de São Paulo* reported the censorship and printed the translated document itself.

Arts and Entertainment

Because artists, film makers and musicians usually have much less political influence in Brazil than do prominent newspaper editors and novelists, they have appeared to be the most vulnerable of the groups restricted by censorship. The quiet despair of such people after the death of their brainchildren is a familiar theme in Brazil.

In part their susceptibility arises from the fact that they are open to attack on two fronts—politics and morality. Since there are few agreed-upon rules for moral control, it has often been used to obscure what is really political restriction. Speaking of the arts in general, Veríssimo observed: "The excuse for censorship is control of pornography, but it is really just a pretext for censoring political information."[34]

The vagueness of the obscenity concept led censors into the spectacle of, in the same year, banning Picasso and an angel. The Picasso work that came to grief was his erotic drawings, which had been sold for $5 in Brazilian bookstores for three years. But in 1973 the ministry of justice decided they were "contrary to public morals and good behavior." The action brought down a storm of protest by the country's sophisticates, including Rio's *Jornal do Brasil* and the resident erotic-surrealist school of painting, but all to no avail.[35]

The angel case involved a boutique in a fashionable section of Rio. Police closed it down because it displayed the statue of a nude angel in the window.[36]

Despite the confusion, censors have shown signs of struggling to develop a reliable rule of what constitutes lewdness in showing the human body. Like an army retreating to new lines, they started by allowing magazine editors to show one female nipple coyly airbrushed. Then they fell back to two nipples, not always brushed out. At the farthest extent of their retreat, they allowed a glimpse of pubic hair, but then they began to recover lost territory, pausing at one point to permit wet T-shirts. Toward the end of the 1970s the one-airbrushed-nipple position had been regained.

Since the earliest days of Brazil's dictatorship, censors have shown constant worry that artists will make them look foolish by getting away with material that has double meaning. Most keenly watched in this regard is popular music, where poetry, passion and slang can all produce ambiguous images.

A prime target of the censors has been Chico Buarque de Hollanda, an enormously popular singer-composer in the *bossa nova* style. At one point, two of every three of his songs were failing to get clearance. Censors became even more irate when they suspected the musician was chiding them with the lyrics of one of his hit records which says: "In spite of you, tomorrow will be another day. You sinned but you forgot to say 'I'm sorry.' " Buarque refused to say what he meant, but the censors took it personally and raided record stores to scoop up all the copies.

Buarque's quiet warfare with the censors became a laughing stock in Brazil. Another song with suspicious lyrics gained such popularity that police invaded the stage where Buarque was only strumming the melody on his guitar and asked him to stop.

At first censors were content to inspect the written lyrics of a song, saving the expense of record production if it failed to pass. But they began to fear, with good reason, that musicians would give a different meaning with the way the song was performed. For example, a song describing "a strong little rain" became a boast of male sexuality with an altered emphasis on syllables. Another spoke of "looking for you," but the tune made it sound much bawdier.[37]

Record sales were going up about 50 percent a year in the early 1970s, and producers were struggling to meet the demand. To cut their losses, the censors demanded that the companies furnish not just the written lyrics but the completed master tapes of musical performances. Then they fell far behind in returning the tapes to the owners, due to shortage of personnel and, according to rumor, the fact that they had only one tape deck for listening.[38]

The ardor of the censors even reached into a 15-nation international song festival, somewhat of an Olympics of music, being held in Rio. They banned a song from Portugal which referred to colonial war in Africa, speaking of "someone imprisoned for stealing a piece of bread, another one for having just said no."[39]

The slang of the drug subculture also disturbed the censors greatly. They heard about the tricks that rock singers had pulled in the United States and Europe by promoting drugs through disguised references in songs. So they drew up a list of all the unacceptable words, depending on what sense they are used in," such as the word "trip." The inspectors still were smarting from the tardiness with which they had discovered that a hit song about a Brazilian road called "BR3" really referred to one of the three veins where heroin is injected.[40]

Stage performances regularly have been canceled by censors, often after the producers have invested heavily and started the run in a nightclub. Sometimes, though, the officers seem satisfied if the act is exhibited only to small, high-paying audiences and kept away from the masses. Mercedes Sosa, an Argentine folk singer known for protest lyrics, was turned down in her application to perform in a 300,000-seat stadium but was approved for a nightclub in a stylish suburb of Rio. Similarly, permits to present plays in the slums of Rio are nearly always refused.[41] All-female audiences also are in disfavor as indicated by a women's liberation play which was a box office hit before censors banned it because men were refused tickets.[42]

Television is largely confined to entertainment and culture because the news and public affairs content is censored even more severely than the print media were. Even those in government who argue for a return to a free press never urge this reform for the broadcast media, as they are considered public utilities. The view is strengthened by the overwhelming dominance the Globo network has won in the television market, and it is an appendage of the staunchly conservative Rio newspaper *O Globo*.

The greater latitude of newspapers to cover sensitive news compared with television became evident in May 1977 when 10,000 students marched through the streets of São Paulo in the largest such demonstration since the turmoil of 1968. Newspapers had massive coverage; broadcast media had none.[43]

The Globo network is so careful that it has hired its own censor, the former head of the federal censorship branch in Rio. But this by no means averted difficulty, as the system lost about $1.7 million in 1976 on productions that were banned. These included a soap opera, for which 30 episodes were made before the ax fell; the loss was figured at half a million dollars.[44]

Films

Brazil has long been considered abroad as having the most creative movie industry in Latin America although, as in Italy and Argentina, most of its products are mindless sex comedies or other B-grade efforts. So it is ironic but perhaps inevitable that Brazilian films which win international honors are seen everywhere but in Brazil, thanks to censorship.

Such was the case with "All Nudity Will Be Punished," which won second place in the Berlin Film Festival for what judges called its "remarkable depiction of social problems in burlesque form." Despite the title, it concerns the tragedy of a prostitute who marries well but fails to make the middle-class social grade.[45] It was removed from circulation so abruptly that in one theater lights were turned on in the middle of its showing and the audience was told to leave.

If some observers saw an easing of controls on books as the 1970s wore on, there was little consolation for film makers. "All Nudity" was one of 10 films withdrawn from circulation when a tough new censorship chief was appointed in mid-1973. The justification offered by the new chief was that the films ran into "accusations made by highly qualified persons." He did not specify the accusations.[46]

When a censor inspects a film, he works from a check list. Among the criteria are:

1. Does the movie harm the family, democracy or social equilibrium?

2. Does it induce free love, deal with generational conflicts, show shocking and immoral scenes, contain Marxist propaganda, or depict racial problems in Brazil?

3. Does it deal with black power in the United States; try to demoralize or ridicule police, the military or the church; or distort Christian doctrine or incite religious conflict?[47]

Even after censors ban a certain film, the police sometimes meet frustration because of clandestine showings. When "The Last Tango in Paris" was at the peak of its popularity, Rio residents deprived of seeing it in their theaters could still seek it out in an aristocrat's residence where it was being offered at $16 a seat.[48]

Censors also were expected to protect the government from exposure of Brazil's poverty-stricken masses and beleaguered Indians. A highly poetic "docudrama'' about the intense misery of the country's northeastern drylands was invited to Critics' Week at the Cannes Film Festival, but the master film was locked up in Brasilia after the censors saw and banned it. The producer denied that it contained any criticism of the government.[49] Another film about the Amazon basin, widely seen abroad, was banned in Brazil because it showed too many naked Indians.[50]

Film makers who collaborate with the censors can salvage part of their expense and effort by cutting some scenes and refilming others with an officer's advice. Then, before it gets final clearance, it must be shown to the most privileged audience in Brazil. This is a panel of high-ranking military and government officials, plus sometimes church dignitaries, who screen the films in Brasilia. After watching the films through to the end, they decide that many of them are too dangerous for the general public.[51]

After losing too many investments through censorship, movie producers often look for safe ways to make money, putting their creativity on the shelf. Two favorite outlets are the banal sex farces, which hint at but do not show immorality, and films based on books or plays which have already escaped punishment. Even the latter holds out hazards, as was seen in the cuts ordered in a film version of the Brazilian classic *Saint Bernard*.

Censorship at the Frontier

Twenty men sit in a room in the Rio international telephone exchange. Their job, according to one of the operators, is to randomly listen in on international calls for anything amiss. The operators have to join in the censorship, she said: "We have to write down the name and number of everyone who makes or receives a call, and we are told to listen very carefully for anything suspicious." The mail is no more private; people living in Brazil are accustomed to getting letters that have been opened and resealed. One São Paulo resident was arrested and beaten after receiving a letter from a friend abroad who complained about Brazil.[52]

Censorship of messages coming into Brazil is an integral part of the overall plan—a link in the chain of control often missing in other authoritarian countries. The curtain around Brazil is by no means impregnable, and actions by the censorship service often are more symbolic than real. By one means or another, Brazilian elites remain notably well-informed about the world around them.

Censors have never conceded that they are using political criteria for censoring incoming materials. Rather, a crusade against pornography is the banner raised.

In the first eight years of the military regime, foreign sex magazines such as *Playboy* and its imitators were allowed to be sold freely in Brazil so long as they were sealed in a plastic sack and marked for sales only to adults. Then, in 1972–73, prior censorship was started, and U.S. and European publications by the dozens were prohibited. Most were strictly entertainment magazines, but the victims included the respected German news weekly *Der Spiegel*, along with several German middle-class picture magazines. This hit hard at the large German-speaking communities in Brazil.

Under the system adopted at that time, all imported publications had to be registered with Brazilian authorities, and three copies per issue had to be submitted. If after the first censorship the inspectors decided there was no danger, the publisher could get a certificate of exemption from further regular checking.

The irritation of losing the sex magazines was relatively minor to Brazilian readers, and they were consoled with Brazilian imitations which bought reprint rights on articles from *Playboy* and the like, sanitizing them somewhat and combining them with more demure photos made in the country. Meanwhile, more substantial magazines continued to be brought in—even an issue of *Newsweek* in 1976 which ran a cover story about police torture in Brazil and elsewhere.

But a new crackdown in mid-1977 appeared much more ominous. Censors began to talk about keeping out not only publications which "run counter to morality and good standards of behavior" but also those that are "subversive" and "contain material contrary to public order." Thought leaders saw the announcement as a serious danger, and *O Estado de São Paulo* called it "one more document for fattening up international reports on human rights violations in Brazil." A congressman declared: "Brazil has become an island in all but the geographical sense."

It was also feared that supplies of imported newspapers and books would be imperiled. It is common for U.S. newspapers to be brought in daily for tourists, and many Brazilians get them by mail. The list of banned books already was past 350 titles, including titles such as *The Happy Hooker* and *Quotations from Chairman Mao*.[53]

PERSONAL DANGER

Throughout most of the period since the military takeover in 1964, Brazilian journalists have been arrested and sometimes tortured and imprisoned, resulting in death in more than one case. The fact that the arrests continue underscores the newsmen's tendency to test or even ignore their limits. Since one can find many unpunished examples of offenses at least as severe as those that bring arrests, it must be concluded that the elaborate laws are failing because they do not deter violations.

Perhaps the strongest weapon the journalists have is their assumption that it is still possible for them to do an honest day's work. Even though this often brings them to grief in the short run, it puts a constant burden on the government to reassert its control. For example, in the case which has brought most disrepute to the government—the Herzog affair—the suspect voluntarily walked into the police station when he heard he was being sought.

Another factor tending to frustrate controls is the willingness of some editors and union leaders to publicly protest incursions on the rights of journalists. This response varies widely, but most who get into trouble can depend on it.

The situation has become snarled in another issue—subversion. Even though aggressive opposition to the government was stamped out by the early 1970s, several layers of underground activity remained, and, according to observers, many journalists have been involved. Because editors do not want to put their heads on the block to protect a communist cell, some have stood by while their reporters went to jail.

Editors cannot rely on the law enforcement system to produce the objective truth about such cases in the course of a trial; thus few editors feel certain of the facts. They discount the government's charges, which often are used as subterfuges to punish news-gathering. But word-of-mouth reports among newsroom insiders conform that underground activities exist.

Such activities range in seriousness from communist plotting to operation of a home mimeograph to distribute stories censored from newspapers, although some police interrogators treat all of them with equal urgency.

Such arrests tend to come in waves because, nearly a decade after terrorism effectively ended, police still speak in terms of militant threats to the state. Particularly sweeping were the crackdowns in 1968, 1972 and 1975. Often several hundred persons are caught up in such campaigns, because the police suspect anyone associated with the prime offenders. Mailing lists of clandestine publications are favorite weapons of investigators.

State action against working newspaper reporters has ranged from formal court charges to random brutality. An example of what reporters can expect from police is shown in the case of Antonio Carlos de Carvalho, a reporter from *O Estado de São Paulo* working in Rio. One night in 1975, political police burst into his apartment and demanded to be told where his wife's cousin was. When he pleaded ignorance, the police put a hood on him and dragged him to a car. They drove a while, stopped and beat him for two hours. Then they put him in a cell six feet square and turned on a siren which shrieked in his ears all night. They released him the next morning; anyone asking about the case was told there was no record of it.[54]

The Carvalho incident apparently was the result of a widely publicized government crackdown on clandestine printshops. Since finding such facilities was not rare, there was wide speculation that the crackdown was an indirect warning to the legal opposition party, which had scored heavily in elections. Rio's best-known newspaper, *Jornal do Brasil,* editorialized that the announcement must be viewed in comparison with "illegal arrests, tortures, disappearance of people, and suppression of free thoughts."[55]

The Herzog Case

It took a martyr to turn the protests into a rebellion of public opinion, however. Before the episode was over, a general had been transferred, people of three religious faiths had stood together to hear their government condemned, and the Brazilian regime had fallen into international disgrace.

Liberals in late 1975 were still putting their hopes in the new general-president, Ernesto Geisel, but it became apparent that he was having trouble with army hard-liners who were panicked at the example of communist successes in Portugal.

The most feared of the regional military commanders, Ednardo d'Avila Melo, had São Paulo as his headquarters. He had just said publicly that Brazil was "fighting a war against Red fascism" and that "traitors and maniacs" were getting help from abroad.[56]

Meeting in São Paulo at the time were the Inter-American Press Association and the American Society of Travel Agents. President Geisel, speaking to the travel agents, was bragging that Brazil did not have riots, unlike other countries. He welcomed tourists to come see Brazil's "humanistic understanding of life."[57]

But the IAPA convention turned into a bitter embarrassment for the government, because delegates in public sessions were given frank descriptions of how journalists were abused in Brazil. The convention was not molested, but local newsmen began getting anonymous phone calls saying they should enjoy themselves because after the "IAPA party" would come a "suppression party."

What followed was a wave of more than 200 arrests of supposed tools of communism in the city. These included lawyers, leaders of the permitted opposition party, labor officials, doctors, professors, students—and 14 journalists.

One of the persons on the arrest list was Vladimir Herzog, the 38-year-old father ot two sons. A Yugoslav Jew, he had fled the Nazis with his parents when he was a boy; they found a new life as Brazilian citizens.

His career had been brilliant. He had been a reporter for *O Estado,* which had the most prestigious news staff in Brazil. Then he had gone off to Britain to become a producer and announcer for the British Broadcasting Corp. Brazilian service. Returning home, he became cultural editor of the news magazine *Visão* and made television documentaries on the side. One of his films, about the fishermen of Copacabana Beach, won wide acclaim. São Paulo's state educational station had set out to approach BBC's category, so it hired Herzog as news director just two months before the police crackdown. He had undergone a security check, getting complete clearance from the federal intelligence service.[58]

When he went to his office early on a Saturday morning, he was told that military security was looking for him.

"I'll go see what they want," he told a colleague. "I have nothing to hide, nothing to fear."

Herzog entered the army offices at 8:30 a.m. By 3 p.m. he was dead. The army announced the next day that he had committed suicide by hanging himself with his belt. He had been confronted with other journalists who had implicated him in their confessions of belonging to a communist cell, the statement said, and Herzog had confessed orally, naming other colleagues, and had been left alone to write out his confession. According to the story, he had torn up his confession, but guards had reassembled it.[59]

The army refused Mrs. Herzog's request for an independent autopsy. She got the body in a sealed coffin.

Monday morning's newspapers reported the case fully, although censors blocked broadcasters from covering it. The papers noted that Herzog's was the third death within a few weeks at the interrogation center.[60]

Although the newspapers did not editorialize about the case, the São Paulo journalists' union, under the new presidency of activist Audalio Dantas, flatly blamed the army for Herzog's death.

"We don't believe the journalists were arrested because of their political activities," Dantas said later. "But we did not judge the merits of the charges against them. For us they were just journalists."[61]

The funeral was held quickly, on Monday, by Jewish custom. All of São Paulo's federal and state legislators were among the 600 attending, along with four of the other arrested journalists, who had been released from jail by a suddenly liberal army headquarters. The Jewish elders had placed the grave in the cemetery's main section, far from the section reserved for suicides.[62]

Then a storm of protest began to break. Legislators went back to their desks to call for investigations, and a senator from a neighboring state interrupted a debate in Brasilia to say the army should not ruin a proud past with such acts as Herzog's death:

"Hitler, when he wanted to practice such ignominious acts . . . did not use the army but the SS, who were dressed in black so as not to compromise the army."[63] Newspapers played up his remark, and they also began to editorialize. One commented:

"It doesn't matter very much if Vladimir Herzog committed suicide or not. The suicide of a man under interrogation is as grave . . . as the killing of a prisoner."[64]

Students at the University of São Paulo, where Herzog had won a doctorate and was a lecturer, went on strike demanding a "full explanation" of the death. Professors voted to join them.

The union organized a memorial service for Herzog, and Paulo Evaristo Cardinal Arns, archbishop of São Paulo, offered his cathedral. He joined Rabbi Henry Sobel of the Israelite Congregation and the Rev. James Wright, a Presbyterian leader, in conducting the service. All the psalms, hymns and addresses were condemnations of repression.

"From the first to the last pages of the Holy Bible," declared the cardinal, "God tells us constantly that cursed is he who marks his hands with the blood of his brother."[65]

About 8,000 persons jammed the seats and aisles of the cathedral, spilling over into a plaza outside. Police had tried to discourage them by setting up roadblocks which paralyzed traffic for miles around. Many motorists just parked in the jams and walked to the cathedral.

The crowd's fury was obvious, but leaders of journalists and students went to pains to avert a confrontation. During the memorial, union president Dantas urged the listeners not to accept any provocation, but rather to accept sadness. Students abandoned plans to carry banners in the street and decided to end the strike.

In newsrooms, the reaction ranged from ridicule to terror. Skeptics noted that photos of Herzog's body showed it hanging from a steel bar 5½ feet off the floor, whereas Herzog was taller than that. Also, the belt around his neck was not the kind he wore.

Others were afraid, because a list of journalists Herzog purportedly had named was circulating. An editorial writer for *Jornal da Tarde* who was named in the list turned himself in, but he was escorted by Dantas and by Ruy Mesquita, director of the newspaper. They were treated cordially by two generals and were told the writer could come back later for questioning.[66]

Shock waves rolled in for several months afterward. Spokesmen for human rights around the world condemned the episode, and Catholic bishops in the São Paulo area set a special day of fasting in defense of civil liberties. They distributed throughout their archdiocese—the largest in the world—a document deploring "flagrant disrespect of the human person."[67]

More than 1,000 Brazilian journalists signed a full-page advertisement in *O Estado* headed "In the Name of Truth." They asked for an effective investigation into the Herzog case. A month later, a military court closed the case and said it had nothing new to add.[68]

Three months after Herzog's death, a fourth prisoner died in the São Paulo army center, again alleged to be a suicide. This time President Geisel transferred Gen. d'Avila Melo.

Shortly after that, an eyewitness account of Herzog's last hours was reported in two newspapers, *O Estado* and *Jornal do Brasil*. The witness, another journalist named Rodolfo Konder, said he had been picked up and tortured at the same time as Herzog. He said that after prolonged pain under electrical shock in sensitive spots, he was taken before Herzog and was told to persuade him to confess to communist work, but Herzog denied it. Konder said that as he was taken away he heard Herzog screaming.[69]

Although journalists continued to find themselves in court for one reason or another, imprisonment of them before conviction almost disappeared after the Herzog incident. And of the 14 arrested during the episode, only one was convicted.[70]

The persistence of Brazilian citizens in pursuing justice was epitomized in a five-year legal crusade waged by Herzog's widow and colleagues. The government tried various stratagems to frustrate them, even to retiring a judge. But in late 1978 the Court of Appeals ruled that Herzog had been killed while being tortured in custody.

Factors Affecting Danger

The degree of official danger to journalists depends partly on whom they work for and where they do their work. Powerful dailies such as *O Estado* and *Jornal do Brasil* have much more influence in freeing their reporters from the snares than do the smaller media. Often simply a protest will bring preferential treatment, as happened when *Jornal do Brasil* reporter Raul Ryff was caught up in an anti-communist drive in 1972.[71]

A few of the dailies, especially *O Estado,* are known for standing behind their reporters even after the initial protest. When *O Estado's* bureau in Brasilia produced a story embarrassing to the government, the bureau chief was told to come in for questioning and to bring the reporter who wrote the story. The chief refused to reveal the story's author, and officials charged him with alienating the people from the government. The newspaper sent the best lawyer in São Paulo to represent the chief, and the charge was dismissed.

"Most importantly," the bureau chief recalled, "my paper supported me and I continued to work. In other papers, the situation would have been very critical."[72]

An *O Estado* executive in São Paulo observed that such incidents would tend to make the average reporter more timid, "so you have to find a man with courage enough." Even so, he noted, employees in remote bureaus often have to be replaced to protect them.[73]

Opponents of the national newspapers take advantage of their relative weakness in the smaller cities. After *O Estado's* correspondent in the northeastern city of Recife, Carlos García, wrote a story that angered local officials, police tortured him in an effort to make him swear that he had acted under orders from a communist cell in the *O Estado* newsroom.

Censors killed an editorial of protest about the affair, but *O Estado's* director sent the message by telegram to the minister of justice. The editorial read, "Not able to touch *O Estado* directly, the authorities avenged themselves against García."[74]

Owners of major media rarely are personally ensnared by the law, although those of weaker ones are considered fair game. Mrs. Niomar Moniz Sodre Bittencourt, owner and director of a financially failing opposition newspaper, *Correio de Manhã*, was kept under house arrest two months. Fernando Gasparián, who had defied censors to start an unapproved press run of his political weekly *Opinião*, spent seven hours at the federal police station. However, Julio Mesquita, whose *O Estado* has offended much more than have the smaller papers, has never been harassed more severely than with a summons to testify in court cases.

Editors who are not owners are treated less politely. Alberto Dines, an internationally known editor and winner of the Maria Moors Cabot Award, was accustomed to spending several days in jail at a time when he was editor of *Jornal do Brasil*. Mrs. Bittencourt's chief editor, Osvaldo Peralva, had to serve out his detention in an army barracks at the same time she was confined to her home.

When a medium has no backers other than the public, the government feels free to take even more sweeping measures. In 1970, the irreverent weekly *Pasquim*, specializing in political satire, was outselling all dailies in Brazil, although it depended entirely on newsstand sales. In one of the government's habitual roundups of supposed subversives, it scooped up nine *Pasquim* editors and writers—nearly the entire staff.

Although the staff spent more than a month in jail, the government reaped more ridicule from the episode than it did from an issue of the always-censored *Pasquim*.

A week after the staff was trucked off to jail, authorities were shocked to see the paper come out on time, full of its usual veiled but sharp humor. Nearly all the stories and cartoons were signed "Sig," the name of the fictitious rat who is the magazine's symbol. Unable to reveal the arrests, Sig bemoaned the "influenza epidemic" that had wiped out his friends.

The real authors were a galaxy of Brazil's best writers, who had volunteered to keep the paper going. Tired of this, the government shut down the paper entirely, sending repairmen around five days later to cut off the phones. A week later, it reversed its field, turned on the phones and allowed the paper to resume publication. Then, after a few days, it freed most of the staff members. They were ordered not to talk publicly about their jailing and to report to military authorities once a week.[75]

Foreigners' Treatment

The Brazilian regime has shown much less hesitance than those in other Latin American countries to intimidate foreign correspondents. Although they have been threatened with quite serious legal penalties, the punishment usually consists of interrogation or expulsion from the country, or both. Contributors to *Time,* the *New York Times,* the Associated Press, *Le Monde* of Paris, and Agence France Presse have been arrested; part-time correspondents have most often been affected, although the AFP chief in Rio was expelled.[76]

The most vicious punishment charged to the government by a foreign reporter has been the alleged torture of Fred Morris, a 41-year-old former Methodist missionary who had sent stories to *Time* and the Associated Press. Morris said he was held without charges for 17 days in Recife, during which he was repeatedly beaten, given intense electrical shocks and threatened with death. Finally, after consular intervention, he was expelled without his possessions.[77]

CLOSURE AND SEIZURE

In keeping with its concern for economic efficiency, the Brazilian military has applied its pressure much more on media supplies (censorship) and operators (legal harassment) than on the finished product or the production unit itself. Thus seizure of issues and closure of the mass medium have been relatively infrequent and usually have been in conjunction with some other control such as censorship.

As noted before, confiscations of issues can come about as belated censorship, as in the case of a book that was recalled after 800 of its 4,000 copies were sold. This also occurred in 1972 when an offensive reference was discovered in *Jornal da Tarde,* afternoon affiliate of *O Estado,* only after 40,000 copies had gone to the newsstands and had to be recovered and destroyed.[78] The company later filed suit seeking financial damages from the government. The paper was under direct censorship at the time, but the objectionable reference had slipped past the censors.

This and also another case underscored the irony that an efficient censor can prevent large losses incurred by the recall of an issue. The second incident involved a statement by Ruy Mesquita, one of the brothers who head the *O Estado* company. He had written a letter saying that press restrictions were degrading Brazil to "the status of a banana republic." It was censored from his own papers but appeared in an uncensored daily, *Correio do Povo* in Porto Alegre. Police surrounded its plant and seized all copies of the issue before they went on sale.[79]

Pasquim, the weekly whose stock in trade is satire, discovered that it had generated some unintended humor when it ran an editorial just after the lifting of its censorship in 1975. "Uncensored does not mean free," the article said, and it noted that the paper "could be seized while you are reading this." This is just what happened; all copies were confiscated.[80]

Despite the government's strong interest in educational broadcasting, it has shown little inclination to enlarge its radio and television holdings by ousting private licensees from assigned frequencies. Broadcast newsmen know how to muzzle themselves much better than those in print media.

The most celebrated case of political retaliation in broadcasting concerned the radio station of the Catholic Church in São Paulo, whose license was lifted for several years because of church leaders' protests against the government. Another station, operated by *Jornal do Brasil,* was put off the air for several days for broadcasting a message from terrorist kidnappers.[81]

FOREIGN DEALINGS

Although the main power brokers in Brazil's military government are clearly rightist and fanatically anticommunist, the regime has adopted a number of nationalistic communication measures which bear a startling resemblance to those advocated by the most vehemently leftist Third Worlders. These efforts by Brazil concern exclusion of foreign ownership, limitations on imports of cinema and television films, and subsidy of local productions of such films. Some antiforeign laws exist in regard to news sales, but these have made no change in previous practices.

Brazil's leaders were reinforced in their drive against foreign ownership by the success that Time-Life Inc. had in invading the country's television market. Time-Life had joined forces in 1962 with the Rio daily *O Globo* to form the Globo network, which soon came to heavily dominate competition in cities all over Brazil. New York executives and technicians poured in, installing a heavy investment in American equipment. The network quickly acquired the most polished U.S.-style production techniques in Latin America.

This raised fears on both right and left that Brazilian television would become an extension of the U.S. video industry. So a ban on *any* foreign ownership or management, even minority control like Time-Life's 49 percent interest in Globo, was included in the package of media laws decreed in the late 1960s. Foreigners could not evade the law by becoming citizens; "Brazilian" in this case meant native-born.

The move did not distress Time-Life greatly, as it like other U.S. investors had already decided to pull out of Latin American properties; the market had become vastly overcrowded and unprofitable. Time-Life completed its pullout from Brazil by 1971, announcing that it had sold its holdings for $3,850,000, which it took home to invest in cable television.[82]

The government has been trying to limit imports of foreign films and give Brazilian films an advantage on movie bills since 1939, when theaters were required to show domestic films seven days a year. As production increased, the quota rose steadily until it reached 112 in 1970, when only 72 were produced. This meant theaters had to force-feed domestic films, good or bad, to their customers and lose money, or evade the law. The latter occurred more often than not, and the government backed down to a requirement of 84 per year by the mid-1970s. By that time production had leveled off at about 100.[83]

Occasional efforts would be made to enforce the quota by closing down movie houses that violated it. In 1972, police in Rio shut 28 theaters for up to 30 days.[84]

Similar pressures have been put on broadcasters. The government's favorite argument for requiring more locally made shows is to cite unemployment figures among Brazilian performing artists. The minister of communication went so far as to hint that the 25,000 out-of-work musicians in Rio would turn to a life of crime, all because of imported tapes and records.[85]

Broadcasters were protesting that Brazil did not have the technical equipment to produce enough programs without spending a lot more on them than they would on imports. The minister answered this by saying in effect that broadcasters would have to settle for a lower profit. Besides, the government was committed to decreasing the violence on television, mostly derived from imports.

Brazil went through most of the 1970s with a law requiring that broadcasters fill half their time with domestic material. But little was done to enforce the rule, and it was widely violated, some radio stations using nearly 100 per cent imported music. Even so, the government was considering an increase in the domestic minimum to 70 per cent.[86]

PROPAGANDA

Although sociologists have never agreed what makes up the Brazilian national character, none puts forward self-discipline and a sense of civic responsibility as the most notable traits. Yet these are among the elements the military regime has been ceaselessly trying to build. It can be argued that this propaganda campaign is the most vigorous one ever waged outside the communist world since Hitler's, yet it differs completely in tone, technique and content.

Several themes have emerged as dominant goals as to what Brazilians are supposed to think:

1. National pride expressed as a quiet, not belligerent attitude about Brazil's place among the family of nations. The nation's recent economic progress is the main point of pride.

2. A desire to work harder for the national goals, particularly in teamwork. "You build Brazil!" is emblazoned on big conspicuous posters.

3. Satisfaction with the job the present government is doing. The appeal does not stress dogma and never stresses identities of leaders. "There isn't a people on earth that won't collaborate with a well-intentioned government," a radio and TV announcement constantly declares.

4. Willingness to carry out specific civic reforms such as cleanliness. The slogan "A developed nation is a clean nation" appeals to Brazilians' desire to lose the banana-republic image.

To implant these ideas, the government has formed a federal public relations agency which is known for soft-sell, slickly modern approaches to mass persuasion. Headed by a colonel who avoids the public eye, the agency staff includes a journalist, a psychologist, and a sociologist. It sets the general themes and then contracts the execution of them to some of Brazil's highly competent private advertising agencies. Its budget figures are kept secret; one staff member says they are relatively small but "well-used."[87]

The messages, nearly always delivered in a few seconds on broadcast media or in simple phrases on billboards or bumper stickers, follow the format of modern commercial advertising. Visuals on television are often brightly animated, tunes are irresistably hummable, and slogans are often clever. Occasionally they are very sober, as when an appealing young boy asks his father "What is nationalism, Dad?" and gets a chummy lecture on Brazil's mission in the world of tomorrow.

Little complaint of brainwashing is heard from the Brazilians, who generally consider the ads harmless.

"We don't have any Goebbels-type radio here because the government isn't interested in that type," noted one radio executive. "It is very cost-conscious and pragmatic—very management-oriented."[88]

Like all advertising, it can get under the skin. One opposition candidate at a rally in an affluent Rio suburb got his best applause by calling the television spots "a consistent annoyance and invasion of our privacy."[89]

Best-known of the slogans is the endlessly repeated "This is a country that is moving ahead!" The satirical weekly *Pasquim* spoofed it with a cartoon showing Brazil fleeing a pack of foreign creditors. When the president declared "No one can hold this country back!" and the propagandists picked it up as a slogan, *Pasquim* ran it under a sketch of a sleigh plunging out of control over a cliff.[90]

Other than the spot announcements and printed sloganeering, government propaganda plays a small role in Brazilian public life. The president pre-empts television time three or four times a year for speeches, patriotic holidays are covered extensively and the federal publicity bureau, Agencia Nacional, sends out a steady flow of releases which major newspapers take great pride in ignoring; smaller papers use them to fill space.

The federal government owns 54 of the 994 radio stations in Brazil, but they are used almost exclusively for educational purposes. Although the state has reserved a number of television channels, it has not exploited them yet and funnels its educational programs through other owners.[91]

A nightly low-key propaganda program has been required of all radio stations since the mid-1930s; thus it has lived through a variety of dictatorial and democratic governments. In many ways it is just what the "people's journalism" forces in UNESCO have been demanding recently as an alternative to private ownership, because it gives the government's side of the news, untouched by commercial hands.

Sent live by phone lines or shortwave, the program runs from 7 to 8 p.m. The first 10 minutes is for the president's use, the next 20 for ministries and the last 30 for congress and the courts. Embarrassed by the extremely low ratings of the program, the military government has tried to replace it with five-minute segments, but congressmen are reluctant to give up their part of the platform. The program's official name is "The Voice of Brazil"; since unhappy listeners have no option except to turn off their radios, it is popularly known as "The Hour of Silence."

Brazil entered the international shortwave propaganda arena in May 1972, modeling its service after the Voice of America. It began by aiming its signals at the United States and Europe, transmitting news, cultural and economic items, and music. The goal was to enhance Brazil's image abroad and promote its exports.[92]

GOVERNMENT ADVERTISING

Although the federal government owns well over half of manufacturing industry in Brazil, it makes relatively little use of this to control media through placement of advertisement. This would be contrary to its basic policy of favoring whatever tactics makes for better commerce, undistorted by political preference.

Officials of the various states, being closer and often more sensitive to their areas' mass media than the grand strategists in Brasilia, are more likely to manipulate advertising for enterprises under their control.

A dispute between the governor of Bahia state and the daily *Jornal da Bahia* went on for several years in and out of court. The wrangling arose over charges of corruption against the governor and was fueled by the paper's protests when he canceled all official advertising in it and pressured private advertisers to do the same.

Larger, wealthier newspapers can resist such attacks more easily, but none has gone so far as *O Estado de São Paulo*. In 1973 the state governor there became enraged over an exposé in the newspaper about a life insurance monopoly which had defrauded railroad workers and which the governor had headed. He struck back by cutting off the state's advertising in both *O Estado* and its affiliate *Jornal de Tarde*.

The papers' management countered with two moves aimed at humiliating the governor. First they said they would never accept the state's ad order while the current governor was in office, even if asked to. Second, as they said in a report, "Considering that the main victim of this pressure would be the people, we decided that both *O Estado* and *Jornal de Tarde* would publish every advertisement and edict of public interest, free of charge."[93]

ELECTION CAMPAIGN CONTROLS

Few governments have ever been so assiduous as the military regime in Brazil at maintaining the appearance of democracy while preventing the reality of it. Since 1970, it has held regular elections at all levels from city councils up to the federal congress, which in turn goes through the motions of choosing the presidential candidate already anounced by the military.

After outlawing 13 political parties which existed before the 1964 coup, the regime set up two official parties, one for those favoring the government and the other for those against. Although the largest bloc of voters cast blank ballots at first, the trend moved steadily in favor of the opposition party, the Brazilian Democratic Movement (MDB).

The pro-government party, the National Renovation Alliance (ARENA), has little role in national administration. But the regime has made clear that, while it will continue to count votes honestly, it will not permit ARENA to lose a majority in the national congress. In addition to a welter of harassments and punishments meted out to MDB politicians before and after they win elections, the mass media are used as a control mechanism.

Ostensibly, the government seeks to prevent the campaign hysteria which was familiar in pre-coup days. It prohibits candidates from buying advertising and gives them equal time on television to state their cases. Each candidate is watched closely for libel and is cut off the air abruptly if the censor feels he is defaming his opponent. In 1974, an ARENA candidate was cut off for accusing the other side of getting funds from Cuba, while an MDB candidate suffered the same fate for saying his opponent was fleecing the public treasury.[94]

These appear to be democratic measures, but they put MDB at a disadvantage because it is the challenger. The government campaigns constantly with propaganda about its achievements and also can curry votes with official patronage at the local level. MDB has to prove that it will continue the economic strides made under the military and provide liberty besides. Stigmatized by its past as a sham opposition, it needs the public attention much more than ARENA to succeed, particularly in the more conservative small cities.

As MDB has gained steadily in elections, the government has steadily cut down on the campaigning allowed. After combing out the name-calling to the extent of making the debates dull in 1974, it moved on to banning televised arguments completely in 1976, allowing candidates only to submit their photographs and statements to be read on the air. These were to include only party affiliation, the candidate's background, and the time and place of voting. But some evaded this by skillful resumé-writing. One candidate in Rio reported that she was "author of articles on the low income of workers . . . the daily trials of the housewife . . . and the inhuman garbage collection tax."

Even so, the restriction was almost a death blow to electoral competition. *O Estado de São Paulo* editorialized: "There is no media magician capable of giving the slightest liveliness or interest to this monotonous exhibition of candidates."[95]

Still another weakening came the next year when the government suspended a law which allowed each political party two one-hour broadcasts a year to tell about its program. Using such an allowance, MDB had criticized the government and demanded the return of democracy. President Geisel, in stopping the practice, ordered one of the MDB spokesmen removed from office and stripped of political rights for 10 years.[96]

SECRECY

Due more to the diligence of reporters than any openness by officials, a surprising amount of information escapes from government offices into the media. The journalists are helped by cracks in the unity among militarists and bureaucrats in Brasilia, despite intense efforts to stamp out intramural rivalry. This assistance does not take the form of public statements but rather of file cabinets left open. It is noteworthy that *O Estado de São Paulo's* exposé of the over-indulgence of bureaucrats came directly from official records.

Some matters can remain maddeningly hidden to reporters. President Emilio Garrastazu Medici caught them by surprise in 1971 when he revealed that not only would the handling of some national security cases remain secret, but also the laws governing them. He said some decrees would be listed only by their titles in the official gazette. The leader of the opposition party, MDB, said that "from now on, we shall be . . . knocking our heads on invisible and unsuspected walls."[97]

MEDIA STIMULATION

In some parts of Brazil's Amazon basin, which is two-thirds the size of the United States, residents cannot receive a newspaper or a television signal, and the only radio signals come from the Voice of America, BBC and Radio Havana. Since six million Brazilians live in this area, the rulers in Brasilia are gripped by the fear that the Amazonians will be alienated from the nation.

The projected solution has been to build immense radio transmitters, a saturation of television stations and a satellite communication system rivaling the best in the world—all at government expense or with its help. (Message transmission is a federal monopoly.)

Plans were announced in 1972 to begin installation of three 250-kilowatt medium-wave stations along the Amazon River; they would be five times the power of the strongest signal allowed in the United States. The locations would be Belem, at the river's mouth; Manaus, the capital of the state of Amazonas; and Porto Velho, near Bolivia.

Television expansion had reached the point by the mid-1970s where every state and territory in the Amazon region had at least one television station—often more—in its capital city. Television sales in Manaus doubled in 1976, supplied by set manufacturing there started by Japanese investors.[98]

The government is determined to knit the nation together by making telephone, radio and television signals available to every citizen, no matter how remote in the jungle. Since the country stretches over 2,700 miles—farther than from New York to San Francisco—forging the links with microwave towers every 30 miles would be a hopeless goal.

So Brazil has taken the satellite route. By the mid-1970s it had already become one of the five heaviest users of the Intelsat circuits, and it has placed an order for launching of its own satellite from Cape Canaveral. This would give it 3,756 voice circuits of its own, plus four television channels; 600 more circuits are set aside for the military.[99]

To receive the signals bounced off the satellite, 17 ground stations had already been built by the middle of the decade for the Intelsat system. With the country's own device in orbit, the ground station total is expected to rise to 95, and the most remote Amazon towns will be able to hook in with national networks instead of getting videotapes by air mail. When the president speaks, he will *know* the whole nation can hear and see him.

Another method of official stimulation of media development is subsidies for film making. This started as a form of back-handed censorship, as the government seeks to drive out film makers it dislikes by giving a financial advantage to those of whom it approves. By 1976 such collaboration had resulted in two homemade superproductions rivaling Hollywood's in sophistication and box office sales. The producers, happy with their new riches, shrugged off the censorship they had gone through. One said that his role was "to get along with it—to have the wisdom and the courage to live with it."[100]

While broadcast media were benefiting most from government projects, publications were seeking their market expansion through a vigorous literacy campaign. Recognizing the drop-off in literacy that usually follows crash programs, the program's organizers have set up cultural posts to keep the new literates reading and have even provided eyeglasses to those who need them. According to official figures, the adult illiteracy rate fell from 34 to 19 per cent in the first half of the 1970s, and the goal was to stamp it out completely by 1980.[101]

RESISTANCE TO CONTROLS

Brazilians' interaction with their military regime seems to indicate that they are willing to accept the patronism with which they have been familiar since colonial days, but they will not gladly suffer tyranny, particularly from a government that claims it is not tyrannical. Since the fading of guerrilla resistance in the 1960s the typical form of protest against tyranny, including control of expression, has been one of a wounded sense of fairness. Like the British, the people of Brazil can say, in quite moderate tones, "We don't play the game that way."

Protests of media controls have been heard almost from the start of the military regime, usually coming in waves, but they started with ripples and have successively gained strength. They have come not only from editors but from leaders of private institutions—church, law, labor, intellectuals. They also have come from within the government itself, even from the military. And, as evidence of the inconsistency of censorship, many of these protests have appeared in public print.

The complaints from within government naturally have come most forcefully from the opposition party, MDB. Hardly a year goes by that some MDB legislator does not create a scandal by criticizing the regime's incursions on free expression and other misdeeds. One of the most dramatic was in 1972 when MDB leader Oscar Pedroso Horta, who had been brought down by a cerebral hemorrhage, wrote a speech which was delivered in congress by his deputy. He threw back at President Garrastazu Medici his promises to listen to anyone who wanted to speak up in public. This had been prevented by censorship, Pedroso Horta said, which made it impossible for anyone to "manifest opinions that are not strictly laudatory of the government's work. . . . Does the president not see contradictions between this state of affairs and the promises he made . . . ?"[102]

A similar note was sounded during the outrage over Vladimir Herzog's death in jail when Francisco Leite Chaves, an MDB senator, compared the Brazilian army with Hitler's SS.[103] Also, four MDB leaders used time on national television to denounce the government's record on democratic practices.[104]

Such statements have often been political suicide for the MDB legislators. One of the four who protested on television was stripped of his political rights, and the government said it would put on trial the party's leader because of the incident. Leite Chaves came close to losing his rights, but he was saved when all copies of the congressional record containing his remarks were collected and destroyed, thus allowing the pretense that his speech never occurred.[105]

As indication that some independence remained in the judiciary after the coup, a judge of the nation's supreme court resigned in protest over a decision in which the other eight justices refused to outlaw prior censorship even though the constitution prohibits it. The dissenting judge said he quit because the court's right of judicial review was dead: "In the present regime in Brazil, no one would dare to criticize the constitutionality of laws of a political nature."[106]

Although military courts are given jurisdiction over charges brought under the National Security Law, the military judges have repeatedly expressed their disgust over the harassment evident in some charges they have been asked to try in regard to the press. Sometimes the cases have been dismissed, other times remanded to a civilian court. Whatever the offense, the judges have said, criticism by an editor is not the occasion for a court martial.[107]

Perhaps the most acute embarrassment ever suffered by the government over press freedom also demonstrated that the army is not a monolith. This was the publicity given an official military report criticizing censorship.

The nation's Superior War College, a sort of graduate school and research center for officers and civilians, had ordered a study of social communication in contemporary society, a fashionable topic in all countries at the time. It was conducted by three psychologists and an artillery colonel.

The report specified the ways a government could get a good public image—which included telling of its failures as well as its successes.

"Trying to hide facts . . . cases a loss of confidence on the part of the people in the communications media and in the voice of the government," the report added. "It provokes rumors, veiled comments and scandals. Responsible criticisms must exist." Censorship, according to the study, violates the rights of free expression and could lead to tyranny.[108]

The whole nation learned about the report, because the War College handed out copies to newsmen. A day later, tight censorship was clamped on any further mention of it.[109]

The myriad of devices used by journalists to evade and criticize censorship has been noted earlier, but the role of the Catholic Church also must be considered. Not only have most of Brazil's five cardinals spoken out against the government's suppression of human rights, but as proprietors of church publications they have had to cope with censorship themselves and have had to learn how to get around it. When the censor bars some passage from the church weekly in São Paulo, the cardinal-archbishop can have it read in churches as a pastoral message. Also, he can have it inserted in the church bulletin.[110]

The very existence of Brazil's alternative media—the so-called "midget press"—is itself a rebuke at the government's control on the larger newspapers. The breed has included nationally known publications such as *Opinião, Pasquim* and *Movimento,* but they have their counterparts in every city of any size. They often expire after short lives but rise again overnight. For example, one called *Ex* was so weakened by government harassment that it went out of business. Shortly afterward its editors were back with a paper called *Mais Um* (Portuguese for *Another One*).

Apparently the midget press members owe their existence to the fact that there are too many for the government to cope with and to the gradual lightening of censorship late in the 1970s. One of the most irreverent, the satirical *Pasquim,* saw its direct censorship lifted in 1976.

"I can't explain why we're not under direct censorship any more," its director, Sergio Jaguaribe, told an interviewer. "The censors were taken out just as mysteriously as they were sent in the first place."[111]

Simply ignoring censors was the form of protest taken by Millor Fernandes, former editor of *Pasquim* and one of the nation's most famous humorists.

Fernandes was quoted abroad as saying, "I have never gone to a censor to argue on behalf of a play or a column. I cannot picture myself . . . trying to explain to him that I meant no harm. After all, a censor is a criminal. We mutually think of each other as criminals."[112]

CHAPTER 3

Chile:

Marking Time

UNTIL 1970, Chilean editors could bask in the admiration their country drew from the world. "At least there's still Chile," observers would say as they scanned the junkheaps of democracy in other Latin American countries. Spectacular in nothing, it still had plenty of "good" features—good education, good health, good government, good literature and good mass media. It had largely avoided both the chaos and the brutal dictatorships that had marked its neighbors' history.

But before the decade was half over, hardly anybody had anything good to say about Chile. In the world's view, it stands like a shipwreck against the southern sky, settling into the sand after being torn by two lethal tidal waves—first from the left, then the right.

The view from inside differs only in complexity—Chileans see all the shadings and explanations that escape outsiders. They can also feel the painfully slow recovery from the political warfare of the 1970–73 Salvador Allende presidency and the military repression that followed Allende's overthrow. Some appearance of normalcy has returned. Shops are full of goods, inflation has fallen from 700 to less than 100 per cent, and political prisoners have been steadily freed—except for the 900 who apparently have disappeared forever. For the middle and upper classes, if Chile has not regained its "good" status at least it is getting better.

The mass media have been at the forefront of the wrenching twists in Chile's line of march, and they have suffered perhaps more severely than most parts of Chile's society. For some media, this has meant sudden death; for some, an agonizing withdrawal from an earlier addiction to political invective; for some, the shame of having their servility to outside interests revealed.

While the heavy hand of government harassment is easy to discern, the deeper questions have more long-term relevance. They raise the possibility that, first, the media contributed more than most institutions to Chile's ruina-

55

tion in the 1970s, and second, that the ethical faults of the media played a large part in their own misfortunes. While the available evidence cannot support final judgments on these questions, it can throw light on the need for responsible exercise of the journalist's power and liberties.

MOCKED BY THE PAST

The somber journalistic scene of the 1970s becomes even more bleak when seen through the prism of the previous two centuries. The least populous of Latin America's major countries, Chile had built a media system that was among the best. Its newspapers and magazines were skillfully produced, its book stores were overflowing with locally published and imported volumes, its broadcast media were both lively and socially aware and even a dozen or so movies were made each year. Despite being tucked away on the continent's most remote corner, it was a hungry consumer of foreign media products.

Geography did much to shape the advanced media Chile had in 1970. Being at the farthest reaches of the Spanish empire, it attracted the adventurous types who had left behind the civilized comforts of Lima and Bogotá. Since its arable region consisted of a small area in its center surrounded by the Andes, a desert, the Pacific Ocean and frigid forests, the settlers spent much of the colonial period fighting nature and hostile Indians. Such hardships did nothing to stimulate journalism, but by the time of the first newspaper in 1812 the frontiersmen had developed enough of a sense of political fairness to make a competitive press possible. Chile's leadership in shaking off Spanish rule gave it nationalistic vigor, and the list of newspapers grew rapidly. *El Mercurio* of Valparaíso, founded in 1827, now is the oldest daily in Latin America.

Healthy rivalry among political parties nurtured the press. Newspapers' main reason for being always was as spokesmen for political parties or factions. Whenever a newspaper was sold, onlookers would ask not who was making an investment but who was running for president. Democracy was always less than perfect, the poor being largely excluded from the ranks of the competing political parties. But the steady spread of public education and literacy eroded this elitism, and Chile had a far more popular base for its press than most countries in the area. Even the Penny Press sensationalism of the United States invaded the country in 1900 when Augustín Edwards McClure started a Santiago edition of his family's *El Mercurio,* styling it on the lines of the *New York Herald.*[1] Later as the leading paper in the country, it was to become distinctly conservative in both methods and politics.

Escaping most of the controls that held back other press systems on the continent, the Chilean media forged ahead like those in educated, somewhat prosperous European countries. Radio started in 1922 and by 1968 had grown to 150 stations, ranging from enterprising news operations to those specializing in soap operas, sports or classical music. Trying to reach the 2,650-mile length of the country, a fifth of the stations duplicated their medium-wave signals in short-wave.

Newspapers developed explosively, growing to 46 dailies including 11 in the capital. A 1961 poll of U.S. daily newspaper publishers ranked *El Mercurio* of Santiago as a runner-up to the 10 best newspapers in the world, putting it close behind the ranks of *Neue Zürcher Zeitung* of Zurich and *Dagens Nyheter* of Stockholm.[2]

Weekly newspapers and magazines were profuse and varied, totaling more than 700. Weeklies could be found in the English, Italian, Croatian and Yiddish languages. Four national news agencies competed to sell the news to provincial dailies. Several magazines were well-known abroad, including the distinguished journal of news and analysis *Ercilla*. The satirical *Topaze* kept politicians on guard with its barbed commentary. From the estimated 700 printing shops in Chile poured a wide range of other magazines, from sexy to academic, and Santiago was one of the printing locations for the hemispheric business magazine *Visión*.[3]

As one of the continent's leading centers of higher learning, Santiago also was a major source of its books. It was producing about 1,500 titles a year by the mid-1960s, more than half of them in the social and applied sciences.[4]

Television was delayed until 1959 while the political forces debated a format for its control. What they agreed upon was a plan to grant licenses only to universities, which were to broadcast both entertaining, commercial programs and educational and cultural fare. Once started, the system grew rapidly, supplemented in 1969 by a governmental network which operated the same way but built enough transmitters to reach nearly all the population. Transmissions from around the world were brought in to Chile by a satellite ground station completed in 1968, the first such in Latin America.

Although the Moscow-affiliated Chilean Communist Party remained small in membership, it was allowed full legal rights and thus could circulate its own publications. It also brought space in non-communist newspapers and radio stations.[5]

Generally the government adhered scrupulously to the constitutional protection of the media. This guaranteed "freedom to express, without prior censorship, opinions, . . . through the medium of the press or any other form, without prejudice to liability for offenses. . . ."[6]

Like so many such basic codes in Latin America, this exception for "offenses" meant the guaranty was only as good as the intentions of the current president and congress, but these proved reliable. A sedition law was passed in 1949 allowing six-day closure of a mass medium which threatened internal security, but this was not utilized.

Thus Chile was one of the few Latin American countries where the extinction of press freedom in the 1970s was a definite reversal of an established norm. It also had developed, far more than most of these nations, a media system which responded to a wide range of political impulses. This chapter will trace (1) the change of the media system first into a battleground of political warfare and later into a depoliticized support mechanism for the government, (2) the instruments used by the military government to purge the media and (3) the few elements of resistance to professional collapse of the system.

In analyzing a vast array of data, much of it not presented here, the writer has concluded that the tragedy of the Chilean media cannot be understood with a devil theory which puts all blame either on the Allende government or the military regime. It is submitted that the controls imposed after Allende's death of September 11, 1973, were the inevitable outcome of the media's orgy of verbal conflict during the previous three years. No society would have tolerated a continuance of this frenzy; if the media had not lowered their own voices, the ruling power would have forced them to do so, whether that power had been a dictatorship of the left or right or even a democratically elected congress.

A CRISIS OF IDENTITY

In 1970, after nearly two decades of trying to win a presidential election, a socialist physician-turned-senator, Salvador Allende, finally gained a plurality in the public voting. He had campaigned under the banner of the Popular Unity Front (UP), a coalition of leftists ranging from communists to splinters of mainstream parties. Its election manifesto spoke in both positive and negative terms when it came to the mass media.

On the positive side, the manifesto described the media as "fundamental aids in formation of a new culture and a new man," echoing the credo of all those in other countries—Cuba and Peru, for example—who saw the ideal role of media as being tools, not opponents of the government. To achieve this in Chile, the UP had housecleaning to do. The media, according to the manifesto, must be "imprinted with an educational orientation" with the purpose of "liberating them from their commercial character." But the most pointed hint of the UP's plans was its declared purpose of "eliminating the sad presence of monopolies" in the media.[7]

"Monopolies" could mean only one thing to the knowledgeable Chilean reader—the chain of 10 dailies headed by *El Mercurio* of Santiago. Although the chain's three units in the capital and seven outside had ample competition from other newspapers, their professional competence and wealth of news gave them circulation totals which overshadowed the others. There simply were no other highly prestigious newspapers.

El Mercurio, which had been on the winning side in most elections until Allende's, was caught off balance when the votes were counted. Then a few days later its director, Augstín S. Edwards III, picked up the gauntlet that UP had thrown down. "We will stay and fight," a spokesman for Edwards announced. "We will stay until freedom ceases to exist."[8]

It is noteworthy that both sides had prepared for battle in the name of democracy, and each saw the other as a mortal threat to the nation. Expectations of a fight to the death held out slim prospects for the give and take of democratic debate.

Even though Allende's selection still had to be confirmed by the congress, jockeying for position started on media staffs as the Marxists and their opponents tried to solidify their defenses. The Inter-American Press Association, of which Edwards had just retired as president, stepped forward with a charge that press freedom in Chile was "being strangled by communist and Marxist forces and their allies."[9]

Allende's election was confirmed October 24, and he took office 11 days later. By that time the lines of battle were clearly drawn. On the government's side was an uneasy coalition of old-line leftist politicians, university intellectuals, vagrant reformers from many countries, and union and peasant leaders. Facing them were the operatives of the largest single party, the Christian Democrats, who controlled congress; smaller parties of the center and right; and a large part of the professional and commercial classes.

Warfare Under Allende

Both sides in the conflict during Allende's three years in office made heavy use of mass media to achieve their ends. The struggle took the form variously of verbal exchanges, competition to own and control each media unit, blockage of professional activity, economic pressures, violence and sabotage, and legal measures.

The government (meaning here the presidency but not the congress) had a built-in advantage in many respects, but the opposition forces kept up an unflagging effort. It has been widely observed that, considering the *exercise* of vigorous journalism as a gauge of liberty, Chile had the freest media system in its history during the Allende period despite the government's attempts to throttle the other side.

Verbal Exchanges—The war of words was possible because each side had both publications and radio stations at its disposal. The administration also had the newsworthiness of its official statements as a weapon, since the opposition media often lapsed into objectivity and printed what the president and his ministers said. Unconventional media such as bumper stickers also were pressed into service; one such label declared: "Chilean: *El Mercurio* lies." It not only adorned bumpers but also walls of government offices. This same theme was taken up in radio spots in which a voice intoned "Chilean doctors no longer use thermometers because the mercury (*El Mercurio*) lies."

During the first year of the regime, words largely took the place of actions, as the government refrained from any direct moves against major print media. Threats from government officials alternated with new claims from the opposition that the media were being taken over and with government denials that this had happened. An example was the confusion over what Allende had said about taking over *El Mercurio.* Several versions had been reported, and four months after his inauguration he stated in a television interview: "I said *El Mercurio* was a Yankee paper written in Spanish and that we were not going to expropriate it but rather nationalize it. I still hold that point of view." His semantic tangle only stirred up more dispute.[10]

Allende repeatedly voiced his refrain that press freedom was not being stifled and would not be. This continued throughout his regime, and the estabishment press reported the claims. Often the statements reponded to attacks by the IAPA, which routinely reports its views on media freedom in each country at six-month intervals. After a year of such quarreling, Allende surprised the press by cordially receiving an IAPA delegation, assuring its members that "freedom of expression will be maintained in Chile at all costs."[11]

The officialist media apprently went well beyond Allende's desires in savaging the opposition. *La Nación,* the outlet closest to the presidential office, was the most sober, although its charges often were drastic. One of its early campaigns was against Chileans in the United States and Argentina who it said were creating economic sabotage against the Allende regime.[12]

But during 1972 the surprises became more shocking. One sensational magazine published a photo of Britain's Queen Elizabeth superimposed on the body of a nude swimmer as its idea of humor.[13] The huge publishing house of Zig-Zag, which the government had taken over and renamed Quimantú early in its term, started pouring out propagandistic comic books by the tons. Its most talked-about product was an attack on a cartoon character from the enemy camp—Donald Duck. A Chilean literary critic teamed up with a Belgian sociologist to write a polemic called "How to Read Donald Duck."

"As long as the smiling face of Donald Duck parades innocently throughout Chilean cities, as long as Donald Duck means power and collective representation, then imperilism and the bourgeoisie can sleep peacefully," the authors warned. They set about to find capitalistic plots and hidden symbolism in all the characters and stock situations of Disney's duck, which was enormously popular with Cilean children—both before and after the assault.[14]

In the two years before Allende's overthrow, the war of words stepped up to a feverish pitch, but by this time the accusations usually had basis in fact, as the abuses that each side had predicted early in the administration were actually taking place. The Allende forces had a field day with the documents which American columnist Jack Anderson revealed, showing the efforts by International Telephone and Telegraph Co. to sabotage the 1970 election. Quimantú flooded the newsstands with Spanish translations of the documents, and the officialist media trumpeted summaries of them and promoted sales of the book.[15] One of the favorite themes of the opposition was the real and imagined preparation by leftists for a civil war.

Although the UP media regularly blared forth with charges that the U.S. Central Intelligence Agency was implicated in the anti-Allende maneuvers, it never was able to produce reliable evidence, so these charges were much smaller issues than those against ITT, which were well supported. One can only speculate how differently Chilean and world public opinion would have been affected if the 1975 testimony before the Church Committee of the U.S. Senate had been revealed while Allende was still alive and in power rather than two years after his death.

But when the staff report of the committee was published it painted a vivid picture of CIA involvement in the verbal warfare of the Allende period.[16] Actually the report said CIA support for propaganda occurred as far back as 1953, when leftist strength was beginning to become significant. But the agency's efforts intensified with time, and covert American activity was credited with being a factor in "almost every major election in Chile in the decade between 1963 and 1973."[17] Although direct support of political organizations and factions played a role, the report calls propaganda the "most extensive covert activity in Chile." Furthermore, this option was "relatively cheap," the staff added. Among the specific communication-related stratagems during the Allende presidency alleged by the report were:

1. Payment of $1,665,000 to *El Mercurio* on the theory that it, the main opposition organ, was in danger of succumbing to pressure from the government.

2. Subsidies of a wire service, intellectual magazines, and a right-wing weekly newspaper.

3. Financing of Chilean groups which put up wall posters and distributed leaflets, sometimes prepared by the CIA.

4. Development of "assets" (sympathetic journalists) in media organizations who could be expected to publish desired stories.

5. Distribution of "black propaganda," which is falsely attributing embarrassing statements to the other side.

6. Planting articles in European and Latin American newspapers which predicted economic collapse under the UP government.

7. Arrangements for "cables of support and protest from foreign newspapers, a protest statement from an international press association, and world press coverage of the association's protest." [18]

8. Sending to Chile, to cover the Allende election for foreign media, journalists from 10 countries who were really CIA agents. Eight more journalists were sent by "high-level agents who were, for the most part, in managerial capacities in the media field. [19]

9. "Support for an underground press, . . . indirect subsidy of Patria y Libertad, a group fervently opposed to Allende, and its radio programs, political advertisements, and political rallies; and the direct mailing of foreign news articles" to opposition politicians. [20]

10. Secret briefings given to U.S. journalists who requested them. One such briefing to *Time* magazine when it was preparing a cover story about Allende's electoral victory "resulted in a change in the basic thrust" of the story. [21]

11. Subsidies to opposition parties to pay for purchase of their own newspapers and radio stations.

12. Publication of books and special studies, plus production of television programs.

13. Funding of an opposition research organization which conducted polls and wrote bills introduced in congress.

Much of this activity was concentrated in the six weeks between Allende's election and his inauguration in a desperate attempt to carry out President Nixon's order to promote a military coup, the report said. This was long before Allende had had an opportunity to take belligerent actions toward the media. However, all told, the CIA was reported to have spent $8 million in Chile between Allende's election and his death. [22]

The role of CIA money in driving a wedge between traditional and leftist newsmen is unclear, but a split decidedly occurred. The Colegio de Periodistas, which had set the pattern for working newsmen's guilds in Latin America, continued to protest against government incursions on the privately owned media. Journalists who supported the government collaborated in an official persuasion campaign called "Operation Truth," designed to refute what Allende called "lies and falsehoods" reported about the regime at home and abroad. They also banded together at a convention, "the First National Assembly of Leftist Journalists," five months after Allende's inauguration. The president, addressing the 340 delegates, grudgingly renewed his pledge to respect freedom of information; his administration was "fighting the battles within the limits of bourgeois democracy and the laws which this bourgeois democracy has dictated,'' he said. Even so, the delegates voted to reject objectivity as a relic of bourgeois tradition.[23]

One of the victims of the war of words, heavily mourned by some, was basic decorum even beyond political matters. The tabloids plunged to unprecedented depths of sensationalism with sex and gore, and the violence they committed on the Spanish language was spectacular. In the name of cleverness, any street slang or solecism was blared forth in headlines.

Ownership and Operation—As has been noted, Chilean media had always had a penchant for choosing up sides politically. But direct control of media by parties had been minimal before the Allende period. The Christian Democratic Party, with funds supplied by the Catholic Church, had bought the vast publishing house called Zig-Zag in 1967 while the party's leader, Eduardo Frei, was president. This gave it supervision over the leading news magazine, *Ercilla,* and a variety of other nondaily publications. The party faithful also owned Radio Balmaceda.

When Allende became president his political bloc could count on *El Siglo* and *Puro Chile,* doctrinaire daily organs of the Communist Party, and *La Nación,* the state-owned daily which always was an apologist for the government in power. Also in the ranks was the state television network, Channel 7, but law required it to remain neutral.

Allende's electoral victory opened a furious competition for control of media by the opposing forces. The Christian Democrats, apparently having little hope for the coup that President Nixon was trying to promote, started building a fallback line of defense, and mass communication was intended as their chief weapon. They also assured protection of their investment by forcing Allende, as the price for allowing him to take office, to accept a constitutional amendment which reinforced the guaranties of human rights such as freedom of expression.

Working in most cases through sympathetic entrepreneurs instead of direct purchase, the Christian Democratic leaders started bringing media into their camp. They acquired the Sopesur chain of daily newspapers, headed by *Diario Illustrado* in Santiago and including four provincial papers in the south. The capital-city daily was renamed *La Prensa* and was placed under the editorship of a former cabinet minister. Another anti-Marxist paper, *Pueblo Libre,* was founded, to be printed in the *La Prensa* plant.[24] Two other tabloids, *La Tarde* and *La Tercera,* also supported the cause.

The most substantial journalistic ally of the opposition forces was the *El Mercurio* chain, with its 10 dailies and a radio network, even though they were not under direct party control. *Orbe,* the largest Chilean domestic news agency, was another vehicle of support for the Christian Democrats.

The party resurrected a picture magazine its Zig-Zag company had published earlier, called *Vea,* and acquired another publishing house, Editorial del Pacifico. It also launched an effort to start its own newsprint factory. In the broadcasting field, the Christian Democrats bought several Santiago radio stations.

The Allende forces made little headway at first in the print field. Rather than acquiring ownership of media, they concentrated at first on infiltrating staffs and exerting pressure on owners to add reporters and commentators sympathetic to the UP cause. They attempted this at *El Mercurio* and largely failed, but it worked at the tabloid *Clarín,* which then had the country's largest circulation. After a bitter struggle between Marxist and Christian Democratic staff members of *Clarín,* the latter conceded defeat by resigning to join the new party daily *La Prensa.*

Pressures from the government did have as a sequel the retreat by the Edwards family, owners of *El Mercurio.* Once Allende's election had been confirmed by the congress, the paper went into a lull in its editorial campaign against the UP. Augustín Edwards, chairman of the paper's governing board, was living abroad, as were his brother and mother, also board members. Apparently seeing themselves as targets which would bring Allende's retribution onto the paper, the three resigned their positions, although Augustín Edwards remained the principal stockholder and chose the replacements on the board; all were loyal employees. Augustín's sister Sonia, an Allende supporter, remained on the board but did not take control. The new chief executive did offer the government an olive branch, saying the paper must "respect the institutions and the office of the presidency."[25] It also offered space on its editorial page to left-wing writers.

The Christian Democrats' dominion over the Zig-Zag publishing house lasted only a little more than three months after Allende's ascension to power. The union printers, feeling their new strength under a communist labor minister, initiated a wage demand which was arbitrated by a board headed by the minister. It awarded an increase averaging 67 per cent, which was twice the inflation rate and a mortal blow to the company, already enfeebled financially. A month later, it sold its physical equipment to the government, which set up its own publishing house, calling it Quimantú, dedicated largely to pouring out an endless stream of Marxist classics and modern interpretations such as textbooks and comics, much of it exported. Zig-Zag kept title to its name and to its magazines, the printing of which it contracted to Quimantú. Rather than castigating the government, the Zig-Zag president hailed the sale agreement as "an equitable solution to the problems of our firm." It would allow the company to "continue carrying out journalistic and information activities with the most absolute freedom and independence," he predicted.[26] This is largely what did happen.

The UP leaders, knowing that broadcasting would affect the masses far more than print journalism, directed most of their energies to solidifying control in this field. They had a large head start when they came to power, because both television and radio in Chile had long put political function above commercialism, and the UP had its firm supporters even in the 1960s. Soon after the founding of the two main Santiago television channels in 1959—the University of Chile's Channel 9 and the Catholic University's Channel 13—leftists began infiltrating the stations' news departments despite opposition from the parent institutions. Only Channel 4, operated by the Catholic University of Valparaíso and received by Santiago viewers, remained outside leftist control. So when the Christian Democrats saw they were in danger of losing the presidency, they put through congress in 1969 a measure establishing a state television network which brought a signal to the entire nation for the first time. More

important to the party, the law setting up the network was an effort to perpetu-
ate its control by the Christian Democrats even if they lost the presidency. This
was done by placing all television under the regulation of a board, to which the
outgoing administration would have a chance to name a majority of members.

Struggles by each side to gain internal control of the broadcast media took
the form largely of continued infiltration of staffs, counter-measures by owners
and managers, founding and licensing of new stations, cancellation and reassignment of frequencies, and purchase of existing stations. The UP forces had
the upper hand, of course, since the stations were regulated by an agency of the
executive branch, the Office of Information and Broadcasting (OIR). The more
disciplined political operatives also were on the UP side. However, the opposition's control of the congress and the independence of the judiciary often frustrated UP efforts to carry out its plans.

The pattern was set for UP pressure on radio stations when a communist
congressman visited various Santiago stations the day of Allende's electoral
victory and suggested that they hire commentators who supported his cause.
The campaign started by this putsch was so successful that by the following
January an opposition senator lamented, with only slight exaggeration, that "all
the important radio stations have been, in some form, submitted to the government through pressures or the expedient of denying them advertising the public
services can place." After two years of the Allende regime, one historian
counted 20 radio stations which UP supporters had acquired and five more
which obtained new licenses. The most persistent effort was directed toward
Radio Balmaceda, the principal Christian Democratic station. It was repeatedly
closed, its frequency was invaded by a leftist station, and loss of its license was
threatened. However, after constant efforts by its party's congressmen, it received a 30-year license renewal in 1972.[27]

A drive to dominate the news and public affairs departments of all three
Santiago television stations also redoubled after Allende's election. The opposition never conceded defeat, and lively debates and forums were aired throughout the administration, although these were often canceled because of presidential anger.

Nowhere was the struggle more intense than in the administration of Channel 7, the state network. The Christian Democrats soon found that the legal
protections they had set up in 1969 and 1970 were less than watertight. Although they had an even chance with the National Television Council, which
governed Channel 7, they also had to contend with the presidential power and
also the staff infiltration. They were constantly protesting polemical programs
which variously offended the Arabs, the Christians and other groups.

Leftist control of the University of Chile's Channel 9 became so complete
that the university rector actually started another station in competition with his
own kidnapped channel. The new one, Channel 6, was strongly opposed by the
presidency as a dispute arose over whether the basic broadcasting law gave the
universities unlimited authority to operate new stations. The rector also waged
a court battle for many months to regain control of Channel 9, winning the
case, ironically, the day before Allende's overthrow.

Another irony was that the students and professors of the two Santiago
universities raised the first effective opposition to the Marxist television con-

trol. Anti-Allende factions won dominance of their campuses in 1972 elections. This had a direct influence on the founding of the "pluralistic" Channel 6, and it also led to a clean sweep against leftists at Catholic University's Channel 13. A resilient anti-Marxist priest, Raúl Hasbun, gained the directorship and set about removing the leftists who had run the news department. The Catholic Student Federation, a strong backer of Father Hasbun, also agitated loudly throughout the capital against bias on the state's Channel 7, gathering petitions and condemning the station as "the channel of the lie."[28]

Blocking of Activity—The feverish exercise of free expression up to the day of the 1973 coup was evidence that the traditional mechanisms for blocking media activity—censorship and closure of media—played little or no role in the verbal conflict. Allende repeatedly claimed that he was following constitutional norms, and, with rare exceptions, he had the laws on his side—laws that were in most cases passed during earlier presidencies. When the opposition challenged the legality of Allende's actions, they often found relief in the courts.

In fact, it was a full year after the 1970 election before Allende's opponents found serious grounds for claiming abuse of the laws. This was when he flared up in anger and canceled the license of United Press International, an American news agency, to do business in Chile. UPI had filed a story in Colombia for its international wires, including those received in Chile, quoting a report by the Bogotá daily *El Tiempo*. It had claimed that a Chilean government airplane had secretly carried arms to Colombian guerrillas. After a chorus of protest at home and abroad and an apology by a high UPI official, Allende rescinded the order. But, to make his point, he expelled Martin Houseman, the UPI bureau chief. It was a nearly perfect preview of a similar incident five years later in Bogotá, in which the UPI bureau there was temporarily put under a closure order for a false story. There, too, the bureau chief was the scapegoat.

Allende's administration did discover one device to control the content of radio stations that was perhaps unique in the history of Latin America—the use of nationwide hookups not simply as a propaganda medium but also as a way to block the opposition's attacks from being aired. Pre-emption of the airwaves by the presidency is a common and legal stratagem in most countries of the area, but it nearly always lasts no more than an hour except during a natural disaster or civil war. In Allende's hands it served to keep opposition voices muzzled for weeks on end during economic crises such as the bitter trucking strike of 1972. This was so galling to one station owned by Christian Democrats, Radio Minería, that after being furnished a diet of music and news from the presidential office for 12 days it broke away from the hookup. Its officials knew that this would incur for them a six-day suspension under the 1949 sedition law.

"Radio Minería cannot go on chained to an illegitimate muzzle," the station's manager, Gustavo Palacios, declared on the air just before the government silenced it. "We prefer enforced silence a thousand times more than being part of a network of falsehoods."[29]

Imports of media materials were rarely restricted, partly because the opposition press stood ready to ridicule the government for such sensitivity. This was what occurred when several films embarrassing to the leftists were refused entry into the country—at the request of the Communist Party, according to opposition newspapers. Focal point of the controversy was the banned film "L'Aveu," made by Henri Costa-Gavras and depicting Stalinist repression of Czechoslovakia. The opposition press turned the banning to their advantage by printing excerpts from the Costa-Gavras script. Allende countered that he "fully understood" why his film should not be shown there at such a "sensitive" time.[30] Oddly enough, other Costa-Gavras films have been banned by right-wing governments in various Latin American countries.

Restrictions on media activity came much more frequently in the panicky three months before Allende's overthrow. In some cases, the presidential office motivated the actions; in others, the impulse came from the army, which was torn by factional dispute and was trying to fulfill its constitutional duty to protect the president. When some army units conducted an abortive coup, loyalist officers accompanied their counter-action with censorship of newspapers and temporary closing of seven opposition radio stations. The army also was responsible for the suspension of the rightist newspaper *La Tribuna* on a charge of carrying "false and alarmist" news.[31] But when the tabloid *La Tercera* published an advertisement placed by fleeing leaders of the coup, a six-day suspension was ordered by the interior ministry. The government also brought about the closing of *El Mercurio* for one day before an appeals court decreed the order null.[32]

Economic Pressures—Financial effects on the media vividly illustrated political realities during the Allende period. In this respect, however, power did not necessarily loom largest on the government side. Each faction had its funds with which to subsidize media—or buy programs or space—and each had advertising with which to reward its favorite organs. The $1,665,000 allotted to *El Mercurio* by the CIA played no small role in keeping it afloat, and the fact that much of the remainder of the agency's $8 million investment in Chile went for propaganda no doubt was beneficial to the fiscal health of other opposition publications.

The peculiarities of newspaper economics brought different fortunes to those newspapers which existed primarily on per-copy sales and those primarily nourished by advertising. The former—the thin little papers filled with sensationalism, whether of the carnal or the political kind—did quite well during the Allende period because the exciting daily developments promoted a public addiction to newsstand purchasing. Most such papers cost little to produce, and their owners had modest demands as to profits. The best of them, the tabloid *La Tercera,* rose from obscurity to a half-million circulation by the time of the coup, putting it among the two or three largest in Latin America.

But if a newspaper depended on advertising in the U.S. style, it was in for hard times, because the country's deteriorating economy steadily reduced the capacity of businesses to promote themselves. *El Mercurio* was practically the only publication in this class, and its accustomed 48 pages shrank to 24 or fewer.

Direct economic actions by the government stirred protests by the IAPA early in the regime, although these had much less impact than the positive and negative influences mentioned above. The IAPA centered its complaints on what it considered excessive wage increases for media staffs sanctioned by the government, the spreading state ownership of businesses and thus of advertising sources, and a freeze in the sale price of newspapers.[33]

Publicity abroad about economic actions against the press focused on *El Mercurio*. However, there were few drastic confrontations between the famous newspaper and the government until the last few months before the coup. In fact, impartial observers were puzzled over the paper's oscillations in its editorial line until it settled down to a dignified defense of legal institutions. Despite fears that the government would bring labor strife to *El Mercurio* and thus pave the way for its takeover, the paper quietly reached a wage agreement with official blessings early in 1971. It was much less burdensome than those in other industries.[34]

The problem that made headlines around the world concerned a so-called "raid" on *El Mercurio* offices by tax inspectors. They announced that the paper was $380,000 delinquent in taxes, which was common among Chilean businesses during the commercial slump that followed Allende's election. Legal means to force *El Mercurio* to the wall were available, but the government compromised on a long-term repayment.[35]

In a strange sequel to the tax case, the IAPA charged that press freedom was being "oppressed" in the episode, but *El Mercurio's* director and those of other publications declined to join in the protest. "If there are any direct government pressures against *El Mercurio,* the employees have not been able to find them," Héctor Precht, head of the paper's journalistic union and an Allende opponent, said.[36]

Other than *El Mercurio's* tax problems, the most-publicized area of economic conflict involving the media was the government's persistent but futile effort to nationalize the paper-making industry. This was one of its earliest goals and was consistent with its socialistic policy of acquiring the country's major means of production. The dense conifer forests of Chile's sub-Antarctic zones poured forth a rich supply of paper products, making it the only substantial exporter in this field in Latin America. With the international price of newsprint soaring, the hard-pressed Allende regime could use this income to stave off economic disaster.

But the opposition saw the move as an effort to control the press, since as proprietor of the paper mills the government could also manipulate the domestic supplies. The record of the Mexican government in this respect stood as a constant warning. Allende repeatedly denied that press control was the purpose of nationalization, but it steadily became a rallying point for more and more groups to oppose the president throughout his term. Not only the publishers and the IAPA but also some paper industry unions and unrelated groups picked it up as an issue.

Outright expropriation of the industry was Allende's first hope, but this was blocked by action of congress. Then the government tried a stratagem it had used to nationalize the banks—buying up shares on the open market. It started off with about 10 per cent of the shares, having acquired them as part of the bank assets. Offering seven times the market value of shares, it started moving toward its target of 51 per cent majority control. Then it faltered in the face of stockholder resistance, which the opposition equated with patriotism. A campaign to buy up shares to keep them from the government got under way, particularly among paper industry workers.

Then inflation, bounding to triple-digit heights, took a role in the drama, abetted by the government. Enormous surges in production costs made it necessary to raise paper prices, but the government, in the name of inflationary control, granted only small fractions of the requested sums. As a result, the industry suffered losses which were driving it to bankruptcy. This, of course, made shares less attractive to hold and thus easier for the government to buy.

A curious spectacle ensued: The publication industry—that part of it not controlled by UP forces, at least—began demanding that the prices of its principal raw material be raised. The publishers believed this was the only way to keep the paper industry out of the hands of the government. The feud dragged on throughout the three years, with much protesting by all sides, continual demands for higher prices, and repeated rejections. Allende never achieved his goal of nationalization, but the industry paid a price for its independence. By the time of the coup, its losses were calculated at $30,658,125.[37]

Violence and Sabotage—Chile's tradition of peaceable and sportsmanlike politics, which persisted until the 1970s, stood as a bulwark against the physical conflict that has dogged the media in other countries. But the passions of the Allende period eroded even this barrier. Although this was a relatively minor part of the over-all struggle between media and government, it constantly posed the threat of even graver trouble.

One thing that promoted this climate of fear was the frequent discovery of caches of weapons. One such collection was alleged only a year after Allende's election when dismissed employees of *El Mercurio* complained to the government, which set about launching an investigation. As the foreboding of civil war grew, rumors spread that other media were harboring arms deposits. Many of these were found to be true after the coup; the Quimantú publishing house was one of the planned citadels for government defenders.

The key role that the government's information office (OIR) was expected to play in such an anticipated civil war was indicated when *El Mercurio* reported what it said was an OIR staff memorandum in 1973. Generally the document was a plan for political sabotage and agitation.[38]

In the last year before the coup, outright violence began to afflict the media as a carry-over from more general conflicts. After several months of strikes and demonstrations, it seemed natural when a mob gathered outside Radio Minería's studios to sympathize with its decision to quit the government hookup. The protesters clogged a major street, lit bonfires and threw rocks through nearby windows. Soon, though, police sent them fleeing with tear gas and high-powered water hoses.[39]

Four other radio stations were briefly taken over by wives of striking truckers shortly before the coup. The government stymied their broadcasting efforts by turning off the electricity to the best-known station, Agricultura, for 14 hours.[40]

Although the feminine presence in this takeover was unusual, in other respects it was following the pattern that became familiar in Chilean newspapers and radio stations throughout Allende's last year. Most often the invaders were government supporters of various kinds who acted in the name of union protests, and typically they would be dislodged by order of a court. In one case—the takeover of the daily *El Sur* of Concepción—they published one issue of a clandestine newspaper.

The most dramatic of the broadcasting conflicts involved the efforts by two Catholic universities to expand their television service's reach, particularly after the leftist forces were ousted in 1972 from the Santiago station. The universities claimed the government had no legal right to stop them and the National Television Council agreed. So without licenses they moved ahead. The university in Valparaíso stretched northward, using homemade microwave equipment because it could get no permits for importing what it needed. Channel 13 of Santiago's Catholic University set about building southward through auxiliary and repeater stations. Its showdown with the government came in Concepción, the nation's third-largest city.

In Concepción, Channel 13 director Hasbun had to face threats from all sides. Catholic students came to his defense to hold off Marxist attackers at the construction site and city officials who tried to shut it down for lack of a building permit. The state electricity company cut off the station's power supply briefly. Then the interior ministry ordered it off the air because it had no concession grant; Father Hasbún defied the order.[41]

Next the electricity company started broadcasting a signal to jam the Concepción station's transmission, letting up only for programs favorable to the government party. Three weeks later the company discovered its jammer had gone off the air; investigation showed that two vital parts of the mechanism had been stolen. The next day, in a bizarre sequel, authorities found the body of a house painter in a house next to the company offices; he had been bound, gagged and suffocated.

Legal Actions—Despite the Allende government's frequent efforts to use the sedition and libel laws against its opponents, the actions usually came to naught because of hostile courts. Among those arrested were Marcelo Maturana, editor of the conservative weekly *P.E.C.*, who was faced with a complaint brought by the armed forces for reporting schisms in their ranks; and Mario Carneyro, editor of *Le Segunda, El Mercurio's* tabloid affiliate. Carneyro's alleged offense was defaming the interior minister in stories about secret arms imports. Both went free through court action.

El Mercurio itself had to fight a charge brought by the government, claiming violation of the internal security law. The cause of action was a story claiming that Chile had only enough dollars to last 45 days.[42]

The Harvest of September 11

When the military junta overthrew Allende's government on September 11, 1973, it clearly had no intention of allowing conflict to continue in any phase of Chilean society. The constitution, which had shielded the constant feuding among politics, labor and journalism, was a dead letter.

Scores of publications and broadcasting stations were either closed or suddenly drained of all leftist influence as more than 500 newspaper journalists found themselves out of work; the more fortunate marked time at home while others fled the country or disappeared into jails. In Santiago alone, four dailies were shut down permanently the day of the coup. This left seven, one of which was owned by the government and two of which died later. The four which survived were under only two ownerships, both of which were willing supporters of the new regime.

Even if the purged media and their employees had been allowed to remain, it was questionable whether there was enough market demand for them to survive. In the months that followed the coup, the basic function of Chilean mass communication changed from frenzied pluralism—both politically and economically—to a one-color conformity to rules.

The commercial media had not become organs of the state, but neither was there any room for the open debate that had swirled into an orgy under Allende. The leftist media had existed to speak for a political faction, and that faction no longer existed.

The Economic Toll—While the rest of the world deplores the loss of freedom in Chile, most journalists there feel that the deepest tragedy of the media is the economic gutting the media have undergone. One set of figures indicates the starkness of the loss: Chile, traditionally one of the most educated countries of the hemisphere with about 92 per cent literacy, now is one of the world's poor countries in newspaper sales. Although its government does not release figures for total copies sold, newsprint consumption indicates the number of pages passing through readers' hands. These show that from 1973 to 1974, the per-capita consumption rate dropped by more than a third. This put Chile at less than three-fifths the consumption level of Trinidad and Tobago and less than one-fifth that of Japan.[43]

Most media spokesmen agree that Chile lost more than half its newspaper sales and advertising between 1970 and 1976. After holding up well during the Allende days, circulation soared just after the coup to the point where one newspaper sold nearly 600,000 a day, which was approximately the total for the entire country three years later.[44]

"People just don't consider newspapers essential," a diplomatic observer noted. "They used to buy two or three to get different viewpoints; now the papers are all the same, so they buy one."

Since Chilean newspapers have to pay the international price for their own domestically produced newsprint, they charge the equivalent of 24 American cents for a 30-page paper. With personal income being drained by double-digit inflation, a housewife hesitates at such a luxury at six times the cost of a pound of sugar.[45]

Television is taking a growing share of the advertising outlays, getting about 50 per cent of the placements from ad agencies. The novelty of world news via satellite built television's audience at the expense of newspapers in 1974, and the arrival of color transmission in 1978 was expected to increase its advantage.[46]

New Roles—With a political role removed from their options, the media have been forced to develop a new identity alien to any they have known before. Since the government has shown little interest in extending its ownership or even actively managing the media, this role decision has been left to the private owners. They, after the removal of the political publishers, consist of the old-line journalistic establishment. One editor, with only slight exaggeration, maintained that by the third year of the military regime there remained only five media owners of any consequence, and all were families in a sense.

These were the Edwards family, owning three of the five Santiago dailies and major ones outside the capital; the Picó family, which owns the largest daily, *La Tercera;* the government "family" of media—television and radio groups and a newspaper; the clan of Christian Democratic politicians who own a large provincial chain of dailies, called Sopesur; and the family of churches, holding a large television network and other media.[47]

One basic decision forced upon the owners by circumstances was to live on commercial income rather than political subsidies. This lesson was driven home for the Santiago press in the first half-year of the military regime, when both the two anti-Allende party papers which had survived the coup disappeared—the Christian Democrats' *La Prensa* because of financial problems, according to the announcement; and the National Party's *La Tribuna* because of a shutdown by the government.

The decision meant that for the first time in their history the majority of newspapers would have to please wide bands of readers with some other attraction than the favorite political slogans, because that was what advertisers wanted in exchange for their keeping the papers alive. The tabloid *La Tercera* had always been far less political than the other Santiago dailies, and it is significant that it absorbed most of the readers displaced by the defunct papers.

Chile still has not moved far into retail price advertising as opposed to manufacturers' brand-name promotion. However, in the late 1970s supermarkets were beginning to expand, and this is expected to generate more business for all media.

Some hope is directed also toward the growth of the provinces as a market due to a government policy to increase regional self-sufficiency. This would run counter to a centralizing economic trend which has resulted in 66 per cent of the population's being gathered in the 300-mile strip from Santiago and Valparaíso to Concepción.

Publishers are fighting hard to make newspapers more of a practical tool for the customer. They print descriptions of school entrance examinations, plus textbook material. A war of special supplements has begun to rage, with topics ranging from horse racing to women's fashions.

La Tercera emphasizes reader-service material for a wide variety of audiences, running special pages for groups as diverse as labor unions and Protestant evangelistic sects. (Since the unions cannot have mass meetings, this is their only effective means of internal communication.) The most ambitious project of this kind is *La Tercera's* weekly 12-page supplement crammed with university-level lessons which supplement the state television's video classes on Channel 7. The paper's circulation jumps 50,000 when these are printed. The subjects range from business administration to German.[48]

TOOLS OF CONTROL

The Chilean military regime has never developed an elaborate dogma of communication. Its concern has been mostly negative—to rid the media of leftist influence, which was done in a few months, and to yank the leash on the rare occasions when a mass medium irritates the authorities.

Out of the uncertainty following the 1973 coup, a Department of Social

Communication has emerged, housed behind the protective guns of the high-rise building that is Chile's Pentagon.

Gastón Zúñiga, a uniformed army colonel, built the department to its present prominence before being promoted and moving on to higher duties. Not only did he act as spokesman to announce government decisions but also as chief theorist on mass communication. He would fervently maintain that Chile has "full liberty of the press—within legal bounds." These bounds were set, of course, by the ruling junta on Zúñiga's advice. At other times, Zúñiga would qualify his claim by saying that true liberty of the press exists nowhere in the world—"It is a utopia that was lost long ago." He justified the measures his government has taken toward the media by noting that the adversaries—Cuba and the Soviet Union—act similarly.[49]

The colonel also would talk grimly of the "international communist conspiracy" he said is using foreign news media against Chile. This inspired him to lead the Chilean delegation to the 1976 UNESCO conference on communication in Costa Rica, and he found himself in unaccustomed agreement with Fidel Castro, to the effect that the power of the major U.S. and European news agencies should be limited. He agreed in principle with a proposal to set up a Third World news agency but abstained because he feared some aspects of the plan.

By the end of the 1970s, as the threat of physical danger to newsmen waned, the Chilean government was controlling the press by at least five distinct methods—closure and suspension of media, seizure and destruction of printed matter, expulsion of foreign correspondents, state ownership of some media units, and limited propaganda activity.

Closure and Suspension

Direct censorship disappeared a few days after the coup, to be replaced by self-censorship, which, as one agonized editor told this writer, "is something that I as a journalist do not understand." Just what is forbidden has never been defined, but since the military uses its claim that a state of siege exists to justify itself constitutionally, anything the generals or admirals feel offensive can be deemed punishable.

Even so, some adverse material does appear in the print media. The government invites a certain amount of restrained criticism, muffled in the turgid prose favored by editorial writers. Some foreign criticism of Chilean human rights violations has appeared in Santiago newspapers, usually accompanied by the editors' condemnation of the "lies and calumny."

Such was the case when the Organization of American States met in Santiago and issued a report which, citing numerous examples, charged the Chilean government with abuses of human rights. After the report had circulated widely by hand among the delegates, *El Mercurio* reprinted it in 7½ pages of small type, followed by 4½ pages of the government's reply. "It is necessary," the reply said, "to maintain legal and administrative measures that limit the freedoms and rights of man in order to protect precisely the most important right of all, the right to a secure life."[50]

Another unexpected breach in the wall came when a former president of the nation and leader of the only major political party, Eduardo Frei, wrote a book criticizing the junta's program. The government allowed it to be printed as an exception to the rule against political journalism, Zúñiga said, but the episode could not be "coverted into a violation of the recess on party politics."[51] Later the government changed its mind and banned the book.

A definite upswing in journalistic temerity came in 1977, mostly in the form of interviews quoting civic groups or their leaders in protesting some government policy. Headlines such as "Aggressive Protest by Farmers" were appearing; they were remarkable in comparison with earlier years under the military but mild in relation with the Allende period.

Boldest of all media is the weekly news magazine *Hoy,* founded in 1977 by journalists who had worked for *Ercilla,* another magazine which had set a standard of competence and frankness far ahead of other media. When a group of investors bought *Ercilla* its editor and many staff members transplanted its reputation to the new publication. Besides running news analyses similar to *Newsweek's, Hoy* seeks out the opinions of those free-thinking Chileans who remain in their country. It created a minor sensation by printing the views of 40 thought leaders who expressed a wide range of opinions, including those calling for a return to elective government.[52]

Another magazine, *Qué Pasa,* has shown notable enterprise even though it is a staunch supporter of the military government. When it printed an article showing a linkage between the security police and the torture of a 16-year-old boy, its editor was beaten in the street by two men who escaped.[53]

However, the usual penalty for guessing wrong on self-censorship is the closure or suspension of the offending medium. Chile's 1925 constitution went to great length to restrict the possibility of punishments against the media, and in no case could they result from political expression.[54] Later laws made a string of exceptions to this guaranty, but they rarely were used abusively. Most notable was the Law of Internal Security passed in 1949, which more than two decades later Allende tried to wield against the press, although he was stymied by the courts.

But the law the militarists rely on to keep the media in line is a creature of their own making. They brought it forth, they said, because of the vagueness of the previous laws worked an unfairness on journalists, and its provisions were less harsh that the ones it replaced. The difference, of course, was in the degree of enforcement. In common with most Latin American countries, Chileans had not feared the overly strict laws they had on the books so long as no one paid any attention to what was written.

But when the junta issued Decree Law 2181 early in December 1975, it apparently meant business. Under the law, any local military commander could shut down any mass medium in his district for six issues or, in the case of broadcasters, for six days. He was to be the sole judge of whether the medium committed one of the proscribed offenses. These were emitting news, opinion or other communications which tend to "create alarm or disgust in the population, disfiguring the true dimension of the facts, whether they be manifestly false or contravene the rules given for internal order." Repeated offenses would lead to permanent closing. Offenders would be warned of their misdeeds before punishment, and appeals were allowed.[55]

For journalists who had patiently endured and often assisted the military revolution, this law came as a staggering insult. They lofted a chorus of protest with a unity unseen in years. Owners fired off editorials, and newsmen pushed resolutions through their national association and their *colegio,* a council for ethics and education.

One phrase in the law particularly piqued them. " 'Creating disgust' is something that many news items cause, even those which emanate from the government, like rises in the cost of living or taxes," the association noted. "Alarming, vague and unjustified," said *El Mercurio.* "Manifestly unconstitutional," added *Qué Pasa.* The annual Press Day celebrations soon afterward were somber.[56]

Colonel Zúñiga reacted to the protests with dismay.

"Law 1281 has not created restrictions on the press but has clarified them," he said in an interview. "It put limits on the power of the state as compared with the previous Law of Internal Security, which allowed greater controls under a declared state of emergency." What the government had really tried to do with the law was to rein in some local commanders and make the language more precise, he added.[57]

The injured feelings caused by Law 1281 led to a stiffening of the journalists' resolve to be heard in the long-term project of writing a new national constitution. The commission in charge of this suggested that the 1925 concepts be restored with an important qualifier—the so-called García Doctrine. This holds that "only in a normal society can there exist full freedom of the press." The *colegio* roundly opposed this, saying that it would mean permanent control, because who could tell when Chile would be normal again?[58]

Whatever the reason, closures of mass media were rare after the decree. The most celebrated case involved Radio Balmaceda, backed by Christian Democrats; a local commander charged it with causing panic buying of sugar. The station was closed for six days, and the manager was banished to a remote desert village. It soon returned to the air but was repeatedly suspended and finally closed permanently in 1977. The actions were widely regarded as warnings to the Christian Democrats to stop their political activity, not as punishment for journalistic crimes.[59]

Although the newspapers could work up little sympathy for a rival medium, both *El Mercurio* and *La Tercera* chided the government for the Balmaceda closing. *La Tercera's* main argument was that it would give the "enemies of the fatherland" material with which to attack.[60]

Even less notice was taken when the government expropriated a minor daily in Concepción called *Color,* claiming that the owners had acted as fronts for Marxist organizations.[61]

Seizure of Issues

It had appeared that the Hitlerian spectacle of books' being burned in the streets of Santiago was a passing aberration of the post-coup mentality, but isolated events in the next three years indicated that this soldierly way of eliminating opposition had remained in the weaponry of the junta. Columnist Jack Anderson, bearing good credentials from his exposure of the ITT scandal, reported in August 1975 that he had brought to light a letter proving that book burning had become a routine academic procedure. The letter was allegedly from a public university official to a subordinate listing 60 library books which must be burned; besides works by communists, they included titles by economist John Kenneth Galbraith and sociologist Gunnar Myrdal.[62]

One of the decade's most controversial acts by the government was the confiscation of all the approximately 60,000 copies of what was then the leading Chilean news magazine, *Ercilla,* the day before it was to go on sale March 23, 1976. The local commander issuing the order explained only that the publication contained ''tendentious articles destined to disfigure the image of the Supreme Government.'' Editor Emilio Filippi was quoted by a newspaper as saying he was at a loss over what article bothered the government; he also cited earlier government declarations that constructive criticisms were allowed. He later decided that a story in the seized issue about political dismissals of university professors was the problem.[63]

The National Press Association and the *colegio* issued polite protests, and *El Mercurio* mused about how hard it was for the press to guess what the commanders would object to.[64]

As for *Ercilla,* it lost $45,000 on advertising and sales.

Expulsion of Correspondents

Having made it clear from the start that foreign correspondents would be viewed as necessary evils, at best, the junta approached the end of the decade still determined to seal the national borders against those who persisted in incisive reporting.

None of the major foreign news media other than news agencies keep correspondents permanently stationed in Santiago. But all try to send in roving reporters. And with steadily growing frequency beginning in 1974, the reporters would arrive at the Santiago airport only to find that they must get back on the plane. They were *non grata*. It soon became a mark of distinction, because the government concentrated on the best-known byliners—people such as Jonathan Kandell and Juan de Onís of the *New York Times,* Joseph Novitski and Joanne Omang of the *Washington Post,* Rudolph Rauch of *Time,* William Montalbano of the *Miami Herald* and James Pringle of *Newsweek*. Rarely would the government specify the charges against the correspondent, saying only that his stories had been ''false'' or ''tendentious.''

The general decree law covering such cases forbids entry to ''those who propagate or foment . . . doctrines which tend to disturb or alter by violence the social order of the country or its system of government; those linked to or having reputations as agitators or activists of said doctrines and in general those who do things that the Chilean laws describe as violations of national sovereignty, internal security or public order; and those who act contrary to the interests of Chile or who constitute a danger to the state.''[65]

Usually the employing medium has played down its reports of the ousters hoping to get the order lifted, as often happens, either for unrestricted entry or special occasions such as the 1976 OAS meeting, when all was temporarily forgiven.

An exception occurred after Novitski of the *Post* angered the military by filing a story about a summary execution of two Chileans, and it ordered his expulsion and briefly kept him under house arrest. In this case the *Post* ran a substantial story on his troubles and protested to the Chilean ambassador in Washington. Within a day he found himself free of restrictions.[66]

Conceding by 1976 that the government had banned a "small group" of foreign correspondents. Zúñiga indicated no acceptance of the adversary concept of journalism. He repeatedly emphasized in an interview that the *Times* and the *Post* had printed "negative" news about Chile. "The government gave these journalists all the facilities they could expect," he said, "but they lied, they wrote only to do wrong to the country." The doors of Chile are always open to those who have not offended the country, he added, but "if you visit my house and blaspheme, would I let you visit again?"[67]

State Ownership

Hewing to 19th Century principles of private ownership, the junta generally has minimized its role as proprietor of media. In fact, it has done less in this direction than the Allende or Christian Democratic governments did. However, the civilian regimes tended to exercise their proprietor role through political fronts, a strategy shunned by the junta.

Even so, the military government could count a Santiago daily, television and radio chains and a publishing house among its assets.

In its democratic days, Chile had piqued the world's interest with its practice of maintaining a newspaper called *La Nación* as the spokesman of whatever government was in power. It competed commercially, but it was always a weak sister among the dailies, especially so during the Allende period.

Sensitive to *La Nación's* bad image, the junta handed it over to the *colegio* and renamed it *La Patria*. It became an attractive, slickly edited paper but still was stigmatized, and the *colegio* tired of being cast in the role of government lackey. So it pulled out in 1975, the government resumed control and the name changed again to *El Cronista*. A leading journalist, Silvia Pinto, was brought in as editor, and she reshaped it as a slightly more folksy tabloid. But the circulation continued to sag well below 5,000. Some people bought it to get the government line, but it differed little in this from the other dailies.

While the government's newspaper has little significance as a propaganda organ, its radio network does loom large in this respect, but only in regard to its international shortwave service. Headed by a young escapee from Hungary, Gabor Torey, the voice of Chile by 1976 was using five shortwave frequencies in seven languages—the main European ones plus Arabic and Russian. Plans were being laid to add Chinese, Japanese and Portuguese. Although listeners find it difficult to tune in, Torey receives mail from 63 countries and has extracted government promises to vastly expand his transmitting power.[68]

Chile's international message has had little to say about the global protests of her human rights situation even when they have been loudest. Instead it tried to boost trade and tourism. Torey marks the protests up to Soviet agitation and predicts that "people will find out for themselves that they are lies." He sees little profit in answering Radio Moscow, "especially with the immense transmitting power they have and the little I have."

The military acquired its radio stations by default when it expropriated the property of various communist and socialist organizations banned in the coup.

The main unit was Santiago station Radio Corporación, once owned by *El Mercurio* and, before Allende fell, by the Socialist Party. It is across the street from the presidential palace where the besieged Allende died, and 16 of his supporters had been living in the station with a small arsenal. After four days of fighting and looting in the offices, it was a wreck.

The operation became called Radio Nacional with the grouping of 14 government-owned stations with 25 affiliated ones blanketing the country.[69] The generals had wanted a BBC-type operation at first, but this failed to catch on with the public. Torey, who had worked in commercial radio, turned the network to a popular format and started fulfilling the government's order that it be self-supporting nine months after the coup. Its only domestic propaganda role is to act as the originating station for countrywide hookups when a high official speaks to the nation.

The government's publishing house is the continuance of what had been called Zig-Zag in democratic days. Renamed Quimantú when bought by the Allende government, it took the name of poetess Gabriela Mistral when the military took it over. It turned aside from the propaganda role assumed under Allende, and the junta tried to find a buyer, meanwhile redirecting it toward making a profit as a commercial publisher.

Although the military inherited a nation-blanketing chain of five originating television stations with 65 repeaters, its greatest concern has been to keep this gigantic apparatus from being an economic drain. Retaining only the right to name the director of the group, called Televisión Nacional, it cut off all special subsidies and ordered that it stand on its own feet financially. This meant allowing the station to fill most of its time with cheap popular entertainment; revenues responded, and advertising rose from $400,000 to $1 million by 1976. It still has to borrow money, but it is approaching self-sufficiency.[70]

Propaganda

Apparently remembering the rampant propaganda spewed by both sides in the Allende days, the military has de-emphasized internal persuasion. Public slogan-posting is kept to a minimum, as is the personal posturing that most dictators succumb to. Presidential speeches are rare, and press releases are straightforward accounts of spot news events, albeit ones that reflect well on the junta's programs.

Editors are under no legal compulsion to print government releases, and they pride themselves on exercising some discretion in rewriting, but they know better than to ignore the urgent matters.

"We don't accept handouts verbatim," said Arturo Fontaine, subdirector of *El Mercurio*. "But we do run the government's declarations. We also distinguish government releases from our own copy."[71]

A convenient method for the government to distribute its handouts is through the teletypes of Orbe, a Chilean national news agency founded in 1955. Just as any client can, the government pays Orbe to carry its stories; this makes up 60 percent of the agency's revenues.

Perhaps the most visible figure in the military government is the first lady, Lucía Pinochet, whose pictures show up almost daily in the press or television as she dutifully opens schools and public events. Because Televisión Nacional's newscast is especially prone to this, detractors call it ''The Lucy Show.''

Conspicuously absent for the Chilean media is any massive appeal to national pride of the sort often manipulated by dictators. The government has made no demands on broadcasters to carry a high proportion of Chilean music, apparently recognizing the resentment this would stir. ''Never are more than five of the top 50 popular songs Chilean,'' a broadcaster noted. ''It's not that we feel culturally inferior—we're just internationally minded and prefer the best in the world.''[72] The fact that the country lost the bulk of its leading composers and performers during the post-coup purge also played a part in this policy.

A FRAGMENT OF RESISTANCE

Remarkably, the military government has not wielded one of the most familiar weapons of dictatorships such as those in Peru and earlier in Spain—manipulation of the staffs of the media. After its initial purge, no efforts were made to erect a system of licensing or blacklisting. In fact, known leftists from the Allende period quietly began reappearing in newsrooms once the initial excitement was over, although they knew better than to bring their politics with them.

Because of peculiarities of its history, Chile witnessed a surprisingly large residue of resistance to government controls, not among the owners of the media but among the professional workers. This determination to keep the flame of integrity lit was especially evident in the *colegio* and in the university journalism schools.

Chile probably can claim the distinction of being the Latin American country with the earliest substantial efforts to develop education, licensing and professional ethics in journalism. Much of the impulse for the colegial concept's spread throughout Latin America in the 1970s originated with experiments in Chile.

The country's first journalism school started at the University of Chile in 1953, and three years later the strong-handed government of Carlos Ibáñez pushed through congress a law which sought to achieve ''responsibility'' in reporting. The mechanism was the *colegio,* which would arbitrate complaints about supposed breaches of ethics and would regulate the issuance of licenses which would be necessary for work in news media.[73] All persons beginning journalistic work would have to earn a journalism degree from then on, although the *colegio* was empowered to waive this requirement in exceptional cases.

Despite fears that the law might be used as a weapon of state control, this has never been threatened. In fact, none of its provisions has been strictly enforced. The *colegio* failed in its purpose as a watchdog of press standards because the law did not define the boundaries of ethics. As for the licensing system, a ''transition'' period still was in progress two decades after the law was passed, which meant that a waiver was relatively easy to get, particularly for jobs in the provinces, where few newsmen wanted to work.[74]

But the law has resulted in the mutual strengthening of journalism education and practice. Catholic University of Santiago started its school in 1961 and provided strong competition for the national university.

"Most editors are journalism school graduates now, and we have been getting a good reception from them for five or six years," Professor José Ortíz observed in 1976.

In the mid-1970s Catholic University overhauled its journalism curriculum to put more emphasis on training in practical skills, the almost universal weakness of journalism education in Latin America. It required students to work on the school newspaper and to serve internships on professional news media.

Over the years this emphasis on academic training has raised the general level of competence to the degree that Chilean journalists find it relatively easy to secure jobs in other Latin American countries. Aside from political reasons, many Chilean journalists have sought better pay in countries such as Venezuela, Argentina and Mexico. Certainly there was an ample supply of such job seekers. Three years after the coup, it was estimated that the journalistic unemployment list included 500 from newspapers (400 for political reasons and 100 because of the economy), not including mechanical workers. Out of work in television were 600 full-time workers of all types, plus 1,500 freelancers such as entertainers. Figures were not available for radio.[75] Although as many as 40 journalists had been killed after the coup, professional leaders believe that few if any remain behind bars.

Even though many of those fired from media work went abroad, the general shrinkage in positions has resulted in furious competition for each opening. Some optimists believe this will result in a better quality of performance, and journalism schools began restricting enrollments in the late 1970s.

Meanwhile, the *colegio* devotes most of its efforts to trying to preserve what is left of Chilean press freedom. It protests the more blatant abuses of power and tries to assert its views in the writing of a new national constitution.

CHAPTER 4

Cuba:

Right Arm of Revolution

by John Spicer Nichols

WHEN CUBAN REVOLUTIONARIES Fidel Castro and Ernesto (Ché) Guevara discussed Guevara's proposal for establishing a rebel radio station, the guerrilla movement was faltering. Castro's troops were not properly fed and equipped and were desperately short of weapons. They had suffered a succession of military setbacks and could not break out of their rebel stronghold in the Sierra Maestra, a mountain range in the southeastern part of the island.

The purchase of even a small, dilapidated radio transmitter would be a major investment for the revolutionary forces. It would mean the continued shortage of arms and other basics. But Castro, having a keen sense for the value of propaganda, concluded that in the long run a radio station might be more critical to the success of the rebellion than guns and ammunition. Guevara was authorized to start the station.

The clandestine radio station, housed in a shack with a grass roof, was not an instantaneous success. An early attempt to pick up its signal from 300 yards away failed. The equipment was continually breaking down. But on February 24, 1958, most of the technical problems had been solved and, preceded by the tune of "Invaders' Hymn," Radio Rebelde officially went on the air. "This is Radio Rebelde, voice of the 26th of July Revolutionary Movement and the Rebel Army, transmitting from Free Territory of Cuba in the Sierra Maestra."

Before the end of the year, Radio Rebelde could be heard throughout the country and much of the Caribbean. Each night, eager to hear something not censored by the incumbent government of Fulgencio Batista, a growing number of Cubans would listen to a barrage of bulletins recounting the military victories of the guerrillas, manifestos, and patriotic poems and music on Radio Rebelde. Castro frequently polished his oratorical skills over the air, and by the time the revolutionaries took control of the government, he had refined his ability to the point that many analysts already considered him the greatest political speaker of this era.

Not only was Radio Rebelde an effective news and propaganda medium, but it eventually became one of the most important operational tools and integrating forces of the guerrilla movement. After the rebels suffered heavy battle casualties, Radio Rebelde appealed for doctors and several rallied to the cause. Arrangements with the International Red Cross for prisoner releases were made via the airwaves. Personal messages ("Mama, this is Pepito. Don't worry, I'm fine.") were frequently heard. And when the rebel forces split into several fronts throughout the country, Radio Rebelde and a growing string of stations in its network kept each military unit apprised of the activities of the others.

"Thus [Radio Rebelde] was a center of military communications of the utmost importance, in addition to having been an instrument for informing the masses which played a political role of great significance throughout the war," Castro concluded in a television speech honoring the 15th anniversary of Radio Rebelde.[1] The radio station became so vital to the guerrilla war that the rebel forces defended it with the same priority they gave to the defense of their hospital and their munitions workshop. And as Radio Rebelde grew in importance as a revolutionary tool, the organizers, news writers and announcers of the station increasingly joined the inner group of decisionmakers in the revolutionary movement. Correspondingly, the military and political fortunes of the rebels grew until January 1959, when the Batista government collapsed and Fidel Castro took control.

A MEDIATED REVOLUTION

The lessons that Castro and his lieutenants learned from their success with Radio Rebelde have not been forgotten. In fact, more than anything else, except the charismatic leadership of Castro himself, the clever use of the mass media (especially the broadcast media) has been responsible for the survival and the continuation of the Cuban revolution into the 1970s.

In the months following the fall of the Batista government, Castro monopolized the broadcasting channels. Night after night he appeared before hundreds of thousands in Revolution Plaza in Havana to explain the goals of his revolution. Millions more heard Castro's performances via radio and television. Castro, according to one historian, is "a latter-day version of William Jennings Bryan able to talk four hours at a stretch and hold the attention of 90 percent of the adult population."[2] Castro's introduction brought several minutes of cheers, singing, dancing and chanting of revolutionary slogans. In those marathon speeches, he informed the public of every new development or setback, no matter how insignificant it appeared. He expounded on everything from lofty and abstract sociopolitical goals to the artificial insemination of cattle. By most accounts, his people were mesmerized. They frequently interrupted with more singing and dancing and with shouts of "Viva, Fidel!"

Herbert L. Matthews, veteran correspondent for the *New York Times* and chronicler of the Cuban Revolution, describes the emotion as

. . . a religious faith which came pouring over the radio waves and through the television screens in the words and presence of Fidel Castro. I coined a phrase at the time: government by television. The Revolution came in a flood of talk, as Fidel exhorted, explained, reasoned with, and aroused Cuba's millions day after day, night after night, four, five, six hours at a time. The world was amused; Cubans listened enthralled.[3]

"Government by television" is an apt description. Castro and his cadre knew that for the Revolution to survive an alliance between the urban middle class and the rural poor had to be forged, and collectively they had to be mobilized against the domestic elite and foreign hegemony. The media became prime tools in this process. As the economic, civic and social structures of the old Cuba were rapidly dismantled, the media were substituted as the major integrating force, linking together disparate groups and prodding them down the path to communist revolution.

A Technological Windfall

The revolutionaries were fortunate in that they inherited a relatively advanced mass communication system. In 1959, most homes outside Havana lacked running water but not a radio receiver. Cuba also had more television sets per capita than any other Latin American country, although most were concentrated in Havana. In all, Castro took control of a developed broadcasting system that, although unevenly distributed, linked most populated areas of the island.

Most Cuban journalists initially hailed Castro's victory and, as a result, were rewarded with a certain amount of independence during the first 18 months of the Revolution. But the emotional fervor that accompanied the transfer of governments waned and Cubans eventually had to face the realities of economic chaos, political upheaval and one diplomatic crisis after another. Under these conditions, Castro felt that an adversary press (like many other civil liberties) was not contributing to revolutionary goals. The few remaining papers that opposed Castro were starved out of business by the end of 1960, and two years later, the revolutionary government had complete ownership or control of all the media.

Pragmatic Goals

Government control of the media served several purposes. The most obvious were to eliminate verbal opposition to the Revolution and to promote greater unanimity of public opinion. More important, monopoly allowed the government to use the media to achieve the major revolutionary goals of mass integration and mobilization.

"If we want to overcome the gap which separates us from the developed nations," Castro said, ". . . our resources [must be] used in a rational, organized way. There is no room for waste. We don't have the luxury of following the path of free competition to achieve economic development."[4] As he had learned in the Sierra Maestra, the mass media are precious resources for the continuation of the Revolution. They could not be left to the helter-skelter management of independent owners under a libertarian press system.

Thus, in what Castro believed was a tradeoff between the importance of the media to political, economic and cultural development versus independent critical analysis of the government, independent analysis was clearly secondary. "What is freedom to write and to speak for a man who doesn't know how to write, who doesn't know how to read?" Castro would ask those who questioned his decision.[5]

Castro's public appearances and television addresses are less frequent and there is some indication that the enthusiasm he once commanded has diminished somewhat. Nevertheless, he still captivates the Cuban masses. In late 1974, Western diplomats estimated that Castro still had the support of 80 percent of the population. When the Cuban people are wronged by or dissatisfied with the government, rather than blame Castro, they are inclined to say, "If only Fidel knew about this."[6] The success of the media (or Castro via the media) to enlist broad public support for the Revolution has allowed the government to minimize the use of repression and terror normally associated with communist revolution (e.g., Stalin in Russia). To be sure, hundreds of so-called "war criminals" were executed in the opening weeks of the revolutionary government, hundreds of thousands more left the country, and a substantial (but widely disputed) number of political prisoners, many of them journalists, remain in Cuban jails today.

But in comparison to Eastern Bloc nations and in contradiction to much that is reported in the North American press, Cuba is not a particularly repressive society today. There are no visible signs of military or police oppression. Neighborhood committees watch out for counterrevolutionary behavior at the local level, but in their homes, people speak freely, without fear, and they walk the streets without looking over their shoulders.[7] Foreign correspondents residing in Havana report that Cubans listen to the Voice of America and other foreign radio broadcasts without penalty and openly discuss the programming with their friends.[8] American-style blue jeans are popular among the Cuban youth. Pop music from the United States is commonly heard in Havana night clubs, and bootleg Hollywood movies frequently appear on late-night Cuban television. Business executives, congressmen, reporters and a smattering of tourists returning from Cuba in the late 1970s have reported many signs of totalitarianism, but few signs of repression.

Ingredients of the System

The Cuban political system is a curious configuration. It draws on some of the features of old-fashioned Latin American dictatorship, in the sense that one charismatic leader dominates. At the same time, it rather awkwardly employs the rigid organizational structure and rhetoric used elsewhere in the communist world. So too, the media are a hybrid of Marxist-communist philosophy and Latin American *caudillismo*. Generally speaking, Cuba subscribes to Lenin's directives about the purposes of the media in a communist state: to help organize the Communist Party, educating members and the public about the aims of the government, and agitating the masses to sustain morale and support.

But communism is merely an attribute of the Revolution, not its essence. Therefore, to better understand the role of the media in Cuban society, one must understand the revolutionary philosophy of Fidel Castro. Probably Castro's most revealing quotation on the media was written in a letter to fellow revolutionary Melba Hernández in 1954, long before the beginning of guerrilla activity in the Sierra Maestra: "Propaganda cannot be abandoned for a single minute, because it is the soul of every struggle. Ours should have its own style and adjust itself to the circumstances."[9]

In this simple statement, there are two elements that have had a decisive impact on the Cuban media since 1959.

First, mass communication is not only important to revolution, but Castro considers it the very soul of the process. This view has been demonstrated in the preceding pages and will be elaborated on later.

Second, mass communication in a revolution must be flexible, able to adjust to changing circumstances. It must be remembered that revolution is a process in which there is rapid change in the fabric of society. The Cuban Revolution, like most true social revolutions, is characterized by volatility, trial and error, instability, fits and starts, appalling human injustice and impressive social gains. In short, the Cuban Revolution has zigzagged through several phases during the past two decades. Accordingly, the role of the Cuban media has frequently changed.

Flexibility Is Basic

The Cuban view of the media is not etched in stone. This Cuban-style flexibility allows the media, under certain circumstances and under careful supervision, to participate in a public dialogue with the leaders of government, to contribute to government decision-making, and to serve as a forum for citizen complaints about the operation of government. During much of the Cuban Revolution, the major media have been nothing more than a loudspeaker for Castro and his inner circle, but the current political and economic atmosphere apparently is encouraging a more active press. In the later half of the 1970s, the Cuban Revolution entered a new phase. Cubans now are experimenting with a new grass-roots political movement known as the *poder popular* (people's power) intended to communicate the needs of the people to higher levels of government.[10] Likewise, the press is gingerly experimenting with a new critical function. It is now a channel through which citizens can register complaints about the tactical operation of the government. However, criticism of the strategic goals of the Revolution or of Castro himself is still not permitted.

"You can dissent within the Revolution," Castro told ABC newscaster Barbara Walters.[11] "In our party you can dissent, you can discuss, and in our assemblies people can dissent."

What Castro ostensibly has established is a Caribbean version of Lenin's doctrine of democratic centralism. Under this doctrine, public issues may be discussed until settled by party authorities. But then all party members are bound by discipline to support the official position. Not only is it permissible for the Cuban populace to debate public issues, but, according to Castro's philosophy, such discussion is necessary to the vitality of the Revolution. But once the central authorities, usually meaning Castro, have made their decision, all dissent must stop.

The following pages trace the media's constantly changing relationship with the Cuban government since Castro's takeover in 1959. The task is difficult because of the complexities of the revolutionary process, the mysterious personality of its leader and the limited evidence available to North American scholars. The task of predicting the future for the press-government relationship is not only difficult but probably impossible.

NEW TRADITIONS FOR OLD

When Castro took increasing control of the Cuban media, critics around the world charged him with destruction of a free press system. In reality, Castro had merely substituted one type of strict government control for another. In the prerevolutionary years, freedom of the press meant a censored, venal and subsidized press responding to government and industry. Nowhere in Latin America was there a more tightly controlled press.

Every Cuban president since national independence at the turn of the century had exercised either overt censorship or the more subtle control of bribing most editors and reporters into submission. In the period immediately before the overthrow of dictator Fulgencio Batista in 1959, press censorship and corruption reached their worst. The government was paying the press approximately $450,000 a month in bribes. Individual journalists were pocketing tens of thousands of dollars per month as so-called public relations consultants to the government.

Only six of the 58 newspapers in Cuba were surviving without government subsidies and advertising. Many papers that were not cooperative with the government were quickly starved out of business through corporate income taxes or import duties on newsprint. Still others were simply owned by Batista and thus unlikely to criticize his administration.[12]

A very few publications, however, managed to survive even though they criticized the Batista regime. Among them was the weekly magazine *Bohemia*, which was consistently hostile to the dictatorship, printed articles by opposition leaders and ultimately contributed to the revolutionary cause.

The government censorship actually worked in favor of Castro's revolutionary movement. Cuban audiences were eager to hear news not censored by Batista and therefore were more attentive to Radio Rebelde and a series of crude underground newspapers printed by the guerrillas and other opposition groups. Further, government censorship of the press was a convenient issue for Castro to exploit in his campaign to bring down Batista. In early interviews with North American journalists, Castro repeatedly promised to end "arbitrary censorship and systematic corruption" and to restore "full and untrammeled freedom of public information for all communication media."[13] He repeated those promises the day he victoriously arrived in Havana.[14]

Castro's Concept

In the first years of the Revolution when the privately owned press quickly fell into government hands and many Cuban journalists were either jailed or left the country, Castro was charged with betraying his promises of democracy. The truth is, according to journalist Herbert Matthews, that Castro never understood the concept of liberal democracy in the Anglo-Saxon sense and "believes with all his heart . . . that his system is democratic because it is a true expression of the will of the masses."[15]

Years later, Castro defined his concept of freedom to another North American journalist:

> I think there are two different concepts of freedom. You believe that freedom can exist in a class society, and we believe in a society without classes. . . . I wonder if you can compare the freedom of the millionaire with that of the beggar or the unemployed. Within the [North] American concept, they are all equal. They are all free. But we believe this is false. We believe that without equality, there is no freedom.[16]

An adversary (although progressively cautious) press operated in Cuba during 1959 and much of 1960, the beginning years of Castro's regime. During this initial period, the press had greater latitude to comment on government action than under Batista's censorship. The non-revolutionary press openly criticized Castro's rule, through 1959, without official repression. But after the honeymoon, Castro began to replace Batista's combination of press controls with his own. The overwhelming majority of newspapers closed during the first year, some due to government intimidation or expropriation, most for economic reasons. The new government immediately ended all bribes and subsidies to the media (except to the official paper, *Revolución*) on which most were totally dependent. Further, as the government rapidly nationalized private industry, the remaining media found it increasingly difficult to find advertising revenue to support themselves. The print media were particularly hard-pressed to find readers and advertisers. Cut off from most official news sources, publications were relegated to rehashing Castro's speech on radio and television the previous night. All the action was in broadcasting media and that is where the public attention was focused.

The denunciations of the Revolution by newspapers such as *Diario de la Marina, Prensa Libre* and *Avance* were generally ignored or discredited by the government in its own newspaper *Revolución* or in the Communist Party paper *Hoy*. The editorial attacks against the government continued without reservation until 1960. In January, Castro required objectionable dispatches appearing in the newspapers to be accompanied by rejoinders (nicknamed *coletillas* or "little tails") prepared by the printers' union. Later that month, militant trade unionists backed by the Communist Party took control of *Avance* and the publisher fled to the United States. The remaining independent newspapers tempered their criticism, although they continued to publish news and editorials unfavorable to the government. Televised retorts from Castro grew more hostile and frequent.[17]

The highly conservative *Diario de la Marina,* the oldest newspaper in continuous circulation in Latin America at that time, became a symbol of opposition to Castro and communism. It crumbled under government pressure in May, and most remaining independent papers also fell in rapid succession. In August, the weekly journal *Bohemia,* a backer of Castro during the Batista dictatorship and a widely respected voice of the left throughout Latin America, was taken over by "revolutionary management." *Bohemia*'s editor, who had suffered under Batista's rule for his support of Castro's revolutionary movement, fled the country.[18]

About the same time and after a series of incidents in which broadcasters had commented against Castro or his policies, virtually all radio and television stations were nationalized. The stations were immediately formed into a government network appropriately called FIDEL, an abbreviation for *Frente Independiente de Emisoras Libres* (Independent Front of Free Stations). Castro's favorite forum had been consolidated under his direct control.[19]

Toward a New Scheme

By February 1961, only six newspapers were being published in the capital city. Five of those newspapers were either government-owned or semiofficial papers under the control of government supporters. All previously independent magazines, publishing houses and film companies were then controlled by the government or had disappeared entirely. Only nine North American correspondents remained in the country, and they were harassed by everybody from government officials to bellhops in the hotels.[20] The closing months of 1960 and the beginning of 1961 also marked the transition of the Cuban Revolution into a new phase.[21] In 1959 and 1960, Castro had effectively liquidated the prerevolutionary order and needed a new governmental structure to replace it. In early 1961, he declared his faith in socialism and began introducing a Soviet system of government. Only a few months before, the United States severed diplomatic relations with Cuba and was preparing its Bay of Pigs invasion. The missile crisis, trade embargo and other confrontations between the two countries were to follow shortly.

Although the mass media were directly or indirectly controlled by this time, independent writers were not restricted and the public was allowed to read freely. Bookstores imported and sold "counter-revolutionary" books, magazines and newspapers. And the literary supplement to the government newspaper *Revolución* was publishing within a wide leftist spectrum. Cuban vanguard writers and foreign contributors such as Jean-Paul Sartre appeared frequently in the supplement in addition to the works of Marx and Lenin.

The editor of *Revolución* was Carlos Franqui, a close ally of Castro, early collaborator on Radio Rebelde and editor of a mimeograph version of *Revolución* in the Sierra Maestra days. In January of 1959, Franqui had arrived in Havana to assume the editorship of the Havana edition of *Revolución* even before Castro himself triumphantly entered the city. Under Franqui's direction, the literary contributions to *Revolución* were eclectic and not particularly dogmatic. Cuba's new Russian patrons and the domestic communist old-guard were disturbed by Franqui's doctrinal deviations and began to pressure Castro to intervene. In June 1961 before a congress of writers and artists, he ended the quarrel and introduced his own dictum: "For those within the Revolution, complete freedom; for those against the Revolution, no freedom."[22] This somewhat nebulous statement became the catchword for journalists, artists and intellectuals until the next phase of the Revolution in which a new combination of circumstances would require a new role for the media.

Schism in the Press

The new phase came in 1963 when failures in development strategy led Cuban leaders to question the applicability of the Soviet system to an island plantation economy. A lively debate ensued between Ché Guevara, who proposed changing to a Maoist "Great Leap Forward" approach, and the more

pragmatic pro-Soviet faction. In June 1963, Castro went to Moscow to repair
the strained relationship with Russia. The day after his return, Castro appeared
on the Cuban broadcasting network to sharply attack *Revolución*. His listeners,
especially journalists, were undoubtedly shocked.[23]

Castro's displeasure has been attributed to *Revolución*'s Moscow correspondent, Juan Arcocha.[24] The young reporter was a strong supporter of the
Cuban Revolution and Castro but had no roots in Marxism and was hostile to
Stalin. Arcocha's coverage of the state visit heaped praise on Castro and con-
veyed the enthusiasm of the Soviet masses for the Cuban leader. But in so
doing, he implied that the Russian man on the street preferred the unorthodox
and flamboyant communism of Castro instead of the rigid, conventional communism in the Soviet Union. Both Castro and the Russian leaders were embarrassed. Cuban foreign policy had been seriously compromised at a critical junc-
ture by the official paper of the Cuban government. Franqui was dismissed
from the editorship, and both he and Arcocha eventually went into exile.

The ideological debate broke out again in the press six months later. It
started innocuously when the Communist Party paper *Hoy* published an editorial questioning whether Federico Fellini's movie *La Dolce Vita,* which portrayed decadence in contemporary Rome, was appropriate entertainment for the
Cuban workers. This brought an immediate response in *Revolución* by a group
of movie directors from the government cinema institute charging that *Hoy*'s
editorial was a "deformation of Marxist-Leninist philosophy."[25] The traditionally avid Cuban filmgoers, having experienced a movie drought because of
the U.S. trade embargo, went scrambling for the usually dull Havana newspapers to follow the debate.

Castro was upset with the role of the press in this controversy, not because
of the impact of Fellini's film on Cuban audiences but because it had provoked
a public debate between the two ideological camps in Cuba. And again it happened at an inopportune time, shortly before another visit to Moscow. Castro
extinguished the flare-up by dismissing another prominent writer for *Revolución,* but this was only a temporary solution. The press, although clearly within
the parameters of the Revolution, could not be allowed to stir up internal debate
or jeopardize foreign diplomacy. More centralized control of the press would
be needed once the ideological differences were settled.

The debate between Guevara's group advocating Chinese-style mobilization of Cuban society and the proponents of an institutionalized revolution followed by the Soviets continued until 1966. Castro did not take sides publicly in
the matter and tolerated a certain amount of discussion in the secondary media,
such as journals, books and cinema. The newspapers were held in tighter rein,
although the rival staffs of *Hoy* and *Revolución* occasionally sniped at each
other in print. There is no known record of open discussion in the broadcast
media.

An End to Debate

As the debate neared its conclusion and Cuba embarked on a new revolutionary phase commonly called "Sino-Guevarism," Castro moved to consoli-
date his direct control of the media. The time for discussion of new directions
had ended. The first step came in October 1965 when *Revolución* and *Hoy* were
merged to become *Granma* (from the name of the boat Castro's guerrillas used

to sail from Mexico to begin their jungle warfare), the official newspaper of the newly reorganized Communist Party of Cuba. Editor of the newspaper was, after 1967, Jorge Enrique Mendoza, member of the central committee of the party, former news reader on Radio Rebelde and Castro's favorite government troubleshooter. No government censorship of *Granma* was required. With Mendoza as editor, *Granma* was an integral part of government. Also in 1965, Guevara heralded the impending victory in the internal ideological struggle by harshly attacking writers and intellectuals in an essay, *Socialism and Man in Cuba.* He charged that the intellectuals' desire for freedom was actually a reflection of "bourgeois idealism."[26] According to Guevara, a "new Cuban man" would be forged in an egalitarian society, and all would mobilize behind revolutionary goals. To do this, mass consciousness had to be raised through education and politicized media. All debate, even in the secondary media, was coming to an end.

For example, a very popular periodical, *Cuba Socialista,* which carried news of the party and analysis of political, economic and social conditions, was terminated in 1967. Officials said that Cubans did not have sufficient political education to appreciate the monthly and that debate on the subjects it covered should be postponed.[27] The following year, a relatively autonomous yet non-controversial newspaper, *El Mundo,* was turned over to the University of Havana's journalism program and a year later merged with *Granma.* The newspaper, which covered world news more objectively than *Granma,* apparently had earned enough from classified advertisements and its circulation of 158,000 to achieve financial independence but did not exercise much editorial independence.[28] Also in 1969, Castro closed down the bureaus of Associated Press and United Press International and expelled their correspondents.[29]

The Sino-Guevarist phase of the Revolution was a disaster: Cuban-Soviet relations reached a low ebb, Guevara was killed in Bolivia while trying to transplant the Sierra Maestra success into South America, and the Cuban economy was in chaos. The focus of the mass mobilization of the late 1960s was to harvest a phenomenal 10 million tons of sugar in 1970. If the Cubans succeeded, they would be able to exert their economic independence from Russia. The attempt to reach this unrealistic goal not only failed but seriously damaged the neglected portion of the economy. The government was nearly bankrupt, the Cuban people were dissatisfied and the survival of Castro's Revolution was in doubt.

Surviving Disaster

Castro responded to the crisis, according to most analysts, with his greatest speech. On July 26, 1970, before a national radio and television audience, Castro admitted failure. He maintained that the failure, in part, was due to an inbreeding of ideas. For the past few years, he had been hearing nothing but his own echo within his inner circle of advisers. His proposed solution was greater independence and democracy, decentralization of government operations and increased public participation in decision-making. He called on the masses to criticize government inefficiency (although not revolutionary goals) and to propose solutions to domestic problems and suggested that the press should be one of the channels for this new public dialogue.[30]

However, use of the media for public feedback, as well as other "democratic'' reforms Castro proposed, was not immediately forthcoming. Skeptics claim that his speech was nothing more than a grandstand play to compensate for his administrative errors, prevent erosion of his charisma and ease public disenchantment. Another possibility is that Castro faced a dilemma. He knew that closed decision-making was partially responsible for the current problems, but at the same time he was faced with the greatest crisis of his Revolution. Open debate could not be tolerated until the crisis had passed; therefore, the promised reforms would have to be postponed.

Eduardo Vergara, the subdirector of Havana's other daily, *Juventud Rebelde*, seemed to confirm this suspicion when questioned by a North American journalist in 1970. Vergara said that the press had a particular role to play in each stage of national development and that there was ''no need'' for it to fulfill the role of critic at that time. It was more important for the press to develop communist ideology and integrate the masses. He added that there were other mechanisms for dealing with differences of opinion and complaints, such as mass organizations, and therefore newspapers would not be used for that purpose.[31]

A New Clampdown

Regardless of interpretations of Castro's speech, the new phase of the Cuban Revolution (1970–1975) was characterized by Soviet-style institutionalization, centralization and continued tight control on all forms of expression. The sensational case of Cuban writer Heberto Padilla was the most notable example of this continued repression of the media. Padilla was a correspondent for the Cuban news agency Prensa Latina and *Granma* in both Prague and Moscow but lost his job following a run-in with the government in 1968. The disgruntled Padilla continued as a poet and novelist to write what some considered veiled criticism of the government.

In March 1971, Padilla was jailed without charges. The word of his arrest filtered abroad, probably via Carlos Franqui, the deposed editor of *Revolución*, then in exile in Paris, and in April a large group of European and Latin American leftist writers and intellectuals (among them Jean-Paul Sartre, Gabriel García Márquez, Carlos Fuentes, Octavio Paz and Mario Vargas Llosa) published an open letter to Castro expressing concern over the imprisonment and ''the use of repressive methods against intellectuals and writers who exercise the right of criticism.''[32] After being held incommunicado for more than a month and after writing a long, abject confession of his ''errors against the Revolution,'' Padilla was released from jail. Two days later, he appeared before the Cuban Congress on Education and Culture and read his letter of self-criticism. The congress responded with a hard-line declaration on the mass media and cultural affairs. Among other things, the assembled writers and artists said that the mass media ''are powerful instruments of ideological education whose utilization and development should not be left to spontaneity and improvisation.'' Control of the media should not be dispersed within the government but centralized under ''a single politico-cultural leadership.'' And in staffing the media, ''political and ideological conditions should be taken into account.''[33] All the suggestions immediately were accepted by Castro in his closing speech to the congress.

A month later, the international group of writers answered Castro and his congress in a second letter charging that Padilla's confession had been obtained through torture and likened the affair to "the most sordid moments of Stalinism."[34] Both Castro and Padilla denied the charge, but worldwide criticism of the repression continued.[35]

Cynicism about Castro's promise to open up his government to criticism only increased in the following few years when Castro built what the *New York Times* called the "Cuban Wall." Writers, artists, and scholars of varying nationalities and political persuasions were denied visas to enter Cuba.[36] North American and British pop and folk music (including protest songs) were temporarily banned from Cuban radio as an alleged cause of alienation of the youth.[37] Herbert Matthews, who visited Cuba during this period, reported:

> Castro decided that he could not get a fair break from writers; he preferred to let unfolding events do their own talking in good time. He was anyway fed up with all authors and intellectuals after the sensational [Padilla] affair. . . .
>
> Between the restrictions and the censorship, Cuba is singularly isolated from the world. Cubans must rely on the shockingly inadequate, censored and biased news of their journals and radio.
>
> So long as Fidel Castro and his associates are convinced that the Revolution cannot expect fair coverage in the American and Western European press . . . Cuba will remain a closed book to the rest of the world. This suits Castro. He believes that time is on his side and that the longer Cuba is left alone the better the picture will be when the moment comes to open up.[38]

Doors Open

The moment of opening came in 1975. Castro had re-established rapport with Russia, negotiated several favorable trade deals with it, eased tensions with the U.S. and stabilized (although not solved) Cuba's grim economic problems. Emerging from an era of isolation and, according to sketchy evidence, severe repression of any form of free expression, Cubans were able to boast of substantial social gains. Most observers recognize that in the availability of education, health care and housing, profound improvements have benefited the common man. The success in the field of education, probably the greatest and least disputed accomplishment of the Revolution, is due, in no small part, to coordinated efforts through the mass media. For example, Castro's old station, Radio Rebelde, became an educational channel teaching the Russian language and offering literary and political commentary.[39] It also has, incidentally, the most powerful signal in the country.

The extent to which Cuba has broken out of its long siege of isolation is demonstrated by the legions of diplomatic, trade, sports, cultural, scientific and technical missions that wended their way toward Havana from all corners of the world. Even Cuba's archenemy, the United States, has had vastly greater access. A covey of prominent U.S. reporters (including Dan Rather, Bill Moyers, Frank Mankiewicz and Barbara Walters), previously *personae non gratae,* paraded to Havana for interviews with Castro and returned with, if not agreement about accomplishments of the Revolution, at least universal praise for Cuban hospitality.

An interesting sidelight to Barbara Walters' celebrated 1977 interview with Castro helps define a basic difference between socialist and capitalist press systems. Cuban editors and other officials gleefully pointed out that while only a condensed version of the total interview was aired on ABC television in the United States, the entire interview was shown on Cuban television, not once but twice. "The U.S. press, because of its commercial nature, cannot fully develop a story," explained Jorge López Pimental, editor of *Juventud Rebelde*. As a result, he said, the U.S. media are filled with "hot" news and not with background information necessary for people to function satisfactorily in society.[40]

Although reopening Cuba's doors to the world was undoubtedly a conscious decision on the part of Castro's government, total isolation from the United States was never a realistic possibility. Cubans can and frequently do listen to Miami radio stations (only 225 miles away) on their car radios while commuting to work, and with a good antenna and favorable weather conditions, they can pick up U.S. television programming in their homes. Even in the midst of its isolation, Cuba never attempted to jam foreign broadcast signals.[41]

CRITICISM IN THE CUBAN PRESS

The showpiece of Castro's new Cuba is the *poder popular* (people's power), a political structure meant to give the government face and ears at the local level. Established by the new Cuban constitution, which was resoundingly approved in a popular referendum in February 1976, *poder popular* theoretically links the people directly into government via a system of elected bodies that begins at the neighborhood level and continues to a national assembly. Despite these political innovations, the basic framework of a highly centralized administrative and decision-making apparatus has not changed.[42]

The most significant part of the *poder popular* experiment is the assignment of ombudsman functions to the neighborhood delegates. Each of these elected representatives is required to hold public meetings at established intervals, listen to his or constituents' complaints, contact the appropriate government agency attempting to solve the problem, and report back to the local assembly on the results. These public meetings have been described as enthusiastic,[43] voluble and critical participation by large numbers of citizens.[44] However, the discussions are not concerned with questions of policy but rather with the efficiency with which established policy is implemented. Thus the people have the opportunity to criticize the performance of government agencies and bureaucrats at the local level without challenging the central government's decision-making power.[45]

New Role for Journalists

In 1974 the Cuban press began publishing reports of these meetings, and the following year *Granma* launched a "consumer action" column used to force bureaucrats to account for their mistakes and inefficiency and to relay reader concerns to the government. Editors of the column, titled "By Return Mail," invite readers to blow the whistle on unresponsive administrators, long waits in the local hospital, lack of garbage collection or any other cases of negligence and waste. A team of reporters is then assigned to investigate the charges and report on their findings.[46]

These Cuban-style investigative reporters have no special authority, but their work has impact because they are on the staff of the newspaper of the Communist Party. As the column continues to build a reputation and wide readership, it increasingly has been demanding "accountability," in essence fixing blame for the abuses that are uncovered.

For example, an investigation initiated by the column staffers led to the firing of three top officials in Havana's sanitation department after a reader reported that two department vehicles were abandoned for months on a city street. Another letter to the column that caused a lot of comment around Havana came from the vice minister of the Cuban national police force. The police general criticized traffic officers for "negligence and insensitivity in failing to crack down on government functionaries who violate laws."[47]

The column was so successful and popular with the readers that Havana's other daily, *Juventud Rebelde,* newspaper of the Young Communist League, started one of its own. The idea is now spreading to newspapers in the provinces. *Juventud Rebelde* editor López reports that his paper receives 800–900 letters per week and part of the reason for the daily's expansion from four to six pages is to handle the influx of letters. "There is nothing that we do in which the people's hand is not present. The people are the government. Therefore, the press criticizes from within and not from outside."[48]

Lionel Martin, stationed in Havana as a correspondent for the Canadian Broadcasting Corporation and a stringer for ABC and the *Washington Post,* believes that the "consumer action" columns have not only brightened up the generally dull Cuban newspapers but also represent a broader effort by the government to use the press in its move toward increased public participation in running the government.[49]

Consistent with Theory

This critical function of the press is completely consistent within a Marxist perspective, according to Mendoza, *Granma*'s editor:

> The tank is [the Cuban worker's] tank. The machine gun is his machine gun. The school is his school. And the factory is his factory. So if the factory is not operating correctly then he will criticize it. The state is his state. Therefore it is only logical that he criticize it. This is the best way he can help the state.[50]

Of course, this freedom of the Cuban press to criticize government operation and to discuss public affairs is not absolute and is tempered by a host of factors. The most prominent are:

1. As has been abundantly demonstrated in Cuban history, the critical ability of the Cuban press is directly related to the political and economic stability of the Revolution. When the continuation of the Revolution is threatened, the government is unlikely to allow dissent, but when the Revolution is on course, a certain amount of public debate, Castro believes, adds to the vitality of his government. This type of relationship is neither new nor reserved exclusively for Marxist-communist press systems. Professor Frederick W. Siebert,

after studying the freedom of the British press, advanced the postulate that "the area of freedom contracts and the enforcement of restraints increases as the stresses on the stability of the government and of the structure of society increase."[51] Siebert's postulate, which has been tested in a wide variety of press systems throughout much of the world, has clear applicability to the Cuban mass media.

2. The major media with the largest audiences, particularly radio and television, have the least potential for contributing to the debate on the public issues. Although Cuban newspaper editors, for the most part, deny it and Cuban broadcast executives only smile when asked about the concentration of government resources in radio and television, it seems clear that there has been and will continue to be a government priority on broadcasting.

The extent of the government's commitment to what Matthews called "government by television" is apparent from studying Cuba's five-year trade plan. One of the top priorities is the importation from Russia of about a half-million radio and television sets. This goal will be particularly costly to meet considering that Cuban television operates on a 525-line system built by the United States in the 1950s, and therefore the regular TV sets manufactured in Russia (and all socialist countries) for use on its 625-line system are not compatible. The Soviet Union is currently manufacturing 525-line sets, at a substantially inflated price, solely for sale in Cuba. The Cuban government places such a great emphasis on having a developed broadcasting system that it is willing to make large sacrifices in other areas of its delicate economy, and accordingly it will retain strict control over the content aired on that system. Little debate has been heard on Cuban television in the past, and the situation is not expected to change. Braodcasting is Castro's forum.

The latitude is greatest for the limited-circulation magazines and journals appealing to specialized audiences. Because they are not as closely tied to the Communist Party as *Granma* and *Juventud Rebelde,* these smaller and more obscure publications provide more in-depth coverage of certain critical issues than the newspapers. Book publishing and film production, both of which have expended greatly since 1959, are largely confined to education and ideological formation; however, the percentage that deals with entertainment or sociopolitical issues also has some flexibility to comment independently.[52]

3. Local issues can be more openly and critically discussed in the provincial media than can national issues in the national press. Political scientist Richard Fagen maintains that there has always been a "subculture of local democracy" in Cuba and therefore concludes that the more parochial the issue, the more vigorous the debate and democratic the approach to decision-making.[53]

4. Consistent with Castro's version of democratic centralism, the media may discuss any issue (within revolutionary parameters, of course) before it becomes a matter of policy set by the central government. Theoretically, debate on any issue is unrestricted until a decision regarding it is made. The problem with this approach is that most important decisions in Cuba, particularly at a national or international level, are made before the people have a chance to discuss them. For example, Cuban troops had been transported to Africa long before the Cuban people were informed of the military venture. "It had to be kept secret for elementary military reasons," Castro said.[54] "Be-

sides," added *Juventud Rebelde* editor López, "The people have a right to be informed about the underlying principles [of the Cuban action] before they start reading the battle reports."[55]

Structure of Media

The *poder popular* movement has also had an impact on the organization of the Cuban media. For the past decade, the Cuban media have monolithically represented all segments of society. The party, state, army and mass organizations, despite their differing functions in society, have all had a unified voice in the media. "We are the newspaper of party," said *Granma* editor Mendoza. "But we are often compelled to publish things of the state because it does not have its own newspaper."[56] Both he and López agreed that there might be situations in which the party and the state disagree, and therefore to protect the critical ability of the press, the functions should be separated. Thus, plans are being drawn to give each major organization or political division its own voice. *Los Trabajadores* (The Workers), the newspaper of the trade unions, is being upgraded from an obscure weekly to a daily. A newspaper of the state, apart from *Granma,* is expected to follow. The ultimate goal is for each major segment of Cuban society to have its own medium to represent it in the public dialogue.[57]

Despite all the protestations of press criticism and other reforms, there should be no doubt about the fact that the Cuban media have been totally absorbed into the government. As long as Castro and his disciples are in charge, there will be no independent ownership of the media and no criticism of revolutionary goals and the inner circle of government. Or, as Castro has said:

> If you asked us if a newspaper could appear here against socialism, I say honestly, no, it cannot appear. It would not be allowed by the party, the government, or the people. In that sense we do not have the freedom of the press that you have in your country [the United States]. . . . Our mass media serve the Revolution.[58]

Thus the ability of the Cuban press to criticize the government or to report public dialogue about the needs of Cuban society is strictly circumscribed by the goals of the Cuban Revolution as set by Castro and his cadre. Even within the boundaries of the Revolution, as past experience demonstrates, the critical content of the media may be further restricted depending on a nexus of conditions of the country. In reality, Castro's dictum to the press appears to be an even more ambiguous "For those within the Revolution, *some* freedom; for those against the Revolution, no freedom."

CHAPTER 5

Mexico's
Undying Myth

THE CLAIM THAT a revolution is still going on years or decades after the fighting stopped has become an accustomed means to keep the people motivated, to allow a regime to stay in power and to postpone a day of reckoning on how many of its goals *the* Revolution has fulfilled. Such a concept has become ingrained in Soviet and Cuban life, for example.

The talismanic phrase leaps at one constantly in Mexico also; it is difficult for any public figure to get through the briefest of speeches without reference to *the* Revolution, which started with the overthrow of a dictator in 1910. But somewhat distinctive to Mexico is the fact that most of its citizens, from the very start, have carried the flag of idealism in one hand and that of cynicism in the other.

Novelist Mariano Azuela expressed this dualism through the words of a rebel soldier as he pauses after one of the revolutionary battles. "How beautiful the revolution!" he exults as looters strip the bodies of the dead. "Even in its most barbarous aspect it is beautiful." Then he turns melancholy:

> A pity what remains to do won't be as beautiful! We must wait a while, until there are no men left to fight on either side, . . . we must wait until the psychology of our race, condensed into two words, shines clear and luminous as a drop of water: *Robbery! Murder!* What a colossal failure we would make of it, friend, if we, who offer our enthusiasm and lives to crush a wretched tyrant, became the builders of a monstrous edifice holding one hundred or two hundred thousand monsters of exactly the same sort. People without ideals! A tyrant folk! Vain bloodshed! [1]

The edifice the heirs of the Revolution have built for mass communication is an impressive one. Mexican newspapers are technically among the best in the Third World, and high quality can be found throughout the provincial cities, not just in the capital. Movies, television programs, books and magazines sent

96

abroad from the fertile workshops of Mexico City make for the kind of cultural imperialism that the country's leaders often denounce in others.

But as reliable sources of information about important things happening in Mexico, its mass media are held in widespread disdain by citizens at all levels of life. They see the shortage of freedom in journalism as part of a general scarcity of democracy. But, curiously, Mexicans somehow find enough freedom to complain about the shortage.

Octavio Paz, Mexico's most honored poet and essayist, points out that the country has been run by one political party since the Revolution, although it goes through the "fiction" of elections each six years. The mission of the legislators, he says, is to "applaud and praise the president," and the judiciary is only an "appendix" of the executive power. Most mass media are not owned by the government or main party, and they would seem to be able to supply the competition of ideas lacking in politics. But Paz sees little hope here:

> Our fictitious political life would be incomplete if we did not have a liberty of the press equally fictitious. Theoretically our newspapers can say what they want to say; in practical terms, they say what they can. And what they can say is what the government wishes them to say. Or what is wished by the big interests that dominate the country—from the private corporations to the powerful political and labor bureaucracies.[2]

The conflict between theory and reality, between a search for light and a retreat into obscurity, has marked Mexico from its earliest days. The nobles and priests who grafted Spanish civilization onto an Indian root appreciated both the status and delight promised by the printed word, and poets and scholars were not slow in developing in the van of the conquistadores. In 1539, only 18 years after Cortez vanquished the Aztecs, an Italian immigrant whom the Spanish called Juan Pablos founded the first printing press in the Western Hemisphere.

But the appearance of intellectual competition in the colonial press was belied by the reality of strict control by the government. For nearly 200 years, the printing shops were confined mostly to publishing pious devotional books or occasional handbills retailing some remote news event such as a foreign battle. Not until 1722 was a periodical newspaper published, and journalism continued to be a tepid affair in the century leading up to independence, even though rebellious talk had been welling up for several decades before the break with Spain.

The 100 years following the birth of a revolutionary paper, *El Despertador Americano,* in 1810 have been called the political period of Mexican journalism. Fierce battles of doctrine and personality were fought out in print as well as in battlefields. But again the press was frustrated in its attempt to fulfill its chosen role. Much of the century was occupied with a succession of dictatorships and only brief interludes of liberalism. Most of the known devices were used against the press—licensing, censorship, fines, prison terms, bribes, boycotts, confiscation, closing, exile, good-behavior bonds, even personal assault and execution.[3] Never before and never since has Mexico seen such daring editors, as they repeatedly invited doom with their attempts to publish. But again it came to naught until the last few years before the Revolution started in 1910.

The seven-year scourge that swept across Mexico then had among its victims nearly all the previous newspapers. Two of today's three best-known Mexico dailies were born in the last year of the fighting, and the early exhilaration of the new order brought an onrush of others. Like the government, they saw themselves as vehicles of democracy and spokesmen for the masses.

But reality again overtook idealism, and Octavio Paz' contention that the media are free from neither the state nor special interests is widely supported. So far had free expression ebbed that when one president decided to restore it in the 1970s (briefly, as it turned out), his press secretary justified it not in libertarian but in practical terms. "The decision to allow public opinion to express itself freely implies recognition of the impossibility of ruling a country of this dimension and complexity through authoritarian means," he declared.[4]

This implies that in Mexico the two-way flow of influence beteeen government and media is particularly significant. The media are shaped by the special nature of the Mexican state, but the political power structure would be quite different with a different media system. We shall look at these contrasting effects separately.

MEDIA EFFECTS ON STATE

The burning issues of the Mexican Revolution were who was to own the land, how power would be divided, and what the role of the church would be. The press was given little more attention than other economic institutions such as the railroads. The 1917 constitution in effect declares that there shall be freedom of the press except when it offends society. Unlike those in the Soviet Union, the Mexican media had no assigned role in building the new order other than the vague hope that they would enlighten the people.

Here again reality intruded upon theory. In the hands of Mexico's abundantly skilled politicians, the media became a weapon for each of them for making the country and its goverment conform to his wishes. Consequently, the dominant effect of media on government has been nonprofessional instead of operating through independent criticism and reporting, although isolated instances of these have occurred in recent years.

Image-Building

Each Mexican president gains his office not by winning the favor of the public but by being chosen as the ruling party's candidate by his predecessor, somewhat as in the military regime of Brazil. So long as his identity remains secret, he is referred to only as *El Tapado* (the hidden one). But once he is unveiled, custom calls for him to become the subject of a massive campaign to "sell" him to the public, even though he has no effective opposition. When the paroxysm of praise has peaked, hardly a flat surface remains in Mexico without a slogan of adulation; even the roadside boulders and hillsides are called into service.

Mass media are prime instruments in this effort. Not only advertisements but news stories and photographs are vehicles for incessant coverage of the candidate's every movement and all the panegyrics heaped on him by news sources, such as a message in 1970 by a labor union to candidate Luis Echeverría that "we are fully confident that you will be the flagbearer and guide of the progress and advance of the new Mexico." The candidate provides ample opportunity for coverage, making speeches and other public appearances and giving interviews as frenetically as if he were in danger of losing the race. Since the constitution prevents re-election and tradition decrees that ex-presidents give up political power, it would appear that the newly-elected candidate would forgo further pursuit of popularity. But two factors conspire against this: (1) The ineffectiveness of the legislative branch means that any governmental dialogue with the people must be conducted by the president, and (2) because recent presidents have tended to choose unknowns as successors, the new officeholder must continue to develop the public personality he started while a candidate.

Thus the *jira de trabajo* or working tour. It resembles presidential tours in other countries, but nowhere is the practice so intense and complex as in Mexico.

An example was the *jira* that President Luis Echevarría went on to southern Mexico 14 months after taking office. It was his fortieth such trip, and it maintained his average travel mileage at 4,000 per month.

Each place the president went, he was cheered by thousands released from jobs or schools; he was greeted by all types of local leaders—political, military, professional, labor, business, peasant. His days were an endless series of ribbon-cuttings, delivery of land titles to poor peasants and inspirational speeches. He held audiences for individual citizens, even to the most humble peasants, who would tell him their problems, sometimes quite bluntly. Often he would make the grand gesture by ordering a local official to grant relief to the complainant.

In the president's party were a large part of his official family and cabinet ministers—plus about 60 reporters, photographers, TV cameramen, radio crews and all their helpers.

The presidental press office did everything it could for the journalists to facilitate the flow of their copy back to the national news centers.

> They were provided in advance with a detailed breakdown of each day's movement and activities, plus copies of prepared addresses. At each overnight stop, pressroom facilities were established in which were typewrtiers, telex and photographic transmission systems, long-distance telephones, duplicating equipment, messenger service and quantities of hot drinks.[5]

Meanwhile, the front pages of newspapers all over the country were festooned with lavish headlines, pictures and lengthy stories which treated the tour with all the drama of a military campaign. Television and radio did no less.

Even in the interludes in the capital between *jiras,* reporters depict the president as constantly receiving callers and visiting with delegations, the emphasis being on the ceremonial rather than the substantial aspects. Despite their fabled cynicism, Mexicans exposed to such coverage must eventually conclude that the president *is* the government.

Although the president receives by far the greatest image-building attention, the media also do a remarkable job of keeping alive the myth of the Revolution in regard to public agencies. Due largely to generous payoffs to reporters, offices such as social security, health, housing and education are constantly presented as symbols of the Revolution's populism.

Political Haven

Media have also served as a haven for politicians out of office, although in this, Mexico differs from other countries. Since it essentially has only one party, politicians usually do not oscillate in and out of office, using the media as a temporary power base while in the outward swing. Instead, the usual trajectory of a Mexican politician's career is a simple matter of up and down. He tries to make his rise as fast and steep, the fall as slow and shallow as possible.

While some politicians have used media as launching pads, more frequently they have gone into publishing or broadcasting after reaching their crest in politics. These fields assure a comfortable income and a graceful posture for an elder statesman.

Some of the more recent presidents who followed this pattern were Miguel Alemán, who acquired part ownership of the television network centered in Mexico City, and Luis Echeverría, who became a newspaper magnate even before he left office. The building of his post-presidential empire will be detailed later.

Reporting and Criticism

In the far northwest of Mexico, a rancher and fishing camp operator named José Toscano operates an eight-page tabloid newspaper, *The Parrot's Godmother (La Comadre de la Cotorra)*. He writes the entire paper, and a large part of it is satirical insults, blunt and ribald, aimed at objects most complained about in Mexico but rarely criticized in the mass media. These include the ruling Partido Revolucionario Institucional (PRI), the rampant demands for bribes, graft, and corruption of all types.

Toscano began his paper as *The Parrot* in 1956. The federal education department, in charge of licensing newspapers, closed it down, but a week later the editor was back with a paper called *The Son of the Parrot*. The next year brought another closure and another resurrection, this time as *The Mother-in-Law of the Parrot*. Another year, another closure.

"That time I went to Mexico City and told the minister of education that it only cost me $5 to make a new masthead and they might as well kill me or leave me alone because I plan to continue publishing," Toscano recalled.

Since 1960, Toscano has published *The Parrot's Godmother* without interruption since, as he observes, "politicians . . . don't kill reporters any more—they train them instead." The latest masthead shows the three previous parrots with their beaks tied shut.

Problems with officials have faded away, Toscano observed. "In fact, they are very attentive. Whenever a candidate comes into town, the secret police always invite me to go hunting and fishing with them until he leaves."[6]

Although *The Parrot's Godmother* is too small for the powers in Mexico City to bother with, its survival does indicate that under some circumstances the inhibitions against the free exercise of journalism can be ignored. Since 1971, at the urging of then-president Echeverría, the press has been cautiously moving toward frank criticism and reporting, albeit with severe setbacks. Relieving the pressure on the media was an Echeverría campaign promise, and he shocked most people by honoring it. He promptly freed several persons who had been jailed for their writings. He built honest research into his own regime and encouraged criticism of government programs from within as well as from the media.

"This is the most important change that has occurred under this government," a journalist commented at the time. "There is still pressure on us, but there isn't the heavy-handed intimidation of the past. And almost all important news finds its way into print."[7]

The new policy met with loud grumbling from the conservative elements in Echeverría's government, and even some of the journalists were uncomfortable with the new uncertainties. The presidential press secretary, Fausto Zapata, remarked that, "in a country with limited experience of freedom of expression, some people became easily alarmed."

The more aggressive elements in the press, as it happened, shared many of the president's early targets for attack—such as corruption and inefficiency in government, big business, and the U.S. State Department. The most lively of the journalistic crusaders, editor Julio Scherer García of the Mexico City daily *Excélsior,* was a close ally of Echeverría and was rumored to have frequent conferences with him.[8] So much did Echeverría rely on Scherer, one observer noted, that "as soon as a public figure begins being attacked in *Excélsior,* everyone knows he will soon be out of a job."[9]

Abuse of power at the lower levels of government, particularly by the police and the military, has been a special target of the media's experimental crusading. A series of revelations about police misdeeds in 1974 gave readers a type of fare totally new to them. One experienced foreign correspondent noted that two of the cases were "extremely significant—both because of what they revealed about the excesses of local officials in Mexico, and because they came to light at all."[10]

In one of the cases, the press revealed that the brutal death of a labor organizer in Yucatán had been solved with the arrest of the state police chief and six subordinates. The other episode involved the murder of a man who was a local newspaper editor and *Excélsior* correspondent in a remote border city. The editor had been exposing a smuggling gang, and he was machinegunned in his office. The local police chief and 30 policemen were charged in the case, which was believed to extend to nearly 200 murders. When the facts were revealed in the nation's press, the leftist magazine *Siempre* declared: "Against tradition, the truth has been published."[11]

A perfect illustration of how the media can help reform government arose from enterprising news coverage in *Excélsior* a few days later. It revealed that gun-carrying men in plain clothes had broken up a youth meeting of the tiny opposition party in Mexico City. To document its story, it printed five pictures clearly showing the invaders, and their faces betrayed them as "special services" policemen. After *Excélsior* printed the material, the state governor quickly suspended 10 policemen and ordered an investigation.

The publicity rather than the harassment surprised the opposition political leaders, who said such aggression was an "everyday" matter. But the coverage was a distinct change.[12]

The media's euphoria over their new-found liberty led to a willingness not only to expose specific cases but to do depth reporting about law enforcement. A public discussion developed on why Mexico has few writers of detective fiction. One answer, widely accepted, was that Mexicans could not conceive of honest and competent administration of justice. According to an *Excélsior* columnist, "In view of the way the police operate in Mexico, it is impossible for writers to create inspectors of faultless rectitude. . . . In Mexico, everyone trafficks with justice. It is bought, it is hidden, it is manipulated in all imaginable ways." [13]

In one case in which a prisoner died mysteriously, the media refused to accept the police explanation. Also, the commercial television network Televisa produced a precedent-setting documentary probing into the problems of the police forces. It detailed not only the officers' complaints—low pay and dangerous work—but also the complaints against them, particularly the practice of *la mordida,* which is the extracting of payoffs for official favors such as canceling traffic tickets. The tone of the documentary was one of helping the government to overcome its image problem rather than attacking it. [14]

Newspapers have occasionally reported messages from terrorists, which is flatly forbidden in countries such as Argentina, Brazil and Chile. Ransom demands have appeared in print, as have letters from guerrilla chiefs gleefully reporting victories which they say the army has covered up. [15]

Since it is possible for the president and other PRI leaders to escape blame when the sins of the military, police and lower officials are exposed, the media have largely confined themselves to these levels. But exceptions have occurred, and whether these will set the mold for the future remains to be seen.

One such breach of traditional self-censorship was the publicizing of the selection of the PRI presidential candidate in 1975, which was tantamount to election since there was not even token opposition in the election the next year. Just as in Brazil, the leading editors felt that even if the people could not participate in the selection, at least they should be able to observe it and hear comments about it.

So the sort of discussion that in earlier decades had taken the form of rumor came out into public print in 1975. The papers excitedly identified whom they considered the seven men the president was considering as his successor, and their qualifications and beliefs were reported at length.

A series of five comic books discussed various candidates, and the cartoonist, a noted satirist called Rius, got in his blows at the system of leaving the choice up to the president. "In Mexico," he wrote, "we have perfected the electoral system so well that we are going to reach the point of having elections without electors (except for a single elector whose vote counts)."

The power of that elector, the president, to point out his successor was always referred to by Rius as "the big finger." Ridiculing the adulation that the chosen one traditionally received, Rius said that it made no sense to list his strong and weak points in advance: "In the precise moment that the big finger tells us who is the good one, we will know all his virtues and forget all his defects, as if by magic." [16]

The same cynicism showed up in the major media. Columnist Vicente Leñero ridiculed the game of concealing the president's choice: "With hidden ones or without hidden ones, democracy continues to shine only by its absence."[17]

Another heresy committed now and then in the 1970s was direct criticism of the president, who had always been considered to be above such things. This came mostly in the last years of Echeverría's term when his self-made image as a liberal miracle-worker began to fall apart. Daniel Cosío Villegas, one of the country's most respected political analysts and formerly an ally of the president, accused Echeverría of a warped understanding of liberty and carefully documented his charges in a much-discussed book.[18]

Perhaps a more hurtful blow at Echeverría was one which questioned his gallantry. A magazine writer said he had botched the state visit of British Queen Elizabeth II by parading her in something that looked like a fire truck and by committing such gaffes as kissing her cheek, taking her arm and saluting in a lounge suit.[19]

The media also have shown less reluctance to interfere in diplomatic matters. *Excélsior* editor Julio Scherer García created a sensation with a provocative interview with the late Chou En-Lai, then premier of China. The newspaper also ruffled Mexico's relations with the United States when it reported—incorrectly, as it developed—that the northern neighbor planned to build a 2,000-mile fence along their border to shut out illegal aliens and drug runners.

But the press also has supplemented its reporting with bitter criticism of U.S. dealings with Mexico. After the *New York Times* revealed that Mexican and American officials were collaborating in questionable tactics to deport illegal immigrants back to Mexico, a wide range of newspapers lashed out at both partners in the deal. A chorus of outrage also went up from the editorial pages when President Nixon appointed as ambassador to Mexico a man who had supposedly helped overthrow the elected government in Chile.

GOVERNMENT CONTROLS ON MEDIA

Journalism professors from all over the United States gathered in 1974 in Mexico City to study the mass media of that country. They heard a panel of speakers made up of some of the most knowledgeable specialists on the subject—a Mexican publisher, foreign and native editors working in the country, researchers.

The publisher, a staunch defender of the system, declared that "freedom of expressing ourselves—that is, freedom of opinion and even of dissent"—was alive and well in Mexico and there was no indication it would die. Then most of the other speakers detailed a welter of controls on the circulation of information in Mexico. The publisher showed no signs of irritation, and he did not attempt to refute the other speakers' assertions. They parted cordially, and the question of who was right remained unresolved and even undiscussed.[20]

The Mexicans' notable capacity for living with contradictions has been pointed out in the historical sketch. But this juggling act goes on today, particularly in the search for information about government. As one careful observer notes:

Mexican politics have long been a mystery, not least to the Mexicans themselves. No ordinary citizen can really make head or tail of anything that happens in Mexico, and following current events is a popular guessing game, which no one ever loses because the truth is never fully revealed. The players are provided with overlapping, conflicting and incompatible tag ends of information which defy confirmation, yet are impossible to disprove.

At times the government joins in, the account adds, as when official spokesmen blamed the 1968 student uprising on both the CIA and Mao Tsetung.[21]

All this inhibition of fact-finding does not discourage communication but rather stimulates it in the form of rumor. Because distrust of what the media say is common, even the legitimate efforts at reporting previously described can meet with an unreceptive audience. One long-time foreign observer described it as chain causation: "Cynicism breeds incredulity, which breeds rumors."[22]

Why does Mexico, a country that yearns to emulate the Western democracies, lack for the most part an adversary relationship between media and government? Unfortunately, the answer cannot emerge from a direct look at governmental clamps on the press, of which there are few. Rarely is it self-evident that the government took a specific action to achieve a specific communication goal and that a specific journalist responded in a specific way. But qualified observers voice two almost universally accepted conclusions:

1. Mexican journalists are generally among the most cooperative in the world in regard to the government's desires.

2. The government has a variety of devices to manipulate the media—most of them benign.

Self-censorship has been generally accepted at all levels from reporter to director. Although in other countries this results in shame and despair, in Mexico it tends to be harmonized with a fairly cheerful outlook. According to one analysis:

> Most reporters and contributors either know how far they can go, or do not feel the temptation to go very far. This enables many of them to state publicly that *they* never had anything censored. And the fact is that a great deal *can* be said in Mexico. The government is discreet in its demands.[23]

At the management level, the process is even more efficient. The *New York Times* has noted that most newspapers "respond principally to conservative business interests," which themselves are interwoven with the political elites. "The editors," says the *Times,* "exclude all information they judge to be annoying to the authorities or favorable to the left."[24] An American who has worked 15 years in Mexico City media observed, "The press is pretty well run by the Establishment," and most dailies are owned by wealthy, influential families. Editors, he said, "know it's to their advantage to print what the government will like and spike copy that might be displeasing."[25]

Even under Julio Scherer García's direction, *Excélsior* was known to be highly selective in its exposés. "You never will see anything published that is unflattering to the Mexican president," a Central American editor maintained. "When the cartoonists draw him, one can be sure the sketch will be flattering."[26] A wire service executive said that *Excélsior* often ducked investigations of actions against guerrillas. "If the soldiers or the police kill three or four persons, they will give the information in one of the inside pages and that will be all. No editorial of *Excélsior* will ask for an investigation. No reporter of *Excélsior* will be assigned to investigate what really happened."[27]

When defining the controls the Mexican government exerts on the press and the results it gets from them, one must emphasize the extreme subtlety with which these controls operate. The government generally shuns the more overt forms familiar in countries such as Brazil and Chile (with notable exceptions); these include direct censorship, closure of mass media, confiscation of issues, and police harassment of journalists. The carrot is much preferred over the stick to get the journalistic donkey to move.

Furthermore, because of the shortage of information, very little direct evidence of the operation of government controls can be obtained. The analyses below have been drawn from people directly involved in the operation of the media, with many confirmations in each case.

Government Purchase of Space

Existing in a country whose official mythology celebrates some of the most socialistic ideals in the political world, Mexico's news media are among the most commercially realistic to be found. Their first precept is to stay in business, and to accomplish this is a miracle, at least for the print media, in the face of hyperactive competition (23 daily newspapers in Mexico City, for example).

To make this miracle happen, the newspapers have felt it necessary to set their advertisement rates extremely low, to fight for subscribers with expensive give-away campaigns, to pay absurdly low salaries and to earn money in any way not forbidden by law. One of these ways is to largely remove the distinction between news and advertising space.

The ethical implications of this practice are not lost upon Mexican journalists. Despite protestations that one cannot judge Mexico by other countries' standards, no Mexican has come forward to defend the practice on any but practical grounds. One leading magazine commented:

> Journalism is not a profession that is very well regarded in Mexico. Frequently editors are considered as lackeys under the orders of vested interests. Directors with the crusading spirit or courageous reporters seem to exist only in novels. Actually the category ranges from extortionists to commission salesmen.[28]

A leading newspaper editor conceded that sale of news space has been widely reviewed by news executives and advertisers, and that the owners have tried to get away with it. Some papers distinguish paid-for material by setting it in type different from normal news stories, and some have put "I.P." (paid insertion) at the foot.[29] However, the latter practice died out in 1976.

Such purchased news space, called a *gacetilla*, is available not just modestly tucked away on an inside page but, in a Mexican newspaper, anywhere from front to back. It is frankly offered in rate books, and it was going for about $12 a column inch in *Novedades*, a leading Mexico City daily, in 1973; in *Excélsior*, it ranged up to $29 a column inch, depending on position. These are approximately triple the usual rates for ads.[30]

Space on the front or editorial pages brings premium rates, of course. Reformer Julio Scherer García, four years after taking over as director of *Excélsior,* still was trying to persuade his employees, who own the paper as a cooperative, to even slightly modify the *gacetilla* policy. He had succeeded in removing the "for sale" sign on the principal news story and all of the editorial page. However, the second news story, with a headline running across the front page, still sold for $8,000.

Aside from *gacetillas,* the government pumps substantial amounts of normal advertising revenues into the media, primarily through state-owned enterprises such as Aeromexico, an international airline; the National Lottery; the National Development Bank (Nacional Financiera); and the large government-owned movie theater chains. Large display ads from these businesses are quite evident in the media, but it is difficult to assess their exact impact on publishers. Romulo O'Farrill Jr., director of *Novedades,* reported that no more than 20 per cent of his ad revenues come from this source; a spokesman for *El Universal,* another large Mexico City daily, said his figure was 18 per cent.[31]

Not only is the insertion of paid and unpaid material confusingly tangled but also the acquisition of it. It is common practice for reporters covering a specific government agency to also handle its advertising orders; the chief reporter for each newspaper can develop something of a fiefdom in his agency, with proprietary rights. One publisher who tried to eliminate such middlemen reportedly had to pay the chief reporter in a certain agency nearly $170,000 to get him to resign.

Government Payments to Reporters

A variation on this practice is that of the journalist's acting as a jobber of space. He pays the publisher for a certain amount of editorial lineage regularly and then resells it to customers, mixed in with unpaid material which he also gathers. This is a favorite arrangement for columnists.

Ostensibly, when the government buys space in media, it is seeking to publicize or promote its programs. But the expenditures also can have the indirect effect of rewarding and protecting friends. Early in Echeverría's presidency, *Excélsior's* experiments in investigative reporting and forthright editorials brought down on it the collective wrath of the business community, which organized an advertising boycott in an effort to throttle the criticism. Echeverría, who depended strongly on *Excélsior's* support, simply filled the gap left by the boycott and increased government advertising. When the businessmen saw they were suffering more than the newspaper, the boycott ended.[32]

A movement toward centralizing government advertising orders has posed a threat to the web of special privilege covering all the various departments and reporters handling such orders. The national congress late in 1975 voted to set up a commercial agency with a majority of stock owned by the government. Called the Central de Comunicaciones, it was to be the funnel for all payments the government makes for "advertising, communication and propaganda."

The Inter-American Press Association said this had raised fear among the Mexican media in that "the government and its 800 para-state agencies—representing 50 per cent of the Mexican economy—would become the country's largest advertising agency, whose economic power over the mass communication media could be a determining factor.''[33]

Central de Comunicaciones had a short life, expiring in 1977 at the hands of the new López Portillo government. The action showed, according to the IAPA, that the new president was ''breaking with the policy of earlier regimes that sought to control the press.''[34]

Payments for Services

Reflective of the dualism in Mexican public life is the custom of payment for services that ostensibly should be free, such as a government agent's processing of documents, or for favoritism in services that are supposed to be impartial, such as the handling of a traffic offense. News reporting often fits into both categories, and the payments usually are made directly to reporters rather than to owners.

Such a payment is called a *mordida* (bite) when involving petty officials; for reporters it takes on the more elegant name *iguala* (agreement).

The *iguala* may be paid by businesses, institutions and individuals as well as government offices, although the latter are more usual. It also comes in several forms.

The best-known form is the regular, usually weekly, issuance of a consistent sum, known as ''public relations fees'' or ''parallel salaries.'' By the late 1970s these were reported to amount to as much as $2,000 a month.[35]

The payment also may be for specific tasks of reporting, either in addition to or in place of weekly payments. Many reporters, particularly those coming from smaller cities, expect publicity seekers to pay them to attend news conferences, even when a newsman only picks up a news release. Julio Scherer García of *Excélsior* recalls that in his early days as a reporter, he had just returned from covering a presidential tour when an official handed him an envelope containing pesos worth $80, saying it was for trip expenses. Scherer handed it back, replying, ''My newspaper pays my expenses.'' For this he was ostracized by his colleagues and reprimanded by his editor. He was accused of insulting the official.[36]

Another, less frequent, form of *iguala* is the type extorted under threat. Police reporters in smaller cities are known for expecting a payoff from an arrested person; otherwise he may be described in a news account as a ''reckless, drunken speedster.''[37]

Although not called an *iguala,* one way to ensure journalistic friendship is the government's practice of overlooking debts due it from news media, such as social security payments for its workers. These are commonly left uncollected until the editors irritate the government, when auditors suddenly ''discover'' the discrepancy.[38]

A few reformist editors have tried to limit or even end the *iguala*-taking, with limited success. Scherer threatened to fire reporters who took bribes, a difficult task in his cooperatively run enterprise. Since reporters may pick up *igualas* from several sources, one long-time observer estimated that 50–60 per cent of their income is of this type, and they fiercely resist any change in the system.

Another editor who tried to change it lost his job as a result. This was Benjamín Wong of *El Sol de México,* a large daily. Oddly enough, he was rehired later when the government became owner of the paper, and he reopened his cleanup drive. The outcome was a compromise—the *igualas* continued, but they were pooled and divided equally among reporters, thus removing the appearance of individual corruption. Wong later was forced out again.

Another current of reform came in 1977 from the least-expected source—the presidency. Inheriting outgoing President Echeverría's image-building mechanism, José López Portillo quickly put out the word that favors for reporters and their editor, even the purchase of space, would be drastically reduced during his six-year term.[39]

Control of Supplies

The aspect of the Mexican press best known abroad no doubt is its dependence on a near-monopoly of newsprint owned primarily by the government. Another distinction is that one of the world's oldest unresolved arguments hovers over the agency, which is called Productora e Importadora de Papel, S. A. (Producer and Importer of Paper, Inc.). Its nickname is Pipsa.

Founded in 1935, Pipsa has all the appearance of a Scandinavian consumer cooperative. The individual newspapers affiliated with it are tiny factors in the world market for newsprint, so they would have to pay premium prices and go to the end of the line when shortages occur. But banded together they represent a buyer for about 250,000 metric tons a year, which makes it one of the biggest customers in the world. This means savings, and Pipsa passes them on to its affiliates at wholesale prices, unburdened by import taxes. It not only imports the paper but also grades and warehouses it.[40]

Thus what is usually a publisher's biggest headache magically fades away. Some publishers would have to go out of business if prices were higher, and Pipsa also has proved a most lenient creditor. Many papers would be bankrupted if Pipsa went out of business and they were forced to pay their debts. So an enduring love affair has grown up between major publishers and Pipsa. They petitioned the government to renew its charter in 1965, and they were granted a new term of 30 years starting January 1, 1966. Of the 22 seats on the board of directors, the government has only one and the publishers the others.

But the fact remains that the government owns 60 per cent of the stock to the publishers' 40, and this puts a formidable weapon in its hands. Critics and defenders argue over whether it should have this weapon and whether it has misused it. The major publishers consistently deny any abuse, and just as regularly some renegade among them claims he has been discriminated against in his attempt to buy newsprint. Every year the Inter-American Press Association hears the argument and takes a middle ground, saying that Mexico has press freedom but that Pipsa is a potential danger to it.

If the charges against Pipsa were true, only the major publishers would have the reporters needed to establish proof, and they are unlikely to make the assignment. Meanwhile, rumors continue to spread: "Pipsa is so crude now that everybody knows about it," a journalism scholar noted in the late 1970s. Some specific complaints have come to light, such as:

1. In the mid-1960s, the leftist magazine *Política* declared that Pipsa was exerting pressure on it. The head of the agency denied this, saying Política had received newsprint as long as it could pay for it.[41]

2. The much-harassed *¿Por Qué?,* another left-wing magazine, told the IAPA in 1971 that Pipsa had cut off newsprint sales to it.[42]

3. Julio Scherer García, overthrown as *Excélsior* director in a government-inspired coup, reported that he ran into trouble with Pipsa when he prepared to start his new magazine *Proceso* in late 1976. It was charged that outgoing president Echeverría wanted to prevent *Proceso* from appearing before he left office on December 1. At any rate, Pipsa refused to sell printing paper to *Proceso,* and it was forced to borrow stocks from friendly newspapers or buy it on the costly open market.[43]

Law requires Pipsa to sell paper to any comers unless it can prove that it cannot get the supplies, unless the buyer is breaking the law or unless the paper is being used for some other purpose than that applied for.

A newsprint buyer may ignore Pipsa, apply for an import permit, buy his paper directly from foreign suppliers, and pay the 10 per cent duty from which Pipsa is exempted. Very few publishers have taken this recourse.[44]

A method often used, despite its illegality, is trading on the black market. In fact, it is reported that Pipsa makes newsprint allocations to affiliates in excess of what they need, knowing the paper will be sold at inflated prices to buyers unable to get approval. This often accounts for up to 40 per cent of a publication's revenues, according to the reports.[45]

The rationale of Pipsa is based on its efforts to cope with high prices from foreign suppliers. But in the late 1970s it was completing a huge factory in Veracruz state which would make newsprint from bagasse, the waste pulp from crushed sugar cane. It was to have a capacity of 220,000 metric tons a year, which, added to a small previous production in Mexico, was expected to end the country's dependence on foreign supplies. How this would affect the system of allocations was left undetermined.[46]

Ownership and Investment

Mexico's dualism again appears in its relationship with big business. The country was one of the first in Latin America to proclaim its socialistic goals, and in the early decades of the Revolution it statled the Western world with some of its moves to nationalize industry. The degree to which this wealth has been shared with the common man is debatable, but it is clear that astute businessmen have learned to coexist very profitably with the government.

Two national federations—of chambers of commerce and of industry—have won from the government protective tariffs, tax incentives, and subsidies. For these they trade their support for socialistic measures such as land reform and welfare assistance.

In addition, collaboration of government with business has shown up in the communication industry through two other means—ownership by state financial agencies and investment by government officials. Where one begins and the other ends, and where both are superseded by private capital, are mysteries which defy any answers but those of the rumormongers. What seems clear is that the state-private linkages have been steadily growing.

The most celebrated case of government takeover was that of the García Valseca chain of 34 daily newspapers and three weeklies. Most are named *El Sol de* (The Sun of) followed by city or regional names. The flagship is a major daily in the national capital, *El Sol de México*.

The chain was founded in the early 1940s by the brother of President Manuel Avila Camacho; he put it in the name of his chauffeur, José García Valseca, who had won the title of lieutenant colonel as a revolutionary fighter. Control quickly passed into García Valseca's hands, and he steadily built up properties throughout the country. Although his editorial pages were ultraconservative, he got along well with the ruling PRI politicians. As for technique, his papers were lively, well-printed and modern in appearance.

The colonel took advantage of Pipsa's liberal loan policy, to the extent of an estimated $12,000,000. Acting through the source of the money, Nacional Financiera, the government called the loan for payment. In turn, the debt was changed into equity of Somex, another state financial agency which has wide holdings in industry.

The reason the government decided to call this loan when others remained unpaid became swathed in a cloud of secrecy. Certainly not to punish García Valseca; his name remained on the masthead, and he reportedly emerged with a sizable block of stock. The government did not try to neutralize the papers but instead put one of the country's most aggressive journalists, Benjamín Wong, in charge of the flagship unit.

Late in President Luis Echeverría's term, reports began to circulate that, before leaving office, he intended to build a communication empire to step into when he departed. According to the reports, the government was disposing of the García Valseca chain stock to private investors, and coincidentally Echeverría's aides began showing up in the chain's management. One of them became executive vice president. More ominously they began looking for more journalistic worlds to conquer. They bought out one of the three traditionally leading newspapers of Mexico City, *El Universal* (although this later was sold). The organization announced plans to build a television network and expand its newspaper holdings, raising its total of dailies to 54 by 1978. Before his retirement, Echeverría also built a futuristic foundation center called the Institute for Third World Studies and offered it as headquarters for a fledgling news agency sponsored by governments of developing countries.

Government takeover of a communication industry has been more clear-cut in the case of motion pictures, although it proceeded in the familiar pattern of the mythical camel who puts his head in the tent, then gradually occupies it. Rodolfo Echeverría, who headed the official National Film Bank while his brother was national president, summed up the process:

> Traditionally, the Mexican motion picture industry had been privately owned. Little by little, the state has come in and taken over different segments of the industry. In [the Echeverría term] the restructuring has been going forward. The principal point of the present administration is that these processes are irreversible. We are entering an important phase of production. Perhaps tomorrow all pictures made in Mexico will be made in coproduction with the workers.[47]

Again, the takeover came about in gradual, legitimate stages. Mexican films had dominated Latin America in the 1940s, along with Argentine ones, producing world-famous stars such as Dolores del Río and Cantinflas and winning international prizes. Studios blossomed in Hollywood-like profusion. But in the 1950s, the spread of television and the growth of literacy brought movies to the brink of disaster. The National Film Bank said it would save the industry but not all the competing studios. So four of them died, and another merged with the lone survivor, Churubusco.[48]

Burdened by a backlog of completed films, the industry hobbled along in the 1960s and, stimulated by government patronage, took an upswing in the 1970s. By then it was a de facto state enterprise, because the film bank was financing nine of every 10 new films. It also was overseeing three production companies, two studios, two distribution companies, 500 theaters, a merchandising group and a film school. Two of the production companies are cooperatives. Workers get half the profits besides their salaries.[49] Management also has turned more to foreign coproductions to finance elaborately constructed movies for the world market.

Although broadcast stations are largely in private hands, the trend toward government ownership quickened in the 1970s as concepts of social engineering through the media spread among intellectuals. A chain of 28 educational and cultural stations had already been forged across the country under the dominance of Channel 11 in Mexico City, operated by the National Polytechnical Institute. It was modernized in the late 1960s, with adoption of color and increase of transmitting power, bringing it to far more homes. The content covered the full spectrum of such stations, from classroom lessons to emphasis on national traditions and arts.[50]

Another case of government takeover through financial default is that of Channel 13 in Mexico City. It was founded in 1972 but soon got too deep into debt to the government, which then assumed control. By 1977 it was directly budgeted by the federal government, although it was under pressure to pay off its eight-million-dollar debt through commercial operations. As a result, it was wracked by internal power struggles and debates among its personnel over whether it ought to be more cultural or more entertaining. Meanwhile, the government was buying up 16 stations in the interior to tie into a chain headed by Channel 13.[51]

In radio, the government keeps a relatively low profile as an owner. It owns a chain of cultural stations much like their television counterparts headed by Channel 11; they are turned over either to government agencies or educational institutions, which get federal funding.[52] These operate through 10 medium-wave, 10 short-wave and 3 FM transmitters. Also, there have been reports that the government is quietly buying up commercial radio stations, concealing the ownership, and that about 10 such purchases had been made by the late 1970s.

As owner of Mexico's telecommunication system, the government is responsible for boosting television signals throughout the country's farflung and mountainous population centers. Catering to the elites, the government had installed one of the world's largest satellite ground stations in 1968, giving it direct television, telephone and telex service to Europe and South America. Loan money for this project poured in from eight of the world's richer countries, and a Japanese company built the station.

When the satellite system was complete, the Mexican president could speak to people halfway around the world at the dial of a telephone or the flip of a camera switch. But he could not speak, except by radio, to nearly a third of his own citizens. Nor, of course, could they be brought into the national community through televised entertainment or advertising.

So the government launched a program to bring telecommunications to every settlement of more than 2,500 people, regardless of how remote and mountainous. This is to be done through an expansion of a microwave system which already links the major cities. When finished, it is to include 203 microwave repeaters and 55 terminal stations.[53]

Secrecy

Leaders in most democratic countries have come to realize that the liberty to print any information a news medium possesses means little if there are no ways to obtain the facts, either because the government conceals them or because reporters make little effort to get them. The latter two problems have been more the rule than the exception in Mexico. "While there is freedom of the press, there is no freedom of information," one long-time observer of the media noted.[54]

Government officials in Mexico have never shown a propensity for openness with the press, but during the Echeverría presidency another step was taken with the creation of a sub-secretariat of the press, attached to the president's office. While this agency received high marks from reporters for its helpfulness in arranging appointments with officials, it also made more efficient the monitoring of information going to the press.

The personal style of Echeverría's successor, José López Portillo, was even more reticent. He put out the word that reporters no longer would be welcome to wander in and out of presidential meetings but would have to get their news on the street outside the National Palace, waylaying guests as they left. Reporters grumbled about the hazards of being run over by cars or being shot by a bodyguard. They chased one quarry, a leading banker, 300 yards into the cathedral before he would talk with them.[55]

Laws Affecting the Media

Commentaries on restrictions on the Mexican media nearly always give short shrift to formal laws, for two reasons. First, governments prefer to use the positive impulsions noted above—the various kinds of favors—to win the press' cooperation, and they like to give the appearance of carrying out the libertarian ideas of the constitution. Second, when the law is used, its lack of explicitness "permits the government to shape it, to interpret it according to the case."[56] More exactly, press freedom follows a six-year rhythm like other aspects of Mexican public life, changing its complexion with each new president.

In their frequent moments of patriotic fervor, Mexican journalists like to cite the eloquent guarantees of their revolutionary constitution. Its Article 6 speaks of freedom of expression:

> The manifestation of ideas shall not be subject to any inquest, judicial or administrative, except in case it attacks morals or the rights of third parties, provokes any crime or disturbs the public peace.

In the next article, the constitution deals specifically with the press and spells out its rights:

> The freedom to write and publish writings about any matter is inviolable. No law or authority can establish prior censorship or demand a bond from authors or publishers, nor can it restrain freedom of the press, which has no limit other than to respect private life, morals and public tranquillity. In no case can the press be seized as the instrument of the crime.

Like most Latin countries, Mexico has a basic press law, passed as an emergency measure in 1916 during the tumultuous last days of the revolutionary fighting. It is basically a law prohibiting *desacato* or disrespect for authority. It bans "malicious expressions calculated to excite hatred of the authorities, the army, the national guard, or the fundamental institutions of the country." [57]

An even broader net was cast with a 1951 penal code which punished with 12 years' imprisonment any expression which sought to "disturb the public order." It, however, was repealed in the liberal early years of the Echeverría presidency.

Newspaper publishers thought the time was ripe in 1975 to get the 1916 law replaced by something more tolerable. They approached federal senators about it and were advised to drop the idea. One sympathetic legislator told them that lawmakers had considered revising the old law but had decided against it. Even though they admitted the law was outdated, according to their logic it was better to "tolerate abuses of freedom of expression than to exercise even a minimum of restrictions." [58]

Laws which publishers considered dangerous were surfacing with dizzying regularity in the national congress during the 1970s. Although most of these died for lack of support, a few became law. Among them was a consumer protection law passed in 1975 which required a government permit to advertise any product. [59] Publishers feared that this would bring about censorship, but no abuses followed.

Although government control of print media varies from a hands-off constitutional stance to political seduction in the real world, broadcasters fall under laws which take an idealistic view of what their media can do to help society. One researcher states that "both on paper and in practice the Mexican government exhibits a high awareness of the social significance of broadcasting for the people and the country." [60]

Mexican lawmakers, having the U.S. model close at hand, have tracked rather closely the developing broadcast law of their neighbor. Both countries' codes recognize a special obligation of broadcasters to operate in the public interest, and both concede the role of private enterprise in the operation. They require government approval of sale of stations, and they pass laws restricting program content despite basic guarantees of free speech. [61]

The main differences lie in the far greater detail with which the Mexican laws put positive and negative requirements on television and radio.

Among the positive injunctions are:

1. Broadcasters must give the government 12.5 per cent of their air time. In theory, ministries pour forth enough educational or cultural material to fill this, but it rarely happens. The only predictable such program is the National

Hour, aired on radio at 10 p.m. each Sunday and ranging from poetry and music to political speeches.

2. Giving priority to military or police bulletins.

3. Joining networks for programs the government thinks are important, such as presidential speeches.

4. Maintaining a "prudent balance" between advertising and programming.

5. Airing audience age ratings for television programs and scheduling those for teenagers and adults after 9 p.m.

On the negative side, the regulations say broadcasters cannot:

1. Transmit films, series or game shows which have not been censored by the government.

2. Air programs transmitted directly from abroad or any programs in foreign languages without government approval.

3. In the case of television, devote more than 18 per cent of their air time to commercials (or more than half of this after 8 p.m.); in the case of radio, the limit is 40 per cent.

4. Corrupt the language, violate community mores, belittle national heroes or religious beliefs, promote violence, alarm the public, encourage racial discrimination, or stimulate addiction to alcohol, tobacco or drugs.

Four cabinet ministries can separately regulate broadcasting, and all four get together as a coordinating council. Thus the control is very responsive to political pressures, the regulators of the industry serving at the whim of the president.

Since Mexican television is dominated by one huge commercial combine and by government stations, official control is made easy. The four commercial channels of Mexico City act as network centers for the country, and they are banded together into the Televisa combine. Closely allied with leaders of the governing party, Televisa has loudly boasted of a self-imposed operating code which purports to carry out the goals of the most forward-minded public television systems. This move was coordinated with President Echeverría's 1973 code of regulations, which made little basic change in previous law but was phrased in more revolutionary rhetoric.

Perhaps the most dramatic action taken to control the content of television has been the banning of 20 American serial programs on the grounds of violence. Some, such as "Kung Fu" and "Mannix," later returned to the air.

Harassment of Journalists

Mexico is not immune to the anonymous terrorism that has plagued journalists throughout Latin America, although there is little evidence to connect the Mexican variety with the central government. When a Guadalajara editor and his wife were killed on the steps of their house late in 1973, it was seen as part of a wave of antigovernment subversion. Also, the central government acted against the corrupt local officials who had murdered a crusading Tapachula editor the next year.

Use of the law enforcement system to harass journalists has been rare but has clearly shown that the government will use this tool when necessary. Such a necessity arose when a shrill weekly opinion journal of the far left, called ¿Por

Qué?, was on the verge of printing a story embarrassing to the government. The story presented evidence, supposedly verified by witnesses, that army spokesmen had lied in explaining the recapture of a colorful politician, Rubén Figueroa, who had been kidnapped by the country's most famous guerrilla chief, a Robin Hood type named Lucio Cabañas.

The army's version was that it recaptured Figueroa after a pitched battle. *¿Por Qué?* had gathered documents which indicated that Figueroa had told Cabañas about rampant corruption, drug trafficking and land-grabbing among elites in his state. According to this story, the army had recaptured Figueroa after paying a ransom and ambushing the emissaries who brought him.[63]

When the army and police heard of the impending exposure, they raided the *¿Por Qué?* office, smashed its presses, carried off its files, and arrested all 33 staff members, according to the paper's owners. The detainees were held for two weeks at a torture center, and all were beaten and threatened with death if they resumed publication, the report continued.

Another occasion when legal processes were used to intimidate a journalist was the filing of fraud charges against Julio Scherer García after his government-inspired ouster as director of the daily *Excélsior*.

The Excélsior Case

"We gave you press freedom and now look what you do!"

A Mexican official was commenting on the rash independence the Mexico City daily *Excélsior* had been displaying in the 1970s. Fraught with all the elements of Greek tragedy, the conflict of concepts led, just as Mexican media were honoring 200 years of free institutions in the United States, to the muzzling of their own most free-spirited news medium. Within 24 hours, *Excélsior* changed from a critic and investigator of the government into a cheerleader for it. And, although it later tried to regain some of its lost luster, its transformation brought down almost unanimous expressions of disgust in both leftist and rightist media around the world.

The episode not only forms a milestone of history but also shows how a broad assortment of government control devices can be brought to bear on one news medium. Most of the devices most familiar in Mexico were evident—government financing and advertising, involvement of state officials in private business, payments to journalists, and control of supplies. Others also were present, such as governmental secrecy, propaganda campaigns, manipulation of laborers, legal harassment, pressures toward self-censorship and outright suppression of information. It also demonstrates the ways in which politicians' and journalists' careers intertwine.

By the 1970s, *Excélsior* had become one of the two most admired newspapers in Latin America, along with *O Estado de São Paulo*. Unlike some of the weakening giants, it was becoming stronger by the day.[64]

What made *Excélsior* respected were its aggressiveness (if not always accuracy) in reporting at home and abroad, its criticism of the government, and the fact that it had made a financial success out of being a worker cooperative. Ironically, these were the elements that led to its fall from grace.

Rising from the ashes of the Revolution in 1917, *Excélsior* became a cooperative in 1932 to avoid financial collapse. It called itself "The Newspaper of the National Life,'' and gradually it became just that, always ranking just above two other aspirants for national prestige, *Novedades* and *Universal*. The opinions voiced in its signed columns were its best-known feature, rivaled by its often biting editorial cartoons.

Until 1968, however, *Excélsior's* worldwide prestige was relative largely to other Mexican newspapers, not to global standards of excellence. One commentator noted that it, along with its serious competitors, often ran ''foolish speculation-type sensational stories.''[65] It also was unexceptional in its governmental criticism.

Julio Scherer García, whose political reporting had won *Excélsior* much of the prestige it had, became director in 1968 after 21 years of working up through the ranks. Soon *Excélsior* began to garner a new reputation for quality, this time based not just on Mexican standards. As poet Octavio Paz recalled much later, it ''was transformed into a newspaper different from the others: *Excélsior* started to say what many others wanted to and could not say. The daily was converted into the center of convergence of the free and dissident opinions of Mexico.''

Luis Echeverría became president in 1970, and his offer of liberty to the press was like oil poured on Scherer's fire. So closely did the Scherer editorial demands coincide with Echeverría's professed policy that the two men were accused of conspiracy. Even *Excélsior's* exposures of corruption in government were in line with Echeverría's reformism.

But as it became clear late in the presidential term that Echeverría's practices were quite different from what he professed, his patience with criticism ran thin. Echeverría wanted to step from the Mexican presidency into the office of United Nations secretary general, and this required a favorable international image. *Excélsior's* steady series of attacks on diplomatic moves reached a climax when it denounced Mexico's support for a U.N. resolution equating Zionism with racism. A boycott of Mexican resorts by American Jews forced Echeverría to reverse his field and seek Israel's forgiveness. *Excélsior* demanded that the foreign minister resign, and Echeverría, seeking a scapegoat in his disgrace before the Mexican public, let the minister go. But he did not forget the humiliation the paper had dealt him. Besides, he had become a professional rival to Scherer by buying into the immense García Valseca newspaper chain.

Early in 1976, government agencies began placing hundreds of thousands of dollars worth of advertisements in other media, charging that *Excélsior* was unpatriotic and irresponsible. Some went so far as to insult the editors personally, such as claiming that Scherer's father had been a gold smuggler. The attacks were particularly severe from the giant Televisa combine, whose newscasters joined the campaign with zest.[66]

Many *Excélsior* reporters found their governmental news sources drying up, one of them being told it was ''necessary to cancel our friendship for political reasons.'' Others were tempted with lucrative offers to join the García Valseca chain.[67] Meanwhile, *Excélsior* kept up its embarrassing disclosures of government activities, including some by Echeverría's chosen successor as president, José López Portillo.

After six months of artillery fire from the media surrounding it, *Excélsior* was literally invaded. About 300 slum dwellers, riding buses owned by a state governor, moved into a vacant 218 acres in the Mexico City suburbs owned by *Excélsior*. Government trucks brought them hot meals and materials with which to build shacks. Leading them was a politician of the official party.

Excélsior had bought the land in 1959 as part of a program to diversify the company and protect it from advertiser boycotts. The land was to be developed as a middle-class housing project, with profits going to build a printing plant and to dividends for members of the *Excélsior* cooperative.

Squatter invasions are familiar occurrences in Mexico, and just as common is the police response—to expel the intruders violently. *Excélsior* had a government certificate clearing its title to the land and thus exempting it from invasions. Armed with this, its lawyers went from office to office seeking to get the squatters expelled, only to be repeatedly refused without explanation. Finally, the attorney general said he would enforce the law only after a general assembly of *Excélsior* cooperative members was held. As it happened, a dissident group of members had called such an assembly for July 8. The lines were drawn.

Now the attack on Scherer and his associates moved within the cooperative. The editor of *Excélsior's* afternoon affiliate, Regino Díaz, began trying to persuade the members, most of whom were printers and had little interest in the issues raised by Scherer, that Scherer was destroying the cooperative's financial health by failing to get the squatters evicted. According to a *Washington Post* correspondent, Díaz was "coordinating his campaign with senior officials of the Interior Ministry and . . . he had ample funds with which to assure cooperative members' votes. . . ." [68]

Mexico takes pride in its intellectual elites, and their statements carry weight. So when 50 such leaders signed a full-page ad to be carried in *Excélsior* the night before the cooperative's meeting, condemning the plot against Scherer, his opponents acted. Sixty men took over the printing presses just as they were to start the day's run. The ad read in part that "a grave aggression against the free press is about to take place." It was yanked off the press, and *Excélsior* appeared on the streets with a blank page. [69]

The cooperative had 1,302 members, and a large part of them gathered for the climactic general assembly at noon. (Reports of the numbers involved in various factions vary widely even among objective reports of the meeting.) As identifying marks, white straw hats and red armbands were worn by many of the dissidents. But also wearing these badges were many burly strangers with weapon-like bulges in their clothing.

Whenever the editors tried to speak, the dissidents drowned them out with jeers and slogans. Finally giving up, the Scherer partisans left the hall and went to their offices. Scherer and six others were ousted from the cooperative's membership by shouted vote. He called the police for protection, but an hour passed without a response. Seventy men, some of them armed, moved on the offices, and Scherer and 200 journalists left the building to avoid bloodshed. [70]

News of the Scherer ouster, one of the most talked-about events of the year, was blacked out of the city's usually competitive major media. Only from foreign publications and from newspapers in Mexico's interior could residents of the capital get reports.

The day of the coup, messengers carried a steady stream of copy from *Excélsior's* former rivals, the García Valseca papers, and it appeared the next morning in thoroughly sanitized form. To replace the celebrated columnists who had quit en masse, rightwingers such as a former official in Cuban dictator Fulgencio Batista's government were hired. Later it tried to repair its liberal image by running criticism of the government, but its credibility had been lost.

With no platform left for debate, the Scherer-Echeverría dispute disappeared overnight. The president was irritated by criticism abroad, though, and issued a formal denial that his government was involved. Scherer went about forming a new company to publish a news magazine and, he hoped, a wire service and daily newspaper later. Relying on word of mouth, he attracted 3,000 persons to a cocktail party at which he reported selling $120,000 worth of stock, with more money pouring in. However, the government reportedly threatened to cut off the Scherer group from their assets in *Excélsior* unless Scherer cancelled a trip to the United States to tell his story to congressmen and editors.[71]

Echeverría gave signs that he was determined that Scherer would not launch his magazine before the December 1 inauguration of the new president. There were rumors of peasant rebellions and even an impending army coup. So Scherer found himself entangled in a fraud indictment for allegedly stealing money from *Excélsior*. Also, the government newsprint agency Pipsa decided there was no paper for the new magazine. However, it did emerge on November 6 on open-market paper, its main article contrasting the "words" with the "deeds" of the Echeverría presidency.

The next May, the *New York Times* reported that the new president had offered to turn *Excélsior* back to Scherer and his crew. Oddly enough, the offer was made through a cabinet minister who was being approached by Scherer for credit to start a new daily, according to the *Times*.[72] However, no action ensued, and Scherer said he would prefer to recover his position through legal action.[73]

CHAPTER 6

Peru:
Reweaving the Fabric

THE EDITORS OF the government-controlled press of Lima, Peru's modern capital on the Pacific coast, didn't know what to make of it. The news filtering out by radio from Lamas, a jungle town 450 miles on the other side of the Andes, was unlike anything they had heard, particularly since they had become accustomed by that time—1975—to filling their pages with highly predictable accounts of the government's glorious advance toward its socialistic goals.

The news was that one of their own, the editor of the Lima daily newspaper *Expreso,* had been kidnapped by the people of Lamas and was being held as a hostage.

Francisco Landa, the editor, had flown out to Lamas—there were no highways—with a group of Lima journalists to attend a seminar on provincial news communication, which the townspeople saw as an effort to make the flow of official boasting to them larger and faster. So they invaded a ceremony in the town square, grabbed Landa and paraded through the downtown by torchlight to dramatize the fact that the town had been without electricity for two months.

They sent a message to an official in Lima: "Enough of deceit and our being ignored by the technocrats. Enough of promises that have only served to make us among the most abandoned people in this area."

In place of promises and seminars, the people of Lamas demanded a new generator, a better hospital and a paved road to the next town.[1]

Landa soon was freed, but the memorable showdown at Lamas pointed up conclusions that many observers of the Peruvian Revolution of 1968 had already reached:

1. Editors had lost all semblance of being adversaries of the government; rather, they were considered agents of it.

2. After six years of claiming that it was the champion of the little man, the government still had not won the affection of the people, even though it had most of the mass media in its hands.

3. No amount of words would take the place of deeds.

4. The people had little patience with grandiose social plans if they did not produce quick results in satisfying the necessities of everyday life.

But back in Lima, where nearly one of every five Peruvians lived, it was difficult to tell whether the lessons of Lamas had been heeded by the generals and admirals ruling the country. This was because there were very few independent journalists remaining to find the answer. Whatever its long-term effects on the ballot boxes and dinner plates of Peru, the Revolution had effectively destroyed daily journalism—both printed and broadcast—as an institution. The press had lost its separate identity and become an appendix to the government. Never had this occurred on so sweeping a scale in Latin America except in Cuba under Fidel Castro.

It could be argued that the Peruvian Revolution's policy toward the mass media was even more original and ambitious than Castro's. The Cuban leadership simply replaced the previous apparatus of journalism with its own voice, while in Peru the newspapers and television and radio stations were integrated into the state machinery, retaining as much of their surface appearance as possible. The casual reader or viewer could ignore the deft changes that had transformed the media into imitations of themselves.

The approach to the media differed from historical models because the Revolution of 1968 itself did.

First, the Revolution was completely dominated by the military—but these men had a makeup which departed from the stereotype of the uniformed brutes who set out to enrich themselves and their collaborating aristocratic allies. This could be said of the Brazilian military revolution of four years before, but the Peruvian one had a vital distinction—it was openly and passionately leftist, even though the rulers included many scions of the elites as well as men of the masses.

Furthermore, the Revolution's ideology was a concoction never seen before in this hemisphere, although similar to experiments that had become familiar in Africa and Asia. Dedicated Marxists were scattered through its lower ranks. Despite this, the majority of the decision-makers were homegrown reformists who wanted to try out techniques borrowed from all over the world, and some that had never been tried anywhere. They endlessly swore that their revolution was "neither capitalist nor communist, but socialist and humanist."

Such sloganeering often has taken the place of action as the first flush of armed victory has faded in various revolutions. But Peru provided a third distinction—its leaders actually carried out some basic reforms which had only been talked about elsewhere. The structure of industry, agriculture, mining, education and finally the mass media was completely and perhaps permanently transformed. A decade after the start of the Revolution, however, these structural changes had not substantially improved the lot of people like those in Lamas—the nearly one-half who were Indian and poor and mostly illiterate. For the similar number who were of mixed blood the results were varied, but Peru had fallen so low in the world marketplace that the reforms were obscured by the rising living costs. And for the one-tenth who were white, it meant either a government job or the loss of their property through expropriation.

THE ROAD TO REVOLUTION

It is a consummate irony that a country which had contributed very little to Latin America's political ferment over three centuries suddenly, in the late 1960s, began rapidly unfurling such an original and dynamic transformation. As it faltered toward the close of the 1970s, the question arose as to whether the Revolution's curse was that it had gone too fast for the Peruvians or whether it had been too timid by not emulating Fidel Castro's decisiveness.

Perhaps history is with the first argument. Peruvians—even the Indians, rooted in village authoritarianism—have tended to cling to conservative principles since colonial days. Conqueror Francisco Pizarro wanted only to extract what gold he could from the country, and the habit lingered after him. As neighboring nations later sought independence from Spain under banners of idealism, the Peruvian elites could see only their Spanish-given perquisites slipping away; Argentine and Venezuelan generals had to thrust liberation upon them, albeit with some native help.

For a century and a half after independence, as some other Latin American nations forged bold new concepts of organizing society, Peru caromed between conventionally liberal civilian governments and military dictatorships which often undid what the civilians had started. The country's one infusion of ideology came in the 1920s with a reform movement called the American Popular Revolutionary Alliance (APRA), which offered a definite program to uplift the Indians and to nationalize the foreign-owned companies which had made Peru one of the world's prime examples of economic imperialism. The military stepped in every time it appeared APRA would win an election.

This dreary pattern was shattered in 1968 when the military again ousted a civilian president. But this time, instead of rolling back the reforms, it promised a sweeping socialization and said it would not go back to the barracks until its reforms were "irreversible."

The Peruvian mass media developed along lines similar to those of the government. Printed journalism began in 1790 as part of the buildup of pressure leading to independence, just as in most other countries of the continent. Such periodicals were published by and for the elites, who were the only ones who could read write and argue about the fine points of political philosophy. Because there was little market for books, the literary figures of the Nineteenth Century had to publish their works in newspapers, even to serializing novels. When the proprietors died, lost an election or left the country, the papers would disappear.[2]

The main exception is *El Comercio,* which has been the gray eminence of Peruvian journalism since its founding in 1839 (making it the oldest *major* daily in Latin America). It was founded to defend the interests of the "liberal" or importing faction—the merchants, intellectuals and anti-clericals who wanted to modernize the country and benefit from the most advanced technology of Europe and the United States. They were locked in political struggle with the "conservatives," who preferred the old colonial ways of feudal agriculture and an economy based on exports of raw materials.

A small number of families—40 according to legend—have dominated Peruvian public life for a century or more, and one is the Miró Quesadas, who had become the sole owners of *El Comercio* by the end of the century. Even a Marxian critic conceded that their influence rivaled that of the owners of *El Mercurio* in Chile and *La Prensa* in Argentina.[3] Unlike most newspapers baronies, however, the Miró Quesada family did not own outside industrial holdings, and a company rule banned political office for top staff members.

El Comercio so overshadowed its competition until 1950 that its name became the common slang for "newspaper"; people would speak of "the comercios" to indicate the entire press.[4]

The recurrent dictatorships of Twentieth-Century Peru employed the usual arsenal of weapons to control the press—closure, seizure of issues, jailing of editors, etc.—without the brutality found in some countries. But the various factions of organized politics nearly always had newspapers to speak for them.

In fact, the various publications did little more in regard to domestic government than report their allies' opinions and their own. The concept of employing the news columns to report the full spectrum of politics had not taken hold.

This began to change in 1950 when Pedro Beltrán, identified with industrial agriculture interests, took full control of another Lima daily, *La Prensa*. Beltrán had earlier joined other landowners in buying the paper to defend their political interests.[5] But while ambassador to the United States he had become fascinated with professional journalistic techniques, particularly the idea of appealing to all political factions with one newspaper. So while maintaining the partisanship of the editorial page, Beltrán created a sensation with the news pages. A colleague from those days recalled the reaction:

> What was an accepted thing with the publics in other countries like the United States was new and revolutionary in Peru. . . . Then when *La Prensa* appeared with that new philosophy . . . the friends of Beltrán told him, "Listen, you've gone crazy! Why do you let that communist speak those things in *La Prensa?*" [6]

La Prensa also confounded its critics by sometimes experimenting with social reporting. It publicized a massive invasion of vacant land by squatters outside Lima in 1954, and it went on to promote competitions among architects for the best design for a poor people's hut. Another of its projects was to start the savings and loan association movement in Peru. At the height of its activism, Beltrán and nearly his whole staff were sent to a prison island for opposing a dictator's bid to continue in power.[7]

The 12 years before the 1968 Revolution were placid ones for the press except for one year of military rule. Since the civilian governments were moderately liberal, most media had little to quarrel with, although they maintained a loyal opposition.

El Comercio, which had veered so far to the right in the 1930s that a columnist had praised Adolf Hitler, moved strongly to a modernizing, nationalistic stance in the 1950s. Then occurred one of the strangest episodes in Latin American history—the struggle between two examplars of the establishment, *El Comercio* and the International Petroleum Co., subsidiary of the Rockefeller interests. The paper had been mounting an editorial campaign against concessions the government had given IPC, which extracted 80 per cent of Peru's oil. Charging the Miró Quesadas with being communists, IPC lashed back by organizing an advertising boycott of *El Comercio* properties by American-owned companies. The newspaper sustained such losses that it was forced to sell off its profitable broadcast stations, in which it was partner with National Broadcasting Co.

The Peruvian mass media arrived at the eve of the 1968 Revolution as one of the most vigorous systems in Latin America, if not uniformly professional. There were six independent morning newspapers in Lima which circulated over the whole country, reducing provincial dailies to minor status; five of the dailies had afternoon affiliates. Broadcasting had evolved with much of the commercial tinsel of the U.S. models and Peru had become a busy exporter of canned soap operas. There also was an ample range of magazines devoted to subjects ranging from politics to sex.

But the most remarkable aspect of the pre-revolutionary media was their identification in the public's mind with certain baronial families. At *El Comercio,* there were up to 45 members of the Miró Quesada group. *La Prensa* bore the face of Pedro Beltrán, who had been in and out of government, rising to the prime minister. Among the other dailies, *Expreso* was owned by Manuel Ulloa, who had been a cabinet minister, presidential candidate and associate of a Rockefeller banking house. *La Crónica* was the property of the Prado family, which had produced four presidents. *Correo* had been founded recently by the chief magnate of the fishing industry. *La Tribuna* stood alone as a party paper, representing APRA interests. Even in broadcasting, four families dominated through control of Lima television and radio stations which fed programs to networks in the provinces.

IDEAS FOR THE MEDIA

The Revolution in Peru, like most others, has not produced a complete code of explicit attitudes and philosophy about the media. But it has gone much further than is usual in spelling out its beliefs. Because Peru has been taken as a beacon for a growing Third World movement to support Western models for media systems, these beliefs are most significant on a global rather than a local basis.

Taking their lead from Marx, the Peruvian ideologues do not look at the media as a separate institution but rather as a tool to achieve the goals of the Revolution. So the place to start in understanding Peruvian policy on the media is the basic concepts of the Revolution itself.[8] These concepts, as laid down in a carefully phrased manifesto, are a mixture of religious idealism, prickly defiance of political enemies, xenophobia and specific plans. While the manifesto draws from a variety of sources, including both Marxism and capitalism, it pointedly rejects many of their crucial ideas. It has won praise from establishment leaders in the Catholic Church, the press, business and the intelligentsia, although many have opposed actions taken to carry it out.

Another reason to take the ideas seriously is that they, not violence, have been the force behind the Revolution. The Peruvian journalist does not go to bed at night wondering whether the dawn will find him in jail or in a morgue, as is common in some nearby countries. With rare exceptions, the closing of a publication is a calculated act of administration rather than a momentary peevishness. In some cases decrees have legitimized actions after they have been taken, but this has been a matter of ensuring necessary surprise rather than cynically covering one's tracks.

Ideological Bases

The manifesto, called the Ideological Bases of the Peruvian Revolution, has three sections of "whereas" statements and a fourth one of "therefores." In highly summary fashion, they are:

1. Whereas the Revolution is nationalist, defending the nation's personality, customs, natural resources and right to choose its own way of life;

2. Whereas the Revolution is independent, rejecting any foreign dogma, opposing control by or dependence on any other power, and embracing Latin American integration and Third World identification;

3. Whereas it is humanist, blending socialist, libertarian and Christian thought and standing for democratic processes, a variety of forms of business ownership, and the right to disagree except when attacking the foundation of the Revolution;

4. Therefore, the Revolution adopts as its goals "a participatory political system grounded in the masses," a pluralist economic system giving preference to "social ownership," and a social system emphasizing justice, freedom, work, participation, solidarity, creativity, integrity and respect for dignity.

It is notable that the only case of double talk in the manifesto comes when it speaks of the mass media; the rhetoric in this case is similar to countless other emerging nations' credos which state absolute principles and then negate them with exceptions. "Pluralism" of thought is defined as letting all citizens disagree, criticize and organize, even to forming political parties to "express a diversity of political alternatives." But then it states: "In the face of these alternatives, the Peruvian Revolution propounds its own standards, coherent and homogeneous, and does not accept within its ranks positions which contradict or devalue its own ideological and political foundation."

Media Plan

The government needed something more precise than the manifesto to map its course, and nearly six years after the Revolution started President Juan Velasco claimed that the state had been operating under just such a plan from the beginning, but it had been kept secret until then. What he revealed was Plan Inca, an elaborate timetable for nationalizing industries such as petroleum, mining, banking, insurance, finance—and the media. Of course, by the time of the disclosure much of the takeover had been accomplished.

Even though the government's media credo never came forth in one piece, it can be reconstructed from a variety of official statements. All of it clearly was rooted in the Ideological Bases and Plan Inca:

1. Freedom of expression is not lost where it has never existed, and such was the case with Peru. "What this country always knew was freedom for businessmen and for small families and groups," said President Velasco in 1974 after taking over the Lima dailies. "There were newspapers of bankers,

newspapers of exporters, newspapers of great landlords, and each one of them served to defend the interests of its owners and of ruling groups.''[9]

2. The government must have its own public voices, and these must consist of some of the most important media. "We have no press in our favor," complained an official just before expropriation.[10]

3. Nongovernmental media are allowed to exist, owned by capitalists, by employees of the media or by public organizations.

4. The nation must achieve "full popular participation." To see that this happens, the government must expropriate some media and give them to "organizations that represent the majority of the population: Farmers, labor communities, universities, artists and intellectuals, etc." (The "etc." does not include owners of businesses.)[11]

5. Criticism of the government is encouraged, but within boundaries which the government sets and interprets. This criticism, Velasco warned, must be "an authentic expression of the great organized social groups that constitute the Peruvian nation."

6. Theoretical support for the communication model is derived from UNESCO studies, "modern schools of thought" and persons who see the press as a public service.[12]

Although the Peruvian combination of the above ingredients must be viewed as unique, each of them evokes a memory of some earlier experiment, such as the corporate states of Benito Mussolini (Italy) and Getulio Vargas (Brazil). In these, the objective was to organize citizens by work categories rather than by political parties—the so called corporate state—and these groups would have their own mass media. Since leaders of the groups would be part of the government, they would not be inclined to overthrow it with their criticism.[13]

Crucial Laws

After its coup in October 1968, the military government showed its mettle by decreeing the first really effective land reform in Peru, breaking up the large estates and putting them in the hands of peasants. Not until the final day of 1969 did it start putting its ideas and plans into laws affecting the media. Then, in a series climaxing in 1974, it took actions which completed the destruction of the major media's independence. These were the Law of Freedom of the Press in 1969; the Law of Industries and the Law of the Journalist, both decreed in 1970; the General Telecommunications Law of 1971; and the Press Law of 1974.

The Freedom of the Press decree, whose name stirred widespread derision, had the effect of putting publishers on notice that the government's needs would take priority over theirs. It tightened the law of criminal libel or disrespect (*desacato*), providing fines or prison terms for insulting the government. It also required that government press releases be printed on the front page, and it barred both Peruvians living abroad and foreign citizens from owning any share of the media. The latter provision was aimed at several rich publishers who spent most of their time in Europe and the United States.[14]

Although intended to change all large companies into "worker communities,'' the Law of Industries was to have a curious effect on the press later when two worker-owned newspaper groups were expropriated by the government. The law said that 25 per cent of any company's profits had to be given to the employees, 10 per cent going in cash payments and 15 per cent in stock purchases. This formula was to be followed until workers owned 50 per cent of the stock.

Under the Law of the Journalist, a newspaper was required to make available a full column of space to writers who wanted to use it for signed articles; newspaper directors who refused would be fined. The law also virtually did away with the firing of journalists, prohibiting work contracts which ran for a fixed period and requiring that only ''grave fault''—an undefined term—would be grounds for dismissal.[15]

The next year saw the most drastic action up to that time—the Telecommunications Law. The broadcast media had little originality in journalism, taking their lead from newspapers, and none of the commercial television stations in Peru had their own news departments; they sold time to producers of *teleperiódicos,* packages of news and advertisements. But the government reformers were eager to use this instrument of mass appeal to promote ''culture'' and nationalism. They declared in the law that the electronic media were ''of public necessity, utility and security, and of preferred national interest'' and that the state must ''direct, promote, carry out, regulate and control'' broadcasting.[16]

More to the point, the government took over 51 per cent of the stock of all television stations, with a pledge to repay the private owners, who would retain the other 49 per cent. The government was authorized to buy into radio stations to the extent of 25 per cent at its option and exercise a veto on all decisions. But all commercial television and radio stations, whether involved in the stock purchases or not, were classified as worker communities and workers would eventually acquire the private owners' 49 per cent.[17]

Other provisions of the Telecommunications Law included requirements that:

1. Owners had to live at least six months of every year in Peru.

2. No private owner could have stock in more than one television and one radio station in each province.

3. All owners and employees must be Peruvian-born (not just citizens), and foreign entertainers would be allowed ''only at the convenience of the authorities.''

4. Imported program material must be reduced to 40 per cent of the air time (from the prevailing 64 per cent).

Thus, with the Telecommunications Law, the military rulers nudged the media another step away from traditional private ownership. First had come the 50-50 partnership of management and labor—the ''worker communities.'' Now it was the 51-49 and 25-75 arrangements, but with the government having the upper hand.

When the broadcast takeover occurred, the minister of transport and communications, who would become the new czar of the airwaves, said that the object was to see that all of the Peruvian people be served. But ''all of the people'' obviously were not running the media under the new arrangement, which did not approach the much-discussed goal of ''full popular participation.''

It was under the banner of this goal that the next and climactic step toward a communication policy was taken. The generals in the presidential palace appeared to be driven by two concerns about the national newspapers in Lima— their determination to rid the nation of press barons and the necessity to make good on their promise of ''full popular participation.'' According to President Velasco, what the country needed was ''a press which was authentically independent, the expression and reflection of great social sectors and diverse tendencies.''[18]

Velasco was enough of a realist to know the typical Peruvian would never believe in a press which was, in his words, ''servile, regimented and laudatory.'' He knew that to avoid an explosion of pent-up public resentment, the people had to have access to a press that was ''pluralist and open to dialogue.'' But, like all authoritarians, he could not take the decisive step and allow criticism of the governmental system itself. All criticism, he said, had to be based on ''ideological viewpoints which fall within the parameters of the Peruvian Revolution.''[19] (The label ''parametered press'' soon became a sarcastic favorite of the public.)

So if the press was to be taken from the hands of the barons, someone else must be found to receive them for ''the people.'' The answer was to establish the occupational organizations so long spoken about. All the peasants would form a ''civil association'' to run their own newspaper, the industrial workers would do the same, and so on through as many categories as the planners could devise.

Unlike the Russian and Cuban revolutions which swept away the old press and founded new publications, the Peruvian leaders chose to hand over existing newspapers intact to the ''organized sectors of society,'' as the civil associations became known. And until the sectors organized, the government would tend shop for them.

These were the principal points of the Press Law of 1974. With either malicious humor or profound stupidity, the framers of the law assigned the eight nongovernmental dailies in Lima to all the wrong kinds of people. *El Comercio,* which had always stood up for the merchants against farming interests, went to rural organizations, along with its afternoon affiliate. *La Prensa, El Comercio's* opposite number on the agricultural side, was given to industrial workers. *Correo,* the sensational standard-bearer of the fishing industry, became the property of the professional sector including doctors, lawyers and engineers. *Ojo,* a scruffy journal of sex and violence, was turned over to cultural and fine arts workers; *Ultima Hora,* another cheap tabloid, to workers in banks, insurance companies and hotels; and *Expreso* and *Extra,* the former voice of the Marxists, to school teachers.

The law was drawn so that only these eight ''dailies of national distribution,'' plus four provincial subsidiaries of *Correo,* would be caught in the net. To be taken over, a daily had to have 20,000 circulation and be sold in half the provincial capitals. The resulting ownership was the first application of a new concept laid down in law two months before—social property. Compared inaccurately to systems used in Yugoslavia, social property was to be owned by an entire organization, but no member of it would have any individual rights to it. It was actually closer to the corporate state ideas than to Yugoslavia's brand of communism.

The state, however, was itself an owner of media which would be in competition with the jointly owned broadcast stations and the social-property newspapers. These state media were a Lima television station (Channel 7) with its provincial repeaters, a radio network and three Lima dailies—*La Crónica* and its afternoon edition *La Tercera,* and the official gazette, *El Peruano.* These, of course, were exempt from the transfers to "full popular participation." This was because, according to the law, the state needed its own media "to explain, disseminate and defend" national policy.[20]

Thus with the expropriation of the eight Lima dailies, the range of types of ownership seemed to be complete. They were state ownership in the case of Channel 7, Radio Nacional and three dailies; mixed state and private ownership (worker communities) in the case of most television and radio stations; social property in the case of the eight formerly independent Lima dailies; and private ownership in the case of the non-daily Lima press (weeklies and magazines), the provincial press, a television station in Arequipa, some radio stations which the government did not want, and a few small media owned by university and church entities. On paper, it appeared to fulfill the goal of pluralism, but the free enterprise factor had almost been eliminated from the major media.

Aside from the ownership provisions, the 1974 law also made criticism of officials even more dangerous than did the 1969 measure. It provided sentences of up to three years in prison for writings that "threaten the security of the state or the national defense" or that "in any way offend the dignity or decorum of high state dignitaries."[21]

Toward the end of the 1970s, the more moderate Morales government began making vague promises about an eventual return to free expression. It appointed a commission made up of journalists and militarists to draw up a new press law which included enough warnings to the non-daily press to keep them on their good behavior and thus avert their frequent closures.[22]

THE TAKEOVERS

The ideas of the Revolution concerning the media have been treated separately because they often get confused with the ways they were carried out. This is unfortunate, because the Peruvian communication ideology ranks with the half-dozen most complex in history.

The unfolding of the Revolution also is significant in its human, practical effects on the media. And as often happens, the reality developed at a different level from the ideas.

Unlike many pseudo-revolutions in Latin America which are really palace coups, the Peruvian experience has been a massive change from earlier ways, motivated by a sincere concern for the good of the poorest classes. But it also had its underlying strands of factional rivalry and of lust for power.

The story of the Peruvian Revolution has been largely one of the military's effort to destroy or reshape other institutions of society (with the notable exception of the Catholic Church). This has its base in ideology, as has been seen, but also derives from the jealousy which the more leftist wing of the military—the one which was in control during the first seven years—holds for the elites of other institutions. While the navy and air force officer corps tend more toward traditionalism, the dominant army has drawn in a steady flow of upwardly mobile men from the lower classes. Thus it was that Juan Velasco, the son of a street sweeper, became the military president of Peru. He and those like him were the most determined to humble the elites, including the media barons. When the Inter-American Press Association protested the 1974 expropriation of Lima dailies, Velasco showed no little class consciousness in his reply: "The organization of owners of newspapers in the continent should know now that today their opinion matters very little in Peru and that their members no longer give orders here."[23]

Peru entered its revolutionary period with the standard communication paraphernalia of a Latin American government—an official gazette, the government broadcast stations and the usual claque of respectful reporters who would dutifully carry the official pronouncements back to their media for publication, even if the editorial pages raged in opposition.

But even some of the editorial pages, considered the heart of the newspapers, did little to oppose the basic goals of the Revolution. Its two earliest thrusts were to nationalize some foreign companies and to carry out land reform, both of which had long been advocated by many orthodox politicians. Among the morning dailies, none was more supportive the first year than *El Comercio*, the most prestigious. From its head offices of marble, velvet and gilt went forth editorials calling for restructuring of the government. Also generally on the government's side were the morning-evening combinations headed by *El Correo* and *La Crónica*, at that time still in the hands of the aristocratic Prado family. *La Prensa* and *Expreso*, along with their afternoon editions, were mostly in opposition.[24]

Issuance of the Law of Freedom of the Press at the end of 1969 marked also a close to the honeymoon between government and press. The departure of *El Comercio* from its camp was especially hurtful to the government, since this paper was a favorite even of some leaders of the military itself. Now its editors saw in the Revolution a threat to "fundamental values of Western Christian Civilization."[25]

The First Wave

To adequately reply to such attacks, the generals felt they needed a better platform than *El Peruano*, the official gazette filled with texts of laws. This was remedied in 1970 with the expropriation of four second-rate Lima dailies—the morning-evening combinations of *Expreso* and *Extra* and of *La Crónica* and *Tercera*. (The same year, the APRA party paper *La Tribuna* was closed for nonpayment of taxes and its printing equipment sold.)

The takeover of *Expreso-Extra* was notable because it set the pattern for many others to come. Its director, Finance Minister Manuel Ulloa, had fled into exile after the military overthrew the civilian government in 1968. He left the papers in the hands of his brother, who stayed in Peru, thus avoiding the absentee landlord prohibition. Its editorials had bitterly attacked the government, and it found itself in trouble with its employees, led by Marxists who were patronized by powerful people in government.

Without prior notice, two truckloads of soldiers rolled up at the newspapers' plant early one morning and seized it. *El Peruano* appeared on the streets shortly afterward with the expropriation decree emblazoned on its front page.

The government did not keep the company formally in its own hands but organized a cooperative of the employees and gave it to them. Supposedly the cooperative was to "assume the obligation of payment" to the former owners at a price set by a judge.[26]

Although the new owners of *Expreso-Extra* were sure to be enthusiastic boosters for the government it was not the same thing as having one's own paper. That was accomplished when the state became the owner of the *La Crónica* properties, seemingly in a most equitable manner. The company had been owned by a bank which was the property of the family of former President Manuel Prado. The business combine went bankrupt, and the state acquired the media through a public auction. Of course, the reason for the bankruptcy was that the state had expropriated the Prados' land and financial interests in nationwide reforms.[27]

La Crónica turned into a slickly edited apologist for the government, running only a few advertisements. *La Tercera* became a lighter version of the morning paper.

Broadcasting's Turn

When the government converted television and radio stations into "associated state enterprises" late in 1971, the action had less impact than the takeover of newspapers because of the relatively lower journalistic profile of the broadcast stations. Much of the operation stayed under management by the new junior partners (the former private owners), although their latitude of decision was increasingly hemmed in by official rules. The government began censoring domestic news and choosing the newsmen; forbidden subjects were violence, strikes and party politics.

In the entertainment programs, pressure was put on the managers to increase the Peruvian-made content to 60 per cent, but they were still 10 per cent short of the goal five years later.[28] Vague controls were put on those aspects of television content disliked by the reformers, such as violence and rich living. Peruvian television had been one of the major exporters of soap operas before the Revolution, a famous one called "Simplemente Maria" having brought in more than $2 million from abroad, but the heavy hand of official controls reduced this activity to the point that most soap operas had to be imported.

Although the social planners behind the broadcast takeover had talked expansively about the future of this instrument as a mobilizer for development, the government did little in this direction, showing more interest in newspapers. It filled its own non-commercial Channel 7 with amateurish local performances of classical music and ballet, which pleased neither aesthete nor peasant. As a result, the commercial stations continued making profits while the newspapers ran deficits once they left private hands.[29]

Despite the slowness in television's creative growth government planners have been projecting a vast increase in production and coverage. They hope to set up new production centers in Lima and three distant provincial cities and also to install about 30 originating stations and several repeaters.[30]

On to La Prensa

Less than a year had passed before the next big move in the campaign to dispossess the media barons. This time it reached one of the "Big Two" Lima newspapers, *La Prensa,* which had livened politics for decades with its editorial duels against *El Comercio.*

In his old age, after serving as prime minister and having made *La Prensa* one of the best-known dailies in Latin America, director Pedro Beltrán had begun spending much time abroad for health care and to teach economics at the University of Virginia. He knew of the provision in the 1969 press law which said newspaper stock could not be owned by anyone who was outside Peru more than six months in a year, and he held 16 per cent of the shares. A court had interpreted the rule as meaning the owner had to be in Peru at least once in each half of the calendar year.

So when Beltrán returned from the United States on January 21, 1972, having left home the previous July 10, he thought he was within the law. Not so, said a government decree—he had been gone more than six consecutive months and must sell his stock, giving the employees first option to buy it, and relinquish the directorship.[31]

A court set the shares' value at $163,000, only $16,000 less than Beltrán had asked. But the employees, most of whom were fiercely loyal to Beltrán, got little help from government banks in borrowing the purchase money. Finally the publishing company itself loaned the money at no interest. As Beltrán stepped down as director at age 75, the president of the employees promised that the "close unity" with their former boss would continue. Beltrán's nephew and namesake succeeded him as director, and the nephew was harassed by a series of criminal charges growing out of *La Prensa* articles; he resigned a year later.[32]

The Final Solution

With the conquest of the Beltráns, there remained in private ownership only the Everest of the Lima dailies, *El Comercio,* along with the lower summit of the *Correo* and *Ojo* combination. With steadily increasing pressure, *El Comercio* found itself under attack from government leaders and from the officialist press. More seriously, the management fought an uphill battle against labor unionists inspired by the government, with wage increase demands ranging over 100 per cent. The only reason the paper continued to hold out was that its survival and that of the remaining private press became a bone of contention among the military rulers.

Strikes became a way of life at *El Comercio* in the early 1970s. The grounds ranged from salary demands to a bizarre episode in which the union first struck to force the owners to revive an unprofitable afternoon affiliate, then struck to stop its publication. In the latter case, the complaint was that the owners had decided to make the paper a sports and entertainment publication without politics, and the printers wanted to insert political comments of their own.[33]

During one month-long strike, the printers surprised the management by putting on the streets a bootleg issue of *El Comercio,* printed in its own shops, with a dedication to the military government on the front page. It carried the full text of the president's latest address.[34]

Toward the end of the strike the founder of the union, who was not in sympathy with the Marxist instigators, pleaded publicly that they put an end to the walkout and buy up the stock in the paper themselves. He accused them of disguising an expropriation effort with the appearance of a labor complaint, and he added a prophetic comment: "Silencing a newspaper is like silencing a man, and the only way to silence a man is to cut off his head."[35]

As the dispute moved to a climax, reports of sabotage began to come out of the newspaper offices. The most common form was to deliberately distort news stories about the government in an effort to stir up the conflict with the press even more.[36]

A major cause of the conflict was President Velasco's extreme sensitivity to criticism. He frequently warned the newspapers in speeches that his patience was growing short, accusing them of "moral and journalistic" delinquency.[37] Indicating that he feared the criticism was causing problems with agrarian reform, he declared that the press would not slow down the Revolution.[38]

The verbal crossfire built up in the spring of 1974, and it became clear that the issue of press freedom was being used within the government as a symbol of the internal feud over general dogma. The man who was later to overthrow Velasco as president and pull Peru back toward the political center, Gen. Francisco Morales Bermudez, had twice threatened to resign from the cabinet if the government went ahead with a planned expropriation of *El Comercio.*[39] Then leaders of navy, the most conservative branch of the military, took up the defense of the press. The federation of journalists had met to protest against press controls, and President Velasco had denounced the meeting as an antigovernment plot. Then Adm. Luis Vargas Caballero, navy minister and a member of the ruling junta, clearly rebuked Velasco by saying in a speech: "Anyone has the right to differ, doubt and criticize. . . . When someone expresses a different opinion we qualify him as counter-revolutionary, anti-Peruvian and so on. This is a mistake."[40] Velasco angrily called a press conference and demanded Vargas' resignation, claiming that the minister had no right to make political statements. The navy's council of admirals voted to support Vargas, but he and two other admirals resigned from the cabinet the same day, apparently to avoid a violent schism in the government.[41]

As opposition to expropriation faded inside the junta, attacks on the independent press by officialist papers increased. Then, in what had become a well-rehearsed routine, policemen geared for a riot swept down in the early-morning hours of July 27, 1974, on the eight Lima dailies still outside government hands. Because of the Peruvian aversion to violence, everyone went home without injury.[42] The only arrest was of the 93-year-old patriarch of *El Comercio,* who was confined to his home to keep him from going to his office, thus creating a sticky diplomatic problem.

For the owners, all that remained was a government promise to pay them

10 per cent of the value of their properties per year, with 6 per cent interest. (Several years after the expropriation of newspapers and broadcast properties, payments to former owners still had not started.)

The takeovers, carried out in the name of the working people, ironically were as hurtful to many newspaper employees as to the remaining press barons. Four newspapers, the *La Prensa-Ultimas Noticias* and *Expreso-Extra* combinations and, partially, *El Comercio*, had been owned by the employees for several years. Now they were to be dispossessed with little hope of payment.

Government-appointed directors immediately took over operation of all eight expropriated papers. They were expected to serve only a year, by which time the government had promised to have organized "civil associations" of various occupations to take over ownership and control. Avoiding the policy it used in television takeovers, the government refrained from appointing military men to the jobs, choosing instead civilians known to be loyal but having some standing in the community.

The takeovers came on a Saturday when most of the Lima population was distracted by Independence Day celebrations. Cuba's military chief, Raul Castro, was in town to help review the Peruvian forces parading through the city in their Soviet-built tanks. By Sunday night the impact of the actions against the press had been felt, and demonstrations erupted for two nights in the upper-class suburbs of Miraflores and San Isidro. Mobs of students roamed about shouting "Elections!" and "Free press!" Pictures of Velasco were burned, and finally the protests turned into a riot of bus-burning and window-smashing. Police broke it up with tear gas and water hoses. They hauled off more than 400 persons to jail, and a communist-led labor federation demanded that the government confiscate the rioters' personal property. Little came of the incidents, but it is notable that protests over press controls set the stage for more violent outbreaks in the next few years.[43]

Protests which were more polite but just as horrified welled up in editorial pages around the hemisphere, and the Peruvian government said "representatives of the world press" would be welcome to visit Peru and debate the matter with local journalists. But when the Inter-American Press Association said it would send a delegation to do just that, President Velasco said the visitors would be barred from entering the country. He called the IAPA "a club of people without a country, mafiosos and market vendors who only defend news businesses and never have defended newsmen, their own workers or their own countries." The new director of *El Comercio*, which was a longtime pillar of IAPA, tried to pull it out of the association, but IAPA refused the resignation.[44]

Peruvian ambassadors quickly defended the takeovers in neighboring countries. The envoy to Colombia denied any communist influence and said the expropriation was "authentically Peruvian." His colleague in Brazil called it "an act of courage, a part of Plan Inca." The prime minister, on an official trip abroad, tried to distinguish the Peruvian approach, which he called "new and different from everything done so far in this field," from the familiar paths to control in other dictatorships. To support his claim, he declared that the expropriation was "in accord with regulatory criteria set by international organizations such as UNESCO."[45]

True to its word, the government took the formality of transferring ownership of the expropriated press to civil associations—at least to those which had
been organized—a year after the takeover. But control was another matter. The
government seemed incapable of laying it down once it had picked it up. There
had been a pyramid of elections in the "organized sectors"—votes first at the
local level, then regional and so forth until a national board was elected to run
each newspaper. But there were indications that the process was not consistently bringing politically reliable people to the top. Troublesome groups such
as the Confederation of Peasants of Peru and the Lima Association of Lawyers,
both of which had opposed some government plans, were excluded entirely
from the civil associations representing their occupations. Even this did not assure obedience.

So when the government began handing over the newspapers in 1975, it
kept the right to appoint the directors for another year. Continual internal warfare developed in some papers between directors of the association boards,
whose members began to feel they were being kept around only for display purposes. A journalist at *Correo* described the process as "a manipulated thing,"
and much of the attention of the boards was taken up with power struggles
within their occupational groups.[46]

When the delayed deadline to release control came in 1976, the government again said the time was not ripe. But this time it made no pretense that it
would feel the annual pressure to carry out its promise.

The civil associations continued to lose any appearance of influence on the
newspapers. "The civil association has no duties, no function," an editor of a
principal daily said. "They collect their salaries regularly." The association supposedly owning *Correo* declared itself in suspension.[47]

"The government now realizes that sectorization was a mistake," Luis
Jaime Cisneros, director of *La Prensa,* said. "It is looking at various alternatives."[48] The fact that the state had 10 money-losing Lima dailies on its hands
was beginning to be a public embarrassment, and among the alternatives being
rumored were a return to private ownership or conversion of the papers into
provincial voices.

THE "NEW JOURNALISTS"

As in many other fields, the hopes and promises of the Revolution to
transform the media have raced ahead of the possibility of carrying them out.
The regime has not attempted to make much use of control devices that have
become favorites in other dictatorships—wide-ranging laws about media content, systematic censorship, closures of newspapers, terrorism, or rigid control
over entry of young professionals into the media.

The principal tool used by the government in its attempt to transform the
media into a revolutionary ideal has been staff control. The junta has relied increasingly on this device as the plan to turn the media over to organized sectors
began to fail.

While staff control has not fully reached the ideal condition, it has been
flexible enough an instrument to allow for the constantly shifting circumstances

in the media on the one hand and the decided changes in the junta's power structure on the other. It also has served the purpose of a political weather-vane; the type of persons put in charge of the press at any particular moment is read as a sure indicator of the "party line" prevailing then. Furthermore, the practice stands as a constant reminder to would-be dissidents of how short the leash from the presidential palace is.

Even before the final takeover of dailies in 1975, the tool of staff control was well sharpened. Less than a year after the government seized *Expresso-Extra* and supposedly turned control over to the workers' community, the editor resigned after being censured by his employees; the main cause of friction was the fact that the government had criticized articles in the papers. Replacing him was a government public relations man, formerly an attorney.[49]

The government had set the stage for its manipulation of the top management in the press when it had gone through the tortuous legal process of forcing Pedro Beltrán out as director of *La Prensa* in 1972. But when it came to the main task with the expropriated dailies, it showed little subtlety. In simultaneous actions, it replaced directors of all expropriated newspapers each year for three years. The most drastic change in the type of directors came as a followup to the ouster of President Velasco; leftist intellectuals were replaced by more moderate thinkers to reflect the government's growing conservatism.

Journalistic staffs below director level also were affected severely. Although journalists did not often attack the government openly, knowing they had to make a living, many of them lost jobs because of their known sympathies; this was made possible because the regime twice suspended its law forbidding dismissals. In a general housecleaning at the time of expropriation, 300 journalists were fired or forced to resign, and many who stayed on were treated with suspicion by the so-called "new journalists"—the appointees who became professionals overnight by official fiat. At one daily, *La Prensa,* older staff members could not afford to retire because the managers used pension funds in desperate efforts to pay expenses.[50]

Professional journalists who continue to work on the dailies generally nurse the hope that the press someday will achieve real independence. "Journalists do not have the vocation to be servants of the palace," one editor commented.[51]

REVOLUTIONARY VOICES

As a whole, the Peruvian press has never placed a high value on objective, probing reportage upon which editorial judgments are based. Instead, reportage tends to grow out of editorial convictions, although this had produced some highly truthful and valuable results at times. Such has been the case both before and after government controls were imposed in the 1970s.

An example was a press crusade against police torture shortly after the eight Lima independent dailies were expropriated in 1974. The practice of torture had been rumored for several years, and finally reports of it broke out almost simultaneously in all media, led by the still unfettered magazines and weekly papers. Two of them, *Caretas* and *Oiga,* published detailed evidence of the torture, including transcripts of taped testimony by witnesses who had been tortured. The government-owned daily *La Crónica* took up the protest, and then President Velasco announced a shakeup in the police high command, admitting that the torture scandal was involved.[52]

Because torture was widely believed to exist before being aired in the press, exposure of it was not what impressed most Peruvians, but rather the denoucing of it and the criticism of the government. It is quarreling with the authorities and with each other that earns high marks for the media with their publics.

Editorial combativeness has been by no means as predictable as with such famous fighting newspapers as *La Prensa* of Buenos Aires and *O Estado de São Paulo*. Lima's major dailies have long been known for softening their voices occasionally, sometimes through fairness and sometimes for self-protection. Such was the case in the nearly six years between the start of the Revolution and the expropriation of the dailies.

A Brief Surge

Strangely enough, one of the liveliest periods in Peruvian journalism was the year following expropriation. The new leftist intellectual editors took seriously the revolutionary rhetoric about the necessity of criticism. The torture exposé was the most talked-about episode in this outburst, but almost no subject was untouched. A *New York Times* correspondent noted:

> Under their new directors, the newspapers have published articles, editorials and letters considerably more critical of the Government than the papers published under the previous owners. Ample space has been given to foreign criticism of the take-overs. Some articles have included remarks by peasant groups impatient with agrarian reform measures. An occasional piece written by an outside critic accuses the government of being totalitarian or even Communist.[53]

This burst of energy was short-lived, however, largely because the Velasco government grew nervous about it and fired all the newspaper directors. When Velasco himself was ousted by his fellow generals and was followed by a more moderate president, the press showed signs of recovering its vitality. But, at least among the dailies, this too soon faded.

Nobody is happy about the daily press, according to Ismael Frias, the editor of the weekly *Equis*. Not only are the newsmen disenchanted but also the civil associations, the reformers and the government itself, he added.

Just why this has happened is widely debated. Frias blames it on the editors, not the government. Others say that independence is impossible under government control.[54] One analyst, after a close study, has decided that the press no longer represents any classes, dominant or lower, but rather that "it is rooted in nothing more substantial than the changing politics of the regime itself." This would indicate that it is only the echo of sounds made by power struggles within the military.[55]

The Fighting Non-dailies

By far the most vigorous sector of Lima journalism has been the non-daily press—the approximately 10 news and opinion magazines and the weekly newspapers that represent every political faction from right wing to communist.

They have consistently been true to their calling, and their only government controls have been temporary shutdown and harassment of their editors in the courts. The generals appear to consider these publications, like television, to be less important than newspapers. New ones are started as often as others are dropped by choice of their owners.

Best-known of the non-dailies for several decades has been *Caretas,* edited earlier by Doris Gibson Zileri and now by her son, Enrique. Although basically leftist in his sympathies, Zileri has regularly mixed criticism with praise of the government. He also has done much of the rare investigative reporting, such as a exposé of filthy hospital conditions. Political humor, often stinging when aimed at the generals, also is one of his strong points.

PUBLIC SUPPORT FOR MEDIA

Not given to public outbursts as much as their more excitable neighbors, Peruvians have rarely expressed their feelings about the mass media with such forcefulness as have the kidnappers of Lamas or the rioters of Miraflores. But neither has the long tenure of the dictatorship snuffed out all inclinations to speak up when aroused.

Although campaigning is forbidden to political parties, they remain opinion-forming centers. After the Miraflores riots, police arrested eight leaders of Popular Action, the party holding the presidency when the military overthrew it in 1968. They were believed to have been charged with helping stir up the riots.[56]

When the military started moving toward a return to civilian rule late in the 1970s, Popular Action also demanded restoration of press freedom. Until it returns, said ex-President Fernando Belaunde Terry, talk of popular participation "cannot be taken seriously."[57]

Literary figures and intellectuals also have spoken up to protest extremes of government repression. When Enrique Zileri was sentenced to prison for his criticism in *Caretas,* a group of literati sent a petition to the government asking amnesty.[58]

By far the most outspoken artist has been Mario Vargas Llosa, one of the most highly regarded novelists in Latin America. Like Zileri a supporter of many of the Revolution's reforms, he also been appalled by its abuses. After the expropriations he wrote protest letters to editors both at home and abroad. He is worried not only about the perils to free thought but also to the Revolution itself:

"With the growing lack of freedom of expression," he told an interviewer, "the Revolution is in danger of becoming fossilized. I don't think there was anything remarkable about the newspapers when they were privately owned. . . . But now the government has isolated itself from public debate."[59]

As president of P.E.N. International, a writers' association, Vargas Llosa is listened to carefully abroad. Newspapers in other countries have given as much attention to his opinions as to the claims of the government. He thinks it is unfortunate that artistic writers are given such political authority in Latin

America but sees it as inevitable because newspapers there "rarely are independent enough to fulfill their role as political watchdogs."[60]

TRADITIONAL CONTROLS

Because the Peruvian experiment is unique, with its destruction of the
daily press and broadcasting as a separate institution, the story of expropriations and staff controls has been described outside the framework of traditional
media controls. The latter also have existed, aimed mostly at the fragments of
journalism remaining outside state supervision—the non-daily press and the
foreign media. While these controls have not been as brutal and extensive as in
some countries such as Brazil, they have been vexatious in the extreme. It is
doubtful that many democratic countries' journalists have the resilience and
persistence of editors in the beleaguered independent press of Peru.

Closures and Seizures

Caretas, the biweekly news and humor magazine of Lima, has bounced
through the revolutionary years like a rubber ball. If anything has been predictable in the Revolution, it has been the fact that *Caretas* will anger the militarists enough to be banned nearly every year. Equally sure has been its return
after the generals have a few months to cool off. During the six years of the
Velasco presidency, *Caretas* was closed three times and its director, Enrique
Zileri, was exiled twice.

Competitors of *Caretas* range from the cautious English-language weekly,
the *Peruvian* (later *Lima*) *Times,* to the doctrinaire Marxist publication, *Marka.*
Numbering about a dozen, they have descended into and fluttered away from
Lima's plazas like its clouds of pigeons. Their lease on professional life has
generally paralleled that of the government-appointed editors of dailies.

The greatest concentration of closings, usually lasting less than a year,
came during the political and economic crises the junta faced in 1974–76.
Caretas was shut down during the tension over expropriation of dailies. Several
others were shut down as President Velasco neared the time of his ouster, and
all the non-dailies were suspended for six months after violent rioting on Lima
streets in July 1976. But leftists had fallen into such disfavor by the latter
period that six of the group, all left of center, were kept closed nine more
months.[61]

The military rarely has given reasons for the closures, nor is it inclined to
go through court procedures. However, a government spokesman announced
after one of *Caretas'* closures that it was being punished for "a frankly an-
tirevolutionary attitude full of insidiousness, falsehoods and insults . . . and
sowing doubts among the people of Peru about the clear and definite position
adopted by the revolutionary government of the armed forces."[62] When such
an order suspended operations of three other publications, the reason given was
that they had revealed a government commercial deal with Japan which they
felt was humiliating to Peru.[63]

A curious turn of events came in February 1975 when the government
closed several of its own radio stations temporarily. It did so to prevent their

falling into the hands of rebellious policemen, who were conducting a violent strike for higher wages in several cities.[64]

Caretas has been the main target for seizure of issues as well as for closures. When it prepared a special section giving facts about the police strike that readers could not get from the dailies, the government seized all 50,000 copies by invading the printing plant and scooping them up.[65]

It agreed to let the issue be sold without the offending pages, then shifted again and confiscated them on the streets.[66] A similar confusion developed the next year when Zileri was allowed to reopen the closed magazine, but when the authorities got a look at 100,000 copies ready for sale, they banned distribution. In the latter case, the government later reimbursed *Caretas* for its financial loss.[67]

Personal Punishment

Regardless of the cause, the dictatorship in Peru has not brought about the police-state atmosphere so familiar in countries such as Chile, Brazil, Argentina and Uruguay. A major reason may be the fact that Peruvian journalists have insisted on holding the government to its pledge of "Christian humanism." Even when journalists are convicted sentences usually are mild. Jail sentences are often suspended, and the government's favorite recourse for ridding itself of bothersome journalists is to ship them into exile. Almost invariably their sins are forgiven after a few months and they quietly return to doing the same kind of things that had led to exile.

Just as the magazine *Caretas* has been closed far more often than others, so its director, Enrique Zileri, has a record of encounters with the police that rivals that of all his colleagues together. His earliest such problem with the revolutionary government occurred in 1969 soon after it rose to power. His offense was revealing a secret pay raise which the military men had given themselves. He was expelled from the country but was allowed to return later that year.[68]

From there on it was a series of arrests, convictions, expulsions, prison sentences, acquittals and pardons for Zileri. Standing behind him always has been his mother, who has pursued his cause in the courts, always on the assumption that justice must prevail. Once when the government offered to relinquish the magazine's building after seizing it, she refused to accept it until her son, then exiled in Argentina, was pardoned from a prison term facing him. The government gave the pardon.[69]

Zileri's immense capacity to embarrass the government rises from his unquestioned credentials as a leftist and the good will in which he wraps his criticism. In normal times, he has said, he would have supported most of the government's programs, but he opposes the military because of its removal of democracy.

> We have always been to the left of the political center . . . long before this government took power. But now, of course, we are the voice of dissent. We are independent. We treasure that. And we believe that governments ought to be questioned.[70]

As part of the game he plays with the police, Zileri has gone into hiding several times while charges are pending against him, then reappeared when the climate was better. Once while under surveillance he escaped by simply climbing over the wall of a friend's back yard. Police have been known to jam downtown Lima traffic while tailing him as he goes to lunch, the pursuit force ranging up to 11 cruise cars. They also follow his wife as she takes their children to school or goes shopping; at one time they requested that she not drive so fast because they were having trouble keeping up.[71]

Other than Zileri, journalists caught up in the legal net have ranged from publication directors to a cartoonist, most of them charged under the disrespect (*desacato*) provisions of the 1969 and 1974 press laws.

For several years in the mid-1970s it was a familiar sight for policemen to force some dissident onto an outbound airliner from Lima airport. In one such case the deportee resisted so bitterly that the other passengers marched off the plane and refused to leave with him. As the crowd applauded and yelled "Fascists!" at the police, they sheepishly led the prisoner away from the plane.[72]

The most spectacular deportation was that of 10 journalists in 1974. They were staffers of two magazines, the leftist *Oiga* and the conservative *Opinión Libre,* which had criticized the government's unfavorable trade deal with Japan. The government warned that "counter-revolutionary action is hiding behind freedom of the press" and that it would not brook any "subversive licentiousness." Five lawyers, leaders of the Lima Bar Association, also were arrested because their group had condemned the trade agreement.[73] At another time, the government sent nearly the entire staff of *Marka,* a Marxist weekly, into exile.[74]

Deportation is a particularly handy way to deal with noncitizens working in the Peruvian media. In one of its earliest acts against free expression, the junta expelled Elsa Arana, a Bolivian who had worked for *La Prensa* 16 years. Her offense was reporting Peruvian press controls to the Inter-American Press Association.[75]

The occasional convictions under the *desacato* laws have been directed almost as often at persons outside the profession as at journalists, under the concepts of criminal libel. An example was the six-month sentence levied against a former labor minister for attacking the government in the name of the Popular Action Party.[76] But because of their relative rarity such punishments cannot be predicted even by the most cautious. A magazine cartoonist did not escape charges with subtlety when he joked that "the solution to the economic crisis rests in the creation of a tax against stupidity." For this he was accused of "having offended the honor of the masses" because the cartoon supposedly insinuated that most people were idiots.[77]

Charges under the press laws also were used to harass the nephew of Pedro Beltrán when he took over the directorship of *La Prensa* following the uncle's forced resignation. The cases generally involved objective news stories which contained facts offensive to someone in government.[78]

Economic Controls

Government pressures affecting production and sales of mass media offerings have been used as a way to punish the regime's enemies through the pocketbook, as is common in dictatorships. The most usual of these devices have been newsprint allocations, labor strikes and price controls.

But the rulers also have used their power to combat some economic damage wrought by modern media systems in underdeveloped countries. These have included advertising techniques damaging to national development and the hard-currency drain caused by imports of supplies such as newsprint.

The rules about advertising, in many ways less restrictive than those in democratic countries, generally reduce high pressure in the appeals. ''The government believes the public is gullible,'' an advertising executive noted. It bases this assumption on the clear fact that nearly half the population is Indian, illiterate, and unschooled in the ways of modern commerce. It also has set out to protect children from exploitation; they cannot be shown or their voices used in ads. Exhortations urging the consumer to do something—''buy this'' or ''drink Coca-Cola''—also are forbidden.

The reformers also are worried that ads imported from the United States with only the words translated will result in ''foreign patterns of alienation.'' Put simply, this means leading poor Peruvians to yearn for goods or ways of life they cannot or should not have. It does little for the mountain dwellers' ego to be told even indirectly that the good life is sailing yachts, driving big cars and going on ski vacations, according to the theorists.

For these reasons—and to give Peruvian advertising people more work— the regime has required that all advertising be prepared in Peru, whether for print or broadcast. Imported ideas can be used, but they must not follow those ''foreign patterns.''[79]

The danger that tastes for imported goods pose to the national economy became clear in the mid-1970s when the country's foreign trade imbalance reached a critical point. For this reason the government announced it would clamp down on ''advertising which stimulates nonessential consumption.''[80] This apparently was the reasoning also behind a move early in 1975 to prohibit the surge of luxury-goods advertising that always occurs before major holidays such as Christmas.[81]

The same desperate effort to cut the outflow of hard currency from Peru has led to construction of one of the world's first mills for producing newsprint from sugar cane pulp (bagasse). Built by the state, the plant was to begin production in 1977 moving toward a peak output of 110,000 tons. This would satisfy the 1975 consumption level of 72,000 tons, eliminate a drain of nearly $30 million and even make possible an export income of $20 million. The soaring cost of newsprint had tripled Peru's import expense for this item in three years.[82]

As for economic measures to penalize the media, these of course have diminished since the expropriations of broadcast stations and Lima daily newspapers. While the newspapers were in private hands, they were being bled into insolvency through controls. Newsprint was allocated and withheld according to which company needed to be rewarded or punished; government advertising was manipulated the same way, and with the increasing government takeovers of industry, this became substantial. Price controls for newspaper sales and on advertising were leveled on all media, but they served to make economic survival uncertain for nongovernmental ones.

Private ownership of newspapers also was undermined by labor problems inspired by the government. *El Comercio* had nearly 20 such work stoppages in two years, and salaries amounting to triple the company's capital were ordered.[83]

Although the regime has been less systematic in using economic devices against the non-daily press, they can be even more hazardous there because of the slim resources that most magazines have. Newsprint control is a constant worry for their directors.

Prohibited Content

The Peruvian military regime has only rarely gone to the extreme of directly censoring media material—that is, regularly inspecting the material before publication. But is has enacted a number of rules prohibiting certain types of content, and these require self-censorship by journalists to stay out of jail.

A censorship commission does stand ready to strike out material when it is deemed necessary. One such episode occurred during economic rioting in July 1976, when the interior minister warned editors against publishing stories that might "undermine national unity" or "promote subversion." Then the censors went to work on the independent magazines. They seized an issue of *Unidad*, a Communist Party organ; sliced out half a page from copies of *Equis;* and delayed the distribution of *Oiga*.[84] Another weekly, *El Tiempo*, suspended publication as a protest against the censorship of its competitors. The interior minister, making what he considered an important distinction, denied any repression because, he said, the publications were not inspected before being printed but only afterward.[85]

The Peruvian upon whom censorship has fallen most heavily is Mario Vargas Llosa, the country's renowned novelist. He has been in disfavor with the armed forces since, at age 25, he published a novel about his years at a military school. It was considered so damaging that 1,000 copies of it were burned at the school, and high officers claimed the author was an anti-Peruvian communist.

So when another novel by Vargas Llosa about the military was made into a movie 15 years later, the stage was set for trouble. The story was a ribald satire about a young officer whose job was to procure prostitutes for soldiers. Various review boards watched the film, then deferred to higher authorities for a decision. Finally President Morales and his cabinet viewed it and decided to ban it in Peru. Even worse, the government put diplomatic pressure on Panama and Spain to obtain its prohibition there, and the international film distributor gave up trying to market it in fear of reprisals in other countries.[86]

Prohibited content has ranged widely from criticism of laws to underwear and Santa Claus.

Although general press laws are quite strict enough to provide grounds for punishing any criticism of government actions, specific regulations have been decreed in some cases. These singled out the Law of Freedom of the Press and the agrarian reform decree as particularly dangerous for anyone to criticize publicly.[87]

After expropriation was completed in 1974, the media apparently could be controlled internally. Some evidence of this was the fact that during the violent police strike in several cities early in 1975, not a word about it appeared in television, radio or the "parametered" press.[88]

Moral censorship has been wide-ranging but erratic. Acting under the Press Law of 1974 which provided for the mass expropriation of Lima dailies, the general who headed the education ministry announced he was taking steps against "erotic and pornographic literature," although anyone searching Lima's streets would have difficulty finding anything salacious. Only a few months later, the porn fighters specifically ruled out advertisements showing men or women in underwear, requiring that sales appeals for such garments "respect morals and good custom."[89]

Even Santa Claus fell victim to the cleanup campaign. Like the Cuban government, Peru's education ministry decided that the jolly old elf, who had been accepted by modernizing Peruvians along with other North American symbols, was a "foreign influence." The ban applied only to advertisements, and it reaped so much ridicule that in 1976 the government blithely denied that such a prohibition had ever existed.[90]

Although the Peruvian regime has not shown as much paranoic fear of foreign journalism as have the rulers of Chile and Brazil, it has used its authority to suppress imports of media material which it feels are a waste of foreign currency and a bad influence on domestic customs. Within two months in late 1975 and early 1976, the supposedly more moderate government which overthrew President Velasco showed that it still was intensely nationalistic. First it banned the Peruvian editions of 23 foreign magazines such as comic books, *fotonovelas* (soap operas in still pictures), and luxury-oriented fashion magazines. The main justification was saving on hard currency—an urgent need at the time. Television felt the brunt of the restrictions, when a group of filmed serials ranging from "Kung Fu" to "Bugs Bunny" were prohibited from entering the country.[91]

Controls on Foreign Reporters

Peru's size and economic importance in world affairs ranks slightly above mid-range among Latin American countries, and this accords with its coverage by reporters from the Western democracies. However, its recent prominence as an ideological testing ground has led it to become a journalistic magnet for the Third World. This is reflected in the sources of its newspapers' foreign news, which vary from the North American services to the Cuban Prensa Latina agency; it provides one of the few outlets in the hemisphere for the PL copy. As the only South American founder of the Third World news exchange led by Yugoslavia, Peru naturally takes a jaundiced view of agencies rising out of capitalist societies.

In spite of all this, business goes on as usual for the bureaus of major Western news agencies and for the newspaper correspondents who wander through Lima every few months. Work usually is not a matter of grim whispers, and the foreign correspondents have adopted a gameness not unlike that of the independent non-daily press.

But all of them have enough troubles to keep them on guard. The Reuters agency of Britain and its regional partner, LATIN, have suffered the most. The LATIN operation was shut down in 1974 after the government accused it of "a persistent and insidious campaign" against the Peruvian regime abroad, apparently referring to a routine news story filed by the Chilean bureau of the agency.[92] The next year, just after the Peruvian police riots, Reuters was shut down and its two British reporters detained.[93] Both operations were later allowed to resume in Lima.

Two Associated Press reporters have been expelled from the country, both of them shortly before they were expecting reassignment and thus were being more bold than usual. One of these was the bureau chief, Edith M. Lederer, a veteran of coverage in Vietnam and Israel. Her ouster was caused by a brief story showing the ineptness of a Peruvian display of military aviation during Air Force Week. As crowds watched, she reported, 30 fighter-bombers made more than 60 runs to attack target boats in the Pacific Ocean; none of the boats was sunk. The story quoted a general's prior boast: "It will be an exhibition of the operating capacity of the Peruvian air force."[94]

Foreign reporters have become accustomed to brief detentions to harass them in their work. This occurred when they were covering the expropriation riots in 1974 and the police strike in 1975. An article in the *Financial Times* of London about Peru's economy got the reporter, a longtime Lime resident, into trouble with the police.

The international press corps also has to contend with false reports by government spokesmen and with informal pressures—usually telephone calls—seeking delays in sensitive news stories. Most foreign reporters steer a middle course between defiance and servility.

Information Control

Peru has achieved the structural dream of many political image engineers—a government public information agency which screens all messages going outward from the government, makes sure that "reality" as seen by the regime is circulated abroad, and controls the major media of the home country, directly or indirectly.

Heading the state's communication apparatus is a cabinet-level agency called the National System of Information (SINADI). It has departments for operating the broadcasting system, placing government advertising, running official news agencies and screening official information (through an office called OCI).

The news agencies, called ESI-Peru at home and ESI-Andina abroad, came into existence only in 1976, on the crest of a wave of such government agencies encouraged by UNESCO. The general who headed them declared that they would "act competitively" with foreign news agencies, putting to rest the fear that they would become a TASS-like monopoly on news going abroad. The foreign agencies also were allowed to continue selling their services to Peruvian media.

But for coverage of their own government, Peruvian editors had to take what the official agencies gave them. For example, when the president would go on a tour of the country, only photographers from the newspapers would accompany him. The news would be sent back by OCI.

One of OCI's main jobs is to maintain control of the Lima dailies through their directors, holding weekly meetings at which the expected editorial policy is explained. During the excitement following the expropriations, some editors made a point of ignoring the meetings. But resistance faded later, and editors merely kept as much distinctiveness in their papers as possible while toeing the government line in broad terms.

The SINADI staffs have made valiant efforts to infuse a revolutionary spirit into the Peruvian people. One cannot look at television or billboards without getting some enthusiastic message. Television spots have been made by show business personalities exhorting support for the various campaigns, always ending with the slogan "Do it for Peru!" The official newspaper *La Crónica* tried to take its message to the "other" Peru—the Indian masses—with an edition printed in Quechua, the tongue of half the population, which has been adopted along with Spanish as the official language. The project was quietly dropped after a few months when it was found that Indians who could speak Spanish preferred to read it and those who spoke only Quechua usually couldn't read anything.

Despite all this vast structure to change people's minds, the military government still has achieved little voluntary following outside its own ranks.[95] It could be argued that its success in carrying out most of its reforms without overt opposition can be credited to the machinery of persuasion. Others would counter that this is simply a result of passivity by the public.

CHAPTER 7

Three Democracies

ATTEMPTS TO CATEGORIZE countries in Latin America as to types of political systems often come to grief over semantics. The concepts of democracy and freedom become tangled with each other. The fact that some majorities can oppress minorities is overlooked sometimes, and at others the truth that dictators can vouchsafe a wide range of liberties.

Most projects to draw up categories in the 1960s and 1970s have agreed that three Latin American countries—Costa Rica, Colombia and Venezuela—can be considered both free *and* democratic, particularly the latter. This, of course, is a dangerous generalization, particularly in regard to government relations with the mass media. Recent experience in all three countries has shown that even the most sincere democrats and libertarians, once in power, find it difficult to resist the urge to discipline frequently unruly editors and reporters.

On the whole, though, the three countries offer one of the world's most interesting laboratories in which to watch the acid of social reform interact with the stone of individualism. The fact that all three have survived while surrounded by a horde of dictatorships calls for a close look at the specific chemicals which have gone into the solution.

THE CRUCIBLE OF HISTORY

Although the three countries' political paths have been remarkably parallel since the late 1950s, they diverged widely before that. The capital of one, Bogotá in Colombia, was one of Spain's richest and most powerful colonial centers while the other two were outposts. This resulted in a relatively glittering intellectual life for Bogotá but no more freedom of public expression than in other Spanish lands. Caracas, Venezuela, lived in Bogotá's shadow in those early centuries but eventually surpassed it in revolutionary fervor.

Costa Rica, having little the Spanish conquerors could exploit quickly, escaped the chasms between wealth and poverty, culture and ignorance that divided most of their neighboring peoples. While this good luck moderated the colonial control, the smallness of the community meant less demand for mass journalism, and handwritten pamphlets served adequately until the first printing press was set up in 1830.[1]

In the post-independence period, all three countries developed press systems that were largely responsive to party politics, although they achieved democracy at different speeds. Colombia has maintained freely elected governments since its break with Spain in 1810, with rare exceptions. This continuity arose from a free play of party competition, involving a public clash of opinions through newspapers identified with one party or another. Brief periods of press restriction did occur, but these were limited by the electoral rivalry.

Costa Rica achieved a similar degree of democracy and civil liberty but only toward the end of the 19th Century after a succession of dictatorships. Except for brief interruptions in 1917–19 and 1948–49, it has had a steady growth of constitutional politics and journalism since 1889.

Until 1958, Venezuela always presented the spectacle of a country whose educated elites supported the principle of democracy but continually brought on themselves dictatorships, including the rule of one tyrant for 27 years. Somehow news media existed, but often for only short periods; a few learned the art of surviving through political discretion.

Amid the painful shifts toward modernity following World War II, all three countries went through a political purgatory. Costa Rica's was brief. When the party in power tried to maintain itself illegally in office by annulling an election, liberal leader José (Pepe) Figueres organized a rebellion which restored the normal succession and installed a moderately reformist constitution. The press, once again with full freedom, moved away from blind partisanship and became somewhat consumer-oriented.

While Colombia endured only four years of illegitimate dictatorship under Gen. Gustavo Rojas Pinilla (1953–57), its transition to modernity was the most bloody. From 1948 to 1957, it was in the grip of civil war called *La Violencia,* fought between the two main political parties, the Liberals and the Conservatives; estimates of those killed range up to 200,000. News media were more partisan than ever, too often fanning the flames of violence. In turn, they suffered grievously, first under an elected president-turned-autocrat, then under Gen. Rojas Pinilla. In the first period, the Conservative president took office while still smarting from the burning of his newspaper plant. Soon his followers were terrorizing the country, even burning out the leading Liberal newspapers, *El Tiempo* and *El Espectador,* along with the home of a former president. The newspapers resumed publication shortly on borrowed presses.[2]

Rojas Pinilla seized the presidency at the insistence of reform-minded centrists and for a while brought about press freedom. Within two years he had become more tyrranical than his predecessor, and he used a broad battery of press controls—censorship, closures, newsprint restrictions, legal harassment, forced publication of announcements. Some of the strictures were part of Rojas' efforts to defuse the civil war, but others were political retaliation.

The Colombian turmoil attracted global attention when Rojas gave vent to his anger by closing down *El Tiempo* in 1955 (*El Espectador* was closed later). The closing of *El Tiempo* came about when it sent a message to an Ecuadorean newspaper contradicting something Rojas had said. The dictator ordered the *El Tiempo* editors to print a retraction on their front page for 30 days, and they refused.[3] Both *El Tiempo* and *El Espectador* soon were on the streets again under false names, *El Intermedio* and *El Independiente*.[4]

After the Liberals and Conservatives called a truce and threw out Rojas, they made a two-decade pact by which they would divide up the public offices, holding elections only as party primaries to decide who within each party would get the appointments; the presidency was to be alternated. At worst, it was a two-party dictatorship, at best it was an unchangeable coalition. Those newspapers which were allied with the Liberals and Conservatives—and these included most of those of any importance—supported the arrangements because their parties did. But they did so by their owners' choice, not by force.

Venezuela's postwar ordeal, unlike those of Colombia and Costa Rica, was not a matter of two-party strife. It was eight years in which all idealistic politicians chafed under one of the last of Latin America's comic-opera, posturing despots, Marcos Pérez Jiménez. He controlled the media through the full panoply of devices, and journalists retaliated with innuendo in the major publications and even by circulating clandestine organs. They went so far as to conduct a national press strike and to refuse to print the government's denial that an obvious uprising had taken place in an interior city.

After Pérez Jiménez' overthrow in 1958, an unbroken succession of free elections started. Two liberal parties emerged as the leading ones, although they did not compromise their rivalry as in Colombia.

The first president after the dictatorship, Rómulo Betancourt, was a sincere democrat, but he faced a Cuban-backed communist attempt to subvert the government. So among his largely successful efforts to turn back their challenge was to suspend communist publications, censor broadcast news, wrest control of the national journalists' association from the communists, and jail some editors. While Betancourt's controls were nearly as sweeping as Pérez Jiménez' had been, they were focused entirely on removing the organized communist threat. Later presidents continued this policy, but there was little need to enforce it after Betancourt's term expired in 1963.[5]

Although democracy is by no means perfect and civil liberties not pure in Costa Rica, Colombia and Venezuela today, they have survived much longer than is common in the area, and they have gone through severe tests. Thus we can examine their commonalities and the ways in which they differ.

THE FORUM FOR DEBATE

Of the two basic media functions of informing and of providing a forum for debate, most Latin Americans traditionally have valued the latter more highly. They have seen it as natural that "the winds of doctrine" should be "let loose to play upon the earth," in Milton's words.

In varying degrees, the three democratic countries have taken advantage of their liberties to stir up these winds of doctrine, and in doing so they have kept alive political competition.

Costa Rica

Nowhere is this truer than in Costa Rica. Not only do the owners of the media take part in the debate but so do politicians up to the president, as well as intellectual leaders and, to a surprising extent, ordinary citizens. The arguments usually rise above the level of petty partisanship, as most citizens have little party loyalty and would scorn a blatant mouthpiece. The battles can be savage, but they stop short of stimulating physical violence and probably even provide a substitute for it.

Tradition has a bearing, because, in the intimacy of Costa Rica's 19th Century small cities, debating clubs (*tertulias*) and wall proclamations flourished. Even in modern times, arguments tend to be settled in family style. When José (Pepe) Figueres, then president, visited the university campus and was insulted by a student, Figueres silenced him with a fatherly slap in the face. The youth was not jailed for sedition, and the president was not charged with assault.

Since Costa Rica does not have an organ for every political faction, persons whose views differ from the editors' must find expression outside the editorialists' and columnists' spaces. Editors are notably eager to quote divergent views in news stories or to provide space for readers' letters. One newspaper director, Guido Fernández of *La Nación,* called the receptiveness to such opinions ''our most conscious policy.''

Other ways of trafficking in opinions are formal interview stories, reprints of speeches and purchases of space or air time.

The stilted approach of the interviews, phrased in wordy questions and answers, is a concession to the rudimentary state of political writing. But they have reader appeal and are, according to one editor, ''a cheap way to get news.''[6] The president's major reports to congress, reprinted in *La Nación,* run four to six tabloid pages.

It is in the purchase of media services that Costa Rica's media debate comes to its fullest flower. The government subsidizes political campaigns, and this proves a bonanza for media both in reader interest and in advertising revenues, keeping some small media from financial collapse. Candidates prefer full-blown discussions of issues rather than the vague images favored by North American strategists.

Even between elections, the warfare continues through bought space or time as well as the other channels of public participation. A classic illustration in the 1970s was the unending controversy over the welcome shown by Costa Rican politicians to Robert Vesco, multimillionaire American financier who was a fugitive from Watergate justice in his own country. Soon every Costa Rican above the age of six had an ardent opinion pro or con, and disputants never tired of trying to change opponents' opinions via the mass media.

News stories about the U. S. case against Vesco preceded his arrival from the Bahamas in 1973. The journalists knew he was avoiding a return home because he was charged jointly with John Mitchell and Maurice Stans in connection with a Nixon campaign donation; a civil suit against him also claimed that he had looted $224 million of assets from mutual funds. Thus the news media had prepared many Costa Ricans to look on Vesco as a financial pirate bringing his gains to a safe haven, and they resented this slur on their country. Others believed his story that he was the victim of a frameup and was only looking for a place to raise his children.

Two other aspects of the affair brought the dispute to white heat. One was the complicity of Figueres, a leader in the majority Liberation Party, who did not conceal that he became a partner in enterprises in which Vesco invested; it was reported also that Vesco had received minor favoritism in enforcement of immigration and customs regulations. Also stirring the furor was the fact that one man—Vesco—was "buying" Costa Rica, scooping up land, businesses and even a school, with tens of millions of dollars. He was believed to have brought with him $60 million, which, as editor Fernández pointed out, was enough to run the national government for three months.[7] Many of his new neighbors thought a rich investor who showed Vesco's obvious fondness for the country was just what Costa Rica needed.

All the standard Costa Rican devices of public debate were brought to bear—editorials, news stories revealing embarrassing facts or just quoting someone, interviews, and reports of speeches and resolutions. But Vesco himself moved the tournament onto relatively new ground—purchased television time. Only a week after his arrival, he bought 60 minutes of prime time for $3,600 on all four of the channels that blanketed the country. He used it to broadly attack his opponents in Costa Rica and later said he would like to "punch in the nose" those who "unfairly" criticized him. This brought a storm of reaction from editors, legislators and reporters, each of whom felt himself to be the potential target of Vesco's fist. But it did not prevent the national congress, controlled by President Figueres' party, from passing a law protecting Vesco from extradition. Nor did it deter a group of prominent Costa Ricans from joining Vesco in a plan to build an empire of newspapers and television and radio stations—two of each, in fact.

Since Vesco's most persistent critic had been Fernández of *La Nación,* he took up the gauntlet and lamented the ridicule Vesco had brought on Costa Rica, demanded that the government refund $8 million in bonds Vesco had bought, and challenged the foreigner to face the nation in an interrogation by journalists.[8] Rodrigo Madrigal Nieto, director of the rival daily *La República,* forsook his editorial columns to go on the same channel Vesco had used and voiced a rebuttal.

Two months later Figueres followed up the Vesco television address with one of his own attempting to explain why his New York bank account had swollen by $325,000 since Vesco moved to Costa Rica. The fact had been unearthed by the *Wall Street Journal* but had been widely reported in Costa Rica.

Another dimension was added to the debate by the willingness of the principals to talk with U. S. reporters who went to Costa Rica to see what all the fuss was about. They returned with depth stories for networks and major publications, and these in turn were quoted in Costa Rica. Not content to speak only for himself, Figueres admitted, after newspapers had quoted a charge by a congressman, that he had helped Vesco write his television speech.[9]

The Vesco controversy continued for years, but it largely returned to the more sedate platform of editorial pages. This was particularly true after the Figueres-Vesco faction founded their own newspaper, *Excélsior,* encouraged by the Mexico City paper of the same name. However, Vesco reappeared on television in late 1974, speaking from his luxurious home and attempting to counteract a petition by 5,000 citizens asking his expulsion from the country.

Although Costa Rica has always had several vigorous daily newspapers in its capital, a movement toward commercialism had drained the acid from their editorial pages by the early 1970s. *La Nación,* owned by large agricultural interests, tried to keep up the fight through constructive criticism written from a conservative viewpoint and often agreeing with the Unification Party, which has controlled the presidency at times but never the congress. Figueres and other Liberation Party leaders had to maintain their end of the debate, as they had no editor committed to their moderate-leftist position. Furthermore, the far left, with a small representation among students and intellectuals, had no effective organ.

Then *Excélsior* was founded to speak for the Figueres sector, and two weeklies, *Pueblo* and *Libertad,* spoke up for the far left. All soon won respect for their professional quality, and *Excélsior* moved into the second-ranking circulation place. (*Excélsior* was closed in 1978.) Fernández of *La Nación* welcomed the opposition, as he acquired clear journalistic targets for the daily debates. However, he continued to print the opinions of leftists. He defended the practice before his doubting board of directors. "These people are working within the system," he pointed out. "If we don't give them a chance they will become *guerrilleros.*"[10]

Experience in the three democracies indicates that the influence of editors in setting the tone and scope of public debate interacts with the influence of politicians and especially the party structure. The optimum condition would seem to be two parties at the forefront, representing distinct viewpoints and confident that they have a chance to win elections by persuading the voters; smaller parties at the radical fringes should have at least a chance to eventually replace one of the leading parties. This describes the party situation in Costa Rica, and it coexists with the most balanced and vigorous public debate.

Venezuela

The two leading parties in Venezuela are fairly equal in strength, but both are mildly liberal and differ mostly in the personalities of their leaders. In fact, the two main parties formed a coalition until the mid-1960s. Also, the leftist fringe parties are much more alienated from the national mainstream than those in Costa Rica.

Although political opinion can be found in the Venezuelan media, it usually is in the form of personal columns or is quoted from thought leaders outside the media staffs, because the major newspapers there present the rare spectacle of not even running editorials. Since they are perfectly free to editorialize, the oddity of the practice is underscored by the fact that even in oppressive dictatorships like Paraguay the editors do their best at giving their newspapers' opinions daily.

Various reasons are given for Venezuela's no-editorial custom.

One diplomatic observer predicted that if the papers were partisan, "it would be precarious financially for them." He referred to the probability that their large advertising linages would be reduced by the ruffling of some political feathers.

The director of one leading daily, Luis Nuñez of *El Universal,* recalled that the press had to stop its editorials under dictatorships and never got back into the habit after democracy was established. Although editors publish their opinions on extraordinary occasions, Nuñez said, "We think if we editorialize every day we would lose the power of the editorial." Besides, Nuñez said, he doesn't like to turn over the task to anyone, and he is too busy to write daily editorials. "I write one when it is in the interest of the public to give my point of view," he concluded.[11]

The largest daily, *El Nacional,* is prevented by its own charter from endorsing presidential or congressional candidates. Besides, said its president, Pedro Penzini, the paper runs two pages every day for opinions other than those of the editor.[12]

Nelson Luis Martínez of *Ultimas Noticias,* another daily, offered the explanation that "readers can make up their own minds without our help." Aware that this view is not shared by editors in most free countries, he added that the press in other countries use their papers for "their own political purposes."[13]

Despite the lack of editorials, the Venezuelan press does present a wide variety of opinion channels. The one that comes the closest to substituting for the editorial is a peculiarly Venezuelan device called the *mancheta,* a one-sentence epigram set in headline type and boxed, running on the editorial page. It is usually a pun and has become a competitive art form. When maddening delays held back the start of construction on the Caracas subway (Metro, which also means meter), *El Nacional* ran a *mancheta* reading, "Al paso que va, será un centímetro" (At the rate it's going, it will be a centimeter).[14]

Opinion columns throng the editorial pages, coming from politicians, political publicists or journalists. As bylines some of them use fictitious names—not clever nicknames as in some countries, but ordinary pseudonyms. Editorial cartoons and slanted headlines and news stories can carry the editor's opinions. Space purchases (*remitidas*) also are increasing.

In addition to the standard news story in which the reporter draws out the opinions of a public figure, there is the custom of running roundups of a variety of spokesmen. This is a favorite way to respond to events outside Venezuela, particularly in the United States.[15]

Colombia

The "two-party dictatorship" in Colombia—the equal division of offices between Liberals and Conservatives—was carefully dismantled in the 1970s according to the original plan. But during its existence many obstacles were put in the way of completely free public debate. The greatest of these was voluntary self-censorship. Next came a siege mentality on the part of the govern-

mental leaders who shuddered at the nine years of *La Violencia* and still faced
armed subversion that persisted decades after the supposed end to the civil war.

The self-censorship grows from the fact that the major newspapers in
Colombia have always been admittedly party organs, even in modern times
when such labels are unfashionable. (In fact, the two Bogotá dailies which
dominate the national press scene, *El Tiempo* and *El Espectador,* both are Liberal Party adherents.) Because leaders of these newspapers were instrumental in
founding the National Front—the coalition of Liberals and Conservatives—in
1957, they considered themselves obligated to support the government. One of
the more severe commentaries on the situation maintains:

> The national press in Colombia needs no restraint—it is almost entirely in the
> hands of leading figures in the Liberal and Conservative Parties and managerial
> control makes the censor virtually redundant. Investigation and campaigning in the
> press are non-existent, and with the exception of the Communist Party's *Voz Pro-
> letaria,* the far left-wing magazine *Alternativa* and the tabloid *El Bogotano* there is
> no critical reporting or muckraking.[16]

Although the tendency noted exists, the above exaggerates it. The press
often publishes material embarrassing to the government, one diplomat points
out, but it does so "with the attitude of a loyal opposition." An editor never
mentions that some government official represents a certain political party. Instead, if the editor is upset over that official's actions, he will seek a whipping
boy—the leaders of the erring official's party.

As in China, readers of Colombian editorials learn to read between the
lines. This is because the careers of politicians in Colombia are, perhaps more
than anywhere in Latin America, interwoven with journalistic careers. Astute
readers know that a certain newspaper's saying something is really a polite
disguise for some official's saying it.

The newspapers' willingness to indulge the National Front government
could go so far as to counteract the interests of the press. Sometimes when temporary censorship is enacted, they raise no protest.[17]

The same mildness is displayed toward affairs of the Roman Catholic
Church, which maintains a concordat or treaty which divides powers between it
and the government. Editors rarely criticize the church itself, although they find
fault with some provisions of the concordat. Protestant missionaries, often a
target for physical attacks during *La Violencia,* also are treated lightly except
for the fundamentalist Summer Institute of Linguistics, which gets a "bad
press."

Unlike the editors in Venezuela, those in Colombia do not attempt to
defend their timidity on any grounds other than political necessity, and they see
the fading of the National Front as a new lease on life for them.

"During the National Front," said Enrique Santos, one of the owners of
El Tiempo, "newspapers went all the way from extreme activism to being cozy
with the government. Since the front ended, newspapers have tried desperately
to regain their credibility with the people. *El Tiempo* was losing circulation
because of it, but *El Espectador* changed earlier and was getting circulation."[18]

Governmental and party leaders are not changing so rapidly in favor of
free discussion of ideas. One analyst said the government is "highly intolerant

of any criticism or any research into the uglier realities that local papers do not print."[19] A third-party leader, Eugenia de Montejo, has run into frequent difficulties for the newspapers she publishes because she speaks for radical causes. The government has a "phobia about subversion," she said. "If someone publishes the truth in a newspaper or on television, that's subversion. If the workers strike, that's subversion, If the students don't like the way their university is run, it's subversion."[20]

Joint Careers

Involvement of journalists in political careers and politicians in journalistic careers can increase or decrease the level of public debate depending on the attitudes of the persons following these joint careers in the three democracies.

Colombia, as noted above, is well-acquainted with the interchange of careers. Many of its presidents have been editors, most notably Eduardo Santos, the founder of El Tiempo, who mingled journalism, politics, scholarship and even United Nations work. His brother, the elder Enrique Santos, also was a senator and leader of the Liberal Party. At one time in the mid-1970s, five cabinet ministers were journalists. Mrs. Montejo, who has owned various newspapers and an advertising agency, is the political heiress of her late father, former dictator Gustavo Rojas Pinilla, succeeding him as the leader of the party he founded.

Joint careers of politics and journalism in Colombia have usually resulted in more hauteur for the journalist rather than more openness for the politician. Costa Rica's experience has tended somewhat in the opposite direction. José Figueres has served as president twice and has helped in the founding of two daily newspapers 25 years apart; his ally and successor, Daniel Oduber, also invested in media. But in all such Costa Rican cases the entry of politicians into journalism has stimulated debate rather than diminished it.

Media in Elections

On one subject, the governments of the three countries do agree in encouraging open debate; that is elections. Costa Rica and Venezuela have long done so, and Colombia moved away in 1974 from what had been essentially intraparty decisions. All give some type of assistance to candidates. Costa Rica makes grants to be spent at the candidates' choice in various media, and Venezuela donates free time on the government-owned television and radio frequencies.

While Costa Rica and Colombia exploit their elections as an opportunity for thrashing out the issues, Venezuela has begun edging toward the image engineering which has afflicted U. S. elections. In its 1973 presidential campaign, both major candidates hired North American campaign specialists. Carlos Andrés Pérez, who went on to win, bought the services of three separate promotion firms who had handled campaigns for Barry Goldwater, Hubert Humphrey and Edmund Muskie. His opponent was advised by a former campaigner for the Kennedys. The fever continued unabated in the 1978 election, when four separate consulting firms from the United States took part in the campaign.

THE POWER OF REPORTING

Since reporting is much less developed as an art than is argument in the democracies, it is confined largely to providing a neutral conduit for the thoughts of news-makers. Since all three are relatively open societies and have robustly competitive media jostling for news breaks, the concept of mirroring public events rather then probing into them provides a large mass of usable if not remarkable news.

Reporters can be resolute about their right to the superficial news. When the mayor of a provincial Colombian city, Barranquilla, decided to bar reporters from the swearing-in of a new city treasurer—posting policemen outside to enforce his order—the irate newspaper and radio reporters retaliated by unanimously deciding not to use the mayor's name in any stories. For good measure, they included the new treasurer in the boycott.[21]

Because the two-party system usually brings to light the more notorious scandals, news media coverage of opposition politicians' statements can provide some surveillance over governments. This occurred in 1977 when charges were raised that the Colombian president's two sons were using their official connections for private gain; wide publicity resulted, and formal investigations got under way.

But the Colombian press rose to new heights of enterprise reporting when the country's drug traffic to the United States reached the point of "deterioration of national prestige," as the daily *El Colombiano* of Medellín called it. Various news media launched a campaign of both reporting and editorializing to point out the gravity of the situation, and *El Tiempo* even sent a reporter to Miami for a series on what happens to Colombian drug smugglers arrested in the United States. Although the coverage was not contrary to official policy, it was credited with putting so much heat on the government that for the first time it organized a serious effort to stop the shipments.

"The Colombian press has had much the same results in the drug area as the U. S. press has had with Watergate," a narcotics agent in Bogotá said. "It has created a public awareness of the problem and contributed to the continued government campaign."[22]

Editors on the more prominent media say they want to build up their investigative and social reporting, and some are making attempts in that direction. Television Channel 2 in Caracas, one of the more aggressive media in the area, did a documentary on how people hunt primitive Indians; the hunters were actually shown shooting the Indians.

"We are not advanced enough to do investigative reporting," Peter Bottome, Channel 2's director, said. "But we do have social reporting about problems like the Indian hunting."[23]

Costa Rica, with the stimulation provided by news media in the 1970s, also went in deeper for enterprise reporting. The largest daily there, *La Nación*, has been allotting reporters all the time they need to gather complex stories, but director Guido Fernández has found the reporters reluctant to do this. "It's very difficult to get reporters to stick with a story," he said. "They want to get it printed immediately."[24]

THE NEW VOLCANO

The three democracies, particularly the larger two, have a welter of laws and regulations restricting the media, but in comparison with the other Latin American countries' yokes they are an easy burden. These restrictions will be detailed later, but just proportion demands that we look first at a movement of the 1970s that promises to make the most basic change in press-government relations since the birth of liberal democracy two centuries ago.

Until the 1950s, all three countries adhered to the concept that the best way for the media to do their job was for the state to interfere as little as possible. Any violation of this principle was usually intended to *stop* the press from doing something, not to force it to fulfill some new role.

But leftist political theorists, ranging from Christian Democrats to communists, have begun putting pressures on the state to protect the little man from holders of concentrated economic power, and these include media owners. The theorists argue that the state must ensure that reporters be educated, the content of the media be educationally constructive and the native culture be preserved against domination of foreign (particularly North American) ideas. How to accomplish these miracles remains uncertain, but all the proposals have one thing in common—the private media owners would lose some power to the state. Much trust is put in the power of law, little in voluntary effort.

Some of the proposals have been enacted, and the backers of the others seem ready to persist indefinitely. Among the most favored ideas are government ownership of media or limits on private ownership; the requirement of professional education and licensing; nationalistic measures such as controls on foreign correspondents, limits on foreign investments and efforts to protect the national language from corruption; laws requiring public access to the media; and national or Third World news agencies.

State Ownership

It is in state ownership of broadcast media that the earliest and most concrete reformist actions were taken in Colombia and Venezuela. Colombia's television system, at least in its surface appearance, appears to be the answer to the reformers' dreams. It has produced a steady flow of admiring reports from foreign visitors.

Inravisión—From its start in 1954 in the National Library basement, Colombian television has been the monopoly of a "decentralized" agency indirectly controlled by the government. It is called the National Institute of Radio and Television (Inravisión for short) and is intended to be free from commercial and political domination, existing largely for the cultural uplift of the Colombian people. In reality, it falls far short of that.

In its early years Colombian television experienced something like the United States' so-called "golden age" of originality, with almost half the air time going to broadcast plays, educational fare, ballet, music and children's programs. But by the end of the 1960s, high operating costs and the public's demand for more exciting material had led to an erosion of locally produced cultural material and a drastic increase in North American serials like "World of Disney" and "Bonanza."[25]

Similar in concept to some Western European systems, Inravisión still is unique. Besides maintaining a purely educational service (Channel 11), it has two commercial signals—Channel 7, which reaches nearly the entire country, and Channel 9, going to the main population centers. Inravisión adopted the old Latin American commercial radio practice of selling blocks of time to independent producers and adapted it to a government system. But rather than putting on the air any producer (''packager'') who wanted to buy time, it keeps the supply short of the demand. It sets a price on each half-hour and calls for bids—not with money but with program ideas. The bidder has to describe all his programming thoroughly, pay a $400 application fee and put on deposit enough money to pay for four months of production.

Each half-hour is classified as to allowable content, although the rules are vague enough to allow much latitude. On a national channel, about 90 minutes are reserved for news and the same for children's programs. ''Family'' programs are slotted for 5:30 to 9:30 p.m., and ''adult'' ones (some violence allowed) after that. Six hours a day are reserved for classroom educational programs getting a free ride on the commercial channel.

About 10 packagers have emerged, all frankly committed to making money but also aware of Inravisión's yearning for more culture and more localism. They spend their time producing advertisements for their rented time, importing cheap serials and movies (mostly from the United States) and, in some cases, producing their own programs. The latter tends toward the types of local productions most common in other Latin American countries—live variety programs hosted by a celebrity, game shows, and news and discussion half-hours. One Colombian soap opera has been developed.

Other than the educational programs, the material on the commercial channels falls into these categories: soap operas, 28 per cent; children's programs, 20 per cent; filmed action and mystery series, 17 per cent; opinion, 10 per cent; contests and game shows, 7 per cent; news, 7 per cent; and musical and humorous shows, 6 per cent each.[26]

Despite the flood of trivial programs, Inravisión's executives claim progress in approaching the ideal stated in the 1967 resolution which set up the time-renting system: ''The primordial goal of the public television service is to foment culture; spread and exalt national values; preserve morality, esthetics and the universal dictates of decorum and good taste; and stimulate artistic activities.''[27]

These lofty challenges are accepted if not all fulfilled by Inravisión's energetic director, Orlando Rovira, who has a doctorate in education.

''We are trying to stimulate cultural programming by lowering the price on the air time for it,'' Rovira told an interviewer. ''By cultural we mean history, art, theater, and music.''[28]

By mid-1976 such programming had reached 12 hours a week between the two commercial channels, and Rovira hoped to raise it to a fourth of the total air time. Inravisión also is slowly lowering the reliance on imported material, having reduced it to 34 per cent. One way to inhibit imports is to charge more for their air time.

The educational channel, reserved for adult training not leading to a degree, has pitifully low ratings compared with the commercial channels. It concentrates on subjects such as literacy and health and is aimed at workers and peasants. The fact that fewer than half the lower-class citizens have television in their homes has actually worked to the advantage of this effort. Research has shown that televised education works best in a group situation with a "live" leader, so the government has placed TV sets in communal centers all over the country, where volunteer teachers guide the students in using the program material.

The education ministry feeds the educational material to Inravisión and has become so adept that it has to import only about 20 per cent of the film. The fact that the Organization of American States has placed a regional pilot center for educational television production in Bogotá is recognition of the Colombian leadership in this field. It also provides a continued stimulus to the local efforts.[29]

Technically, Inravisión is well advanced in transmission of black and white signals. The bulk of the population lives in the shadows of mountains that block out the signal from Bogotá, so Inravisión has installed 17 repeater stations to bring service to 84 per cent of the people.[30]

In the late 1970s, Colombia was on the verge of a breakthrough that would make these repeaters unnecessary. This would be the launching of a communication satellite under contract with the United States, thus making Colombia the first country in the Third World with its own. Coverage was to extend from the nation's San Andrés Islands in the Caribbean to its Amazon jungles.

The government was planning to spread the $120 million cost over four years of its telecommunication company's budget. Planned later were two other satellites, one to tie it to the other Andean countries and the other to handle global linkages. Having built its own ground receiving station in 1970, Colombia would be free from dependence on the Intelsat system with its own satellites.[31]

Like most South American countries, Colombia and Venezuela long resisted the tide of color television. They wanted to prevent a sudden drain of hard currency that would occur if North American and Japanese manufacturers should exploit such a new market for color sets; besides, they believed the sets were a luxury their poorer citizens could ill afford. So both banned color transmission, even on closed-circuit systems.[32] This did not deter the upper classes in both countries from buying tens of thousands of color sets in anticipation of the day when lawmakers would reverse the law. Support for such a move was indicated by the candidates who won the presidencies of the two nations in 1978, and steps to implement the change were taken in 1979.

Venezuelan ETV—Despite Venezuela's image as a leader of the movement to use media for national development, its record in exploiting television is unexceptional. The government does maintain one educational channel which attempts to present an "alternative" or cultural service, but it has won little applause from either the intelligentsia or the mass of viewers, who much prefer the commercial channels.

The educational channel was the first television operation in Venezuela, starting as one of the earliest in Latin America, but it was quickly surpassed by the others. Its signal was confined to Caracas until it put up a mountain-top transmitter which carried it to the most heavily-settled areas.

Reform in Costa Rica—Aside from university radio, the Costa Rican government has confined its media ownership to an educational-cultural television station which started late in 1978, accepting advertising only from state agencies. However, a bill was being offered which if enacted would revolutionize the broadcasting system, even though election setbacks dampened its chances. Avowed purposes of it were similar to those of Colombia's state system— education, information, "wholesome" entertainment, human "dignification," protection of national identity, cultural uplift, and development of arts, sciences and sports.[33]

Underlying these bland formulations is the hard-core reason for the new plan—the assumption that broadcasting must be a handmaiden to government policy. This logic starts with the concept shared by every country—that the airwaves belong to the people, society, the nation, the state, or the government in power, all of which are seen as identical. So if the people (that is, the government) decide on a policy, why should they allow their own property (the airwaves) to either act against that policy or fail to implement it? To see that it does not act against policy, according to the argument, the government must prohibit a wide range of evils the commercial users of airwaves are prone to commit. To ensure that the airwave users go further and implement the policy, the government must force them to carry certain material or simply must become a user itself—perhaps the only one.

Expounding this theory, Costa Rica's former minister of culture, Carmen Naranjo, declared that it is "natural" for mass media to be closely linked with a country's policies.

> If the state is carrying out some social program, or expanding public medical welfare, or implementing some economic policy in which saving and more reasonable spending are sought, or discouraging abuse of public services, a mass medium of communication cannot be removed from or indifferent to such ends.[34]

In the case of Costa Rica, the policies in effect at the time put priorities on increasing productivity, encouraging thrift, saving on hard currencies, improving education, stopping the flow of farmers into the city and trying to save Costa Rican customs from dissolving into an alien lifestyle that exalts rock music, hamburgers and blue jeans. Foreign (mostly U.S.) programming makes up 70 to 80 per cent of the fare on Costa Rican television, and this in turn is made up predominantly of violence and North American glamour. Although the policymakers cannot prove that watching "Kojak" makes the Costa Rican viewer lazy, wasteful, ignorant, insecure and unpatriotic, they can mount a compelling argument to that effect.

Like the architects of the Colombian and Venezuelan television systems, the Costa Rican planners accept private commercial participation as an economic necessity, but they would plug it into the mechanism differently. They propose that the state, instead of renting out air time as in Colombia or operating a competitive channel as in Venezuela, should become the senior partner in each television or radio broadcasting company, owning 51 per cent of the stock. Resembling the arrangement which long has been in effect in Italy, the Costa Rican plan entails the curious spectacle of the government's receiving a request for a channel-use license from a company which it partly owns.[35] This raises the possibility of an incestuous relationship between government and business as is frequently seen in Mexico.

The projected law does not offer a formula by which television will create an ideal citizen. But it does seek to remedy nearly every failing which has ever been laid to television. For example:

1. To take the "bigness" out of television and to help the citizen identify with it, repeater stations would be prohibited. This would prevent networks and theoretically would increase local programming, although small independent stations in other countries usually are so poor they cannot afford anything but cheap imports. For various reasons, such an experiment (the UHF project) was abandoned in the United States in the 1950s.

2. To blunt the influence of business motives, control of television and radio would be put into political hands, with great care taken that the power be distributed among the various parties in the national congress and among government ministries. Below two levels of governing councils would come a bureaucracy headed by a director general, and it in turn would be advised by up to 60 members of four consultative committees. The control apparatus is patterned somewhat after that of France, which has an entirely state-owned system.

3. The national president would be able to pre-empt all television and radio time without notice.

4. A cabinet minister could do the same with three-day notice.

5. Two ministries—those of education and of culture, youth and sports—would get two hours of free air time weekly. Two others—health and agriculture—would get one hour each.

6. Each political party would get 15 minutes free per week, raised to 30 in the three months before an election.

7. To meet the objection that television doesn't pay enough attention to what legislators do, the law would require broadcasters to report daily on debates and other activities.

8. So that all the objectionable things in television programs are purged, they must be submitted for prior censorship. Exempted would be news, cultural, educational, artistic, political, religious, philosophical or governmental programs.

9. To limit the addiction to soap operas, they would be restricted to two per day, to be aired outside the midday and evening mealtimes.

10. To cut down on the irritations of sportscasts, rules are laid down for commercials, and announcers would be required to use correct grammar.

11. Newscasts must be fair, objective and complete, with sources indicated.

12. To deal with "advertising clutter," commercials are to be allowed only between programs. They could take up only 10 per cent of air time and not more than 20 minutes in any one hour.

13. To avoid the spread of bad habits, there would be a ban on advertisements promoting alcoholic drinks, medicines or tobacco; subliminal advertising; appeals unrelated to the product; human degradation; or exploitation of sex.

14. Privacy would be guaranteed for everyone except officials performing public actions.

15. Those who feel offended by broadcasters would get a chance to reply on the air.

16. Political parties are to be given equal treatment.

17. Everyone except the broadcasters would be guaranteed a right to give their opinions on the air.[36]

Radio—Although surveys consistently show that radio is the most relied-upon medium for information among the Latin American masses, it has received little attention as an instrument of government in the three democracies. Since the advent of transistor receivers in the early 1960s, almost everyone in these countries hears radio regularly, if not attentively. But despite some government ownership in Venezuela and Colombia, most radio in all three is a mixture of continual commercials, screaming and clownish newscasting, play-by-play sportscasting and specialized popular music (rock for one station, pop for another, etc.).

State-owned radio services have developed alongside the commercial systems in Venezuela and Colombia, as has a powerful university station in Costa Rica. All carry much classical music, discussion programs and documentaries. Venezuela's state network has also conducted ''radio schools'' for the teaching of literacy and other basic subjects to adults, and Costa Rica's university station has aimed its training programs at more advanced subjects such as foreign languages.

Recognizing a wise investment, the Colombian government has started buying the services of a private institute which operates what is clearly the most successful broadcast training program for peasants in the hemisphere. This is Acción Cultural Popular, better known as Radio Sutatenza. Now operating out of a 14-story building in downtown Bogotá, with 700 paid employees, the institute started in 1947 as the effort of a poor parish priest, José Salcedo, to educate children and adults scattered in isolated little farms throughout the mountains. His first transmitter was a 100-watt device hauled by horseback up to Sutatenza, the highest village in the Andes. He sold his parishioners' chickens in the city to get more equipment. Slowly he built up a program which, combining radio programs with communal meetings and cheap publications, began to teach the peasants how to read, build new houses, farm better, have fewer children, and enjoy themselves in neighborhood clubs.[37]

By the mid-1970s, Radio Sutatenza had become a five-station network beaming its signal to battery radios in the homes of 200,000 adult students, who had joined their neighbors in 23,000 ''radio schools.'' The government contracts with Sutatenza to reach the more inaccessible parts of the country where the formal school system does not extend. Sutatenza also gets help from a variety of foreign foundations.[38]

Print Media—Governmental involvement in print media in the three countries has been notably rare. The main exceptions have been the investment by Liberation Party leaders in Costa Rica in a chain of media properties; and the traditional party orientation of newspapers in Colombia. The Costa Rican chain, which included the daily *Excélsior* until its death in 1978, started out with $20,000 of voting stock owned mostly by politicians. But it also issued $3 million worth of non-voting common stock, and this is where an unannounced amount of money from fugitive financier Robert Vesco went. Dr. Luis Burstin, a physician who masterminded the project, explained the motive for the action:

> Our party has gained the government many times, but the opposition—the homegrown oligarchy—has tried to govern through the news media which they control. Now for the first time we will have our own voice.[39]

Colegios

The Latin American movement toward professional guilds for journalists, called *colegios*, had become almost stalemated by the late 1960s. Its components had become familiar to reformist lawmakers in various parts of the region. They included requirements that all new journalists must have a professional university degree and must get a government license to practice; that employers could be punished for hiring anyone else; and that journalists who already had experience when the law was enacted, usually three to five years, would be exempted from the educational norm.

At the same time, the opposition from publishers had become rocklike. They felt that the *colegio* laws would take away their power to run their own businesses and would ruin them financially. The Inter-American Press Association became a sounding board for these fears.

So when the Costa Rican congress passed a *colegio* law in 1969, the precedent was set both for the concept and the opposition to it. Nearly a decade later, when its practical effects were beginning to set in, discontent with it and with the University of Costa Rica Journalism School still was clearly evident.

Venezuela passed a *colegio* law in 1972 and Colombia in 1975, although they were applied gradually over the following several years. The reputation of the journalism schools in those countries was somewhat better than in Costa Rica, particularly in Venezuela.

The *colegio* laws in all three countries assuaged some fears by exempting writers of opinion from the controls. Some protections for professional secrecy also were included, although these could be overridden by courts.

Venezuela's law, unlike the others, was explicit in stating the practices which could cause a journalist to lose his license. They were intentional actions to report lies, misquote sources, harm someone with reporting and depart from objectivity; and to refuse to correct errors. The Venezuelan law also forbade management from falsifying a reporter's copy, forcing a reporter to write lies or altering the work of a columnist.[40]

All three laws also required journalists with three years' experience, during the transition period, to take an examination to get a license. A typical examination, as described in the Colombian law, includes the subjects of Spanish grammar; Colombian and world literature, history and geography; national and world current events; communication law; and Colombian government and economics.[41]

Nationalism

Although the three democracies have traditionally been among the most open in the world to interchange with other peoples, their governments all have moved toward limiting foreign influence on mass communication in recent years. These moves have taken the form primarily of posing difficulties for foreign correspondents, restricting foreign ownership and guarding the purity of the language. In varying degrees, the three countries have been identified also with the movement to set up national or regional news agencies because of dissatisfaction with the major international services such as the Associated Press, United Press International and Reuters.

Underlying all these tendencies is the natural defensiveness of smaller countries when faced with larger ones. Carlos Andrés Pérez, the highly visible Venezuelan president, spoke out often on the subject, as when he addressed the Inter-American Press Association in 1974:

> We Latin Americans have reasons to complain because we are a subinformed region in this developed world. The press of the great countries [does] not publish our realities, our struggles, our purposes and on many occasions they ignore us even though we are struggling, not for a confrontation, but for understanding. There is no Latin American country, there are no Latin American compatriots that do not have the same complaint against the world press.[42]

Pérez' claim that Latins are discontented with the area's treatment by the developed world's press generally is supported by this writer's interviews with hundreds of persons. However, there is less agreement on how to remedy the problem. In Colombia and, to a lesser extent in Venezuela, an apparent hostility to foreign correspondents on the part of some governmental figures has resulted. (No serious trouble of this type has been recorded in Costa Rica.)

Correspondents—Although Pérez has been the most-quoted Latin American leader in expressing resentments against foreign media, he was much more tactful on the subject than his neighbor, Alfonso López Michelsen, then president of Colombia. López was known to engage in shouting matches with the foreign press corps and his attitude left its mark on lesser officials. *Index on Censorship,* an international journal, has argued that Colombia's treatment of foreign reporters, in comparison with that accorded by military dictatorships farther south, is "milder, more insidious, but hardly more tolerant." It goes on to describe various incidents which it said occurred in the mid-1970s in Colombia:

—Free-lance reporter Timothy Ross, a Britisher, found his visa extension delayed after he reported on Bogotá's soaring crime rate for the *Observer* of London. Two years later, in separate incidents, he was interrogated five hours by police about his sources,and he alleged that a kidnap attempt against him was made in downtown Bogotá.

—A *New York Times* reporter was summoned to talk with President López and was subjected to an "angry tirade" about *Times* coverage of Colombia. Later the president's press secretary refused the *Times'* request for interviews and information.

—A reporter for the *National Enquirer,* a U.S. scandal paper, "left the country in a hurry after confiscation of his passport, day-long 'routine questioning' and orders not to write anything."

—Fast-exit visas which the government had traditionally allowed foreign reporters were revoked. These visas had made possible the use of Bogotá as a news-coverage center for neighboring countries, and without them an endless web of red tabe was encountered. (The visas were restored later.)

—United Press International was ordered to leave the country because it erroneously distributed a flash saying President López had been assassinated. The order was lifted after UPI said it would move its bureau chief out of the country.

—Two foreign reporters covering student demonstrations were beaten by police even though they displayed their credentials.[43]

Venezuela's record is much better, but an incident in 1976 indicates that police can be the arbiters of what foreigners may report. Three American reporters—one each working for *Esquire* magazine and for the *Miami News,* the other a free-lancer—had flown into Caracas to cover a sensational and, for Venezuela, embarrassing chain of events involving terrorism by Cuban exiles. The reporters were held incommunicado in their hotel overnight, then shipped out on a plane to the United States.[44]

Foreign Ownership—Another way that nationalists have exerted their influence on press-government relations is through removing any vestiges of foreign ownership from the media. Ironically, the only medium in which such ownership has ever been significant—television—had already been largely abandoned throughout Latin America by foreign investors.

During the early 1960s, the three American networks and Time-Life Inc. had been engaged in what Timothy Green calls "a great, but unhappy, flirtation with Latin American television." They wanted a share of the ownership to sell programs, transmitting equipment and television sets, but they also believed the stations would be as enormously profitable as the ones in the United States had been.

> In Venezuela the American networks bought into every single TV station; NBC joined the local Phelps family in Channel 2 in Caracas; ABC went into Channel 4 with the Cisneros family (which had made its fortune bottling Pepsi-Cola), while CBS and Time-Life linked up with Goar Mestre from the Argentine and the Vollner family, whose main interests were sugar and rum, to open Channel 9.[45]

The result was staggering financial losses for the Yankee investors. "We simply overestimated the market," an NBC executive recalled. "For a while everyone thought it was the new frontier. We quickly found out it wasn't. There were just too many stations." In Venezuela, where the three main channels' budgets totaled $24 million, the entire advertising revenue available was $22 million. Sometimes the Americans held on to their shares only because no one else wanted to buy them.[46]

So when the Venezuelan government ordered foreign owners to clear out of local television companies early in 1974, the effect was negligible. NBC held 10 per cent of the shares in Channel 2, and ABC had about 10 per cent of Channel 4, although the law had allowed them up to 20 per cent. But in one of the first acts by Pérez after he became president, foreign companies were given 30 days to sell out their stocks.[47]

Since Colombia's television has always been government-owned, the investment problem has not arisen in it; radio, on the other hand, operates under a law that prevents foreigners from operating any station or owning more than 25 per cent of it. Nor can a station be subsidized by any foreign government or company.

Costa Rica was one of the few Latin American countries where foreigners had large media investments in the 1970s, and even that was put to an end in 1978 with enactment of a strict law confining ownership of newspapers, television and radio stations, and advertising agencies to Costa Rican citizens. ABC had to sell its 35 per cent share in Channel 7.[48]

Robert Vesco's investment in San José's Channel 11, two daily newspapers and several radio properties has been noted. The operators of the chain were careful to point out that, Vesco's shares being common stock, he had no voting rights. And the very fact that Vesco did not dare set foot in the United States, being under indictment there, diminished his role as a foreign investor.

The crisis posed by Vesco came to an end in 1978 when he voluntarily left for the Bahamas just before a new president, Rodrigo Carazo, who had promised to expel him, was inaugurated. Carazo and his cabinet quickly announced they would deport Vesco to the United States if he showed up again.

Language—Venezuela and Colombia have taken steps also to expel foreign influences in the language—not only in the vocabulary but also in how it is pronounced. Dubbing of television films for the Spanish-speaking markets throughout the hemisphere has long been a specialty of studios in Mexico and Puerto Rico, although nationalists in other countries have smarted over the difference in accents. In 1974 the Venezuelan government decreed that all such films must be dubbed in Venezuela.[49] Four years later the law still had not been implemented.

In Colombia, the purge was applied to foreign words used in advertising in the capital city, Bogotá. The provocation was the rampant imitation of stylish words from abroad, mostly the United States—terms such as drive-in, beauty shop, dry cleaning, delicatessen and boutique. So the mayor declared that business signs and labels must find a Spanish equivalent for all such words.[50] The crackdown failed in its enforcement, however.

The Candia Case—The difficulty United Press International got into after distributing the false "assassination" story merits a closer look because of what it illustrates about the fragility of press freedom even in Latin American democracies and the sensitivity which developing countries feel about their international image. It also poses questions about the adequacy of "fail-safe" procedures in the handling of news at super-speed, and the possibility that such news could cause disastrous panic.

For UPI, it meant a hair-raising six days, because for that period it was under orders to close up its operations in Colombia, traditionally a pivotal point for covering northwestern South America, Central America and the Caribbean—and also a country with 25 million population and many UPI customers. For Pieter Van Bennekom, Colombian manager for UPI, it meant a crisis in his brilliant but uncertain young career. And for Patricio Candia, another young journalist, it meant being portrayed before his colleagues as a fool at best or a poisoner of the news at worst. For all of them, it meant struggles to prove that their penalties were unmerited.[51]

Candia, a 25-year-old who looked younger, had been a sports writer in Cali, a provincial Colombian city, and he was passionately devoted to journalism. He had followed his father in the profession, working on a leftist newspaper and radio station in his native Chile. Both father and son had left the country after Salvador Allende's fall, although they were not fugitives.

Having done well working for a Cali newspaper and acting as sports correspondent for UPI, Candia was offered a job in the Bogotá offices. For the youth
who had already seen his career collapse once because of his employers' politics in Chile, it was the chance of a lifetime. He was to start work on Monday,
July 5, 1976. But he was stretching his luck, because he was living—even
worse,working—in Colombia illegally, as his tourist visa had expired.

Candia was so eager to start with UPI that he showed up at its offices two
days early—around midday on Saturday. Things were quiet, and a Colombian
reporter and the copy boy were the only ones around; they were playing chess.
Fascinated by the clattering teletypes scattered along the walls, Candia asked if
he could practice typing on one, as every wire service reporter must do. Material typed into the machine would go nowhere unless switched through to
Caracas, which was a control point before reaching New York. From there
copy is distributed to selected parts of the world or all of it. A switch on the
right side of the teletype stand made the difference between the typed material's
going out of the country or going in the wastebasket.

What happened next is the nub of an argument that reached global proportions. The reporter on duty, Fabio Castro, said he flipped the switch into the
"Bogotá" or harmless position and went back to his desk; a half-hour later, he
went to inspect Candia's work, and, as he scanned the material, the copy boy
pointed to the dancing needle of a meter and exclaimed that Candia's writings
were being transmitted.

Various versions of what happened to the switch surfaced later in the fran-
tic efforts to escape blame. One was that Castro had failed, intentionally or not,
to flip the switch; another, that Candia had moved it to the "Caracas" or transmitting side, by accident or intent; still another, that the copy boy had done it.
All three denied any guilt.

But what Castro had noticed an instant before the copy boy's alarm was
that Candia had been writing short, imaginary news stories in Spanish, all
badly typed but harmless except for one line among the garbles: "The president of Colombia, Alfonso López Michelsen, was assassinated."

Castro stopped the transmission and rushed to inform the UPI office in
Caracas what had happened. But it was too late.

"The news had passed like a comet past Caracas and from there to New
York," he recalled later. "At that moment there arrived a flash from New York
with the news. That meant that the false news had already been retransmitted
by New York to Bogotá and was spread through the world."[52]

Suddenly all four office phones started ringing. A telex message came
from New York UPI asking for more details. Castro, almost immobilized with
panic, told New York over and over to correct the falsehood. It had gone out
from New York at 1:54 p.m.; four minutes later it was "killed" on the same
wire.

But the spark of rumor was not put out so easily. The Spanish news
agency Efe, which has an interchange with UPI, picked up the news in New
York and sent it on to Madrid, where it was put on the worldwide wires. The
Madrid operatives threw in a little imagination. Using a Bogotá dateline, they
said the murder was the work of terrorists and that the death had been officially

announced. However, Efe also transmitted a denial, quoting a presidential aide as saying López was alive and in his palace.

López was not in his palace—he was in seclusion at a country estate, writing a speech. But he was livid with rage when the messages of condolence began coming in from around the world and he learned of the false news. He told reporters he was "profoundly disgusted" and that he did not believe it was an accident since it followed the lines of sabotaging and confusing the country.[53] He immediately ordered UPI expelled and the Efe correspondent in Bogotá, who had nothing to do with the case, stripped of his credentials as a journalist. Candia, who had left the UPI offices in a daze, soon returned to face the consequences. Police took him off to jail.

By Monday, the two top UPI executives in Latin America, Claude Hippeau and Martin McReynolds, had flown in from Buenos Aires to help Van Bennekom unsnarl the tangle. They filed a court appeal and the next Friday secured an interview with López. He lectured them on what he saw wrong with UPI's coverage of Colombia but then cooled down and told them not to worry about the ouster. By that night it had been revoked, and UPI announced it would reassign Van Bennekom to another country. (He was assigned to Buenos Aires, but Argentina refused him a visa, apparently because of contacts with the Colombian government. He later became Caribbean news editor in Puerto Rico.)

Candia, who had spent the week behind bars while the Colombian press heaped abuse on him, was deported to Chile by a judge who cited his visa violation. Since critics had accused him of plotting the López incident as leftist sabotage, he kept a low profile in the military-ruled Chile, rejecting speech invitations. Soon he left for Spain, where he had relatives.

Even though the crisis quickly subsided, there was a general feeling that it would be used for years to come to prove various points. It preceded by only a week the UNESCO meeting on communication policies in Costa Rica, and the UPI executives held themselves ready to go there and defend their position if the issue arose. It did not, but the alleged mistreatment of small countries by the international wire services was criticized with new vigor.

Questions remained after calm returned—some with implications for the future. Answers that emerged were at best only tentative or in some cases confusing:

1. Even if Candia's motives were innocent, does this case prove that a saboteur could get into a position to make people around the world believe some dangerous falsehood, such as a nuclear attack?

Van Bennekom said that Candia had an outstanding record with a right-wing newspaper in Cali and that Candia's previous part-time work for UPI also was good.

2. Why was no discretion exercised at the "control point" in Caracas?

Responses as to this differ. Martin Houseman, the UPI chief in Caracas, said his office has no editorial responsibility over Bogotá—only mechanical. Although Bogotá was supposed to move stories only on the hour, the switch was open to New York in case Bogotá had anything to send. Van Bennekom said that his helper, Fabio Castro, had been eager to make a good impression for the office and had been pushing Caracas for more wire time, but that he had told Caracas to follow proper control procedures.

3. Why did UPI New York refile the false news on other wires even though it was not introduced with the required codes?

The flash was translated from Spanish by the Latin American news desk, then relayed to several other regional desks, which sent it over worldwide wires which reached about 3,000 UPI clients, about half the total. It was carried by many radio stations, including one in Bogotá, although CBS radio in the United States killed it in the same broadcast in which it was read.

H. L. Stevenson, UPI president, concedes that the agency's own rules were violated in Bogotá, Caracas and New York. Editors in New York had ignored the jumbled nature of Candia's transmission because they had been having trouble with garbles caused by mechanical problems.

4. Why did President López and the Colombian press react so vehemently to a false report of death—something that has occurred countless times and usually is laughed off by the public figures involved?

A close look at the language of the protests indicates that the resentment focused not on any imagined insult to the president but on the idea that such a savage thing could happen in Colombia. Also, there seemed to be a nervous look over the shoulder at Colombia's nine years of civil war, which was started by the murder of a popular leader, leading to vicious street fighting.

5. How could anyone be forbidden to practice journalism in a democracy with personal freedom?

This brings to light the fact that the licensing provisions in Colombian press law can be used to muzzle a person who does something to anger the public or even just the authorities. Permits are required both for wire services to use telecommunications and for their reporters to do their work. Such permits can be removed by executive order, although appeal to the courts is allowed; the UPI case did not reach this level before the order was revoked.

Access to the Media

Venezuela, while not requiring public access to the media as such, has included among the journalist's obligations the duty to "rectify the errors of fact which may have been committed in reporting about persons, events and declarations." He also is required not to "corrupt intentionally the opinions and declarations of third parties."[54]

Colombia requires radio broadcasters to air, free and without comment, corrections or explanations resulting from news, speeches, lectures or commentaries. This must be done whenever the affected person considers the material incorrect or injurious.[55]

Efforts to pass a law in Costa Rica giving lawmakers free space in newspapers failed, but there is some indication it could surface again. Congress is the dominant force in Costa Rica, more so than the president, and most of its members have a high regard for what they and their colleagues say. Even though the Costa Rican newspapers print an unusually large amount of such pronouncements, there is never enough to satisfy all the legislators.

So a law was proposed to require newspapers of 50 pages or more to give over 6 per cent of their space to verbatim statements from officials; those with

20 to 50 pages would have had to devote 4 per cent to this purpose. This would mean three full pages taken from a 50-page newspaper.[56]

One of the dailies, *La República,* said the law would force newspapers to run "everything coming from the pens or typewriters of public officials, from a love letter written during the heat of the long and tedious parliament session, to a doctoral thesis." *La Nación,* the largest daily, called it "a flagrant violation of all laws that govern private property in Costa Rica."[57] Finally, the majority of legislators agreed and the project was dropped.

Area News Agency

Political leaders in the three democracies were speaking up with growing frequency in the 1970s about their image problems in the developed countries. The complaint of Venezuela's former president, Carlos Andrés Pérez, has been noted earlier.

The root of the problem, as Pérez and others see it, is the indifference of the major international wire services and large news media to "our realities, our struggles, our purposes," as Pérez puts it. Correspondents on the scene are not to blame, he has said.

> They send their news to the central office, but the centers of these great news agencies publish what they want to, and in so doing, the news which Latin America is interested in having published to the world is not divulged, and in this way news of less importance is published. The same thing is being done by large newspapers; these great publishing houses throw away the greater part of material received from international agencies.[58]

Pérez' former minister of state for information, Guido Grooscors, has called the international wire services "the multinationals of news." Among Latin American reformers, this is a grave condemnation.

The solution to the problem, according to Pérez, is the formation of a Latin American news agency backed by governments. The area already has an agency cooperatively owned by some large newspapers and affiliated with the British agency Reuters; it is called LATIN. But Pérez dismisses it, saying it "has not gained the strength, neither the significance it should obtain."[59] Even many of his opponents join him in this judgment.

Pérez has been vague on how he proposes that his new agency would be organized and financed, considering the fact that some of the strongest backing possible has failed to bring notable success to LATIN. Grooscors has mentioned the possibility that it could be organized by governments, by private business or both.

The main object of Pérez and his allies has been to get general agreement on the need for a new Latin American agency. With only Argentina dissenting, he got solid backing for the concept at the San José, Costa Rica, meeting of UNESCO in 1976. Grooscors dropped the hint that Venezuela would put its oil riches behind the agency, saying it would make the greatest possible contribution "in line with the integrationist policy of the country." His reference to Latin American integration raised the fear of Venezuelan imperialism among some leaders of the region, although others were content to let Venezuela have its agency if it would pay for it.[60]

The Pérez plan calls for the agency to be formed step by step, starting with national agencies and then groupings of several countries before developing into one entity for all of Latin America.[61] Whether each country would be represented by an independent agency or by its own propaganda office is to be left to each government.

Costa Rica and Colombia have averted the pressures to establish information ministries, although public relations offices have sprouted in many government agencies. Any dealings the Costa Rican government has in communication—mostly confined to minimal regulation of broadcasting—are handled by the minister of the interior. In Colombia, the minister of communication concerns himself largely with the mechanical operation of telephones, television and radio.

Communication policy moved into a major place in Venezuela's government when Pérez became president in 1973. Grooscors, an experienced diplomat and bureaucrat, was named minister of state for information. His job was running the Central Office of Information (OCI), which had aspirations of being just what its name said but was prevented by lack of authority. Gooscors set about pushing through Congress a bill establishing a "Ministry of Information and Tourism." He justified it mainly on two grounds—the efficiency of centralizing many agencies' publicity offices and the public's need to know about government:

"We believe that democratic government must satisfy the public with what is happening."

Grooscors conceded that opposition parties were accusing OCI of being a propaganda agency—"but we try not to do that."

The Pérez government saw itself as a trailblazer for all developing nations in the use of information as a "resource," as Grooscors called it. He noted that each country must find its own special way toward an information policy.[62]

However, Venezuela's leadership in this field makes a look at its new information ministry worthwhile. These are the ministry's duties:

1. Coordinating all information, advertising and public relations of the government agencies. The law establishing the agency concedes that a citizen has the right to ask for information but that some things cannot be revealed because this would "endanger the national sovereignty, dampen investigations or ruin goals."

2. Projecting a "favorable image to the different nations of the world" by running fairs and expositions, planning publications and sponsoring visits by "personalities or representative groups" to Venezuela.

3. Managing all the printing and audio-visuals of the government. It is argued that the various agencies over-produce these, do not distribute them and then burn them.

4. Manage all advertising campaigns for the government.

5. Do research on public opinion for the government.

6. Form and administer a national cinema policy.

7. Fix rates for commercial tourist services.

Venezuela's ministry is not unique, as its structure and concepts resemble those of authoritarian countries such as Peru. However, by the late 1970s it remained unclear whether the other democracies or even the Venezuelan public would accept the basic change it implies.

TRADITIONAL CONTROLS

It might be argued that Venezuela and Colombia have more democracy than freedom. Although their electoral processes have unfolded without interruption since the late 1950s, both have been afflicted at times with subversion. During these periods, governments have turned to controls not unlike those wielded by dictatorships farther south. But it would be difficult to prove either that these have been continuously applied (most have dealt with relatively brief crises) or that journalists have been severely intimidated by them. It also is clear that at no time has the majority of the populace opposed the controls. Most of all, the citizens want to avert a return to chaos, and if journalism promotes chaos, they feel it must be restricted.

Costa Rica, having lived a quarter-century without serious threat to internal stability, has had far less resort to the traditional controls than its two larger neighbors. It would appear that the people loathe strong controls of any kind too much to permit the media to suffer alone.

Censorship

Colombia has a strong heritage of prior restriction on media content, and it has not rid itself of the practice yet. By the late 1970s, it was almost entirely confined to the broadcast media, however.

Even before the harsh dictatorship of Rojas Pinilla during the civil war, other Colombian presidents used censorship either to maintain order or to handicap political opponents. During Rojas' regime, censorship was extended to nine major newspapers at one time in 1955, partly to keep the public from knowing why he had closed down the liberal daily *El Tiempo*. He also put out a decree forbidding publication of anything "directly or indirectly disrespectful of the president of the Republic or the head of a friendly nation."[63]

While the print media no longer are troubled in this manner, radio and television are bound by a web of rules. Most of the time radio is under self-censorship rather than inspection, and it has its own list of forbidden material:

1. Any material telling about "crime against the family or against sexual liberty and honor."

2. Information that can impede judicial or police investigations.

3. Any crime news which is not objective or which has "crude or morbid descriptions" or which defends the crime.

4. Any transmissions that attack the country's constitution, laws, foreign relations or institutions; the "life, honor and goods" of citizens; or respect due to authorities.

5. False or tendentious news that incites disregard for the law or disturbance to the peace.

6. Any political speech or lecture without 48 hours' notice to the ministry of communications.[64]

For violating any of these rules, the station owner can lose his license for at least two years.

Since the state operates television itself, through producers who buy time, the broadcast agency Inravisión can make its own regulations. In one of these, decreed in 1972, producers are required to submit their material for censorship on these schedules:

1. Filmed programs—films submitted for viewing three weeks before air time.

2. Live programs—scripts submitted 48 hours in advance.

3. Newscasts—scripts and films submitted 30 minutes in advance.[65]

It must be conceded that the government exercises its rights to censor or punish broadcasters lightly most of the time. However, during an extended state of siege in 1975 and 1976, President López twice warned stations to watch their steps. Once he ordered the minister of communications to cancel the license of any radio station that spread reports threatening public order. Later he forbade both radio and television to carry any unofficial reports about kidnappings and election results.[66]

A filmed television series written by world-renowned author Gabriel García Márquez in 1977 caused a furor because it portrayed the atrocities of the 1948–57 civil war and offended Conservative politicians' sense of fairness. Police officials viewed the film because it showed the police in a bad light, and the president's cabinet discussed banning it. But the ministers decided in the end to let it be aired.[67]

A movie producer can run into trouble even in the filming if Colombia's international image is at stake, the experience of an American documentary maker indicates. His film, dealing with hunger in Colombia as well as India and Nigeria, was to involve scenes of the hordes of orphan boys who forage for food in the streets of Bogotá. The producer reported later that Colombian government representatives tried to prevent him from getting his footage, and he succeeded only by shooting from hotel windows and moving cars.[68]

Because Colombia continues to be troubled by terrorism, strikes and sometimes riots two decades after the supposed end of the civil war, "state of siege" legislation was in effect 16 of the 20 years following the truce. It is lifted occasionally and just as quickly reimposed at the sign of discord. Among other things, the legislation gives the government the power to suspend the licenses of professionals, including journalists, for instigating or directing illegal movements.[69]

Venezuela's experience with its dictator of the 1950s, Marcos Pérez Jiménez, closely parallels that of Colombia. Local print media and broadcasters were put under prior censorship by the ministry of the interior, although foreign reporters could operate freely.[70]

Even after the restoration of democratic elections in Venezuela, censorship continued several years. Communists were attempting to overthrow the government, and one of their main strongholds was the press. The president derived his power to censor through Article 56 of the Constitution, which forbids propaganda that "incites disobedience of the laws," which the communists were doing clearly and repeatedly. He also suspended constitutional guarantees several times.[71]

By the late 1970s, other controls had superseded censorship. Broadcasters were aware, though, that a 1937 law still required that all material going over the airwaves be censored, although it was not being enforced.[72]

Censorship on moral grounds continues in Venezuela as in most Latin American countries, although its position as an international crossroads, near the fleshpots of the Caribbean, limits the effectiveness of such controls. When the movie "Last Tango in Paris" was banned from showing in Venezuela, an enterprising travel agent ran heavily-booked planes for two months to Curaçao, a nearby Dutch island, where the movie was showing.[73] Resistance faded during the Pérez presidency, and mild pornography slowly came to Caracas.

Costa Rica's only brushes with censorship in recent times have also been on moral grounds. A censorship department has long operated within the ministry of the interior to stand guard over printed and filmed material; it is mostly a matter of import controls, since Costa Rica produces so little of such content. Guidelines for the censors are fairly specific: "Obscene or pornographic texts . . . the dissemination of antisocial customs, and the presentation of scenes which may lead to vice, criminality, sexual aberrations and the use of drugs or which are contrary to the country's cultural values."[74]

The censorship board is too understaffed to have much effect, although the country is generally free from smut. Arguments sometimes have arisen over the board's decisions, however.[75]

With the new emphasis on the social role of media in the 1970s, a movement built up to pass a new censorship law. The idea was to expand censorship beyond the traditional grounds of sex and gore to protect whatever the censors felt would be distinctive about Costa Rica's way of life. In the words of the bill proposing the law, the censors could ban anything that "might influence the destruction or deformation of the fundamental values of man and the Costa Rican society."[76] However, a counter-measure gained ground later; it would confine moral control to a U.S.-type classification system and would restrict its provisions to entertainment media, not journalism.

Closure and Seizure

Unlike other controls, the device of shutting the public off from some news medium, by either closing it or seizing printed matter, has been on the upsurge in Venezuela.

This measure was taken frequently under the Pérez Jiménez dictatorship and also during the communist crisis which followed. In fact, it was the most effective step taken to purge media of communist influence early in the 1960s. The country's supreme court outlawed the Communist Party and the Movement of the Revolutionary Left (MIR) in 1963, thereby forcing the closure of these groups' newspapers.[77]

Three incidents in 1976 brought the practice back into the forefront of Venezuelan affairs. All were related to the kidnapping of an American industrialist working in Venezuela, William F. Niehous. It was one of the most embarrassing and infuriating episodes the government had faced since the communist crisis.

A principal demand of the kidnappers was to get the manifestoes they continually issued into print or on the air. These statements preached the group's political creed and attempted to justify the kidnapping. Media directors were caught between their news sense and concern for Niehous on one side and the pressures of the government to refuse the demands on the other.

Government officials won the support of major publishers through gentle but firm prodding in meetings. Four such publishers recalled in a report to the Inter-American Press Association:

> These meetings were carried out by the authorities in an atmosphere of respect for the autonomy and independence of the news media. They only expressed their opinion as to what might be construed as a violation of existing laws. The Government . . . maintains that publication of these documents . . . would be in clear violation of current regulations.[78]

But soon afterward television Channel 2, known for its aggressive news coverage, secured an interview with a man who claimed to represent the kidnappers. Throwing caution to the wind, the station put the interview on the air. The minister of radio communications, acting under a 1963 regulation concerning subversive propaganda, ordered Channel 2 to suspend operation for three days.[79]

The action brought down a storm of protest on the government from legislators and other media. No attempt was made to stop the criticism, and Channel 2 added its share when it returned to the air.

The station, in fact, boasts of its punishment. It posted a huge blow-up of the closure order in the focal point of its lobby. "We consider it a badge of honor," station director Peter Bottome said.[80]

Bottome sees the incident as "a dangerous precedent" because the station carried the news in good faith. "Nobody still can prove we were wrong," he said.

The next episode happened the very evening Channel 2 resumed operation. It showed that the central government cannot always control what some agencies such as the police and military do to restrict media freedom.

Just as the Caracas newspapers were approaching their press time, agents of the federal detective bureau (DISIP) swooped down on several newspapers, most notably *El Nacional,* the largest. They had heard that the papers were going to print a manifesto from the Niehous kidnappers, and they intended to stop it. They even took the printing plates off the presses at *El Nacional.*

The minister of the interior, in charge of all law enforcement, immediately got midnight phone calls at home from several *El Nacional* executives. He promptly called the police off.

The government went to great lengths to soothe the press over the incident. It admitted that the police had been "offensive" and later dismissed the DISIP chief from office. But it also said the newspapers had misunderstood the whole operation, which had been intended as an "elementary protective measure" to shield the papers against retaliation from the Niehous kidnappers because their manifestos had not been published.

The publishers reporting the affair to the IAPA assured the world that press freedom existed in Venezuela and they hoped events like the DISIP case would not happen again.[81]

But it did recur, five months later. This time it involved a publication, a political party and a legislator all at the leftist fringe. It was difficult to find a voice from the mainstream raised in their defense.

The legislator, Salóm Mesa, was one of four who had been charged with aiding in the Niehous kidnapping. Stripped of parliamentary immunity, they were turned over to the military for trial because some of the kidnappers had been dressed in uniforms and therefore it was considered a military crime.

Soon after being jailed, Mesa wrote a long and defiant letter to his political party, the People's Electoral Movement. In it he claimed he was arrested because he knew about "inconfessible understandings" between then-President Pérez and the U.S. Central Intelligence Agency during Pérez' election campaign. He hinted that the company for which the kidnapped Niehous worked was tied up in the supposed plot, and he accused Pérez of sending him to a military court "because it is the only one which allows him to advance his grim purpose."[82] Ironically, only five months later the *New York Times,* quoting U.S. intelligence sources, said that Pérez had taken CIA payoffs, but much earlier than Mesa had claimed.[83]

Punto, the leftist weekly publication, ran a story reporting Mesa's letter and quoting it in full. The military seized all copies before they could be sold. The explanation given was that Mesa had criticized the president in his role as commander of the military and thus military justice was in order; however, the letter never made reference to this relationship.

Since the closure of major Colombian newspapers during the Rojas Pinilla dictatorship of the 1950s, this measure and the seizure of editions have been generally discarded in that country. The fact that the government almost shut down operations of UPI demonstrates that it can happen.

Punishments

A strong minus factor in the status of democracy in Venezuela and Colombia is the political strength of the military establishments. Although civilian governments in recent decades have managed to keep the military subordinate, it is only because they have trod lightly on the prerogatives of the generals.

Laws left over from the early 1960s, during the Venezuelan communist crisis, allow military courts to try civilians in any cases involving "anguish" among the people and in many others related to subversion. This does not entail the brutality often associated with military justice elsewhere in South America, and appeal to civilian courts is allowed. But it has special bearing on freedom of expression, as unorthodox journalism can easily be considered dangerous.

This military role caused what amounted to exile lasting nine months for Miguel Angel Capriles, the flamboyant owner of a newspaper chain, who is sometimes referred to as "the Hearst of Venezuela." Capriles published a confidential government report on a boundary dispute with Colombia, adding his accusation that Venezuelan politicians were giving in to Colombian pressure. He was charged with the technicality of inciting the military to rebel but sought asylum in the Nicaraguan Embassy and was allowed to leave the country. The next year he was permitted to return but was whisked off to a military base for questioning when he arrived. The price set for his freedom was abdicating as head of his publishing empire, which he did, but he soon regained effective control.[84]

In another case, a female journalist who interviewed guerrillas, including some prison escapees, was clamped into a military prison while being investigated on suspicion that she had aided the subversives. At the same time, the defense minister warned journalists he would apply military law to them if they impugned the integrity of the armed forces.[85]

The military in Colombia also is not averse to flexing its muscles with the intent to intimidate journalists. In 1976 the minister of defense, a top-ranking general, announced that there would be "regulations" to stop what the militarists considered journalistic excesses. He was referring to some sexy material in a Bogotá tabloid and political accusations printed in the leftist magazine *Alternativa*. Other militarists in turn criticized the two publications of being "apologists for crime."

The Bogotá Journalists' Circle protested in person to President López. He promised them nothing would come of it—at least during his term.[86]

Police in both Venezuela and Colombia are known to be ready to rough up aggressive reporters in crowd situations. Television reporters in Venezuela have been arrested and beaten and their film destroyed by police while covering student riots. Colombian police caused an international incident when they beat up Bogotá reporters covering a visit by U.S. President Lyndon Johnson's daughter Lynda. In both cases, however, the national governments apologized to the press.[87]

Government Advertising

Not having economies that are largely owned by the state, the three democracies have limited amounts of government advertising in comparison with countries such as Peru and Argentina. But all have some socialization of industry, including consumer industries ranging from liquor in Costa Rica to petroleum in Venezuela. Since even state-owned industries are expected to earn a profit, they turn to advertising to move the products off the shelf. This income is particularly important to small publications for whom every issue is a financial crisis. Usually government purchases of space make up a higher percentage of total revenue for them than for the large dailies, which draw on a wide range of privately owned enterprises for ads.

Although the use of advertising as a weapon in the hands of government is not well documented in Venezuela, it is accepted as a way of life among media leaders. The weapon is rarely wielded, they say, but the director of a mass medium thinks twice before risking the loss of government advertising. One widely discussed case was that of a newspaper called *2001*, which was founded while the Social Democrats controlled the presidency but which had a staff loaded with bitter partisans for the opposition party. A phone call to the director pointed out that a continued lack of "objectivity" would mean loss of government ads, and within a few days all the partisans were fired.

This type of pressure is considered important in Colombia, where such ads can make up 25 per cent of the total. Costa Rica also is familiar with it but since the favoritism is handled somewhat quietly, it rarely stirs up protests. It was generally accepted that when leaders of the party in power helped found the new daily *Excélsior* in 1975, it got more than its share of state ads to keep it afloat financially. Oddly enough another new publication in Costa Rica, the radically leftist weekly *Pueblo,* also got nearly all its ads from the state, although its main income was from circulation. The director of *Pueblo,* Javier Solís, never tired of savagely criticizing the government. But with the typically democratic logic of Costa Rica, he reasoned that the government had a special responsibility toward his paper because of its peculiar nature.[88]

Government Pressures

Aside from the specific actions of the government to affect the press noted above, the three democracies also share with their neighbors the indirect pressures which can be exercised with various degrees of severity. These may take the form of publicly criticizing media, influencing third parties who may in turn induce the media to take certain actions, withholding information, or using the time-honored political technique of the "friendly" advice or request via a telephone call.

Venezuelan President Pérez, himself a former journalist and an everflowing fount of strong opinions, was quick to criticize what he saw as misdeeds of the media, although he did not use the belligerent tone so often directed by national leaders at this target. Trying to make good use of the newly expanded Central Office of Information, his office sent a form notice to directors of newspapers asking them to check everything concerning the presidency with the press agents before printing it. Such a storm of protest arose that Pérez had to back down.[89]

Pérez was much less gentle when the *New York Times* reported that he had accepted CIA money while he was a cabinet minister during the 1960s. The president, aiming his anger both at the U.S. government and the *Times,* called publication of the story "a dishonorable conspiracy against the independence and dignity of Venezuela." He implied that "very high levels" of the U. S. government had a hand in the report, and he threatened to pursue the matter to "its final consequences." President Carter later apologized to Pérez for the *Times* story.[90]

The Venezuelan government tried to operate under tight secrecy when it was preparing to nationalize its oil industry, but details of its plans kept leaking out. Pérez responded by severely clamping down on any possible outlets of information.[91]

When Colombia adopted its *colegio* (licensing) law for journalists, the rhetoric used by President López Michelson's government had a strong flavor of retaliation at the press. He conceded that the law was aimed at "the sensationalist press—the press which irresponsibly used headlines to create situations of opinion." He lectured the press that it should not report international politics "with the criteria of a soccer game, as if it were an issue of how many goals one country scored against another."[92]

PART TWO

A HEMISPHERIC
VIEW

CHAPTER 8

Government Effects
on Media

IF ONE WERE to ask the average news reader in the United States or Europe what the main type of government intervention in Latin American mass communication is, the answer probably would be "censorship." Ironically, if this were true—if the degree of official censorship that exists in the area were the principal concern of journalists—a massive upsurge of contentment would occur in newsrooms throughout the hemisphere.

The fact is that the interweaving of government with media has produced a tapestry with a vast panorama of scenes; of these, official censorship occupies one of the least noticeable corners. The means of control at a government's disposal are as diverse as the weaponry of war, ranging from permanent or temporary padlocking to restrictions on what can be said in an advertisement. Measures taken by the regime also can have a benevolent or at least patronizing motive, as when subsidies are distributed or an educational article or program is furnished. Furthermore, the government may take sides in an internal battle within the media, passing laws which require higher salaries or more education for reporters.

Each country has its own particular blend of these measures, as has been detailed in previous chapters. But anyone who studies the situation by going from country to country soon feels that he is entering the same house through different doors. It becomes apparent that Latin American countries share some common grounds in the way their governments deal with their media. This chapter looks at some of these continuities. They are grouped under the broad headings of effects on media operations; state ownership, management and propaganda; controls on content; and personal penalties.

EFFECTS ON MEDIA OPERATIONS

A police officer bearing an official order that a newspaper close its doors and go out of business is a chillingly familiar sight in many Latin American countries. So is the lightning-fast descent of a squad of uniformed men to seize the copies of a publication from its press room or the newsstands.

In these and other ways, a government can intervene in the process of manufacturing and distributing a product, whether it is a sheaf of pages or a broadcast signal. Since Latin American governments tend to have much more sheer power than patience for tedious actions such as censorship, the sudden slash in the medium's operation makes much more sense from its standpoint.

Closure and Suspension

Scarcely a government in Latin America with authoritarian leanings has resisted the temptation to use the padlock in recent years. This use has varied widely in intensity, particularly in relation to how troubled a country's political situation is.

The news media of greatest prestige—usually the traditionally elite dailies—rarely suffer this indignity, although none is immune. The actions rarely are permanent and thus most must be termed suspensions rather than closures. Even so, this type of penalty can be one of the gravest injuries to a news medium, as it can bleed to death economically trying to keep its operation intact in the face of uncertainty.

Apparently the greatest appeal that closure and suspension hold for authoritarians is their flexibility. They can be applied selectively to certain companies, and their application can last for any length of time. They also represent one of the types of repression most easily justified under a claim of national emergency. Thus a government can vent its anger with an appearance of constitutionality, it can repeal the closure and correct a foolish punishment without admitting its mistake, and it can know that it has a handy weapon to adapt quickly to a newly changed policy.

Few political systems in Latin America have been so unstable as the Argentine one, and that country also has been the one most likely to see its journalistic media closed and suspended. This device has been used with equal alacrity by governments of the left and the right, the elected and the usurper.

The tabloids, which include most of the political and sensational scandal sheets of Buenos Aires, have been the favorite target of the padlockers in Argentina. Even the establishment press considers these papers to be expendable, and their closure rarely brings a strong protest from fellow media. The fact that the punished enterprise can go to court and hope for justice there somewhat blunts the effect of protests; in fact, some of these actions have been voided by judges. Of course, by the time judicial relief comes the paper has suffered grievously in the counting office.

Closure also can serve to chastise a news medium which is a sheer nuisance to the government, even aside from the left-right struggle. This occurred when the mass-circulation tabloid *Crónica* was shut down for trying to promote a "people's invasion" of some British-held islands.

Whereas dailies are as likely to be shut down in Argentina as are other publications, the closure-suspension weapon is used in Peru almost exclusively against the weekly Lima press, partly because they make up most of the independent media left in the country. And unlike the Argentine victims, the Peruvian ones are edited by the most respected journalists in the country. Two other distinctions are that the Peruvian weeklies often are shut down en masse rather than one by one, and the reason frequently is preventive—to keep them from worsening a crisis—rather than punitive.

Nowhere is the economic effect of suspension clearer than in Uruguay, where this device is the principal means of state control over media. In the words of one local analyst, "The list of temporary and permanent closings . . . would occupy many columns of a newspaper, even if they were just briefly described."[1] The temporary ones make up a large part of the total, and the public is treated to the spectacle of a publication that repeatedly tries to rebuild its circulation and advertising after shutdowns ranging from a week to several months. Such publications gradually waste away until they die.

Smaller publications have most often been the target in Uruguay, although an incident in 1977 showed that even the most prestigious can be brought low. *El Día,* the gray eminence of the nation's dailies and the nearest approach to an opposition organ, was the victim this time.

Much to the surprise of *El Día*'s readers—and its editors—a line showed up one morning in the "Situations Wanted" classified ads saying, in street slang, "Homosexual military men." The military rulers of the country took offense, even though the editors charged that it was clearly sabotage. After police made a perfunctory search in the printing plant for the culprit, the punishment for the newspaper was announced: 10 days' suspension; expulsion of the director, an Argentine citizen, from the country; and removal of tax preferences which all newspapers received, thus the equivalent of a large fine. *El Día* was already financially anemic, and it approached its centennial date with some doubt that it would survive.

Although shutdowns have been rare in Chile, they have been dramatic enough to draw international attention. Nearly all leftist publications and radio stations were closed overnight, never to reappear, when the military ousted the Allende government in 1973. This lightning action—perhaps the most decisively effective restriction of media in Latin American history—largely eliminated the need for later closures or suspensions. A widely reported exception was the repeated suspension of a radio station speaking for the Christian Democratic Party.

The Chilean junta also has been more assiduous than other governments in making its shutdowns legal, if not constitutional. It carefully reshaped an older emergency-powers law and produced a decree which spelled out the procedures for six-day or six-issue suspension of mass media. The grounds for the penalty remained vague, however.

The Brazilian military government, with its vast apparatus of legalized repression, has largely desisted from shutting down media. Shutdowns would be inconsistent with its great concern for economic rationality in all that it does; rather, it concentrates on making sure the need for shutdowns does not arise.

However, the Venezuelan government, generally considered to be democratic, has shown itself quite ready to halt the operations of a broadcaster or publisher. Officials shut down a television station for three days and raided newspaper plants with intent to stop them in separate incidents in 1976.

These actions apparently are the result of long conditioning of the Venezuelan government during democratic periods. It has had chronic problems with

leftist terrorists, and its use of closure powers against publications aiding terrorism goes back nearly two decades.

In countries where the media are absorbed by the state, as in Cuba, or
highly collaborative, as in Mexico, little need for media shutdowns exists. At
the other extreme, the very existence of a disclosive-adversary stance on the
part of the media is an indication that the government has abandoned the option
of the padlock.

Seizure of Copies

Although always secondary to other forms of control, seizure of a publication's issues stands ready as a weapon for all authoritarian governments and
some democratic ones. It is almost as swift and decisive a control as closure,
although it does put police or soldiers in a comic light when they must scurry
around the city grabbing copies from distribution points and newsstands. It
also is much hard work for an hour or so.

Universal legal customs offer some basis for a claim that such actions are
proper. This is because, when a crime is alleged, officials may seize evidence
of the supposed offense. If a court later acquits the defendant, of course, the
evidence is returned to him. But nothing is so useless as an outdated news
publication, and the publisher must relegate his copies—which cost him tens of
thousands of dollars to produce—to the city dump. Even one such episode can
start him on the road to financial ruin.

Seizure of issues must be viewed as a closely related alternative to censorship. In countries where efficient censorship does not exist, such as in
Argentina, seizure is intended to accomplish the same end—stoppage of specific content. But it is crude and inefficient, because material covering dozens
of pages will be killed for the sake of one article.

Once a government seizes copies of a newspaper, magazine or book, it has
an embarrassment on its hands. This is because, unless it returns the goods to
the owner later, it must dispose of them. Since the brutal bookburning under
Hitler and Mussolini, world public opinion has become so sensitive to the
"murder of knowledge" that Latin American dictators have avoided such spec-
tacles if at all possible. Startling reports of bookburning incidents emerged
from Chile during the post-coup excitement in 1973, although the government
denied—with apparent basis—that it was responsible. Similarly, the supposed
purge of subversive books from a public university library two years later also
went unconfirmed.

In Argentina, the various governments were even more cautious following
the publicity which arose from a bookburning by military officials in 1971.
Seizures continued, but the cases were always taken before the courts, which
retained some independence. Argentines also are familiar with the electronic
equivalent of publication seizure—jamming of radio signals. An Argentine-
owned station across the river in Uruguay from Buenos Aires is well known for
carrying the most unfettered news to be heard in the capital. During tense times
in the 1960s and 1970s, the Argentine government would blot out the alien signal with a constant buzzing sound.

The Brazilian and Peruvian militarists resorted to the seizure device in ways similar to those of their colleagues in Chile and Argentina during the 1970s. The independent media knew that seizure would be invoked with enough provocation but that this came rarely. Furthermore, the generals tried to keep the appearance of justice alive in their courts, and in at least one case the Peruvian government reimbursed a seizure-afflicted paper for its losses.

Somewhat more disquieting to those who equate free elections with free speech has been the experience in Venezuela. Several times during the mid-1970s, publications were either seized or threatened with seizure. In a sense, justice is even more uncertain in this democracy than in the dictatorships, as the military has the legal power to take civilians into custody and try them when the alleged offense is against the armed services. Just how far-reaching is this power was demonstrated when the military seized copies of a leftist weekly in which a legislator had insulted the national president; the rationale was that the president was commander of the armed forces, and so the case was a military one.

Control of Personnel

The specter of government manipulation of the media for its purposes through personnel control has constantly loomed up in the fears of Latin American publishers. They have seen how communist and fascist dictatorships in other parts of the world, particularly Spain under Franco, have insured a complaisant press simply by guarding the door of entrance to the profession. If the state has the power to license these professionals and uses self-serving criteria in doing so, no other controls are needed.

Rightist dictatorships in Latin America have never shown a penchant for exercising this control, although the leftist ones in Cuba and Peru have. The latter do it simply by naming reliable supporters as directors of the media, and the directors in turn appoint subordinates who are of like mind. This does not by any means offer a rigid, unchanging solution for the government; directors have been replaced frequently as national policies change and as the directors show some independence and displease the regime.

Ironically, the most heated controversy about licensing has come from democratic countries. This is related to the movement to establish *colegios,* which resemble the medieval craftsmen's guilds which protected the quality of work by making sure that anyone who entered the craft was qualified—and that once he got in he was paid adequately. The practice in Latin America separates *colegios* from labor unions, which often exist alongside them. *Colegios* usually do not bargain for contracts but rather try to keep an oversupply of poorly educated, low-earning journalists out of the job market. Among other things, they foster education through support of journalism schools and through organizing seminars of their own.

Organizers of the *colegios,* usually those reporters with the most professional spirit, have found most publishers are not inclined to implement *colegio* goals voluntarily. Regardless of which is the cause and which the effect, publishers continue to hire untrained youngsters and underpay them, and youths imbued with the romance of journalism continue to overfill the labor pool. In a sort of occupational Gresham's Law, the few qualified journalists despair of the poor pay and move on to public relations or government, driven out by the less competent. In recent years protests have come increasingly from another quarter—the community being poorly served, particularly the politicians.

Colegio organizers have concluded they can and must get the force of law behind their efforts. They have framed statutes which usually call for professional licenses to be granted upon completing a university journalism degree and/or passing a wide-ranging academic examination devised by educators or journalists (not media directors). Such laws always allow for a transition period during which journalists with about five years' experience before passage of the law are exempt from the requirements. Directors can be charged with a crime for hiring anyone without a license. Furthermore, the *colegio* or a similar group could revoke a journalist's license for breach of ethics.

Chile had the first such law, passed in 1956, although it has never been fully implemented. With the hemispheric vogue of legally enforced journalistic reform in the 1970s, the movement began spreading like wildfire. Costa Rica's law started the new wave, followed by Venezuela and then Colombia. The Dominican Republic was struggling over its law late in the decade, and others were beginning to follow suit.

Publishers, smarting over the prospect of having to pay more for new reporters, looked for a flaw in the plan and easily found it—the inadequacy of journalism schools. Dr. Raymond B. Nixon, commissioned by the Council of Higher Education in the Americas to survey Latin America's journalism schools in 1969, reported a ''marked discontent'' with them in comparison with a survey seven years before. He added that professors, students, working journalists and editors agreed ''to a surprisingly high degree'' on the deficiencies and needs of journalism education.[2] Although it was widely conceded also that the only way to improve the schools would be through collaboration between them and news media, little has been done in this direction.

Another charge brought against the *colegio* laws is that they effectively take away from publishers the sole power to decide who can be hired; it also is often predicted that the government will use the law to allow only its political supporters access to the profession. The first charge is clearly valid, although no publisher has lost real control over his staff. The second one has never been borne out by experience. Even so, many publishers say the danger of the laws lies not in what they are doing but what they *might* do. *Colegio* laws consistently were stirring fiery speeches in meetings of the Inter-American Press Association late in the 1970s. When Pedro Penzini, a Caracas daily publisher and IAPA board member, remarked at such a meeting that *colegio* laws appeared to be a fact of life, he was angrily condemned by several colleagues.[3]

Economic Controls

Although seldom relied upon as a major form of media restriction, economic measures taken consciously to control media are important in nearly all the authoritarian countries. Such measures often result from poor-nation problems as well as efforts to weaken an opposition press, but the democratic countries are notably free of them. At the other extreme, media which are totally absorbed into the state also are not menaced by them, because the government must protect its own family.

As has been noted, national leaders who have wanted to rid themselves of troublesome media—particularly publications—have learned that an overt assault will earn them black marks with world public opinion. But if they simply make it difficult for a publication to cope commercially, it will become too weak to be appealing to the public and eventually will die. This makes no headlines, and observers will pay their respects to the pitiless law of the marketplace and remark that the death of such a weak competitor was a mercy to all concerned.

Censorship and seizure can accomplish this weakening, but they also earn scorn for the government because they deal with content. Economic controls are considered less despicable even though the result is the same. They also can appear to be benign; economic favors can tame a troublesome publication as readily as punishment.

One group of economic controls centers on the money the government itself allocates; these might be called *financial* pressures. Another group, through which the government sets the conditions under which the mass medium must seek its income, has to do with *operational* pressures.

All types of Latin American states are becoming steadily larger participants in business, nationalizing banks, insurance companies, lending agencies, some manufacturing fields, petroleum and mining, and many more. Since such businesses must sell their products, they must advertise. When this vast array of official advertisers is allied with the governmental agencies which constantly publish routine public notices—school examinations, job openings, requests for bids, etc.—the state shapes up as massively important to the advertising media.

So advertising by government agencies and by industries wholly or partly owned by the state makes up one of the largest financial pressures. This can effect the medium by pouring in revenues—and also by refusing to pay its due bills for this service. Tax laws fall into this category. They also have two faces—the government can collect, and it can neglect to collect. Other financial pressures are extending or refusing such assistance as credit, foreign exchange currency allotments, and bribes.

Operational pressures consist of laws or regulations that set the ways the mass medium must handle its advertising, deal with labor unions, import supplies, and determine selling prices. The state also can affect operations by stimulating and controlling the sources of a publication's supplies.

Pinpointing direct effects of government advertising is almost impossible, as no publisher wants to admit that he depends on the official feed trough. Usually he will point to the relatively small role of government agencies but shrug off the large one of state-owned businesses.

However, in at least three countries—Mexico, Argentina, and Brazil—the power of state advertising over publishers is widely acknowledged. In Mexico, where the government wins its way with the media more through the carrot than through the stick, official payments for space form one of the major methods of such influence. Straight-forward advertising comes from state-owned enterprises such as an airline, the lottery and movie theaters. But vast amounts of editorial space is paid for as disguised advertisements by government officials—and anyone else who wants to pay. Cabinet ministers often use this device more for their personal political ends than for the purposes of the general government. However, the president himself can control a large part of the flow when he wants to, as happened in former President Echeverría's successful campaign to depose a combative director of the country's leading newspaper.

Reinforcing the effects of official advertising is the Mexican custom of placing each agency's orders through the reporter covering that agency, thus assuring him of a large commission. This elicits his sympathy as well as that of the publisher.

Another way a government can get extra benefits from its advertising money is to distribute it through an agency which also carries the official news service, which usually has propagandistic overtones. This way the advertising can be used as bait to get the media to buy the news service and publish its stories. Argentina has witnessed this stratagem under several governments; the official agency Telam is the vehicle.

Placing orders for media space or time is one thing, but paying for it is another. Governments have been known to fall behind scores of thousands of dollars in payments for their ads. Both the prestige dailes of Buenos Aires, *La Nación* and *La Prensa,* have suffered from such delays, and when finally paid they usually get currency vastly deflated from what it was worth when the ads ran.

Media must contend not only with national governments but also lower levels of administration which may have the power to advertise. Thus in Brazil, where the federal government has not been a major offender in this matter, state governors have a notorious tendency to punish media by cutting off ads. One rather wealthy newspaper, *O Estado de São Paolo,* retaliated against such a threat by itself banning the state's ads from its pages. When its publishers realized the people needed the information in the ads, they still refused payment but ran them free.

Taxes offer a method both to chasten all the media and, through selective enforcement, to put pressure on individual units. Raids can be carried out against media offices to seize accounting books, and inspectors can find large delinquencies in tax payments. This is basically what happened during the Allende regime in Chile, particularly against the major daily *El Mercurio;* however, the evidence indicates that the charge was true in the case of *El Mercurio,* as it was for many papers which were not raided. *El Mercurio* was allowed to pay off its debt on easy terms, but governments in other countries have used this type of pressure more effectively. They can "forget" to collect such debts as social security payments owed by media. The Argentine government used such delinquencies as one of its reasons for canceling the licenses of independent Buenos Aires television stations. The Mexican government, on the other hand, uses a very long leash. It continues to allow newspapers to fall behind on taxes, and this practice constantly reminds publishers of the financial difficulties that news and editorials could cause.

Mexican politicians also excel at another device for controlling the media—bribes. The custom of officials' offering bribes or journalists' demanding them has long standing in Latin America. It was the favorite control of the old-line despots who began fading from the scene after the 1960s; Fulgencio Batista of Cuba was the best-known practitioner of this art, but there were many others. The more moralistic, nonpolitical dictators of the 1970s shun this as beneath their dignity. Even the strait-laced José López Portillo, who was chosen for the Mexican presidency in 1976, greatly reduced this outlay as a waste, but there was no indication that it was dying in that country.

A slight variation on the bribe system draws on the modern arts of public administration. This is the practice of hiring a flock of "public relations consultants" for every official agency, and who better can perform this job than the reporters assigned to that agency? These reporters have learned that they not only get paid for their cooperation but can get preferences on the release of news. Some competitors of *La Nación* in Buenos Aires ruefully admit that it outpaces them in official news because it has the most reporters on the government payroll.

Media are becoming big business nowadays, and thus they often need credit to operate. Since banking has been a favorite target for nationalization throughout the area, a publisher seeking a loan often must take his request to a representative of the government. This funding power has been used for political ends in many places, and Mexico is the most flagrant example. A state lending agency there became the proud owner of a chain of nearly 40 newspapers—by far the largest in the country—when it foreclosed on loans. But sometimes the credit-giving role of the Mexican state is used simply to enrich all the parties to a transaction—including the private owner. A property can be foreclosed, sold, and resold so many times the observing public becomes cynical about the whole matter.

Since most Latin American governments are chronically short of hard currency, they must ration it among domestic businesses which want to buy this currency to spend on imported supplies. Mass media are considered nonessential luxuries, particularly when troublesome to the government. So media directors constantly face problems—although usually not insurmountable ones—in getting their foreign exchange money; this was notably true in Chile under Allende, when broadcasters were cut off almost completely from their suppliers. Even when the currency exchange is freely granted, media like other businesses often must put their domestic currency on deposit several months before they can convert it.

Controls on advertising, one of the operational measures, reflect a general disgust with commercial promotion which is being expressed increasingly in Latin American public life, particularly among leftist reformers. To them advertising represents all that is greedy and exploitative in native industrial barons and in the reformers' most hated target—the multinational corporations based in the major industrial nations. To some Latin Americans, obeying the command to "Drink Coca-Cola!" is a step toward sophistication; to others, it is cultural treason. One can understand the reformers' revulsion when the panorama of Latin American advertising is viewed. Compared with the North American version which it imitates, it is far more simplistic, repetitious and snobbish. The reformers are particularly anxious to protect the gullible poor from deception.

The Peruvian government has been the most active in devising regulations to this end. It has prohibited the most high-pressure of sales appeals—those which include direct commands. Also, it has insisted that ads go through a cultural translation and leave out foreign symbols of the "good life" such as yachts and U.S. movie stars. Ads must be produced in Peru, thus giving work to local technicians. The government also banned the Yankee super-salesman, Santa Claus, for several years until it had suffered enough ridicule and quietly forgot the ruling.

The second Perón government in Argentina, fighting to control consumer prices, sponsored a law intended to keep advertising from driving the sales tags upward. Since the country's economic chaos already was discouraging the purchase of advertising, the regulations reduced the media's income even more deeply. Furthermore, they did not prevent runaway inflation.

Aside from ceilings on advertising prices, the per-copy sales prices of publications also often are limited while inflation is soaring. This can result in a newspaper's damaging itself with every copy it sells because production costs rise faster than income; such was the case in Peru before the 1974 newspaper expropriation, when the independent press was repeatedly weakened by unrealistic price ceilings.

Labor unions have succeeded in getting laws passed which restrict the management's latitude severely, particularly in Peru, Argentina and Mexico. These laws enable them to sabotage a business for their own purposes or for those of the government, which can manipulate them to undermine the owners. This was a prime technique in the takeover of the independent press by the Fidel Castro regime in Cuba. A variation was seen in the overthrow of director Julio Scherer García of *Excélsior* in Mexico City; the nation's president, Luis Echeverría, arranged for agents to infiltrate the cooperative which owned the paper and vote Scherer out of office.

Governments have been playing a large role in stimulating and controlling the supply of printing paper, both newsprint and the higher grades needed by magazines. Chile is the only country in the region self-sufficient in newsprint, although others are expanding their production. The Mexican and Peruvian governments have actively promoted the use of bagasse (sugar cane pulp) as a raw material in place of the conifer trees they lack. The state has also formed a partnership with big newspapers in Argentina to increase tree production and thus make more paper.

Mexico's long-standing scheme to help newspapers get newsprint through the agency called Pipsa has won it a dubious place in history. The practice is almost universally abhorred by foreign observers, who see in it an incestuous arrangement to subsidize newspapers while making them obligated to the government. Newspapers who cooperate in the plan are given tax rebates which reduce the price of imported newsprint. Since they buy from the agency, they also are constantly in debt to it. This was the major factor in the foreclosure which led to the state's becoming owner of a large newspaper chain.

The Allende government in Chile tried to buy control of that country's newsprint industry but was defeated by aroused newspaper publishers and workers in the industry.

The government's role as an advertiser was noted earlier, but it can also affect the operations of a mass medium by pressuring private advertisers to cancel or reduce their orders to media. This is a nearly universal practice in varying degrees, even in democracies, because the "buddy system" is so widely accepted in all phases of life. It has been particularly useful in Brazil in the case of weekly publications which have disturbed the government.

STATE OWNERSHIP, MANAGEMENT AND PROPAGANDA

Every government in Latin America except Cuba has committed itself to maintaining at least some private ownership in the mass media. Even in Cuba, where public life was slowly becoming more pluralistic in the late 1970s, there have been indications that organized groups—loyal to the regime but competitive intramurally—were destined to get their own media and thus crack the monolith of state-owned media.

On the other hand, every government has to some degree become a media owner. Among the properties are the full range of media—newspapers, magazines, domestic television and radio (either stations or networks), foreign shortwave radio systems, news services and advertising agencies. Almost universally, states have bought transmission facilities—telephone and telegraph—from the former private owners; unlike the mass media, these are considered feasible only as monopolies.

The most prevalent concept outside Cuba regarding state ownership is that the state should be one of the competitors for the public's attention. Just how heavily it weighs in against its rivals varies. In Peru, the state presence towers above the private one, while in others such as Costa Rica and Honduras it is minuscule.[4]

State acquisition of media has not been spreading in most Latin American countries in recent years. Even the one with the most explosive burst of such activity—Peru in the 1970–74 period—has been trying to extract itself from its role as a newspaper publisher.

The reason for this reluctance is that governments rarely can avoid losing large sums of money on media, even when they try to operate commercially. This stems partly from bureaucrats' penchant for content which bores the public and alienates advertisers, particularly in television. Sheer incompetence in management also is a frequent cause for the losses.

Nearly all Latin American governments were facing up to the necessity for financial austerity in the late 1970s. They were having to pay the bills for the reformist splurges of the 1960s and 1970s, and international creditors were demanding that they tighten their belts.

Thus other methods of controlling the media have proved more attractive to governments. Even democratic ones of a liberal bent, such as Costa Rica and Venezuela, are slowing their efforts to make over the media for the purpose of social rather than political change.

Propaganda activities, on the other hand, have been showing a mild increase, especially on the international scene. Having a shortwave radio service to "tell the (Chilean, Brazilian, etc.) story to the world" has become a status symbol among smaller nations as they seek the sort of prominence conferred by Voice of America, BBC, Radio Moscow and Radio Havana on their respective governments. As the various right-wing dictatorships have come under foreign criticism for their human rights abuses and their financial position has suffered, shortwave is seen as a defensive measure.

Internal propaganda has become the most essential function of the media in Cuba, although information and entertainment play small roles. The approach largely follows the one followed by older communist regimes—examples of socialist heroism, heavy-handed theorizing and reports of official celebrations. In addition, the personality of the maximum leader—Fidel Castro—is relied upon to carry the messages, much as was the case with Mao Tse-tung in China.

However, most other governments have proven either too timid or too inept for internal propaganda to become a significant force. Only in Brazil does a longterm campaign have professional polish, although even there the public tends to treat it with no more seriousness than it would a Coca-Cola advertisement. Generally in Latin America, times of crisis such as the aftermath of a coup or the canal treaty excitement in Panama are the only times the output of the propaganda mills reaches noticeable proportions.

The paroxysm of publicity that always accompanies election campaigns is not considered here because this is nominally outside the governmental structure. However, the semi-officialist nature of the leading parties in Mexico and Brazil make their propaganda almost merit inclusion in this category. Mexico has the one-party rule it does largely because of the massive glorification of officials' deeds, snuffing out any sparks of support for opposition parties. Although the Brazilian government has been scrupulous sometimes in giving the opposition a chance to be heard, this leniency has disappeared when it appeared possible that the ''outs'' might win too many elections.

An odd twist on election propaganda occurred in Venezuela in 1978 when outgoing Predisent Carlos Andrés Pérez tried to assure his place in history by a splurge of government advertising during his final months in office. In a sort of serial valedictory, Pérez' aides devoted each ad (placed in a wide variety of media) to glorifying some aspect of his administration. The emphasis always was given to a smiling photo of Pérez and the slogan, ''Step by step the action of the government is being accomplished.''

CONTENT CONTROLS

Latin American governments exert prior control over content of the media—as distinguished from punishment for what they disseminate—in five basic ways:

1. Notifying editors on an ad hoc basis as to currently ''hot'' topics which they must not touch.

2. Passing laws which specify which types of content must not be published or broadcast.

3. Official censorship of the material (inspecting and sometimes killing the copy before it reaches the distribution stage).

4. Forcing a medium to publish or broadcast verbatim releases from the government.

5. Secrecy as to government actions, sometimes called censorship at the source.

The first option is by far the most frequently employed. The second necessitates a stability and preciseness which few governments in the area possess, and the third calls for a bureaucarcy highly trained in a trade for which there are few instructors. So there are few job applicants who have both the qualifications and the stomach for the work.

Forcible publication is a common tool of authoritarian governments, although it is rarely taken to extremes. Secrecy, which is taken for granted in all countries, runs into a cross-current of talkativeness which sometimes negates it.

Notification and Laws

The director of an Ecuadorian provincial daily newspaper was clearly upset as he talked with a foreign visitor. He had just lived through the humiliation of having to censor urgent news from his own newspaper. Police striking for better benefits had battled with troops in Quito, the capital, and a military official had telephoned all news media and asked them not to mention it. The editors agreed, but soldiers came around to double-check their proofs that night anyway. Now the editors, frustrated not only by the request but by the insulting inspection, were organizing a protest against their not being trusted to censor themselves.[5]

The most unusual aspect of this episode was the editors' reaction. Telephone calls asking or demanding that specific stories be deleted from the day's news are common practice in all but the most democratic of Latin American countries. Most often, the editor tries to keep his embarrassment as private as possible and does not publicize the order, even to his colleagues. He simply exercises his prerogative to kill stories without explanation.

The phoned order usually comes only when a crisis is most intense—and thus most newsworthy. Since such peaks are encountered only occasionally in news coverage, editors have time between phone calls to forget the ignominy.

But governments want rules that last longer than a passing crisis, and for this they put their desires on paper. These take the form of laws, usually in the form of decrees, since dictatorships are more prone to such restrictions than are parliamentary democracies. They also are issued in the form of special regulations or "advisories" related to some continuing set of events, such as the visit of a foreign dignitary. If the regulations appear to wear well and the need for them recurs, governments dignify them by changing them into decree laws.

Brazil furnishes the prime example of both oral and written notices. The local military or police authorities frequently telephone editors, and new written rules are always to be expected for such phenomena as a presidential succession, the visit of a head of state, or even a social trend such as streaking. In turn, the ideas behind these rules are put into more general terms as statutes. A final step is to make them amendments to the constitution, which is a simple process under the military regime.

Collecting all the Brazilian laws and permanent regulations that could be found, this writer isolated 47 distinct types, and some of these even had subcategories. (See Appendix.) They touch on almost every type of material that a ruler could object to, although the way is open to provide more if the need arises.

It is notable, however, that the texts of many Brazilian restrictions make gestures at justifying them; for example, they prohibit actions which would have certain undesirable effects on society. Typical are laws which make criminal offenses out of publishing material which provokes "ill-feeling" in the military, damages family morality, prejudices the national economic policy or attracts attention to crimes. But these laws against effects rather than actions alone actually provide an escape route for some defendants with good lawyers. Some impartial judges remain, and they try to extract justice from the constitution, even when their action goes against the interests of the government. So if the lawyer can show that the offense did not bring about the effect—or that the punishment is prohibited otherwise by the constitution—defendants have been known to be released from such charges.

This is equally true in other countries under authoritarian governments. Most of them came to power proclaiming the need for law and order, and they consider it better for their images to lose an occasional court case than to destroy the prestige of the courts. Journalists often see this as their last and perhaps only line of defense. The director of the *Buenos Aires Herald,* Robert Cox, while still under charges of aiding subversives through news he printed, expressed gratitude for the treatment he was receiving from the courts. He eventuallly was cleared of all charges.[6]

In all countries, journalists must abide by general laws of subversion, defamation, pornography or the like. Liberal democracies in the West have generally avoided special press laws in the belief that this would create a precedent for special controls. However, Latin America's traditional emphasis on legalism has led to an almost universal adoption of press laws and, for the broadcast media, additional regulations about use of the airwaves.

Many of these laws and broadcast regulations originated several decades ago and generally are considered toothless because they have been made obsolete by changes in media practices and technology or simply by legal customs. Venezuela, for instance, has a law which says all broadcast material must be censored; this has long been ignored.

Such an arrangement has proved to be a workable compromise. Governments have the comfort of knowing they possess a weapon if needed. Although journalists are left uncertain as to the limits of their freedom, most prefer the unknown dangers of darkness to the clear threat of daylight. Thus when the military government of Chile dusted off an old internal security law passed under a democratic government in 1949 and reissued it as a decree law, the press arose in furious protest. The point at issue was that the junta had put enforcement in the hands of local military commanders, who would not be paralyzed by legal niceties. The government was puzzled at the reaction, because the new law actually gave the defendants avenues of appeal they did not have before.

Costa Rica's press law offers an example of the least restrictive ones. The offenses it punishes are largely confined to defamation of individuals (not the government) and interference with the nation's foreign policy, such as incitement of war or insults to resident diplomats.[7]

Nevertheless, control through notification and laws basically rests with the journalist himself as the enforcer. Its logic draws on two assumptions: (1) the journalist can and will apply the restrictions to himself, a process called self-censorship (*autocensura*), and (2) the government is willing and able to punish him for failing to do so.

To make self-censorship easier for the journalist, governments have adopted the practice of providing "advice" when called upon. Standing somewhat in the role of consulting attorneys, government experts on prohibited content are available with simply a telephone call from the journalist. This way the journalist can protect himself against post-publication punishment.

With rare exceptions, self-censorship *has* become a way of life for journalists throughout Latin America. Governmental pressures account for most of this, although regard for terrorists, for the interests of one's employer and for the party affiliated with the medium plays a strong role. In the author's interviews with hundreds of journalists across the hemisphere, no aspect of the profession was mentioned so universally as self-censorship.

Because of this general acceptance of what is considered as inevitable, the need for punishment is minimal. When punishment does occur, it usually takes the form of closing or suspending the medium or seizing copies of a publication. Terrorism, sometimes inspired by the government, is used in some cases. Officials generally avoid openly punishing an individual for his writings, as this exposes them to worldwide ridicule and makes a martyr of the person.

Official Censorship

Although careless use of terms has resulted in applying the word censorship to all forms of media control, it is intended here only in the strict sense of inspection and possible banning of media content before distribution.

Censorship has been a conventional tool of media control for decades in most Latin American countries, but rarely has it been a significant restraint on journalism. Although entertainment media re policed to some extent in all the countries, governments generally have preferred to avoid the massive problems posed by censorship of news media.

The main exception to this hesitance comes during times of political crisis. It has become almost a cliché for censors to follow on the heels of military coup-makers. Their purpose is to prevent publication of any material that might excite the populace, as the new rulers' primary goal other than suppression of armed resistance is always a façade of calm control. No sooner is the first shot fired than uniformed officers show up in newspaper and broadcast offices. Aside from inserting some of their own pronouncements, they usually leave most of the editing to the regular staff members. After three or four days of reading a newspaper's typewritten copy, galley and page proofs or the first copy off the press, they manage to intimidate the staff and satisfy themselves there is no danger. Then they disappear before international protests have time to take shape.

Short of being a hangman, a censor has probably the least admired job in government. He is the butt of ridicule everywhere, even in dictatorships, because the most intelligent of his breed will inevitably make ludicrous oversights or deletions. For this reason the general level of intellectual and mental health of those who can be attracted to the work is minimal. This was indicated when the news leaked out that 21 of Brazil's 90 censors were being fired because they had scored too low in a psychological inspection test given by the government itself.[8]

One military government, Brazil, and one democracy, Colombia, provide the area's only examples of systematic censorship on public affairs, as opposed to arts and entertainment. Even in those countries it is slowly falling into disuse because of the burden on the government.

Brazil's censorship of journalistic print media was lifted completely in 1978; even before that, it had covered only about a half-dozen at any given time, although the ones under inspection varied from year to year. Among the most consistent were a highly political Rio daily and several of the leading weeklies with national circulation, particularly those emphasizing satire. The country's most famous newspaper, *O Estado de São Paulo,* also was under censorship for three years ending in 1975 because it had refused to censor itself.

Just how, when and where Brazilian censorship would be applied was highly unpredictable. No one knew from week to week which print media would be under inspection. Censors in one city would be more harsh than others, some news stories would be hit harder than others in the same category, and some publication would suffer more than others. Since the government did not talk publicly about censorship policies, some observers speculated that the erratic performance resulted from weaknesses of the system; some said it indicated a deliberate effort to demoralize journalists; some said it was both.

One aspect of censorship in Brazil was clear to all concerned: It, like economic controls, was carefully wielded to slowly exterminate publications which the government disliked. Since the government has avoided controls such as licensing and closure, it waits for indirect restrictions to result in a publication's death by seemingly natural causes. Many times, opposition dailies or weeklies would be told by censors to drop the same story that ran without trouble in other publications. After months during which the publication was unable to print what the public could read elsewhere, buyers and advertisers slipped away and the enterprise collapsed for lack of money.

The Brazilian government provided two types of censorship service—in-house and remote. Larger, more frequent or more prestigious publications such as *O Estado* were honored by assignment of a censor to come to their offices; the Catholic weekly *O São Paulo* also had this privilege. Others such as the leftist weekly *Movimento* and the satirical publication *Pasquim* had to send each week's articles off to Brasilia from their offices on the coast; in a mad panic to meet the press deadline, they had to re-edit their pages at the last minute after a third or more of the material was killed by the faceless censors in the capital.

In the early 1970s, censored Brazilian publications used various stratagems to signal to their readers that some story had been deleted—leaving a blank space, printing some other story in two spaces or simply running comically absurd substitutes such as recipes or cartoons. However, the censors gradually got tougher and stamped out such practices.

In both Brazil and Colombia, regular and thorough censorship of broadcast news is taken for granted. Such efficiency is possible because television and radio process far less news copy than newspapers do. Scripts can be demanded at a fixed time period before air time, such as an hour, and returned quickly to the station with deletions marked.

Aside from material cut on moral grounds, the kind of content most often sought out by censors in all countries is that which would stir up public unrest, as noted above. This is the principal justification for Colombia's restrictions, and most other democracies have been known to resort to it when a breakdown in law and order are imminent.

A variation on this—preventing media from giving information on terrorists and thus presumably encouraging them—has become an obsession with some governments. Several recent Argentine governments' efforts to prohibit publicity for terrorists has become a major point of conflict between the state and the managers of media.

News about conflict among political parties also is a frequent subject for censorship. The kinds of governments which impose censorship are likely to be the ones that want to keep parties' activity either suppressed or tightly controlled, and one of the handiest ways to do this is to keep their pronouncements out of the media.

Censorship on moral grounds—sex and violence—is to be found throughout the area in varying degrees. Since it rarely stirs any protest stronger than grumbling from the publics, it can provide a convenient mask for what is really political censorship. More than once, particularly in Brazil, content has been deleted because it remotely resembles morally offensive material. The film "All Nudity Will Be Punished," a Brazilian product which won praise abroad, was banned from domestic showing ostensibly because it dealt with the life of a prostitute, but its reflections on the Brazilian class structure were generally believed to be the real reason.

Entertainment and the arts have, on the whole, suffered even more from censorship than has journalism. This is partly because persons in these fields usually do not have powerful publishers behind them and partly because almost anything they produce can be attacked on moral grounds, whether the censor is looking for sex, criticism of society, depiction of drug abuse or other crimes, violence, poverty, injustice or any other of the more sordid sides of life. Even internationally famed writers are not immune from restriction.

Unpredictability of censorship can cause financial ruin to producers of art and entertainment, because often the censors will inspect a movie, book, phonograph record, play or stage show only after it is ready for the public and huge sums of money have been risked. If the production is stopped at that point, the producer may never recover from his loss. Thus some of the most creative Argentine and Brazilian film makers have given up in despair, going abroad or confining themselves to safe, harmless, B-grade films.

Indecision over whether to do their best work and risk ruin is a constant dilemma for the area's entertainers and artists, but a surprising number keep their integrity. Brazil's world-famous novelists and popular musicians have deliberately produced work they know will bring trouble, and they often must rely on income from sales and performances abroad. In a similar situation is Peru's renowned novelist Mario Vargas Llosa, who pursues his leftist philosophy on a different track from the socialist generals who run the country; consequently he has run into difficulty getting his books and a movie based on one of them distributed at home.

Forced Publication

A standard article of faith among the media reformers of the 1970s was that a news medium should be forced to give space or air time to be used by anyone who feels injured by the medium, and the editor's pencil must not intervene between writing and publication of the protest. A related proposal sometimes made is that politicians, in and out of government, be given a free platform even if not injured. The main argument supporting these changes is that the largest and most respected media are owned by special interests, political or economic, who use the media to advance or conserve their positions. This is often true, although most of such media gained their followings by being so individualistic and appealing to a certain faction.

An unspoken argument underlying all assumptions about public access laws is that libel statutes play little part in Latin American societies, although all governments have them. Few people take recourse to them, and few court judgments are made against news media. So anyone who feels wronged in the public debate generally seeks justice through reply rather than judicial punishment.

Efforts to require media to give offended parties free space or to correct errors have been made mostly in the democratic countries, although gestures in this direction have been made throughout the region. Venezuela requires journalists of all types to rectify errors they have made and forbids them to ''corrupt intentionally the opinions and declarations of third parties.''[9] Colombia imposes a similar obligation on radio broadcasters.[10]

Costa Rica attracted much attention abroad when a law was introduced in its congress requiring newspapers to devote 4% to 6% of their daily space to verbatim statements by government officials. This would have meant that up to three full pages would be lost to the editors of a 50-page newspaper. After much dispute and after vehement criticism of the measure by the media, the idea was dropped.[11]

Governments of all types in Latin America typically require broadcasters to donate up to two hours a day for official purposes, ranging from pseudo-newscasts to educational programs. These tend to be aired in non-prime time, and little protest is heard. Also, the national president can always pre-empt air time for his speeches, but the disappearance in the 1970s of the personalistic dictators led to a decrease in Hitlerian posturing.

A thoroughly familiar practice in authoritarian countries is the requirement that news media publish or broadcast official statements from the government—verbatim. All dictatorships retain this prerogative, but they were exercising it with steadily less frequency in the 1970s. It smacked of the brutality from which they wanted to dissociate themselves; furthermore, most newspapers were quite willing, even in democratic countries, to quote high officials at tedious length without coercion. Editors did take it as a matter of ethics to distinguish coercive bulletins, when they were published, with typographical signals such as bold type or a headline kicker such as "official space." Generally, such arrangements were necessary only in times of crisis, when the governments did not trust the editors to cooperate.

Secrecy

The idea that government must speak with one voice and that this voice must be tuned seductively has been rejected by most liberal democracies around the world. It has been considered far safer for a variety of spokesmen to be heard, no matter how raucous or confusing the sound may be. Reporters are thus allowed to seek their information where it lies, even to observing the arguments within the government and perhaps taking peeks at confidential documents. Basically their license dates back three centuries to John Milton, who argued that only through the open conflict of various versions could the truth emerge.

But in the 1970s, the one-voice concept was on the rise in the most disparately governed countries of Latin America. The factors at work appeared to be:

1. The eagerness of many university-trained bureaucrats to apply "administrative science," which abhors the untidiness of open doors and file cabinets.

2. The upsurge of military dictatorships in many areas, entailing a philosophy in which information (intelligence) is considered to be a weapon to be protected and to be used against the enemy.

3. The emergence, in both democracies and dictatorships, of those officials who see information as an instrument for social engineering. Since the private media owners who employ reporters usually have no interest in assisting this manipulation, the social engineers ensure that the kind of information that goes out from government offices is not the kind that would put government reform projects in a bad light and thus diminish public support from them.

The mechanisms for controlling information at its source consist mainly of information ministries and official or collaborative news services.

Information ministries still are considered upstarts among the older ones such as defense and foreign affairs. Typically one will germinate in the lowly press office of the president. In the image-conscious 1970s, presidential press agents often had Rasputin-like power, and they would try to convert their offices into secretariats or even ministries, sometimes with success. Meanwhile, public relations offices have proliferated in the other ministries and departments; while these try to shape the information outflow for the benefit of their chiefs, the central information director tries to eliminate them as threats to his own power.

Another way information ministries enlarge their scope is to absorb the functions of regulating the broadcast industry and, in some cases, operating government broadcast systems. Thus what started largely as a technical activity of government—setting channel frequencies and the like—becomes enmeshed in an an effort to influence citizens' thought patterns.

Such ministries also take charge of the government's propaganda activities, previously discussed. Included in this is the authority to administer placement of all advertisement orders.

Aside from the centralized control the Castro government in Cuba has had over media since the mid-1960s, two other experiments with high-level information departments have been witnessed in Latin American. These are in Peru and Venezuela.

Peru's National System of Information (SINADI), while still not at ministerial rank, has sweeping powers approaching those in Cuba. Under its control are the expropriated dailies of Lima, the broadcast system, official advertising, propaganda, governmental information, and two news agencies. While the media—both official and private—have some latitude for independence, SINADI steadily increased its scope of authority in the 1970s. Its argument was that it simply made government a communicator that competed with others in Peruvian society, but any credence is this was fast disappearing.

Venezuela's press office had burgeoned by 1977 into a full-fledged Ministry of Information and Tourism, which has control of all the ways a democratic government can intervene in the information process plus travel promotion and regulation. It lacks the full range of official media controlled by its counterpart in Peru, since the Venezuelan state owns only two television stations and a secondary radio system. But its role in highly vocal support of the Third World media movement has earned it a prominence even beyond its borders.

All other governments in the region have information offices of varying statures. They generally are most active in the military dictatorships such as Chile, Argentina, Brazil and Uruguay, although the peculiar ferment going on inside the Brazilian bureaucracy and political body results in much leakage of information to the media.

It must be conceded that information offices often increase the flow of communication to the media, so long as the reporters do not expect embarrassing material. Also, the press officers sometimes lend a sympathetic ear in government which reporters otherwise would not encounter.

PERSONAL PENALTIES

Although the pattern differs greatly from country to country and decade to decade, generally speaking the profession of journalism has always been relatively dangerous in Latin America. During the various wars of independence and civil strife in the last two centuries, the agitators and leaders have intertwined roles as journalists, politicians and militarists. Thus the profession is well represented in the halls of the martyrs.

But the slow movement toward journalism's becoming a separate occupation in the 20th Century has resulted in more danger with less glory. This is because modern tenets of the profession discourage partisanship in favor of impartial pursuit of the truth. So when a journalist of this era is struck down by a bullet or is thrown in jail, he does so not under the flag of some holy cause but under the less attractive standard of objective news.

Furthermore, the danger no longer comes only from the clear and open penalties of the government. Terrorism poses an even greater threat in some countries.

Brazil and Argentina present the greatest danger for individual journalists, although the dictatorships in Uruguay and Paraguay are not far behind. Chileans have little problem of this type because all opposition journalists are in exile, and the Peruvian regime has been remarkably gentle in its punishments. Rough treatment is rare and erratic in Mexico, as it is in the democracies of Venezuela and Colombia.

While personal repression in Brazil has not been as lurid and constant as foreign critics have often portrayed, it still is the most blatant in Latin America, because the government makes little attempt to disguise it. Trial and imprisonment on stated charges play little part in the process, although some courts retain integrity. Rather, interrogation intended to get a confession is what makes otherwise audacious journalists blanch with fear. Even when the national president sincerely tries to cut down on the brutality, his efforts get diffused through the welter of competing power centers. Somehow the order to go easy rarely gets to the policeman holding the electric prod.

Several factors make personal penalties for journalists in Brazil different from those in other countries, even other dictatorships.

First, angry protests have come from many quarters of society whenever a journalist appears to be unfairly dealt with. Newspaper editors, union leaders and church officials—particularly those in São Paulo, where some of the worst abuses have occurred—are quick to raise their voices publicly, and at least this form of opposition to the government usually goes unpunished.

Furthermore, many of the print media have built for themselves public respect to an extent that the government hesitates to treat their employees unfairly. This is particularly true in the case of large national newspapers such as *O Estado de São Paulo* and *Jornal do Brasil*. Although their workers are not immune from trouble, journalists with less powerful employers are more likely to be arrested.

On the large, influential papers the owners themselves are accorded more deference than reporters and even editors. Very rarely has an owner suffered any real punishment.

The most frequent targets of police action are the journalists who work in the so-called "midget press"—the tabloid weeklies which deal in political theory and satirical criticism. In view of the harassment these staff members continually suffer, their persistence in returning to their posts is remarkable.

In Argentina, journalists in the 1970s have known the most intense, sustained terror perhaps ever recorded in Latin American history. At the same time, the most intractable secret in Argentine public life has been the exact nature and source of the terror. Despite the fact that highly competent analysts have tried repeatedly to put together the most elemental facts about the terrorism, all that emerges is guesswork, rumor and surface events.

Like most of the ailments of Argentine life, this one has not been confined to one kind of government. Most evidence points to a steady buildup starting with a relatively low level under the military dictatorships of the early 1970s. It paused with the democratic election of Juan Perón in 1973, then began mounting again as Perón henchman José López Rega gained influence, particularly after Isabel Perón succeeded to the presidency upon her husband's death. Again it soared after the military overthrew Mrs. Perón in 1976.

One sign of how difficult it is to assess the scope of terrorism is the erratic scorekeeping of its progress. A bewildering variety of "lists" of victims constantly circulates over coffee cups in Buenos Aires. Within 24 hours, two U.S. correspondents came up with widely differing totals—35 and 65—of journalists who had disappeared mysteriously in the decade.[12]

Journalists by no means are the only endangered group, although they are among the most represented. Others include artists, entertainers, intellectuals, educators, labor leaders, Jewish spokesmen and political activists. Besides these, there are two groups who have suffered for quite distinct reasons—the genuine subversives and the victims of kidnappers seeking ransom. It could be said, as many have, that Argentina has been embroiled in a civil war, except that no one was sure who the combatants are, where they are fighting, and why.

Furthermore, to prove that someone has "disappeared" in Argentina means little. He could have been arrested by police for public trial or for secret interrogation and either release or execution, sometimes preceded by torture. He could have been taken by one of the military branches for the same reasons. In all such cases, spokesmen for the agency concerned can say they know nothing of the incident if no one tells them about it or it does not go on record.

Sometimes the captors came from a shadowy world populated by off-duty policemen or soldiers, political fanatics, or bullies with personal scores to settle. Such a group was the dreaded AAA (Argentine Anticommunist Alliance) formed by Perón's friend López Rega.

The scorekeeping of disappearances is complicated by the large number of suspects who simply go into hiding, either after arrest or in fear of it. Others openly go into self-imposed exile.

Amnesty International, a civil rights league which is among the more systematic scorekeepers, published the names of about 200 scientists, teachers, sociologists, writers and students who had vanished or been imprisoned without charge in the first year and a half after the 1976 military takeover.

Although government control of mass media personnel has never been systematic in Argentina as in Peru, journalists have come to expect their careers to be buffeted by political winds. The ones considered most dangerous, if they do not disappear, discover themselves blacklisted in their occupation; this is even more effective in broadcasting, entertainment and education, which are linked with or controlled by the government. Even when one is not blacklisted, he can expect a definite ceiling on his professional success if he is even slightly tainted in the view of the current government; this limit is imposed by superiors and colleagues who in turn fear for their own careers.

Ironically, Argentine journalists have rarely suffered indefinitely at the state's hands when their cases are handled by the courts or when foreign criticism is brought to bear. All recent governments have strained to retain the appearance of legality, and the militarists who took over in 1976 were especially anxious to escape the stigma of brutality their fellows in Chile and Brazil had acquired. The Argentine publishers' association (ADEPA) has consistently complained—albeit in vague and polite terms—against what it considers official incursions. It is backed up somewhat more forcefully by the Inter-

American Press Association, which has strong representation among Argentine members.

One of the most severe—and most confusing—instances of state action against a journalist was the 12-month jailing—reportedly with torture—of a prominent Buenos Aires newspaper publisher, Jacobo Timerman, followed by state trusteeship of his company. Timerman was implicated in a plot to "launder" funds from terrorists' ransoms, although officials never found sufficient evidence to charge him. Timerman, a noted Zionist whose arrest coincided with an upsurge of harassment against Jews, was released after diplomatic pressure from President Carter.

For distinct reasons, both Chile and Peru experienced little of the personal harassment of journalists that Argentina and Brazil knew throughout the 1970s.

Despite the frenzied political conflict during the Allende presidency (1970–73), which was expressed heatedly in the nation's journalistic life, this rarely led to personal penalities against personnel of the media other than loss of jobs in media of which the state could gain control. Even for those persons, there were ample media opposing the government and eager to provide them with work.

Certainly the few weeks following the military takeover in 1973 saw massive retaliation against leftist journalists. It was estimated that more than 500 of them lost their jobs; those of them who had been most audacious fled the country as exiles the day of the coup, and if they failed they vanished into the military prisons.

However, because of that sudden purge the agony of suspense has never been a continuing matter for Chilean journalists during the troubled decade. If they survived the purge, professionally and otherwise, they were little disturbed by the government.

The Peruvian military regime has mingled absolutism with a surprisingly high level of personal liberty, and this has been reflected in the mass media. The police-state brutality of Brazil and the constant terror of Argentina have been unknown in the Andean nation ever since the generals interrupted the democratic process with a coup in 1968. The most extreme penalty assessed against journalists—one that became used with humdrum frequency—has been deportation. Police forcing an offending newsman onto an airliner leaving Lima have been a familiar sight; just as likely is the journalist's ability to return home a few months later after tempers subside. Occasionally an editor or reporter will fall into the snares of the *desacato* (sedition) law and spend less than a year in prison.

Peru had its sudden purge of newsmen after the government expropriated the Lima dailies in 1974, with about 300 persons being fired or forced to resign. These were not permanently blacklisted in the Argentine of Chilean fashion, however, and usually were able to find some sort of media work.

Two decades after the Castro revolution in Cuba, it is moot to speak of personal hazards to journalists in that country, because all dissidents have left the public scene, through force or fear. Those who remain have been chosen for their fervor, caution or subservience, and they pose little threat to defiance against the regime. However, recent investigations show that the officialist editors are eager to exploit any latitude for criticism allowed them by the government.

This is cold comfort for those Cuban journalists who are excluded from professional work at home. An undetermined number, probably ranging over 100, have taken up an emigré existence in Florida, Puerto Rico and Venezuela, with a scattering throughout Latin America. Because few of them have avoided the running debate over Cuba, they live in constant danger from political opponents. Assassinations and maimings are not unknown.

Between the revolutionary victory in 1959 and the effective absorption of the Cuban media by 1965, imprisonment of troublesome journalists became a familiar weapon. Although the number that remains is open to speculation, each issue of the Inter-American Press Association news publication goes through the ritual of printing this boxed notice:

> There are more than 30 journalists in Cuban jails, some since June of 1959 and many without having been given the benefit of a trial. This reminder is published in compliance with a resolution adopted by the XX General Assembly.[13]

Even though nearly all these prisoners were sentenced before 1965, the government has made examples since then of a few deviants, usually working outside the established communication units. Such a case was that of Heberto Padilla, a poet and novelist who was jailed without charges in 1971 after writing allegories which reflected badly on the government. After a month behind bars, he emerged with an humble confession of his "errors." A group of distinguished writers around the world protested that the confession had been obtained through torture, although Padilla denied this.

Although most Mexican journalists, like those in Cuba, work inside "the system," far more deviation occurs. Punishment often comes swiftly, in various forms and from various sources. All political power flows from the national presidency, but branches and levels of government use it in their own ways. So the occasional assassinations, beatings and harassments of journalists often originate in the minds of army generals, federal bureaucrats, provincial officials, police chiefs and local party bosses. Since vengeance and violence are woven into Mexican public life, such treatment of journalists does not depart from tradition in general although the need for it arises in a relatively few cases.

Part of this tradition is that, no matter how turbulent the political brawling at lower levels, the president remains above the fray, at least in appearances. President Luis Echeverría came close to breaking this unwritten law in 1976 when, according to informed reports, he passed the word that the country's leading editor, Julio Scherer García of *Excélsior,* should be ousted. After several months of harassment, Scherer García and 200 colleagues resigned and started a new publication.

Among the democratic nations, the life of a journalist is generally secure from governmental danger, but exceptions occur. Colombia and Venezuela, the largest democracies, still have vestiges of an official attitude that any threat to the state—particularly the armed forces—justifies temporary suspension of normal liberties. The military, although usually subordinate to the elected president, has been known to use its political muscle to bring legal action against journalists. In Venezuela, military courts even have the right to try civilians who supposedly have caused "anguish" among the people or have been involved in subversion. Offences to the dignity of the president also are a frequent reason given for action against certain individuals.

Instances of such episodes persisted throughout the 1970s despite the near-disappearance of guerrilla danger. Often the cases become so enmeshed in other issues that both the issues and the punishment become difficult to isolate. The most famous Venezuelan press magnate, Miguel Angel Capriles, fled into exile after angering the army, only to be allowed to return and turn over title to his properties to relatives. A leftist politician accused of subversive affiliations got into deeper trouble in 1976 for accusing the president in a magazine article of being a tool of the U.S. Central Intelligence Agency.

A year later the director of Venezuela's respected news weekly *Resumen,* Jorge Olavarría, became embroiled in legal troubles after he printed reports from the Italian press that President Carlos Andrés Pérez, a noted bon vivant, had associated with prostitutes during a visit to Rome. Although Olavarría went to jail on charges brought by his wife over a divorce dispute, followed by a libel suit brought by a government official, the journalist claimed he was defenseless against "a power without limits and without scruples." Signs were painted on walls attacking him, and he claimed that the government had scared off his advertisers. He took asylum in an embassy and fled into exile.[14]

CHAPTER 9

Media Effects
on Government

IN LATIN AMERICA, public spokesmen are generally as reckless as their peers in other countries in the matter of attributing power to the mass media. They give it credit or blame for overthrowing governments, corrupting or edifying the national values, impelling buyers into lemming-like madness and seducing the young away from the teaching of home and school.

Social behavior has changed drastically in recent decades, of course, and this is particularly noticeable in more traditional countries. Since many people look to leaders for easy explanations of why the changes occurred, the myth of the media juggernaut makes for good speech material, whether the thrust is leftward or rightward politically.

However, any consideration of the available research would dash cold water on fiery oratory. The basic findings, established by 1960 and often corroborated since, are that the most typical effects of the mass media are reinforcement of existing opinion, or, at the most, minor change. In the rare cases when conversion occurs, powerful influences outside the media must be acting in its behalf.[1]

Thus, the media can play roles in public life, but they are part of a large cast of characters—homes, schools, friendship circles, places of work, churches, parties, etc.

The little basic research that has tested these principles in Latin America indicates that the theory, although developed through studies in the United States, also applies southward. While the opinions of newspaper devotees generally coincide with those of their favorite editorial page, there is no assurance that editorials *caused* such choice of opinions. (It could be speculated that holding the opinions resulted in the readers' choosing their favorite newspaper.) This coincidence of opinions exists only for high-prestige newspapers, however—not for the mass-appeal ones.[2]

Despite these precautions, one must still take account of (1) the persistent faith on the part of political leaders, editors and the public that media do have strong, independent effects, and (2) the research evidence that indicates media have influence when certain optimal conditions exist. Thus the analysis to follow will note the types of overt behavior that has been known to have influence on opinion or that is carried out on the *assumption* that such influence takes place.

POLITICAL ROLE OF MEDIA

Rooted in European customs but strongly linked with U.S. news organizations, the basic role of Latin American media has developed through several stages over the last two centuries. These stages have been similar to—but not identical with—those in the rest of the Western world. From the shipping journals and court gazettes of the colonial period the newspapers evolved into revolutionary pamphlets, then into no less inflammatory vehicles of party warfare. An emphasis on objectivity and accuracy in superficial news coverage followed. In the 1970s demands for new roles for the media began to arise, often calling for opposite changes because the pressures were coming from all sides. One set of critics would urge the media to strive for new levels of scientific accuracy while another would push for more subjective interpretation. From one day to the next, the editor might feel pressure for less sensationalism or for less highbrow obscurantism.

But in the great majority of Latin American countries during the 1970s, the editor's choice as to what role he would stake out for his medium was partly or entirely taken away by the government. This does not mean that he was cut off from the possibility of affecting the government—only that he had to play under game rules that were not of his making.

The two most dramatic instances of this fencing-in of the media have come in Chile and Peru. Chile's press and broadcast industry had advanced the standard of professionalism, based on the modern concept of the information role, to one of the highest levels on the continent by 1970. During the next three years, while the country was administered by a leftist coalition headed by Salvador Allende, the media put aside nearly all roles except that of unbridled party warfare in the 18th-Century style. When military coup-makers took over in 1973, one of their first orders of business was to deny the media nearly all vestiges of their political role. The Christian Democrats, who collaborated with the military for a while, were allowed to keep a newspaper and a radio station as muffled voices, but even they later died off.

All the leftist media were closed overnight, and the only political function allowed for the remaining media was to act as cheerleaders for the regime if they chose—and most did—and, as the years went on, to respectfully suggest courses of action to the government. Any frontal attack on the legitimacy of the junta was out of the question. So as to find some function which would attract enough customers to survive economically, the Chilean media turned to an almost purely commercial function, making a willingness to respond to advertising the only qualification for readers or viewers.

Peruvian media underwent an equally drastic change of life in the 1970s, although at a different pace and in different forms. Military rulers—leftist in this case—gradually chipped away the media's political role for six years, leaving them little reason for existence. As a coup de grace, the state expropriated first the major broadcast properties and then the leading newspapers. Thus their function became closely comparable to that of the Chilean media, even though they were directed by government appointees in one case and private owners in the other.

Other countries under authoritarian rule during most or all of the 1970s saw boundaries set in some manner for the political role of the media. They range from the near-absolutism of Paraguay and Uruguay to the mild strictures of Ecuador, Bolivia and Honduras. Argentina, although ostensibly having one of the least repressive policies toward the media, in reality has one of the most effective boundaries because of the intimidation through terrorism. On the other hand Brazil, with highly restrictive laws, has a press which continues to exercise a political role, straining at the fences if not breaking them down.

Ironically, the country with the media system most tightly controlled by the state, Cuba, also assigns a vital political role to its publications and broadcasters. Under official guidance, journalists labor constantly to keep the linkages between government and people, and among various power centers within the government, in good repair.

Without compulsion as direct as that in Cuba, Mexican journalists fulfill a very similar political function. In theory most of the media units are in private hands, but in reality they are under far more pressure than their colleagues in Chile and Peru to sally forth for the cause of the ruling party and the governments it installs. This is accomplished, in a uniquely Mexican way, without major legal controls or even substantial fear. Rather, the enticement of financial gain through collaboration is the main incentive.

Three democracies—Costa Rica, Colombia and Venezuela—have been the workshop for the forging of new roles for the media. Costa Rica in particular has provided the prototype of a media system which offers ample opportunity for the public to express itself in political and other matters. Colombia until the mid-1970s supported two major parties which had formed a coalition in 1957 after a nine-year civil war; their members in turn operated newspapers devoted to maintaining this truce by down-playing conflict between the factions. (However, they are turning gradually toward open political competition.) Venezuela presents the odd spectacle of newspapers which offer a forum similar to those in Costa Rica but which largely disdain the idea of running editorials themselves, something which editors in other countries fight to their last breath for.

In recent years, however, these three democracies have been the cockpit for a struggle between the classical liberals who operate the media and a new breed of reformers. At the heart of the dispute is a basic disagreement over the ideal role of the media. The reformers see this vocation as uplifting, educating, and politicizing the people—rallying them to the support of government policies, which are assumed to be uniformly wholesome, since they come from officials who have risen to office through popular elections or revolutions. In opposition, the traditionalists maintain that the highest calling of a mass medium is to make money—by pleasing the customers. Only rarely are thoughtful proposals for a compromise between these positions offered, because each side sees the other as traitors to the ideals of the nation.

HAVEN FOR POLITICIANS

Soon after the wars of independence in Spanish America early in the last century, a practice which deeply affected political life solidified. This was the ownership of newspapers by politicians. While in power such a person could use the pages of his journal as an official organ; this allowed him a channel, before the days of radio and television, to defend and articulate his policies. Often, like José Batlle y Ordóñez of Uruguay, he would build a basis of public opinion through such publicity before he introduced a reform. And during the lapses when he was out of power he could direct his inky outrage at those whom he saw as despoilers of the national patrimony.

Newspapers have provided politicians not only with income and platforms but also vehicles for radical change. Both in and out of the presidency, Batlle y Ordóñez campaigned ceaselessly in his famous Montevideo daily *El Día* for programs ranging from divorce to state ownership of key industries.[3] Bartolomé Mitre did much to modernize Argentina through the columns of the daily he founded, *La Nación*.[4]

In the 20th Century, political ownership gradually has been tapering off as the media become more commercially oriented. But the governmental involvement of newspaper families such as the Miró Quesadas and Beltráns of Peru, the Mantillas of Ecuador, the Santos dynasty of Colombia and the Pazes, Gainzas and Mitres of Argentina still is legendary. Other political leaders such as José Figueres of Costa Rica have founded media in modern times without benefit of family tradition, and some such as Carlos Andrés Pérez of Venezuela have used backgrounds as journalistic writers rather than owners to gain entry into public life.

Mexico provides a curious variation on the practice of interspersing media activity with political tenure. Customs growing out of the Revolution of 1910 require that aspiring politicians work their way up through the ranks of the dominant party rather than entering from media positions. However, once someone reaches the apogee of his political orbit he is expected to retire from public office. Since a politician may do this relatively young, he needs a vehicle for the rest of his career; he is barred from politics but is expected to feather his retirement nest while he is in office.

This is particularly true of Mexican presidents. Some have gone into industry, but others have favored the mass media. The most blatant example of this was the final years of the Luis Echeverría presidency in the 1970s. He systematically and covertly set about getting control of major Mexico City newspapers and at the same time insinuating his top assistants into their leadership. To eliminate his principal journalistic competition, he staged an internal coup in the cooperative that owns the nation's best-known newspaper, *Escélsior*, resulting in the ouster of brilliant editor Julio Scherer García and a large part of his staff.

SPOKESMAN FOR GOVERNMENT

No 19th Century architect would have dared design a presidential palace—especially in Latin America—without a balcony facing a public plaza. Continuing a custom stretching back into the dawn of monarchy, this device provided a method for the head of the nation to reveal, explain and defend his actions.

Balcony speeches still play a part in Latin American politics, partly because most of those old palaces are still in service. Mexico's, dating back to the time of the Spanish conquest, provides a platform for the national president to electrify the multitude with the Cry of Independence every September 15. Juan Perón, in both his presidencies, rallied his *descamisados* (shirtless ones) from the balcony of the Casa Rosada, being upstaged in his earlier period by his spellbinding wife, Evita. Fidel Castro has attracted crowds estimated at up to one million hanging on his every word shouted from the Presidential Palace.

But such occasions have become rare and ceremonial, as political leaders find they can reach far more people, more easily and quickly, through the mass media. In many respects Latin America does not differ from other Western nations in this regard. The presidency and every other government department of any prestige has rooms for briefing the press and delivering a broadcast message. The president and sometimes cabinet ministers and state governors can pre-empt television or radio time when they wish.

Thoroughgoing exploitation of the media has not generally resulted, with the notable exception of Cuba. The Castro government's devotion to mass communication was evidenced first during its origins as a guerrilla movement, when it built a radio station at the sacrifice of desperately needed weapons. After its victory, it made the media instruments to win the power over to its programs and to keep itself in power. In particular, its use of television through the personality of Castro probably will stand as the most dramatic demonstration of this medium's potential, rivaled only by the almost instant success of televised advertisements in the United States of the early 1950s. Herbert Matthews of the *New York Times* called it "government by television."

Although not forced to do so, the Mexican media provide their government with probably the most accessible loudspeaker in Latin America outside of Cuba. The frenzy with which reporters can inflate the importance of a presidential tour of the provinces has become part of the national legend.

Most Latin American states own media units in some form, but the public tends to despise them as house pets of the president. So governments have sought out newspapers of some prestige (broadcast stations lack the requisite dignity) as their best friends in the communication field. This gives rise to a frequently heard term in Latin America—"officialist." The editors attempt to maintain the distinction that attracted the government's favor in the first place, even while serving as apologists for those in power. Such dailies have in recent years included *Clarín* of Buenos Aires, *El Mercurio* of Santiago, *El País* of Montevideo, *O Globo* of Rio de Janeiro and *El Universal* of Mexico City, although some have cut the ties.

Aside from Cuba, Mexico and, during the Perón periods, Argentina, most Latin American countries have followed a tendency since 1970 to leave behind the hero worship that was endemic in their political life ever since independence. A brief and rather pathetic exception to this came in the final months of the Carlos Andrés Pérez presidency in Venezuela. Pérez, who had displayed a Kennedy-like flair for publicity throughout his five years in office, cranked up all the publicity and advertising machinery at his disposal in 1978 to put out a paean of praise to his accomplishments. He appeared to be trying to write his own pages in history, and the episode brought much embarrassment to his own party.

CRITIC OF GOVERNMENT

Pedro Joaquín Chamorro, an editor who led the fight against Nicaraguan strongman Anastasio Somoza, criticized his opponent almost to the moment he was shot to death on the streets of Managua.

Alberto Gainza Paz, owner of the famous Buenos Aires daily *La Prensa*, got himself exiled and his paper seized for criticizing Juan Perón incessantly. When the former dictator died, *La Prensa* ran a bitterly critical editorial.

When Haitian dictator Jean-Claude Duvalier eased up on the press for the first time in two decades, criticism immediately sprang up.

Carlos Lacerda, a fiery Brazilian editor, criticized President Getulio Vargas so severely that Lacerda was almost killed in an ambush. Later, Lacerda's criticism drove Vargas to commit suicide.

These are among the more noted examples of the difficulty Latin American journalists willfully invite through their criticism of government. But they are by no means isolated cases; parallels can be found in almost every country, every month.

In the context of its history, political criticism is the most natural function of journalism in Latin America. Throughout their two centuries of independence, most citizens in the area have not acquired the psychological rhythm of other Western nations which develops from regular elections every four or six years, resulting in a peaceful transfer of power. Rather, it has been more usual for this transfer to take place outside the elections which the constitutions call for. An extreme example is Bolivia, which has had more than 180 governments in 150 years.

Thus the most typical time for a Latin American government to change hands is when the general public or one of its subdivisions, such as the military, can no longer endure it. The boiling point is brought about not only by the government's actions but also by the way its critics—particularly those in the mass media—perceive those actions. Traditionally the press has been operated by men schooled not in the objective rigors of the scientific method, which is the philosophical parent of the news concept. Rather, they have been taught to value the classical Greek and Latin rhetoric and argumentation, which led to political criticism and thus to editorials.

Media criticism of governments can have three types of effects—it can anger the leaders enough to retaliate, stir up the public enough to throw out the government by force or election, and spur the government to alter its behavior. There is ample evidence of the first, but the other two are difficult to document.

The 1970s produced a high tide of retaliation, as detailed in the previous chapter—closures, suspensions, seizures, censorship, jailings, beatings, murders, etc. These actions are often channeled through the courts and are explained as the result of legal offenses such as sedition or incitement. But everyone concerned always is aware that the real cause is the fury of a civil or military official who has felt the jab of criticism.

This touchiness is closely related with the emergence of a new kind of national leader in the 1960s and 1970s—the one who is above politics. The wave of military regimes brought with it a horde of technocrats who felt they were sacrificing their preferences to selfishly rebuild their nations after the systems were ravaged by demagogues. Thus they felt they should be exempt from criticism because their motives were pure; they spoke with the most unaffected devotion their peoples had ever seen. In Peru, the generals sounded convincing when they exalted "Christian humanism." In Chile, housewives flocked to contribute their wedding bands to pay for the post-Allende reconstruction.

Thus, in the "national emergencies" that went on for years under the military governments, criticism could logically be viewed as treason. Besides, it was foolish, the generals reasoned, because they had the guns on their side.

As for gaining enough public support to effect a change in government, a direct cause-effect chain cannot be proved. But it is worth noting that all the overthrows of civilian governments in the 1960s and 1970s were preceded by a drumfire of media criticism against their policies. And in the few remaining democracies, millions of dollars are being poured into campaign advertising. Venezuela's exploitation of the media during election periods approaches the complexity found in the United States. Even the limited voting allowed in Brazil brings out sophisticated plans for wooing voters through the news and advertising columns. All this is intended at least in part to combat any effects of editorial criticism aimed at the candidate.

Changes in government behavior brought about by journalistic criticism also can be surmised mostly through circumstantial evidence. Oddly enough, the government which has made the greatest display of responding to criticism is that of Cuba. Since about 1974, the Castro regime has been carefully building an apparatus of criticism within its system. It has reached the point where reporters for the government-operated newspapers are sent out to investigate complaints received from the people—faulty street repairs, inefficiency by petty officials, rudeness to consumers and the like. They can even lay the blame on low-level bureaucrats for allowing the abuses. Criticism of the regime itself and its philosophy, of course, in unthinkable.

Another authoritarian regime—the military government of Brazil—also has been known to react favorably to criticism, which in that country comes from opposition media unlike in Cuba. The general who happens to be president at any given time always must contend with rival power centers within the military, and he welcomes the media criticism if it is directed against something that troubles him also. This was the case when *O Estado de São Paulo* exposed rampant high-living at state expense on the part of Brasilia bureaucrats in 1976.

A similar response occurred in Peru when the state's own daily newspapers launched a campaign against police brutality. The rulers quickly took action to end the abuse and won much favor with the public in doing so.

Criticism also has been welling up in Mexico in recent years, amazing cynical observers who had seen nothing but servility in the media there for decades. President Luis Echeverría, sporting a reputation as a liberal, encouraged the unaccustomed role for the press after he took office in 1970, although he tried to slow it down later.

The Argentine media seem to have an uncanny knack for sensing when to muffle themselves and when they can get away with criticism. Usually the latter occurs when the mark of death is upon a regime. This happened to some extent when the military tired of its dictatorship and scheduled elections in 1973, and it recurred much more strongly after Juan Perón died and left the presidency to his hapless third wife Isabel. The last months before her ouster by the military was a carnival of criticism.

A somewhat similar episode was witnessed during the presidency of Salvador Allende in Chile. He was under constant, unbridled criticism by media throughout his three years, but the final one was an orgy of vituperation.

PUBLIC FORUM

The idea of providing an outlet for ordinary citizens to use in venting a wide range of opinions has never caught on among the majority of Latin American newspapers. Even less have they gone out and solicited such opinion. Rather, voicing opinions has been considered to be the function of the owner or his kindred spirits, the columnists. Letters to the editor, when printed, tend to congratulate the editor on one of his editorials or add supporting data.

Most cities in the region have several newspapers, each representing a party or factional doctrine; broadcast stations have widened this range. So the lack of emphasis on readers' letters has not resulted in any restriction on public debate. A citizen, instead of expecting to get a variety of views from one medium, buys a handful of newspapers and listens to several broadcast stations. In Mexico City, for example, he has more than 20 dailies and a like number of broadcast stations to choose from.

However, the wind is changing. News media of all types are not only accepting the ethic of internal diversity but also are discovering that it pleases customers. This is particularly true in the democracies, such as Costa Rica, Venezuela and Colombia. Where public expression is unrestricted and the people fond of political controversy—the latter is true throughout Latin America—the media can find no excuse not to be channels for this debate.

The competitive spur also has dug into the sides of newspaper directors. Television, lacking the prestige pundits who wrote for newspapers, turned instead to panel discussions, inviting spokesmen from all walks of life to lock horns on camera. These proved enormously popular, often rivaling the soap operas in ratings, and the newspapers got the message. Now the more enterprising ones are trying to pump life into their letters columns, doing opinion roundups in the form of news stories, and mimicking the panel discussions with multiple-interview articles.

San José in Costa Rica, one of the smallest capitals in the hemisphere, clearly leads all the others in development of a public forum through the media. Perhaps the intimacy of the people with their leaders, plus a tradition of yeoman democracy, contribute to this. At any rate, the letters columns have long been crowded with shrill dispute of readers with the editors and with each other. Some readers, wanting more prominence for their opuses, buy advertising space, as do political factions even in years when there are no elections.

For anyone with a pretense to Costa Rican political leadership, it is a simple matter to get his manifesto reported in a separate news story. Since the city has few reporters skilled in interpreting such pseudo-events, what usually results is almost a verbatim quotation of the politician's statement.

One episode which demonstrated the possibility of media as public forums was the Robert Vesco confrontation with Costa Rica. Vesco, under indictment for Watergate complicity in the United States, took up residence in San José and started a pellmell purchasing of property there, including newspapers and broadcast stations. The failure of the government, being run by friends of Vesco, to expel him as a fugitive from justice stirred up the country's hottest public dispute in decades. The media were thronged with opinions of all types and from all sources, high and low. Some occupied bought time—purchases of television time became common—and many were given free exposure. By the time it receded, the controversy had become a model of how to ventilate an issue.

It must be noted that news media throughout the region are feeling another pressure for the forum function. This is the movement for a "people's media system" being pushed by forces aligned with UNESCO. Such proposals are bitterly proposed by most media owners, but some are fighting fire with fire by voluntarily undertaking some of the UNESCO ideas.

REPORTING ON GOVERNMENT

Anyone coming to Latin America from an Anglo-Saxon country and observing the governmental news is struck by the enormous dignity with which reporters vest the most minor functionaries. Their photographs are regal, their statements verbosely verbatim, and their titles overwhelming. And when the subject matter ascends to the heights of the presidency or the cabinet, the reader gasps in the rarefied air.

It is no semantic accident that the persons who write news for the media have often been called *cronistas* (chroniclers). They have not been paid well, either in money or respect, and thus they do not often have that hallmark of substance, a university degree. So it has not been in the scope of either the ability or the job description of such workers to put anything but the most formal or superficial events in their stories.

Thus a reporter assigned to the presidential palace is expected to confine his copy to two types. One is transcribing the pronouncements and speeches of the great man himself, delivered in person or through a mediary such as a press agent. This is common throughout the world, but in Latin America there is much less tendency to find expert backgrounding and placing in context, sometimes referred to as interpretation.

The other type often found is the chronicle of minutiae. This elevates to the status of news the trivial details of a ceremony or simply the traffic in and out of the official's office. Some newspapers give a minute-by-minute account of the identity and description of everyone who comes and goes from the palace, even to printing the license plates of the visiting vehicles.

However, Latin American reporters and editors are becoming acutely aware of the kind of reporting which is winning acclaim in other countries. Traveling through the region at the height of the Watergate scandal, this writer found deep admiration in every editorial office for the exploits of Woodward and Bernstein (and often a keener awareness of the events than most Americans had). There was always the same comment: "But that couldn't happen here."

But on another study tour three years later, I found mini-Watergates emerging in many countries, often in the face of personal hazard to the reporters. The infection had become endemic, and the general consensus was that serious cases would break out sooner or later. Everywhere the assumption was that this trend was permanent, not a passing fad.

Clearly the progress was slow and often discouraging. Each country had one or two media or simply individual reporters who were universally cited as *the* innovators in this field. They excited widespread envy among their colleagues, and many of the younger reporters were determined to do them even better.

This progressive reporting has taken basically three forms—interpretive or analytical, social, and investigative.

Magazines such as *Ercilla* of Chile, *Veja* of Brazil, *Caretas* of Peru and *Resumen* of Venezuela have led the way in all these types, particularly interpretive or analytical. In countries starved for the meaning behind the facts, they usually provide a three-dimensional explanation of what has happened. For their foreign material, most rely heavily on buying publication rights to the copy of major news media abroad, particularly opposite numbers such as *Time, Newsweek,* the *Economist, L'Express* and *Der Spiegel.* Thus they are put on their mettle to come up to the standards of the imported material; they often do, and more. Foreign publications now have begun reprinting *their* copy.

Two newspapers also attracted much attention for their interpretive reporting in the 1970s until they were forced to the wall by their governments. *La Opinión,* a Buenos Aires daily, was founded in 1971 as a frank imitation of *Le Monde* of Paris, as was *Opinião,* a Rio de Janeiro weekly which came along a year later. In each case the paper was the brainchild of a liberal businessman. Both dispensed with editorial pages and instead allowed their writers to analyze the news as they chose. The result was often leftist but usually glittering with intelligence. Newsmen throughout the region, regardless of political bent, envied the two papers' penchant for saying things they had always wanted to but were prevented by professional custom. Both papers faded from their usual role in 1977, however. The Argentine one was put in receivership when its owner was arrested in a financial scandal, and the other was suspended indefinitely because of the owner's despair over governmental harassment.

Social reporting—description of those facets of society which are not secret but simply ignored or misunderstood—has been developing rapidly, perhaps more so than the other types. Most notably, the news media have discovered the poverty that has always surrounded them. One of the earliest forays into this field was in 1958, when a young Brazilian reporter named Audalio Dantas discovered that a barely literate black woman living in the slums of São Paulo had been keeping a diary for years about her daily life. He edited it, keeping intact the raw vigor of the original, and it created an international sensation in book form and in other media.[5] Studies by social scientists from the

United States also did much to lift the curtain on the reality of poverty. Some of these, like the books of anthropologist Oscar Lewis,[6] infuriated the establishment in the countries concerned, but the precedent was set for local reporters to do their own probing.

Since most Latin American governments claim the role of guardian of the poor, any such reporting is quite clearly an indictment of officials' failure. So it provides a way for reporters implicitly to criticize the government in countries where press controls prevail. Punishing the journalists would be an admission of guilt.

True investigative reporting poses a paradox: It occurs only to the extent that the media have some freedom, but is needed only to the extent that someone in power is covering up news of public interest. The investigative reporter must put his shoulder to the barriers that block the normal flow of information.

The fact that isolated instances of investigative reporting are occurring every year in the region thus indicates that some range of freedom exists in all the countries but that corruption exists even in the democracies. Certain media in two countries with the most persistent governmental controls—Brazil and Mexico—have been among the most active in investigative work. *O Estado de São Paulo,* the largest daily in Brazil, has stunned the country with exposures repeatedly. They range from the highest levels, such as a series of lavish living styles for bureaucrats, to everyday concerns, such as failure of inspectors to stop contaminated milk. Mexican media, most notably the capital daily *Excélsior,* began amazing observers early in the 1970s with stories which had been unthinkable in earlier times. While they by no means became the dominant theme of Mexican journalism, it nevertheless was considered a giant step forward to see occasional exposés on such time-honored evils of public life as police brutality, habitual demands for bribes, and suppression of political minorities. Even in Peru, where state controls were steadily engulfing the media in the 1970s, reporters would occasionally lift the lid from something embarrassing to the government; the untamed weekly press was the pacesetter in this.

Oddly enough, the media in the freest countries—Costa Rica, Colombia and Venezuela—have been among the most laggard in forging a strategy of investigation. All have seen rare occurrences such as revelations of drug dealing in Colombia, exploitation of farm workers in Costa Rica, and government waste in Venezuela. But, compared with the opportunity and with the efforts in authoritarian countries, the democratic media have been surprisingly inactive.

CHAPTER 10

Postures of
The Media

As THE NUMBER of independent states in the world has doubled and then tripled during the 20th Century, bewildered readers of the news have tried to sort out the new nations into the cubbyholes of their minds. Since even the best educated of citizens cannot remember all the characteristics of the various newcomers—or even their names—the tendency has been to gather them into categories. Somewhat as we mentally organize the positions of each season's sports teams, we divide nations into those that are in our league or the rival one, or those who rank high, medium or low on scales we consider important.

In comparative studies of media systems, analysts have been no less diligent than sports writers in categorizing the units. Although some attention has been given to "modernization" and "eliteness,"[1] most of the ratings have concerned efforts to measure press freedom, either alone or as a concomitant of such broader concepts as democracy.

THE RATING SYSTEMS

Although few of those who have attempted measurements have consciously tried to construct them so as necessarily to glorify the United States and Western Europe at the expense of other areas, this has been the inevitable result. Semantic problems also sprang up early in the studies.

First, definitions posed problems. How could freedom be distinguished from license on the one hand and licentiousness on the other? Was freedom to be gauged by explicit guaranties by a government or simply the absence of interference? Or perhaps the posture of the government had less bearing than what the media dared to do and could get away with. What was the word "press" to embrace—only printed matter, or radio and television also? Only journalistic content of these media or all content including entertainment and advertising? What about visiting correspondents and imported media content?

Somewhat related to definitions was the question of criteria. Were the factors which make up freedom to be assumed, or should they be specified? Under the first option, ambiguity could arise between different raters and also between raters and readers of the analysis. Under the second, some criteria considered important in some countries by some observers holding some doctrines could be omitted. Such omission could make a large difference in a rating.

Furthermore, how would the ratings be arrived at? Indicators that could be quantified, such as the number of times a problem was reported in some newspaper, would be so crude as to lead to absurd distortions. If the opinions of qualified observers (judges) were to be used, could those rating the various parts of the world be induced to use the same scales and criteria? Would a foreigner judge the freedom in a country with too little understanding and would a native judge it with too little objectivity?

Perhaps most important, what value loading would be put upon the terms, definitions, criteria and indicators? If the investigators are United States citizens, they no doubt would adopt what is called freedom in their country as the benchmark, along with the assumption that, since freedom is good, all the components of this particular type of freedom would be good, and anything Americans consider bad could not be a component.

Lastly, freedom from what or whom? Domestic governments traditionally are cast as the only powers that can restrict freedom of communication. But evidence from recent decades indicates that media owners, labor unions, unidentified terrorists, mobs, suppliers, distributors, religious authorities, international bodies and even foreign governments can influence the amount of media freedom within a country.

THE CHART-MAKERS

Perhaps the earliest substantial efforts to set up press freedom categories were those of associations such as the International Press Institute, heavily oriented toward Europe, Africa and Asia, and the Inter-American Press Association, dealing with the Western Hemisphere. Since reporters have traditionally been averse to joining anything, these organizations have remained the province of media owners and, to some extent, editors. Thus they have taken a rather uncomplicated view of press freedom. The enemy is always the government, private investors are the only rightful owners, commerce is the highest and best calling of the media, society can exert demands on them only through the marketplace, and any legal norms beyond the most basic defamation and pornography laws are unacceptable.

The IAPA began issuing its annual (later semiannual) reports on freedom of the press when it was reorganized soon after World War II. They have the appearance of roll calls, because nearly always the entry on each country begins with the solemn pronouncement that "There is . . ." or "There is not freedom of the press" in the respective country. Often the entry goes no further than this, but sometimes supporting evidence ranging from a sentence to many pages is provided. The "is" or "is not" verdicts are decided by a standing committee, and the evidence is provided by committee members living in the concerned areas, who usually are politically hostile to or defensive against each government. A less developed affiliate of the IAPA, the Inter-American Association of Broadcasters, deals with the radio and television field. Both groups issue regular bulletins giving timely reports of what they consider incursions on media freedom, and both protest vigorously to governments whose actions they disapprove.

The International Press Institute, headquartered in London, operates much as the IAPA does, particularly through its periodical bulletins and through special reports. It did much to set the tone for later freedom ratings through its survey report called *The Press in Authoritarian Countries* issued in 1959.

The report disclaimed any effort to give a "scientific definition" of an authoritarian regime, saying simply that it included those which had had "a permanent censorship or a constant and general control of the press" during the 1956–58 period.[2] With either articles or lists, it placed in this category the Soviet Union and all Eastern European countries; Spain and Portugal in Europe; Egypt, with no mention of the rest of Africa or the Middle East; the communist countries in Asia, plus South Korea, Taiwan, South Vietnam, Indonesia and Thailand; and eight Latin American countries. Evidence about each country's restrictions came from anonymous sources which the IPI described as "experienced journalists who have lived in or visited the countries in question and who are considered as specialists in their field." In some cases, other investigators made further checks.[3]

Spurred on by these efforts, communication researchers carried out a flurry of systematic rating projects in the 1960s. Leading the way was Raymond B. Nixon of the University of Minnesota, a pioneer in international communication studies and a tireless globetrotter.[4] He was interested in press freedom ratings (excluding broadcasting) of 117 countries, not as an end in themselves but rather to test a hypothesis that had grown out of the national development studies of the 1950s. This held that "there is a positive and systematic relationship between the degree of press freedom in a country and three other indices of national development. . . ."[5] He did prove that this correlation existed between press freedom, as he defined it, and per capita income, literacy and radio and newspaper distribution. Although he disclaimed any attempt to prove causation, his results did suggest a relatively sophisticated view of media restriction—that it arises not through the caprice of a ruler but rather from the lack of certain elements of modernity.

Nixon adopted the IPI's definition of press freedom. To apply it, he used what was basically a committee of scholarly experts, mostly alien to but acquainted with the country rated. He used first a five-point scale and later a nine-point one, ranging from "free" at one end to "authoritarian" and later "controlled" at the other. As a concession to communists' sensitivities, he labeled their systems differently from other "authoritarian" or "controlled" ones but ranked them together for statistical purposes. Nixon also tested alternative methods but found they either were impracticable or confirmed his other findings.

Somewhat similar in purpose to the Nixon studies was one by two political scientists, Arthur S. Banks and Robert B. Textor.[6] Seeking correlations, they measured 57 characteristics (including press freedom) of 115 nations. Although the computerized results provided a rich array of correlations, these were largely discounted by communication scholars because the only press freedom indicators used were the year-end reports by the Associated Press, which are sketchy at best and rely heavily on the problems of foreign correspondents.

The first (and last) large-scale comparative study of press freedom for its own sake—not as part of a broader project, as were the Nixon and Banks-Textor ones—came in 1966 and 1967 when Ralph L. Lowenstein of the University of Missouri published precise numerical ratings for 94 of the 115 independent nations then existing. He attempted to overcome all the shortcomings of previous studies by a variety of devices.

In the Lowenstein project, called the Press Independence and Critical Ability survey (PICA), all major media were included—newspapers, periodicals, news agencies, books, radio and television. It used a seven-point scale with "completely free" at one end and "completely controlled" at the other. The former was defined as the media's having "absolute independence and critical ability, except for minimal libel and obscenity laws" and exhibiting "no concentrated ownership, marginal economic units or organized self-regulation." "Completely controlled" was defined as absence of such independence and critical ability and presence of the cited influences.[7]

But the chief departure of PICA from the other studies was that it specified 23 criteria upon which each media system was to be judged. They covered widely varied restrictions, mostly having to do with government policy and laws but also with private ownerships and self-regulatory bodies such as press councils. Also included were some favors such as state advertising which could compromise the media, and two factors having to do with the degree to which the media exercised their critical ability were listed.[8] To cope with the problem of rating media in countries in which most or all of the media were state-owned, Lowenstein simply suspended 12 of the 23 factors in rating them. Different sets of both native and foreign judges were used for each country, although the natives' judgments were discarded if they varied widely from the non-natives'.

Lowenstein frankly ruled several factors outside the range of the PICA study. One was the degree of stability in a press system's freedom; this he left to future measurements like PICA (there have been none). For various reasons, he also decided criteria should exclude constitutional provisions, access to government records, problems of foreign correspondents and imported publications, foreign investment in media ownership, and private advertising as a control device.

The most publicized freedom survey conducted since the PICA project is the Comparative Study reported upon annually or seminannually since 1973 by Freedom House in New York. It subsumes freedom of expression under "civil liberties," one of the two bases for its numerical ratings of countries, the other being "political liberties." Essential to civil liberties, it says, are independent news media.

> This may mean private control of the press or radio, but more importantly it means freedom from any of the various forms of censorship. The Survey is interested primarily in censorship that is applied in defense of a ruling party or its

policies; there is only marginal interest in censorship applied for social or religious reasons.[9]

A well-endowed permanent secretariat, supervised by a centrist sample of prominent Americans, arrives at the ratings through consultation with academic social scientists. It gives seven-point ratings for each country on each of the two kinds of liberties, then boils this down to three categories into which the countries are divided—"free," "partly free" and "unfree."

Freedom House does not offer precise criteria by which countries are judged, and its reports consist of articles which recount assorted events in each major region of the world and give the author's interpretation of progress there. Highly truncated versions of these reports are provided for news media, and a "Map of Freedom" dividing the world into white (free), gray and black areas is sold for $5.

Political competition is Freedom House's main concern, and it concedes that it gives little attention to economic systems. However, it took a brief look at relations between the two aspects in 1978 and arrived at a conclusion: "Capitalist states can be free or unfree; socialist states can only be unfree."[10]

A New Departure

The problems mentioned earlier in regard to press freedom ratings were coped with partially by some of the surveys, but enough of them remain to raise doubts about the entire concept. There is no doubt that the persons who conduct them have put much hard, honest work into them, and the underlying information produced can be enlightening. But when this supporting information is washed out in the attempt at simplified ratings, reality tends to depart with it and we are left with confirmation of the prejudices we have picked up through superficial news reading. The process may reduce the frustration of headline-skimmers, but anyone interested in serious analysis is as poorly served as if given a list of all the pretty, ugly and intermediate women in the world.

Still another problem would remain even if all the others were met: Is it defensible to reduce to two or three words or a few numbers the swirling mass of interactions in a national community of several hundred million persons? Even when speaking of one aspect of this society, freedom of expression, it appears from the studies reported in this book that vastly different patterns will occur within one country. The print media may have far more latitude than television; the same difference may be found between individual newspapers, between national and local media units, foreign and domestic newsmen, editorials and news content, political and nonpolitical material, loyalist and opposition journalists, and peaceful and disturbed periods.

So a systemic look at each country, one by one, seems imperative. Not only must the current work of all levels of the media—from reporter to owner—be investigated, but the media must be viewed as part of a national pattern of institutions—government, education, recreation, religion, etc. They also must be looked at from a historical perspective, with an attempt to discover tendencies pointing into the future.

Even the painting of such a complex portrait can be as useless for the comparative analyst as is the ratings game if it has no relevance to the broader work. But the studies reported in this volume brought to light certain patterns of behavior that occurred, with some variations, in many countries. In the more refined analyses, tracing the incidence of these patterns and contrasting systems in which they are absent would seem to make the spadework of the national portraits worthwhile.

Traditionally, studies of media-government relations have focused only on which restrictions are put upon the communicators. Such studies portray the media operators as helpless victims of rapacious governments—frail reeds which bend to any official wind. Although this can happen, the present studies repeatedly show that two important variations can occur—media can influence or even bully the government, and even when the government tries to restrict the media, their response to the effort often can have more to do with their freedom than any other factor.

In the previous chapter it was seen that development of Latin America has followed its own dynamics and is not simply a defective imitation of processes originating in the United States and Europe. We are beginning to understand that there may be a "Latin American way" for many facets of society, including mass communication. Although it still is not clear—neither to native analysts nor to foreigners—exactly how the area's scale of journalistic values differs from those of other areas, we certainly would be foolish to assume that the free (positive)-unfree (negative) scale used in the United States could be exported southward without adjustment.

It is not the purpose of this study to discover what is *wrong* with media-government relations in Latin America but rather to discover what *exists*. Toward that end, the categories used in this chapter—disclosive-adversary, cautious, collaborative, and absorbed—have been chosen so as to reduce value loadings. Furthermore, these labels describe *postures of the media* rather than government policies; the first three suggest that these postures have been chosen by or at least accepted by the media.

On the basis of the case studies in this book and the author's intensive studies of other Latin American communication systems, attempts will be made to place various parts of these systems into each of the four categories. These placements are based on the situation of the late 1970s, and no claim is made that they are durable. (History has shown how volatile such situations are.) However, the emphasis is on the patterns of action that produce the categories in the hope that these will have long-term usefulness as analytical tools. Placements into the categories are made only to illustrate them, and any resemblance to the earlier rating systems is unintended.

THE DISCLOSIVE-ADVERSARY POSTURE

Latin American news media, at least as early as the dawn of the 20th Century, accepted the norm that their two principal functions were to lead and inform and that content carrying out each function should be segregated from each other. Media, after all, were part of the trappings of modernity, and publishers were keenly conscious that the dual-function concept came as part of the package.

But the concept and the reality diverged widely in Latin America. Because the media had great value as political vehicles for the publishers, they prized the leadership role far more than the informative one. So opinion spilled over into the news columns, whether through selecting and emphasizing stories that favored the publisher's viewpoint, slanting a headline on an otherwise objective story, or lacing the facts with commentary or innuendo. All of these practices were common in the United States and Britain in the 19th Century and even persist in many parts of the world. But rarely have they coexisted so easily with the concept they violate as in Latin America.

The two functions have come to mean quite different things to different journalists. Leadership frequently has meant supporting one political faction or party which existed to advance the ambitions of a charismatic chief and his followers rather than to accomplish an explicitly stated program. When this element is in office, the publisher reinforces the faithful and condemns the supposed treason of the opposition. And when the out-of-office period comes, through guns or ballots, the editorials fall into tepid timidity if faced with a dictatorship or into violent name-calling if in a democracy.

Furthermore, the informative function can take different shapes. It can reflect the editorial line in the ways noted above. More commonly, it also can be a neutral channeling of opinions from political leaders, even to the extent of giving the opposition a chance to be heard. (This is the standard pronouncement form of news story which throngs so many media throughtout the area.) Offering the justification of the freemarket theory, publishers even vary the open-channel policy by charging opinionmakers for space in the news columns, disguising the covert advertisements so as to appear as if they were gathered by reporters.

However, media can carry out the two functions in much more daring, even reckless manners. As leaders, they can habitually take the stance of adversaries of the government, no matter who is in power. Thus, although they may profess loyalty to a doctrine shared by a party or faction, they are not under its control nor does the news medium depend on its fortunes. The adversary posture, if deeply rooted in the medium, continues even when the government makes clear that it will tolerate no such audacity. If this occurs, of course, the medium suffers punishment, is put out of business or, as often results, so intimidates the government that it is allowed to go forward without severe handicap.

In their role as informants, news media can try, at least part of the time, to truly disclose to the public things it needs to know about its government—things that the politicians are not willing or able to disclose through the open-channel activity of the media. Even those Latin American media which have been the most forthright as adversaries often have stopped short of being disclosive. This is not for lack of will but rather lack of ability, because disclosive reporting calls for highly developed skills of fact-gathering and writing, which must be acquired through arduous study, either in journalism schools or through apprenticeship to older journalists who themselves were heirs of such a tradition. It also requires the outlay of much money, and few reporters would endure such preparation, going abroad if necessary, for the pitifully small salaries paid by most Latin American news media.

It must be noted that disclosiveness need not be confined to the so-called "investigative reporting," usually connoting the revelation of corruption in government. It can range across a vast area of sociological, economic, scientific and artistic reporting. Trends, patterns and weaknesses in a system that have nothing to do with a single regime can be exposed. A nation can be educated about itself, including its cultural strengths. But the essential ingredient is the originality that comes from a high degree of education and professional ability, not merely the hackneyed repetition of media messages the public has read or heard a thousand times before.

Where are the adversary and/or disclosive media to be found? Certainly they flourish most easily in democracies such as the ones studied earlier—Costa Rica, Colombia and Venezuela. But form of government seems to have little to do with the existence of these keepers of the flame. This writer, during his visits in all 20 Latin American countries, has taken soundings as to which media command wide respect for fulfilling one or both of the advanced functions. The listing below follows no particular order and carries no claim of completeness. But there is good reason to support all the mentions.

Examples

Scanning the Latin American panorama for media that are both adversary and disclosive (using the definitions just offered), one finds a generally bleak picture, athough those that are one or the other appear more often. Brazil, with one of the most harsh systems of media restriction, presents the most ample array of media fulfilling both roles. The democracies of Costa Rica, Colombia and Venezuela taken together are surprisingly thin in this sector, and another dictatorship, Argentina, is among the most represented, although this is definitely not the predominant mode of the country's journalism. Notable but isolated examples such as the weekly press in Peru can be found in other countries under various types of governments.

Although the adversary-disclosive posture is by no means universal in Brazil, one never has to look far to find such ferment. The prime example in the country—in all of Latin America, in fact—is *O Estado,* the leading daily of a provincial capital, São Paulo. Like most Brazilian dailies, it is generally critical of the government while supporting its basic concepts. What emphasizes the criticism is that this posture has no relation to party rivalry, as the legal opposition party exerts little doctrinal magnetism on either the press or the public other than as a symbol of resistance; thus there is little basis for suspecting that the criticism is a function of loyalty to a party. Ironically, this truly adversary posture is a phenomenon of the dictatorship period itself, as the criticism largely followed party lines until the 1964 military takeover. In fact, *O Estado* and other leading media continued to act as cheerleaders for the government for several years after the coup.

As signs pointed toward eventual resumption of civilian control of Brazil in the late 1970s, there was no certainty that editors would be all-weather adversaries of whatever government ensued. But after more than a decade of being nonpartisan critics, Brazilian editors could reasonably be expected to continue the habit.

The most remarkable aspect of the Brazilian media is their tendency to be disclosive as well as adversary. Never has the country seen so much persistent and highly competent digging for subsurface news as in the 1970s, whether it concerns corruption in government or pollution or abuses of consumers. *O Estado* with its 500 editorial employees has also led the pack in this regard, but others are running close on its heels. *Veja*, a São Paulo weekly news magazine, has consistently probed into domestic and foreign situations with a tenacity that easily puts it in the company of counterparts such as *Time, Newsweek, The Economist, L'Express* and *Der Spiegel*.

The weekly newspaper field—the so-called "midget press"—has provided some of the most enterprising reportage in addition to criticism. Such publications range from the archdiocesan Catholic voice of São Paulo to raffish satirical journals. For several years their standard-bearer was the highly competent leftist weekly *Opinião*, but it collapsed under economic pressure in 1977.

Other newspapers as well as *O Estado* have caught the spirit. *Jornal do Brasil* in Rio contends for the distinctions *O Estado* has won. So did the opposition *Folha de São Paulo* until its owners gave in to government pressure and fired its crusaders in 1977. Smaller provincial dailies also frequently get in trouble because of their criticism or revelations.

Broadcasters, much more vulnerable to official reprisal than the print media, are less bold but still very eager to share in the honors. Radio stations' talk shows often push against the boundaries, and television documentaries have set out to rival programs like "Sixty Minutes" in the United States.

Skeptics say the Brazilian media would not be half so cocksure without the wealth given them by their country's economic boom, and it is true that the upward curve of their aggressiveness closely parallels the "miracle" of the early 1970s. However, other Latin American countries with surging economies have not shown similar outbursts of media activity.

Despite ample opportunity, media in the two largest democracies, Venezuela and Colombia, have shown little inclination to be nonpartisan critics and aggressive reporters. The end of the national front coalition in Colombia has created an appetite for such fare but little in the way of offerings. In Venezuela, the race for the *peso* has resulted in little prestige for this type of content, although television Channel 2 and the news magazine *Resumen* have made some efforts toward disclosive reporting.

Journalism in Costa Rica, while vigorous in other respects, shows only the promise of adversary and disclosive activity. New standards of professionalism are being widely adopted in the dailies *La Nación* and *La República* and in television Channel 6, and this has resulted in material embarrassing for the government.

Equally in flux is the situation in Mexico. Julio Scherer García brought about a flowering of independent journalism during the early 1970s when he was director of Mexico City daily *Excélsior* and touched off rival efforts in other newspapers. This kind of work went into eclipse when Scherer was ousted through government pressures. The Scherer group went on to found a magazine and then a daily, but these were at the fringe of the national life in their initial period.

Surrounded by a sea of daily newspapers and broadcast media operated by the government, the private weekly press of Peru has shown a resilience and freedom of spirit equaled only by its counterparts in Brazil. Perhaps no publication on the continent has taken more chances to be closed than *Caretas* of Lima, the best known of the breed. Its director, Enrique Zileri, also ranks as the most often exiled journalist in the area. But the other Lima weeklies, ranging to extremes of left and right, also have been considered so dangerous by the government that they have frequently been closed en masse. Their editorial criticism has much the same tone as that usually read in Brazil—support of the revolution but opposition to specific measures. Although they rarely exhibit the resources and skills needed for regular disclosive reporting, they produce enough to keep their future in doubt.

In Argentina, glints of independence and enterprise break through the journalistic clouds in a scattered fashion. The most consistent examplar has been the *Buenos Aires Herald,* a small English-language paper that wrings daily miracles from a tiny budget. It quietly acts the role of a thoroughgoing Argentine patriot, dispensing sober criticism without a hint of *gringo* condescension, regardless of the government in power. It does not have the staff for wide-ranging investigation, but it continually prints news that is generally known among the elites but which the other dailies are reluctant to print.

A newspaper that has shown fierce independence from political control if not from doctrine is *La Prensa* of Buenos Aires. It has never hesitated to criticize any government, although it is much more gentle with rightist ones than those of the left. Until his death in 1977, Alberto Gainza Paz, director of *La Prensa,* based his editorial policy on an implacable contempt for Juan Perón, dating from Perón's takeover of the paper and Gainza Paz's exile in the early 1950s. Disclosive reporting was not his strong point, however, and the news columns grew progressively more slanted as he and his staff grew older.

Another Buenos Aires daily, *La Opinión,* gave the country the most penetrating depth reporting it had ever seen, beginning with its birth in 1971 and ending with its near-death in 1977, when its director was jailed in a financial and political scandal. *La Opinión* never ran editorials—only slanted but highly intelligent articles on all facets of national life. These were not totally fearless, as the paper trimmed its sails as political pressures required, but they did excite the envy of journalists throughout the hemisphere.

Another isolated case of notable disclosive reporting is to be found under still another dictatorship, that in Chile. It again demonstrates that a journalistic medium can rise to its highest respect after the political party with which it was affiliated is banned from activity. *Ercilla,* the leading news magazine of Chile, had been a spokesman for the Christian Democrats before the military coup of 1973. Forced to navigate in apolitical waters, it developed its international prestige somewhat like *Veja* in Brazil. When unsympathetic business interests bought out the magazine in 1977, director Emilio Filippi simply transferred the reputation and most of the staff to a new publication, *Hoy.*

Those who value the adversary-disclosive posture can find guarded hope for the provincial newspapers and sometimes broadcasters of many larger countries. Although their aggressiveness often grows from party loyalty, sophistication is to be found in the most remote areas, often as a reaction to the exhaustion which capital-city media fall into because of battles with the government. Particularly notable are the provincial media of Brazil, Colombia, Mexico, Argentina and, to some extent, Chile.

The traits studied here rarely emerge in the smallest countries; courageous opposition to a government can occur, albeit usually in defense of a secondary party. This was demonstrated for many years in the combativeness displayed toward the Nicaraguan dictatorship by Pedro Joaquín Chamorro, director of the Managua daily *La Prensa* who was assassinated in 1978.

Characteristics

If one is to be certain of any generalization about the conditions that produce adversary-disclosive journalism, it would have to be that the practice can spring up anywhwere. Democratic government by no means assures that it will occur. In fact, the Latin American experience indicates that it is more likely to exist under threat than under protection. This is seen on both temporal and geographical scales. The media of Brazil and the weekly press of Peru never displayed nearly so much of these qualities until the 1970s, when they were under most pressure. Furthermore, the adversary-disclosive qualities are notably rare in the democracies of Colombia and Venezuela, particularly in comparison with some of the dictatorships.

The case studies also show a strong likelihood that adversary-disclosive practices will coincide with the removal of party politics as journalism's reason for being. It was only after the Brazilian weeklies, the Peruvian weeklies, and Chile's *Ercilla* had to become essentially nonpartisan that their independence and diligence rose to their highest. The *Buenos Aires Herald,* although never affiliated with parties in recent times, also has flourished most when party competition was weakest.

The concept that party competition may be anything but beneficial to democratic institutions is heresy, of course. But the conclusion that sometimes it can smother independent journalism is inescapable.

Certainly not all editors have responded equally to adversity and partisan nakedness. So it is worthwhile to examine the internal characteristics of the media which have responded with an increase in the professional traits studied here.

One thread that runs through nearly all the outstanding examples is an intensely personalistic orientation of the medium, which means that the director usually is mostly active in journalistic tasks rather than in business management or political maneuvering. Such a journalist-director may have to learn what the inside of jail cells look like, as several have, and he may have to buy his independence at the cost of appeasing his governing board if he is not the owner. The most enviable position, of course, is held by those who speak with the authority of ownership, as do the Mesquita brothers of *O Estado de São Paulo* and Enrique Zileri of *Caretas* in Lima, and as the late Alberto Gainza Paz of Buenos Aires' *La Prensa* did. Exceptions to the general rule may be found in the rare cases in which businessmen have been the driving forces behind publications mentioned above, such as Fernando Gasparián of *Opinião* in Rio and Jacobo Timerman of *La Opinión* in Buenos Aires; it may be significant that both left the journalistic field in 1977, one through financial pressures and the other because of a commercial scandal.

Political orientation of the medium seems to have little to do with existence of the adversary-disclosure posture. The directors can range across the full scope of ideology in their sympathies, except for the far extremes. Rather, as in the case of party loyalties, it is the extent to which the journalist restrains his doctrinal passions that he is able to approach the norm considered here. It was not until the conservative Mesquitas of *O Estado* and Guido Fernández of Costa Rica's *La Nación* rose above ideology that they won professional prestige. On the left, the same could be said of the Peruvian Enrique Zileri and the Chilean Emilio Filippi.

Whether a cause or an effect, international orientation does seem to correlate with being adversary and disclosive. Without exception, those identified with this posture are men with a world view. Although their pages are concerned primarily with domestic matters, in all cases they spend heavily to keep a cosmopolitan dimension. They may do double duty as foreign correspondents themselves, as Julio Scherer García did while director of *Excélsior*.

THE CAUTIOUS POSTURE

By far the most common posture to be found among Latin American journalistic media is that of caution. Whereas the adversary-disclosive mode described earlier involves a conscious decision and overt acts on the part of the publisher, professional caution is a normal, habitual response shaped by centuries of class societies and authoritarian governments. Of course, in all cultures "going along" is considered a wiser course of action than being perverse, but in Latin America punishment for the maverick journalist is considered much more likely to be swift and sure.

Guessing where the danger spots lie has always been a highly developed art in Latin American newsrooms. Nearly every journalist in the region longs to have his moments of audacity, but he wants to approach them with his eyes wide open, not to stumble upon them. The process is complicated by the fact that prior restraint such as official censorship very rarely has existed in recent years, except for the few tense days following a coup d'etat.

So what results is massive *autocensura* (self-censorship), a practice to which a great majority of the region's journalists admit with despair and shame. In practice, it consists of a reporter's leaving out of his stories things he has witnessed or rumors which could be checked out with competent sources. It also means that an editor will backstop the reporter in making sure these deletions are made. From the standpoint of the consumer—both the elites and the masses—this results in daily reliance on the rumor mill.

Being their own inspectors is so repugnant to journalists that they generally welcome official censorship as an alternative. Thus it was that *O Estado de São Paulo* refused to censor itself and tartly informed the government that if it wanted such control it would have to do it. Officials did supply an in-office censor for three years, then mysteriously withdrew him, apparently because of worldwide ridicule.

Another way the cautious posture manifests itself is through obscure writing or broadcasting. Latin America's poets, novelists and essayists have produced some of the most forceful writing to be found anywhere—simple, direct and muscular. But ironically the media that are intended to be understood most quickly—newspapers in particular—are the most difficult to follow. Even news accounts often are tangled in pretentious words, tortured syntax, marathon sentences and irrelevant facts. These devices actually are used for a purpose—to hint without asserting. So those readers or viewers who are among the insiders have learned to extract some meaning—often not the right one—from all the fluff. Editorials and columns, dealing with more sensitive matters, are even more impenetrable.

However, it must be recognized that a journalistic medium which typically follows the path of caution is by definition not an adherent of a governing faction or an active party of opposition; if it had the protection of these, it would have little need for caution. While it does not assert its independence forthrightly like the adversary-disclosive media do, neither is it in the thrall of outside forces like the collaborative ones are.

Examples

Some degree of journalistic caution may be found in every country in the region. It is the dominant mode in most dictatorships, where the great majority of media do not see fit to endanger their lives or those of their employees for moments of glory. However, the publishers typically stand ready to exploit any relaxation of governmental control.

Nowhere is this better demonstrated than in Paraguay, perhaps the most efficiently policed dictatorship in the region. In what approaches true adversary posture, the leading newspaper, *ABC Color,* constantly takes its criticism as far as it can, always staying just inside the safe zone. "We're always trying to move the walls outward bit by bit," its director, Aldo Zucolillo, said in an interview. "We know we are risking ourselves, but this risk decreases the more we test the situation."[11] Other newspapers emulate *ABC* with less fervor and skill.

Uruguay, with a dictatorship almost as rigid as Paraguay's, also has one newspaper which shows the way for others who would proceed in cautious opposition. This is the venerated daily *El Día*, founded in 1886 by a giant of Uruguayan history, José Batlle y Ordóñez. Its editorial writers have become masters of writing criticisms which must be read between the lines. They also haunt the government by each day running a huge blow-up of the founder's picture and a distinctly democratic quote from him.

Besides Paraguay and Uruguay, countries where the cautious posture is the most frequent are Argentina, Bolivia, Ecuador, El Salvador, Guatemala, Haiti, Honduras and Venezuela, even though some of the media in these countries assume other postures.

Anyone accustomed to the traditional categories of "free" and "unfree" will choke at finding the media in democratic Venezuela lumped together with those in dictatorial Haiti. But here we are concerned not primarily with the attitudes of the governments but with those of the media. For quite different reasons, media in the various countries noted above tend to avoid impartial editorial criticism and/or disclosive reporting.

Real or feared governmental pressures are the largest causes for the prevailing caution in Bolivia, Ecuador, Haiti and Honduras. In form, these have been classic dictatorships in which the president—a general in three cases—has ruled without parliamentary hindrance. Mild criticism and some bold reporting was slowly increasing in the late 1970s, even in Haiti, but journalists knew they were on a short leash that could be yanked at any time.

In Argentina and Guatemala, on the other hand, anonymous terrorism looms as the most inhibiting of the worries that bedevil news personnel. A background of governmental pressures still is a felt presence, particularly in Argentina, but it is the hail of bullets in the street, the bomb in the office and the kidnapping, often combined with murder, that have gone farthest in putting journalists on their guard.

A quite distinct form of influence chills the ardor of media directors in Venezuela and El Salvador. Their media systems are rivaled only by Brazil's for financial prosperity. But whereas leading Brazilian media have chosen to risk or reinforce their profits through audacity and enterprise, the principal Venezuelan newspapers have elected not to editorialize at all but rather to print a variety of opinions from contributors. Although editorials are regular features of the press in El Salvador, they rarely are offensive to those in charge of the government or the economy. As for disclosive reporting, the giant Venezuelan enterprises could afford it, although the small Salvadorean economy provides a slender base for it.

Characteristics

As in the case of the adversary-disclosive posture, it is easier to find factors which do not correlate with the cautious posture than those that do. We find it existing under democratic as well as the most dictatorial regimes, albeit more often under the latter. Prosperity also seems to have little bearing, as the range stretches from the lucrative giants of Venezuela to the poverty-stricken sheets of Honduras and Haiti.

Again the needle of the compass points to the type of leadership of the media as the most consistent factor. The directors of the cautious media tend to be persons who see economic fitness of their enterprises as their highest duty. Quite often such directors are faceless to the general public although well known in the business community. In many cases they inherited the ownership but not the professional orientation from their fathers; in others, the owning family has always been primarily interested in the commercial aspects. Still another route to this posture is the purchase or establishment of the medium by men who are investors and have come quite late in their careers to responsibility for journalism. This is by far the most frequent case in regard to broadcasting.

Political conservatism appears to correlate strongly with the cautious posture, and it might be speculated that those who are hesitant to act rashly in politics will be just as hesitant in professional matters. However, this association probably is spurious, because a large part of the exemplars of adversary journalism are conservatives. Furthermore, the overwhelming majority of media directors in Latin American *are* political conservatives, so it is not surprising to find them bulking large in the most common professional mode.

THE COLLABORATIVE POSTURE

Journalism in Europe and the United States emerged as a separate institution in the 19th Century alongside others such as the military and the church. But the process has been slower and less decisive in Latin America; journalism remains to some extent an adjunct of the older groupings. Various reasons might be found, including these:

1. The personnel of the media traditionally have used journalism as an occupational way station, resorting to it between political or academic appointments. A variation on this is the almost universal practice among journalists of holding several jobs, often in different fields, at the same time.

2. Centuries of periodic humiliations at the hands of governments. It is difficult for a profession to retain its dignity when any national leader can whimsically force the members to prostrate themselves, which is what often occurs during the most minor crises.

3. Over-competition for a limited market. In many cases this has prevented an elite stratum from emerging, thus setting a standard for the other units. Instead, the entire system has to jostle for position and even rely on political "angels."

Despite these negative factors that make collaboration with other forces a necessity, some publishers would prefer to make alliances even if they had a choice. The concept of a newspaper's or other medium's isolating itself from other institutions has never become an ethical norm in Latin America.

The most frequent alliance, of course, is political. In an earlier section it was noted that political criticism may arise from more than one motive. It may be truly adversary, which signifies that the medium will play the role of the inspector-general of all political factions in or out of the presidential palace. But more often the criticism is viewed as a tactical weapon to advance the cause of the faction with which the publisher is allied. If the faction is out of power, the target usually is the party controlling the government. But once the publisher's cause triumphs, he becomes the defender and herald of the new governors.

This is not to imply that the collaborative posture always entails servility to political leaders. Quite often the director of the journalistic medium becomes leader of the political movement, as has happened countless times such as in the cases of José Batlle y Ordóñez of Uruguay, Bartolomé Mitre and Domingo Sarmiento of Argentina, Manuel Prado of Peru, Eduardo Santos of Colombia and Carlos Andrés Pérez of Venezuela. Furthermore, the journalist carrying the torch for a political faction, such as Pedro Joaquín Chamorro of Nicaragua, may well become a martyr to the cause as Chamorro did.

The decision of whether to collaborate may in effect be made for the publisher. This occurs when an authoritarian regime takes over through a coup and outlaws opposing media. The only ones allowed to continue in operation are those which opposed the previous governors and are enthusiastic about the new ones; the decision thus is a governmental one.

Money rather than politics may also be the basis for the collaboration. It had been pointed out above that the media owners' orientation to commerce can result in adoption of the cautious posture, which signifies that they weigh their decisions on the scale of profits and do not necessarily made a political alliance with the government or factions. But the commercial collaborator frankly sees the government or party as a business partner or at least a steady customer.

Such an arrangement is becoming steadily more expectable as governments in Latin America become statist in their economies. While they may not absorb the media, they do nationalize or co-invest in many of the largest advertisers—banks, airlines, railroads, factories and insurance companies. This naturally leads to the attitude on the part of the media directors that what is good for the government is good for the journalist.

State-operated credit systems often are another economic linkage between government and media. These lead to considerable mutual back-scratching, and default on the loans may bring about actual joint ownership.

Examples

Perhaps the classic illustration of the collaborative posture in recent times has been the support given the government of Colombia by all its major media. This originated in the devoted loyalty traditionally given by Colombian newspapers to one or the other of the long-established parties, the Liberals and the Conservatives. During the country's nine-year civil war (1948–57), every individual in the country was expected to declare himself for one side or the other, and this reinforced the press' party ties. Then when the warring parties made peace by forming a coalition to run the government, called the National Front, the media accepted the political leaders' decision and closed ranks. Although under no direct government control, the press had much the same slavish attitude as those in a communist country. (All of the television system and part of the radio stations were state-owned.)

As the National Front was being phased out and true political competition was returning to Colombia in the late 1970s, so the posture of the press was gradually changing. However, although the blind support of the government is fading there is no indication that the publishers will cast themselves adrift from the parties they have always been allied with.

The Chilean media, particularly the Santiago dailies, provide an example of collaboration made necessary by a revolutionary coup. After the virulent conflict between media favoring the Allende government and those against it, the military coup-makers eliminated the pro-Allende media by closing them, jailing their officers or frightening them into exile. The junta bluntly made clear to the remaining media that they would fall into line or suffer the same fate. Most of those who opposed Allende favored the military to some degree anyway. Those that were most lukewarm in their support, the Christian Democratic Party's stalwarts, have slowly gone out of existence since the coup because of economic and political pressures.

Because the Chilean military has not built its own political party, its alliance with the collaborative media has always been viewed as a temporary recourse. Mild criticism of government actions has slowly emerged, although it still has the ring of in-house discussion.

Mexico presents the case of a media system which, during the revolution of 1910–17, originally came to be collaborative because of a purge like that in Chile but which since has turned to another motivation—profit. Still a one-party country in essence, Mexico has loosened the negative controls over the media to the point that opposition media are free to operate. The fact that few of them do is a tribute to the effectiveness of the massive buddy system which pervades Mexican public life. One learns early in life that, whether one is a labor leader, businessman or journalist, the way to power and money is through the dominant party, which is identical with the government. These opportunities for enrichment exist at all levels; the reporter gets his fee for favorable news he writes about a government agency, the advertising salesman gets his large commission for official notices, and the publisher profits from cut-rate supplies and loans he gets from state agencies. The question basically is not whether the journalist can be independent from the government but rather whether he wants to be. In the words of one foreign reporter, "Mexico has more freedom than most editors there use." [12]

Collaboration need not be widespread as in Colombia, Chile and Mexico to be significant. It may consist of a partnership between the government and one leading newspaper. This is a relationship prized by political leaders, as it is considered far more effective to have as the official organ a seemingly independent paper than one owned by the state. Dictatorships especially crave such a relationship; they usually resist any temptations to directly bully their chief journalistic collaborators and thus get more willing service. With varying degrees of devotion, this linkage has evolved by the late 1970s for *Clarín* in Buenos Aires, *O Globo* and its television network in Rio, *El País* in Montevideo, *El Mercurio* of Santiago and *Le Nouveau Monde* of Port au Prince.

Several other forms of collaboration to be found currently are notable for their rarity. One is religious affiliation. This rarely occurs among the mainstream journalistic media, although one of the two major newspapers of Bolivia, *La Presencia,* is owned by the Catholic Church. Its editor calls it "the only one of its kind in the world" in that it openly competes with other newspapers and avoids being "ecclesiastical." [13] His boast can be defended at least for Latin America. There are dailies with strong sympathies for the church, such as *La Nación* of Buenos Aires, and parochial publications such as the bold archdiocesan weekly of São Paulo. But they do not fill the role *La Presencia* does.

Radio stations and magazines owned by religious groups are found widely throughout Latin America, but they typically deal with news and public affairs only as a sideline. The most extensive of these is HCJB of Quito, Ecuador, whose mission is worldwide Protestant evangelism through shortwave radio, and Sutatenza of Colombia and Fides of Bolivia, which are "radio schools" designed to help peasants and urban poor improve their lot.

One of the most bizarre forms of collaboration occurs in Honduras, where the two major newspaper groups are owned respectively by leaders of the resident Arab and Jewish communities. This rarely affects the domestic editorial content of the papers, but the affiliations are frequently mentioned in discussions of the press.

Foreign-language publications, which are found in every country in the area, usually collaborate closely with their alien constituencies. However, a movement is afoot among them to build readership among the English-reading natives, and the *Buenos Aires Herald* has largely shed the reputation of being a mouthpiece for *gringos*. To a lesser extent, this could be said for a weekly, the *Tico Times* of San José.

The Spanish-language media of Costa Rica appear to be in a transition phase between their historic mode of being partisan collaborators and a new identification as adversary and disclosive voices. Such ideas are admired by many journalists and could easily become dominant.

Characteristics

The most instructive thing that can be said about collaborative relationships between media and factions is that the linkage continues only so long as the faction has a need for it. The medium rarely breaks up the alliance of its own accord, mostly because it is so advantageous.

The Mexican government is known as the most stable in Latin America because one party has run it for six decades. Consequently the media have had a long time to define their identity, and changes in basic structure come slowly.

Colombia's collaborative arrangement has begun breaking up as the coalition government itself does. As the Chilean military regime gradually has less need of a journalistic claque, so the media there have edged away from full partnership. The alliances between the dictatorships and single newspapers in Uruguay, Brazil and Argentina also have the aura of marriages of convenience.

THE ABSORBED POSTURE

When a mass medium finds itself in one of the other postures, it has gotten there by choice or habit. There is another posture, though, which results primarily from an initiative taken by the government. This could be called the absorbed mode; when it occurs, the operators of the medium make no pretense that they are independent. This type of ownership could be compared with nationalized industries, but mass media rarely are perceived or described the same way as sausage factories. Even dictators have more sensitivity than that.

Thus we find several variations on state-owned status, even though the alternatives result in state control as well as if they were state property. Among these are ownership by (1) parties or civil organizations controlled by the same forces as the government, (2) private business corporations in which the state has invested, (3) government officials acting as private investors, and (4) mixtures of the above.

Furthermore, there is no one process or even motive through which the medium becomes absorbed. In almost all countries the governments accept the concept of private property and pay for confiscated possessions or at least promise to do so. An easy way for the state to obtain media is simply to found them. It also may inherit the property through acquisition of another enterprise such as a bank which in turn owns the mass medium. And organs of a party may become de facto state media once the party assumes power.

Causes for acquisition may range from a desire to choke off opposition voices to sheer accident. In between would be desires to mobilize or educate the people, do a favor for a support group such as a labor union, mete out revenge on media owners who are personal enemies of the rulers, or protect the public from media content the rulers consider harmful.

A state can take over a broadcasting operation much more easily than it can a publication. Universally, the airwaves are considered public property and are controlled by governments, which in some countries may allocate them to private licensees, usually for limited periods. In countries where the state has a right to operate its own television or radio stations, it can acquire an existing operation by refusing to renew a station's license or by revoking it. Nothing is more redundant than the physical property and staff of a station that has no frequency, so the state can quite legally acquire these at distress prices. Or, of course, it can confiscate them if the law is malleable enough.

The state can even get dominion over an audience when it buys a station, because most broadcast units are intended more for entertainment than journalism. This, however, rarely occurs; although the audience may not care who is running the station, governments have a notorious penchant for converting lively and profitable programming into a dull money-loser.

It is even more difficult for a regime to obtain or keep the circulation of its newspapers. Unlike television and radio, which comes without charge to the consumer, a newspaper costs money to read, and few publics want to pay for propaganda.

Examples

A system in which media are totally absorbed into the state is alien to some of the more deep-rooted qualities of Latin American public life—a contempt for organizational and political tidiness, a remarkable capacity for adjusting to new conditions while retaining traditional patterns, and a fervent devotion to the privacy of one's own property. So it is that few unalloyed examples of this posture are to be found, and even the one country whose entire media system is assumed to be state-owned, Cuba, actually has a mixture of forms. All are absorbed into the state apparatus, however.

The Cuban broadcast system is frankly a property of the government. But strictly speaking, the government has no major publication of its own. The major national daily, *Granma,* is a publication of the Communist Party; the second-ranking daily, *Juventud Rebelde,* is published by the Young Communist League. A spate of other national publications are all organs of various political and occupational bodies. Their leadership is intertwined with the personnel of the government and the party, but, as in the Soviet Union, the staffs of the papers feel their first loyalty is to their immediate organization. With pluralism cautiously expanding in the late 1970s, indications were that this rivalry among publications would grow also.

But no matter how much variation exists in the Cuban media, they have disappeared as a separate institution. The military or the universities may have rights of their own, but the media derive their privileges only through the organizations they serve.

This also can be said of the major national media in Peru, the only other Latin American country which has undergone a drastic social revolution in recent times. Television and all important daily newspapers are in effect vehicles of state policy, joined by some radio stations. But they are a far cry from the Cuban media in appearance and content; vestiges of the old days of private ownership remain. Entertaining and sensational material can be found alongside the propaganda, some free thought peeks through the conformist editorials and columns, and news from Western news agencies appears daily.

This journalistic leakiness in the ship of state can be traced in part to the fact that the Peruvian regime has stopped short of complete statism. Private capital still owns 49 per cent of the stock in Lima television stations and exerts much day-to-day control. Ownership of the Lima dailies rests in the hands of vast occupational associations, which have proven to be politically unreliable to a shocking degree. So the government still appoints the newspaper directors. The state itself owns three relatively minor Lima dailies.

Latitude remains for the national non-daily publications in Peru, plus the weak provincial press, to provide enough scraps of independent journalism to discredit the media serving the state. Thus the mixture of property forms which the regime saw as healthy pluralism has turned to its own disadvantage.

Perhaps the most uncomplicated route to a statist press was that taken by the Torrijos dictatorship in Panama, which set up a corporation with mixed state and private ownership—dominated by the state. Then it bought four of the six dailies in the country (all are in the capital). It paid a fair price and has run them as commercial enterprises, albeit poor ones, ever since. One television and one radio station are state-owned, but these fields are dominated by private holdings. This mixture of forms allows the government to say that freedom of information remains. This is a polite fiction, because the private media must censor themselves heavily, although their operators like to think of themselves as an opposition.

In Nicaragua, one of the two dailies in the capital (one of three in the country) is the property of the Somoza family, which has run the country for four decades. However, its circulation is less than half that of the other Managua daily and is generally held in contempt because it has been absorbed into the ruling clique. The other capital-city daily is vehemently combative, so much so that its director was assassinated in January 1978.

Most Latin American states own daily gazettes for publication of laws and official notices, but Chile is the only one besides Peru that owns a general-purpose, competitive newspaper. Although far less propagandistic than absorbed publications in other countries, it is still largely disdained by the public.

Taken as a whole, broadcast media are far more often to be found in the absorbed posture than printed ones. This grows out of tradition rather than power grabs in most cases, as the European tendency toward statist or publicly owned broadcasting has always held a fascination for Latin American planners. This, however, has never resulted in any coherent policymaking in regard to government participation in broadcast ownership, and the range of combinations varies widely. At the extremes would be no state ownership except for educational radio or television stations as in Costa Rica, and total ownership as in Cuba.

Perhaps the most ingenious arrangement of all is the Colombian television system. The state owns all television transmitting facilities and uses them partly for education, but it rents out much of the prime time for commercial use. Thus statist and private television truly coexist in the same system.

Chile blankets the country with state television and radio signals which operate in rivalry with university television stations and privately owned radio stations. All of them seek to be self-supporting through advertising sales, however.

Argentina has seen more movement toward absorption of broadcast media in recent years than any other Latin American country. This was the takeover of all three Buenos Aires commercial television stations during the second Perón government (1973–76) on the grounds that their licenses had expired. Since these stations served as the programming centers for most other stations in the country, the move gave Argentina an effectively statist video system. Even before the Buenos Aires action, Argentine broadcasting was a wild melange of non-commercial and commercial stations, owned variously by the federal government, lower levels of government, universities and private investors.

Characteristics

The absorbed media represent the only posture which has a strong identification with political doctrine. It is much more often to be found in its more extreme forms under leftist than rightist governments. The leftist regime in Cuba and Peru are the leading examples of those that have moved in this direction. On the other hand, rightist dictatorships in Brazil, Uruguay, Argentina, Chile and Paraguay have shunned any increase in state ownership and in some cases have made gestures to decrease it.

Dictators of both doctrinal poles usually share a desire to control public expression, but adherence to the sanctity of private property has inhibited rightist regimes from embracing statism in the media. The Brazilian and Argentine militarists have not been averse to state ownership of industry, but this was done in the spirit of stimulating the economy.

Another characteristic of leftist regimes which has given them a propensity for absorbing media is that they typically have a positive theory of mass communication rather than a negative one. That is, they see the media as necessary tools for carrying out the purposes of the state, whereas rightists tend to view them as potential impediments to state policies. Thus independent media are most likely to suffer through the suffocating embrace when ruled by leftists but are susceptible to the blow on the skull under rightists.

Where absorption of media has occurred, those with the least journalistic prestige provide better targets for takeovers than those which are older, more respected and more vocal. Dictators seem to sense the danger of infuriating the public by taking over one of their institutions too quickly. So the typical pattern is to pick off the weaker members of the media family first. This was demonstrated in Peru, where the more superfluous dailies and the broadcast stations were nationalized in stages leading up to the climactic blow—the absorption of the elite dailies.

CHAPTER 11

Conclusion

LIKE SO MANY buildings in Latin America, the imposing Victorian home of *La Prensa* in Buenos Aires is built around a patio, with interior balconies overlooking it. The elegant offices of the director are on upper floors, and during his long directorship Alberto Gainza Paz had frequent orders to send down to the people producing the paper. These would be put on paper by a male secretary and carried to a uniformed porter standing on the balcony. He would place them in a polished brass box which would be ceremoniously lowered to another porter stationed below. There they would be retrieved and carried to the appropriate hands. *La Prensa* had money to install pneumatic tubes or the like, but that would have been a concession to changing times. Gainza Paz, a man of immense dignity and iron-willed conservatism, approved of few things that happened in Argentine public life during the 1970s.

Gainza Paz's death in 1978 as much as anything symbolized the approaching end of a decade which had made an indelible difference to mass communication in Latin America. Military dictatorships had become the rule rather than the exception around the end of the 1960s, and many observers interpreted this as merely the recurring swing of a pendulum from democracy to absolutism.

But the facts, as they emerged, failed to fit the pattern neatly. These militarists were not content, like earlier uniformed juntas, to restore law and order, eliminate "dangerous" politicians and cool off the national climate. They approached the science of government with dead seriousness; instead of preventing change they intended to foster it, through laws and decrees which they would ensure were implemented, even placed into carefully wrought constitutions.

Mass media directors, like their forebears for four centuries, were accustomed to having to bow to the momentary needs of governments. Their only consolation was that the regulations of today could be forgotten tomorrow and

238

that, even though regimes would come and go, newspapers would go on almost forever.

But by the end of the 1970s, these directors were realizing that their professional world had changed. Just as the national armies had acquired a vast weaponry undreamed of before, so the governments had put together a sophisticated array of controls for the media. In fact, huge portions of the media simply disappeared into the bureaucracy of the state.

It was the fashion at the decade's close to speak of the controls as temporary—something that would melt away when the sun of democracy rose. This assumption posed two problems. First, the controls had been etched so deeply into the institutions of various nations that it was difficult to imagine their being erased overnight, even by elected governments. Second, the concept that absolutism is abnormal and democracy normal in Latin America flies in the face of all recorded history.

A hard look at the realities of Latin America's past shows that, rather than being a cauldron of revolution as the popular image makes it, the region is one of the most conservative in the world.[1] It was thrust into nationhood under the aegis of 16th-century Spanish thought patterns—Catholic, authoritarian and semi-feudal—and has felt only superficially and recently the forces that have made Europe and the United States the grounds for democracy that they are today. Such forces are the Protestant Reformation, the scientific method, political egalitarianism and the Industrial Revolution. As one historian expresses it:

> Latin America . . . remains paternalistic, hierarchical, authoritarian, Catholic, corporate, personalist, and elitist to its core. . . . The clash between traditional and modern has intensified throughout the Hemisphere, raising strong doubts as to whether Latin America's traditional structures are any longer capable of managing and controlling the rising tide of popular demands, and whether its historic patterns and institutions can survive.[2]

Directors of the mass media cannot escape the observation that their business makes up one of the "historic patterns and institutions," and the simple fact was that it was *not* surviving by the end of the 1970s in the same character it had had at the beginning. Governments were no longer treating it like a river which causes trouble regularly by flooding its banks and which must be sandbagged occasionally but generally endured as as a divine punishment. Instead, the river is being diked, damned and harnessed to the needs of the state.

This last point is crucial to an understanding of the change. It is becoming clear that not only do governments affect the media, but media also influence the political process. Some forms of this influence are familiar, but powerful forces are afoot which would find new ways the media can provide services. And if the media directors do not want to do so, they can be forced or their media taken away from them.

Dictatorship was thought of as the hallmark of Latin American government in the 1970s, but perhaps more so was the surge of vast bureaucracies. This generation of generals respects technology, and they have peopled their regimes with technicians. Perhaps oddly, the same could be said of the elected administrations in democratic countries. Above all, technicians want to set things in order, and an untrammeled media system without responsibilities is quite disorderly.[3]

Furthermore, the technocrats realize that controls which punish media after the fact are wasteful and inefficient. Rather, their ideal is preventive or, even better, prescriptive regulation. If the media are told what they should do, the need for punishment diminishes.

Latin America, in one of its brief flirtations with political idealism, had a wave of liberal democratic governments in the late 1950s and early 1960s, before the tide turned toward the military. Leaders of this movement assumed that, in a free partnership between government and business, all forms of justice could be attained. Whether because the idea was impracticable or because the leaders ran short of time, they were left with a record of failure and with disillusionment by those who needed their help.

The new technicians are taking no chances on such accidents of the old systems. Whether called leftists or rightists, they are building dikes that will last, to control the river or even redirect it. Neither they nor their political patrons are given to rhetoric like that of the younger Perón, Vargas and Castro. But when they do talk, it is of ideas such as the corporate state, which does away with the need for political parties and political legislators. The media, like all interest groups, would play their assigned role and, within well-defined rules, would be invited to have some say about government. It has appeared visionary, but actually it recalls the *fueros* of Spanish colonial regimes—those special rights conferred, not by popular will, but by the ruler.

If that were all there is to the political dynamics of the region, the media would have to sit back and wait for the state to work out their destiny. But even while the technicians plan and work to achieve their nirvana, mass media continue trying—often with much success—to have a life of their own. True, they are getting away from the rabid partisanship of yesteryear, in some cases because the parties themselves are dead. But two segments of the media are refusing to be manipulated by others.

First, some of the owners are proving remarkably adaptive to the new times, recognizing that the voices of poverty and frustration must be heard. And, while they passionately hold to the belief that independence is the air they must breathe, they concede that the governments of the 1970s have been much closer to the heartbeat of the people than most past ones.

Second, there is a new yeast in the ingredients of journalism. This is the growth of professionalism among the employees. Swelling in the 1970s like never before, this new element unfortunately has been seen by owners as a threat to their power and independence, partly because the employees have relied on government backing to gain their goals sometimes.

It would appear wiser if the two segments realize that, while both will always seek their economic well-being, it is difficult for either to escape the challenge to bring light to dark places. To keep this flame alive in hostile winds of the future will require many guardians.

APPENDIX

BASIC LAWS AND REGULATIONS CONCERNING BRAZILIAN MEDIA

PROHIBITED EXPRESSION

Agitation

—Material capable of provoking ill-feeling within the armed forces or between them and authorities or the public.
—Propaganda in favor of war, political or social subversion, or racial or class prejudice.
—Incitement to lawbreaking or defense of such infraction.
—Use of false news, or of true news cut short or distorted, to turn the people against the authorities.
—Subversive propaganda, including "adverse psychological warfare" and rallies, and defamation of any official.
—Material from abroad intended to spread ideas incompatible with the constitution.
—Criticism of institutional acts and resulting legislation.

Sensitive News

—Political arrests or censorship unless furnished by a competent authority.
—Statements by anyone stripped of political rights.
—Actions by the government to strip political rights or to fire, suspend or transfer anyone.
—Any news that could create tensions among the authorities or could provoke differences of opinion.
—Any troubles regarding students such as dissolution of student bodies, protests, strikes, demonstrations or students' conflicts with each other, teachers or authorities.
—Workers' movements, strikes or disturbances in Brazil; large headlines or television films about subversion or civil violence in other countries.

—State secrets or any other unreleased information about internal or external security of Brazil.

Morality and Religion

—Offenses against morality and public decency.
—Sexual lust shown in photographs so as to damage family morality, particularly if obscene or depressing.
—Detailed descriptions of crimes; headlines that attract attention to crimes.
—Large headlines or photos about business robberies (such stories are to be short and on inside pages).
—Political attitudes of the clergy "or of third parties which could create tensions or conflicts of a religious nature."

Economic

—Any material that could prejudice the economic policy of the government.
—False information, or true information cut short or distorted, about public disturbances or tending to reduce confidence in the banking system or the credit of any company, institution or government body.

Libel

—Moral offense to anyone in authority for reasons of factionalism or sociopolitical differences.
—Offending the honor or dignity of the president; vice-president; presidents of the senate, chamber of deputies or supreme court; cabinet ministers; state governors; or mayor of the capital city.
—Defamation against anyone dead or alive. Truth is no defense if the libel is against the president or other senior officials or foreign heads of state.

Technical Faults

—Political news whose truth is unproven.
—News reports that are distorted or trimmed.
—Headlines, photos or captions that are malicious or sensational or do not conform to the text of the story.
—Use of these phrases: Reliable sources, well-informed person or politician, official presidential or ministerial sources, and spokesmen. Always try to give the precise source, particularly in political news.

CENSORSHIP REQUIREMENTS

—During a state of siege, newspapers, periodicals, broadcast stations and news agencies may be censored. (State of siege has been in effect since 1971.)
—All books, magazines and foreign publications must be submitted to the federal police for permission to distribute.
—Live telecasting is forbidden except for news bulletins for which scripts have been censored. All other television programs must be given to the censor in finishing videotape rather than as scripts.

—In the case of radio, all scripts must be kept 60 days and tapes of unscripted programs 30 days.

MANAGEMENT REQUIREMENTS

—The minister of justice can confiscate copies of publications, suppress broadcast programs and close down any mass medium.

—Registration of all mass media, printing firms and news agencies, along with names of owners and chief executives, is required. (Clandestine publication is a crime.)

—Besides listing all executives and the printer, editors must keep a register of all their writers' pen names. Names of directors and producers of broadcast news and political programs must be announced on the air.

—A person offended by a mass medium must have a right to reply in identical space or broadcast time. Literary, artistic or sports criticism is exempt except when in "bad faith."

CIVIL RIGHTS

—The president can suspend any citizen's political rights, dismiss him from any job, and "fix restrictions or prohibitions related to any other public or private rights."

—A person may be held indefinitely without charge (loss of habeas corpus right) in case of crimes against national security, economic and social order and the popular economy. These are among the crimes specifically mentioned in the press law.

—For persons arrested under the national security law, military courts may take jurisdiction, defendants may be barred from exercising their professions, bail or suspended sentences are prohibited, and the defense is seriously limited.

—Professional journalists must be held before sentencing in proper accommodations separate from common criminals.

FOREIGN ASPECTS

—The national security law applies to acts committed anywhere by anyone, even foreign citizens in their own countries, "notwithstanding conventions, treaties and rules of international law."

—Imports of publications are forbidden if they offend against state security and public order; deal with war, race or class prejudice; or encourage subversion or moral offenses.

—Foreigners may not share in ownership of Brazilian mass media; the only assistance from abroad may be installation. Exempt are scientific, technical, cultural and artistic publications.

—Foreign companies may not distribute Brazilian news inside Brazil.

OTHER PROVISIONS

—If not written in "bad faith," the following types of material are exempt from punishment: Literary, artistic, scientific and sports criticism; reports on unclassified government decrees; reports on legislation and court proceedings; criticism of laws, legal proceedings and other areas of public interest; and discussion of ideas.

—Efforts to prevent publication of information through bribery or other means are prohibited.

—It is prohibited to form or join any group which, guided or helped by a foreign government or organization, harms or endangers the national security.

NOTES

NOTES FOR CHAPTER 1*

[1] Gabriel Ortíz, ed., *La Prensa Entre la Lealtad y el Miedo* (Bogotá: Asociación Latinoamericana de Periodistas para el Desarrollo, 1976), p. 11.

[2] *Buenos Aires Herald,* Sept. 12, 1973, p. 1, Sept. 13, 1973, p. 9, Sept. 14, 1973, p. 9; *La Razón* (Buenos Aires), Sept. 12, 1973, p. 8.

[3] *La Prensa* (Buenos Aires), Oct. 1, 1973, p. 6.

[4] *Buenos Aires Herald,* Oct. 5, 1973, p. 9.

[5] *Miami Herald,* June 8, 1975; Ortíz, p. 12.

[6] *Miami Herald,* June 24, 1974, June 28, 1974, July 19, 1974; *New York Times,* July 19, 1974.

[7] *Miami Herald,* Sept. 4, 1976; *Los Angeles Times,* Oct. 24, 1976; *New York Times,* Sept. 28, 1977.

[8] *The Economist,* Feb. 1, 1975, p. 40.

[9] *Washington Post,* Dec. 17, 1974.

[10] *Washington Post,* July 11, 1974.

[11] *Miami Herald,* July 4, 1974.

[12] *Miami Herald,* Nov. 22, 1975.

[13] Ortíz, p. 12.

[14] *Miami Herald,* Nov. 19, 1974.

[15] *Miami Herald,* Jan. 16, 1977.

[16] *Miami Herald,* Sept. 14, 1976; *Newsweek,* Aug. 15, 1977, p. 31.

[17] *Miami Herald,* March 1, 1975.

[18] John C. Merrill, Carter R. Bryan and Marvin Alisky, *The Foreign Press* (Baton Rouge: Louisiana State University Press, 1970), pp. 197–98.

[19] *The Economist,* Jan. 4, 1975, pp. 42–43; *New York Times,* Dec. 21, 1974; interview with Amerigo Barrios, managing editor, *La Crónica,* Aug. 13, 1976.

* Most newspaper articles cited are taken from *Information Services on Latin America*, Olinda, California, and may be found in that publication under the date noted. It does not provide page numbers for articles included.

[20] *Atlas*, February, 1971, pp. 46–47.

[21] *Miami Herald*, Jan. 30, 1977.

[22] *Miami Herald*, March 25, 1974.

[23] Editors of *La Prensa, Defense of Freedom* (London: T. V. Boardman & Co., 1952), p. 307.

[24] *Buenos Aires Herald*, Aug. 22, 1973, p. 9.

[25] *Ibid.*, p. 8.

[26] *Ibid.*, p. 1.

[27] *Miami Herald*, May 15, 1975.

[28] *Miami Herald*, March 21, 23, 1974.

[29] *Miami Herald*, Oct. 14, 1974.

[30] *Comments on Argentine Trade*, October, 1972, p. 21.

[31] *Miami Herald*, Oct. 4, 1974.

[32] *Washington Post*, March 29, 1976; *New York Times*, April 4, 1976.

[33] *Washington Post*, May 11, 1976.

[34] *Washington Post*, Sept. 15, 1976.

[35] *Buenos Aires Herald*, Oct. 3, 1975, p. 5.

[36] *Buenos Aires Herald*, Oct. 9, 1973, p. 9.

[37] Editors of *La Prensa*, pp. 9–196.

[38] Interview with Pedro Simoncini, president, Asociación de Teledifusoras Argentinas, Aug. 12, 1976; *Televisión Argentina: un Enfoque Nacional* (Buenos Aires: Ediciones Proartel, 1969).

[39] *Los Andes*, Mendoza, Argentina, Oct. 12, 1973, pp. 4, 8.

[40] *New York Times*, Aug. 1, 1974.

[41] *The Economist*, Jan. 18, 1969, p. 28.

[42] Interviews with Alberto Gainza Paz, Oct. 10, 1973, and Aug. 12, 1976.

[43] *Miami Herald*, May 25 and 26, 1977.

[44] *Miami Herald*, May 26, 1972.

[45] Interview with Robert Cox, Aug. 11, 1976; *Miami Herald*, Oct. 24, 1975, p. 10D.

[46] *Gainesville* (Florida) *Sun*, April 24, 1977, p. 12A; *El Dia* (La Plata, Argentina), Sept. 28, 1977.

[47] *Newsweek*, Aug. 15, 1977, p. 31.

[48] *Miami Herald*, Feb. 10, 13 and 26, 1974; March 1, 1974.

[49] *Miami Herald*, Jan. 10, 1975, Feb. 20, 1975, Sept. 16, 1976.

[50] Interview with Alberto Gainza Paz, Aug. 12, 1976.

[51] *Ibid.;* interview with Fidel Huegas, *La Nación*, Aug. 11, 1976.

[52] Interview with Alberto Gainza Paz, Nov. 2, 1973.

[53] Interview with Alberto Gainza Paz, Oct. 10, 1973.

[54] *Christian Science Monitor*, June 6, 1975.

[55] Interview with Robert Cox, Nov. 5, 1973.

[56] *Buenos Aires Herald*, Oct. 10, 1973, p. 9.

[57] *New York Times*, March 6, 1974.

[58] *Latin America*, Sept. 17, 1976, pp. 284–85; *Miami Herald*, Aug. 2, 1976; *Washington Post*, Dec. 28, 1976.

Notes for Chapter 2

[1] Nelly de Camargo and Virgilio B. Noya Pinto, *Communication Policies in Brazil* (Paris: The UNESCO Press, 1975), pp. 9–18.

[2] *Ibid.*, p. 13.

[3] Helen Miller Bailey and Abraham P. Nasatir, *Latin America: The Development of Its*

Civilization (Englewood Cliffs, N.J.: Prentice Hall, Inc., 1960), p. 535; de Camargo and Noya Pinto, p. 17.

[4] Christopher George, "Press Freedom in Brazil," *Index on Censorship,* Vol. 1, No. 1 (Spring, 1972), p. 43.

[5] John C. Merrill, Carter R. Bryan and Marvin Alisky, *The Foreign Press* (Baton Rouge: Louisiana State University Press, 1970), p. 203.

[6] Antonio de Sousa, "Forced into Silence," *Index on Censorship,* Vol. 6, No. 3 (May/June, 1977), p. 16.

[7] *New York Times,* April 3, 1976.

[8] *Ibid.*

[9] De Sousa, *Index on Censorship,* Vol. 6, No. 3, p. 15.

[10] *Ibid.*

[11] *Miami Herald,* March 12, 1971.

[12] *Los Angeles Times,* July 1, 1971.

[13] *Miami Herald,* April 4, 1973.

[14] *Washington Post,* March 13, 1973, and June 7, 1973.

[15] *Los Angeles Times,* Oct. 16, 1972.

[16] *Ibid.*

[17] Interview with Oliveiros da Silva Ferreira, editor in chief, *O Estado de São Paulo,* Aug. 30, 1976.

[18] *Los Angeles Times,* April 2, 1971.

[19] *Los Angeles Times,* Oct. 16, 1972.

[20] *Los Angeles Times,* June 10, 1973.

[21] *Washington Post,* June 2, 1974.

[22] Interview with Da Silva Ferreira, Aug. 20, 1976.

[23] *Washington Post,* Aug. 6, 1976.

[24] *Washington Post,* June 2, 1974.

[25] *Miami Herald,* June 24, 1973.

[26] *Miami Herald,* April 2, 1977.

[27] *Wall Street Journal,* Oct. 12, 1970; *New York Times,* Feb. 19, 1972.

[28] *Los Angeles Times,* March 16, 1972.

[29] *Ibid.*

[30] *Miami Herald,* July 24, 1971.

[31] *New York Times,* Feb. 19, 1972.

[32] *Miami Herald,* July 13, 1972, and March 2, 1977.

[33] *Christian Science Monitor,* Sept. 26, 1975.

[34] Los Angeles Times, March 16, 1972.

[35] *New York Times,* Jan. 10, 1973.

[36] *New York Times,* May 23, 1973.

[37] *Los Angeles Times,* April 26, 1973.

[38] *Ibid.*

[39] *Miami Herald,* Sept. 20, 1972.

[40] *Los Angeles Times,* Jan. 5, 1971.

[41] De Sousa, *Index on Censorship,* Vol. 6, No. 3, p. 19.

[42] *Los Angeles Times,* Dec. 9, 1975.

[43] Interview with Audalio Dantas, president, Journalists' Syndicate of São Paulo, June 14, 1977.

[44] De Sousa, *Index on Censorship,* Vol. 6, No. 3, p. 19.

[45] *Los Angeles Times,* June 24, 1973.

[46] *Miami Herald,* Aug. 1, 1973.

[47] *Ibid.*

[48] *Miami Herald,* Aug. 8, 1973.

[49] *Los Angeles Times,* May 28, 1972.

[50] *New York Times,* Sept. 9, 1971.
[51] De Sousa, *Index on Censorship,* Vol. 6, No. 3, p. 18.
[52] Timothy Ross, "Information Control in Brazil," *Index on Censorship,* Vol. 1, Nos. 3–4 (Autumn/Winter, 1972), p. 142.
[53] *Washington Post,* June 2, 1977.
[54] *Washington Post,* March 29, 1975.
[55] *Christian Science Monitor,* Feb. 3, 1975.
[56] *Washington Post,* Oct. 29, 1975.
[57] *Ibid.*
[58] *Los Angeles Times,* Oct. 27, 1975, p. 10.
[59] *New York Times,* Oct. 28, 1975, p. 7.
[60] *Los Angeles Times,* Oct. 28, 1975.
[6] Interview with Audalio Dantas, Aug. 27, 1976.
[62] *Los Angeles Times,* Oct. 28, 1975.
[63] *Los Angeles Times,* Nov. 23, 1975.
[64] *Miami Herald,* Oct. 31, 1975.
[65] *Los Angeles Times,* Nov. 2, 1975.
[66] *Miami Herald,* Oct. 31, 1975.
[67] *New York Times,* Nov. 12, 1975, p. 18.
[68] *Los Angeles Times,* Feb. 4, 1976; *New York Times,* March 12, 1976.
[69] *Los Angeles Times,* Feb. 4, 1976.
[70] Interview with Audalio Dantas, June 14, 1977.
[61] Interview York Times, Dec. 7, 1972.
[72] Interview with Carlos Chagas, bureau chief, *O Estado de São Paulo,* Sept. 6, 1976.
[73] Interview with Oliveiros da Silva Ferreira, Aug. 30, 1976.
[74] *Miami Herald,* March 17, 1974.
[75] *Los Angeles Times,* Nov. 14, 1970, and Jan. 3, 1971; *New York Times,* Nov. 22 and Dec. 28, 1970.
[76] *Los Angeles Times,* Dec. 25, 1970.
[77] *Time,* Nov. 18, 1974, pp. 48 and 51.
[78] *Washington Post,* Sept. 26, 1972.
[79] *Miami Herald,* Sept. 22, 1972.
[80] *Washington Post,* April 2, 1975.
[81] *Miami Herald,* Aug. 20, 1970.
[82] Wall Street Journal, July 6, 1971.
[83] De Camargo and Noya Pinto, pp. 47 and 76.
[84] *Washington Post,* Jan. 27, 1972.
[85] *Variety,* June 1, 1977, p. 43.
[86] *Ibid.*
[87] *Miami Herald,* Jan. 6, 1973.
[88] Ary Nogueira, executive, Diarios Associados, Dec. 10, 1973.
[89] *Miami Herald,* Nov. 8, 1976, p. 22A.
[90] *New York Times,* Dec. 28, 1970.
[91] De Camargo and Noya Pinto, p. 71.
[92] Media Survey, U.S. Information Service, Brasilia, Jan. 11, 1973, p. 8.
[93] Report of the Freedom of the Press Committee, Inter-American Press Association, 1973, p. B-16.
[94] *Miami Herald,* Nov. 10, 1976.
[95] *Miami Herald,* Nov. 8, 1976, p. 22A.
[96] *Miami Herald,* July 28, 1977.
[97] *Christian Science Monitor,* Dec. 10, 1971.
[98] *Anuario Brasileiro de Media,* 1975–76.
[99] *Christian Science Monitor,* Aug. 19, 1976.

[100]*Los Angeles Times*, June 25, 1977.

[101]*Wall Street Journal*, Dec. 3, 1974; *New York Times*, Aug. 20, 1975.

[102]*Los Angeles Times*, April 9, 1972, p. A3.

[103]*Los Angeles Times*, Nov. 23, 1975.

[104]*New York Times*, July 9, 1977.

[105]*Los Angeles Times*, Nov. 23, 1975.

[106]*Miami Herald*, March 12, 1971.

[107]*New York Times*, Feb. 19, 1972; *Miami Herald*, July 10 and Aug. 11, 1972.

[108]*Los Angeles Times*, June 21, 1972.

[109]*Miami Herald*, June 23, 1972, p. 16A.

[110]*New York Times*, April 25, 1975.

[111]*Washington Post*, May 6, 1976.

[112]*New York Times*, May 24, 1977.

NOTES FOR CHAPTER 3

[1]Thomas E. Weil *et al.*, *Area Handbook for Chile* (Washington: U.S. Government Printing Office, 1969), p. 242.

[2]John C. Merrill, *The Elite Press: Great Newspapers of the World* (New York: Pitman Publishing Corporation, 1968), p. 41.

[3]Weil *et al.*, pp. 243–46.

[4]*Ibid.*, pp. 247–50.

[5]*Ibid.*, p. 242.

[6]Constitution of 1925, Republic of Chile, Chapter III.

[7]*Miami Herald*, Sept. 20, 1970, p. 2B.

[8]*Ibid.*

[9]*Ibid.*

[10]*Miami Herald*, Oct. 22, 1970, p. 6H.

[11]*St. Petersburg Times*, Oct. 14, 1972, p. 3A.

[12]*Miami Herald*, Jan. 21, 1971, p. 4D.

[13]*Miami Herald*, Jan. 6, 1972.

[14]*Christian Science Monitor*, Feb. 11, 1972, p. 1.

[15]*Miami Herald*, April 10, 1972, p. 15C.

[16]U.S. Senate, Select Committee to Study Government Operations With Respect to Intelligence Operations, *Covert Action in Chile: 1963–1973*, 94th Cong., 1st Sess., 1975.

[17]*Ibid.*, p. 9.

[18]*Ibid.*, p. 24.

[19]*Ibid.*

[20]*Ibid.*

[21]*Ibid.*, p. 25.

[22]*Ibid.*, p. 2.

[23]*Miami Herald*, April 14, 1971.

[24]*Miami Herald*, Oct. 22, 1970, p. 6H.

[25]*Miami Herald*, Nov. 16, 1970.

[26]*Miami Herald*, Feb. 24, 1971, p. 23A.

[27]Tomás P. Mac Hale, *El Frente de la Libertad de Expresión: 1970–1972* (Santiago de Chile: Ediciones Portada, 1972), pp. 134–46.

[28]*Los Angeles Times*, May 14, 1973, p. III 9.

[29]*Florida Times-Union*, Oct. 27, 1972, p. A6.

[30]*The Economist*, April 10, 1971, p. 46.

[31]*Miami Herald*, July 2, 1973.

[32] *Christian Science Monitor,* July 2, 1973.

[33] *Miami Herald,* May 31, 1971.

[34] *Miami Herald,* Feb. 24, 1971, p. 23A.

[35] *Ibid.*

[36] *Ibid.*

[37] Tomás P. Mac Hale, *Poder Politico y Comunicación en Chile: Marzo a Septiembre de 1973* ("Caudernos del Instituto de Ciencia Política, No. 14; Santiago de Chile: Universidad Católica de Chile, 1977), p. 16.

[38] *El Mercurio* (Santiago de Chile), May 19, 1973, p. 3.

[39] *Florida Times-Union,* Oct. 27, 1972, p. A6.

[40] *New York Times,* Aug. 17, 1973.

[41] *Los Angeles Times,* May 14, 1973, p. III9.

[42] *Miami Herald,* June 29, 1972, p. 4B.

[43] *Statistical Yearbook, 1976* (New York: United Nation, 1977), pp. 593–95.

[44] Interview with Alberto Guerrero, director, *La Tercera* (Santiago de Chile), Aug. 3, 1976.

[45] Interview with Fernando Díaz, director, *Ultimas Noticias* (Santiago de Chile), Aug. 6, 1976.

[46] Interview with Gian-Carlo Giardelli, McCann-Erickson de Chile, Santiago, Aug. 5, 1976.

[48] Interview with Alberto Guerrero, Aug. 3, 1976.

[49] Interview, Aug. 5, 1976.

[50] *Washington Post,* June 10, 1976.

[51] *Miami Herald,* Feb. 25, 1976.

[52] *New York Times,* Aug. 26, 1977.

[53] *Washington Post,* July 3, 1977.

[54] Gabriel Ortíz, ed., *La Prensa Entre la Lealtad y el Mieo* (Bogotá: Asociación Latinoamericana de Periodistas para el Desarrollo, 1976), p. 43.

[55] *Ibid.,* p. 49.

[56] *Miami Herald,* Feb. 25, 1976.

[57] Interview, Aug. 5, 1976.

[58] Ortíz, p. 46.

[59] *Christian Science Monitor,* April 27, 1976; *New York Times,* Aug. 26, 1977.

[60] *La Tercera* (Santiago de Chile), March 26, 1976.

[61] *Miami Herald,* Nov. 11, 1976.

[62] *Washington Post,* Aug. 30, 1975.

[63] Interview, Aug. 4, 1976.

[64] *El Mercurio* (Santiago de Chile), March 29, 1976.

[65] Circular distributed to foreign correspondents in Santiago, July 1976.

[66] *Washington Post,* Sept. 2 and 3, 1974.

[67] Interview, Aug. 5, 1976.

[68] Interview, Aug. 4, 1976.

[69] *Ibid.*

[70] Interview with Manfredo Mayol, Aug. 5, 1976.

[71] Interview, Aug. 4, 1976.

[72] Interview with Carlos Wilson, Aug. 6, 1976.

[73] John C. Merrill, Carter R. Bryan and Marvin Alisky, *The Foreign Press* (Baton Rouge: Louisiana State University Press, 1970), p. 207.

[74] Interview with Fernando Díaz, President, Colegio de Periodistas, Aug. 6, 1976; interviews with Professor José Ortíz, Universidad Católica, and other journalists, Aug. 4–6, 1976.

[75] Gabriel Ortíz, pp. 47–48.

NOTES FOR CHAPTER 4

[1] "Fidel en Radio Rebelde," *Granma* (special issue), March 8, 1973, p. 4.

[2] Maurice Halperin, *The Rise and Fall of Fidel Castro—An Essay in Contemporary History* (Berkeley: University of California Press, 1972), p. 227.

[3] Herbert L. Matthews, *Revolution in Cuba: An Essay in Understanding* (New York: Charles Scribner's Sons, 1975), p. 126.

[4] *Cuba and Fidel* (Churchill Films, 1976). Interview with Frank Mankiewicz.

[5] *Ibid.*

[6] Jan Knippers Black *et al., Area Handbook for Cuba* (Washington: U.S. Government Printing Office, 1976), p. 298.

[7] *Cuba at the Turning Point* (New York: Business International Corporation, 1977), p. 2. This chapter draws heavily on the background and conclusions in this source, the best and most current analysis of Cuba's economy.

[8] Interview with Lionel Martin, correspondent for the Canadian Broadcasting Corporation, Havana, Cuba, Nov. 19, 1977.

[9] Fidel Castro, *Revolutionary Struggle 1947–1958,* eds. Rolando E. Bonochea and Nelson P. Valdes, vol. 1: *Selected Works of Fidel Castro* (Cambridge, Massachusetts: The MIT Press, 1972), p. 231.

[10] *Cuba at the Turning Point,* pp. 7–10.

[11] "From the Cutting Room Floor: The Complete Text of Barbara Walters' Interview with Fidel," *Seven Days,* December 1977, p. 20.

[12] Hugh Thomas, *Cuba: The Pursuit of Freedom* (New York: Harper and Row, Publishers, 1971), p. 1136. Also see Black, *Cuba,* p. 318.

[13] Castro, *Revolutionary Struggle,* p. 365.

[14] "Castro Heads Cuba's Armed Forces; Regime Is Sworn In," *The New York Times,* Jan. 4, 1959, p. 1.

[15] Matthews, *Revolution in Cuba,* p. 346.

[16] *Cuba and Fidel.*

[17] Thomas, *Cuba,* p. 1261.

[18] Boris Goldenberg, *The Cuban Revolution and Latin America* (New York: Frederick A. Praeger, 1965), pp. 203–4. A rival magazine called *Bohemia Libre* was later published in the United States and Venezuela.

[19] *Ibid.*

[20] "Fidel's Kind of Freedom," *Time,* Jan. 11, 1960, p. 45.

[21] For an excellent discussion of the phases of the Cuban revolution, see Carmelo Mesa-Lago, *Cuba in the 1970s: Pragmatism and Institutionalization* (Albuquerque: University of New Mexico Press, 1974).

[22] Halperin, *Fidel Castro,* p. 252. Also see Matthews, *Revolution in Cuba,* p. 314, and Black, *Cuba,* p. 252.

[23] Halperin, p. 248, and Matthews, p. 328.

[24] Halperin, pp. 248–53.

[25] *Ibid.,* p. 348.

[26] *Ibid.,* p. 254.

[27] Black, *Cuba,* p. 325.

[28] *Ibid.,* pp. 319–20.

[29] Matthews, *Revolution in Cuba,* pp. 2–3.

[30] Mesa-Lago, *Cuba in the 1970s,* p. 104. Also see Lionel Martin, "Paper's 'Consumer Action' Column Blows the Whistle on Abuses in Cuba," *Washington Post,* Nov. 4, 1977, p. A27.

[31] Black, *Cuba,* p. 321.

[32] Matthews, *Revolution in Cuba,* pp. 322–3.

[33] Mesa-Lago, *Cuba in the 1970s,* pp. 99–100.

[34] *Ibid.,* p. 101.

[35] For an alternative analysis of the Padilla affair, see U.S. Department of State, Office of External Research, *Cuban Revolutionary Ideology and the Cuban Intellectual,* Cynthia McClintock. Foreign Affairs Research Paper, No. FAR 2258-P. Cambridge: July 1975.

[36] Matthews, *Revolution in Cuba,* p. 2.

[37] Mesa-Lago, *Cuba in the 1970s,* p. 102.

[38] Matthews, *Revolution in Cuba,* pp. 2–3.

[39] Black, *Cuba,* p. 333.

[40] Interview with Jorge Lopez Pimentel, Havana, Cuba, Nov. 17, 1977. There have been numerous charges on both sides of the Florida Straits that ABC's editing of the interview erroneously portrayed Walters as a tough, effective spokeswoman for the capitalist world, while Castro appeared to be a dogmatic and unperceptive advocate of communism. To judge for themselves, readers should compare the full and edited versions in "From the Cutting Room Floor," *Seven Days,* December 1977, pp. 10–38. In actuality, what the Cubans and *Seven Days* claim was a complete version of the interview was not. A small portion in which Walters asked some questions about Castro's social life was censored by Cuban television.

[41] Personal interviews. The USIA estimates that at least 40 percent of Cuban adults listened to Voice of America occasionally in 1963. See United States Information Agency, Research and Reference Service, *The Foreign Broadcast Audience in Cuba Today: Estimates Based on Refugee Reports,* R-133-63 (R), August, 1963.

[42] *Cuba at the Turning Point,* p. 7.

[43] Black, *Cuba,* p. 313.

[44] Interview with Martin.

[45] Black, *Cuba,* p. 313.

[46] Martin, " 'Consumer Action' Column," p. A27.

[47] *Ibid.*

[48] Interview with Lopez.

[49] Martin, " 'Consumer Action' Column," p. A27.

[50] Interview with Jorge Enrique Mendoza, Havana, Cuba, Nov. 17, 1977.

[51] Frederick W. Siebert, *Freedom of the Press in England, 1476–1776* (Urbana, Illinois: University of Illinois Press, 1952), introduction.

[52] Interviews with Cuba trade officials. Cuba cannot import television sets from the United States because of the trade embargo and has lost credit with Japan, the only other major manufacturer of 525-line sets, after several broken trade contracts.

[53] Black, *Cuba,* p. 316.

[54] *Ibid.,* p. 289.

[55] "What Cuba Wants," *Atlas World Press Review,* October 1977, p. 20.

[56] Interview with Lopez.

[57] *Ibid.*

[58] Interviews with editors.

NOTES FOR CHAPTER 5

[1] Mariano Azuela, *The Underdogs* (New York: New American Library, 1962), p. 81.

[2] *América Latina,* Aug. 10, 1976.

[3] Albert L. Hester and Richard R. Cole, eds., *Mass Communication in Mexico* (Brookings, South Dakota: Association for Education in Journalism, 1975), pp. 2–7; Erling H. Erlandson, "The Press in Mexico: Past, Present and Future," *Journalism Quarterly,* Vol. 41, No. 2 (Spring, 1964), p. 232.

[4]*New York Times,* June 23, 1974.

[5]*Christian Science Monitor,* April 24, 1972, p. 11.

[6]*Los Angeles Times,* April 6, 1977.

[7]*New York Times,* June 23, 1974.

[8]*Expansion,* Mexico City, May 3, 1972, p. 28.

[9]*Ibid.*

[10] Stanley Meisler, "Two Murders That Rocked Mexico," *Los Angeles Times,* May 5, 1974.

[11]*Ibid.*

[12]*Los Angeles Times,* May 9, 1974.

[13]*Los Angeles Times,* Sept. 4, 1974.

[14]*Ibid.*

[15]*Miami Herald,* Dec. 29, 1973.

[16]*Los Angeles Times,* May 21, 1975.

[17]*Ibid.*

[18]*Index on Censorship,* Vol. 4, No. 1 (Spring, 1975), p. 77.

[19]*Miami Herald,* July 18, 1975.

[20] Hester and Cole, pp. 1–47.

[21] John Taylor, "Mexico: The Guessing Game," *Index on Censorship,* Vol. 5, No. 4 (Winter, 1976), p. 34.

[22] Interview with James Budd, June 14, 1976.

[23] Taylor, *Index on Censorship,* Vol. 5, No. 4, p. 34.

[24]*New York Times,* June 23, 1974.

[25] Hester and Cole, pp. 39–40.

[26] Pedro Joaquín Chamorro, quoted in *Expansión,* Mexico City, May 3, 1972, p. 28.

[27]*Ibid.,* quoting Paul Wyatt.

[28]*Ibid.,* p. 20.

[29] Hester and Cole, p. 41.

[30] Richard R. Cole, "The Mexican Press System: Aspects of Growth, Control and Ownership," *Gazette,* Vol. 21, No. 2 (1975), p. 70; Colin Willis, "Entrenched Press Corruption Challenges Mexican Editor," *Editor and Publisher,* July 8, 1972, p. 14.

[31] Hester and Cole, p. 42; interview with Ariel Ramos, Subdirector, *El Universal,* June 16, 1976.

[32] Thomas E. Weil *et al., Area Handbook for Mexico* (Washington: U.S. Government Printing Office, 1975), p. 243.

[33] Report of the Committee on Freedom of the Press and Information, Inter-American Press Association, midyear meeting, 1976, Aruba, p. 25.

[34] Report of the Committee on Freedom of the Press and Information, Inter-American Press Association, annual meeting, 1977, Santo Domingo.

[35]*New York Times,* Jan. 2, 1977.

[36]*Expansión,* Mexico City, May 3, 1972, pp. 23, 27.

[37] John C. Merrill, Carter R. Bryan and Marvin Alisky, *The Foreign Press* (Baton Rouge: Louisiana State University Press, 1970), p. 181.

[38] Interview with James Budd, June 14, 1976.

[39]*New York Times,* Jan. 2, 1977.

[40] Cole, *Gazette,* Vol. 21, No. 2, pp. 67–68.

[41]*Ibid.,* p. 68.

[42]*Miami Herald,* March 24, 1971.

[43]*Proceso,* Mexico City, Nov. 6, 1976, p. 15; *New York Times,* Nov. 7, 1976.

[44] Weil *et al.,* p. 244.

[45]*Ibid.*

[46]*Journal of Commerce,* Dec. 12, 1975.

[47] *Los Angeles Times*, March 24, 1976.

[48] Weil *et al.*, p. 256.

[49] *Los Angeles Times*, March 24, 1976.

[50] Weil *et al.*, p. 254.

[51] *Proceso*, Mexico City, Sept. 19, 1977; interview with Professor José Rubén Jara, June 19, 1976.

[52] *World Communication: a 200-Country Survey of Press, Radio, Television and Film* (5th ed., New York: Unipub, 1975), p. 178.

[53] Weil *et al.*, p. 255.

[54] Hester and Cole, p. 39.

[55] *New York Times*, Jan. 2, 1977.

[56] Carlos Avila Nieto, "Mexican Communication Policies," unpublished research report, College of Journalism and Communications, University of Florida, 1976, p. 9.

[57] Cole, *Gazette*, Vol. 21, No. 2, p. 67.

[58] Report of the Committee on Freedom of the Press and Information, Inter-American Press Association, annual meeting, 1975, São Paulo, p. B27.

[59] Report of the Committee of Freedom of the Press and Information, Inter-American Press Association, midyear meeting, 1976, Aruba, p. 26.

[60] Dennis T. Lowry, "Broadcasting's Expanding Social Role in Mexico," *Journalism Quarterly*, Vol. 26, No. 2 (Summer, 1969), p. 333.

[61] Walter B. Emery, *National and International Systems of Broadcasting* (East Lansing: Michigan State University Press, 1969), pp. 26–27.

[62] *Miami Herald*, Sept. 24, 1974.

[63] Taylor, *Index on Censorship*, Vol. 5, No. 4, pp. 35–36.

[64] It was ranked as one of the two "elite" newspapers of Latin America by John C. Merrill in 1968, along with *La Prensa* of Buenos Aires. See Merrill, *The Elite Press* (New York: Pitman Publishing Corporation, 1968).

[65] *Ibid.*, p. 245.

[66] Armando Vargas, "The Coup at Excelsior," *Columbia Journalism Review*, September/October, 1976, p. 46.

[67] *Ibid.*, p. 47.

[68] *Washington Post*, July 11, 1976.

[69] Vargas, *Columbia Journalism Review*, September/October, 1976, p. 48.

[70] *Ibid.*

[71] *Washington Post*, July 29, 1977.

[72] *New York Times*, May 14, 1977.

[73] Report of the Committee on Freedom of the Press and Information, Inter-American Press Association, annual meeting, 1977, Santo Domingo.

NOTES FOR CHAPTER 6

[1] *Los Angeles Times*, Jan. 8, 1975.

[2] Thomas E. Weil *et al.*, *Area Handbook for Peru* (Washington: U.S. Government Printing Office, 1972), p. 169.

[3] Carlos Artega and Carlos Romero, *Communication Policies in Peru* (Paris: UNESCO, 1977), p. 17.

[4] Pedro G. Beltrán, *La Verdadera Realidad Peruana* (Madrid: Libreria Editorial San Martin, 1976), p. 50.

[5] Dennis Gilbert, "Society, Politics and the Press: An Interpretation of the Peruvian Press Reform of 1974," Paper Presented at the National Convention of the Latin American Studies Association, Houston, Texas, Nov. 2–5, 1977, p. 7.

[6] Interview with Mario Castro Arenas, Subdirector, *La Prensa* (Lima), July 4, 1973.

[7] Beltrán, pp. 54–63.

[8] Artega and Romero, pp. 63–66.

[9] *Miami Herald*, July 30, 1974.

[10] *Washington Post*, July 28, 1974.

[11] Communique from the Embassy of Peru, *New York Times*, Aug. 1, 1974.

[12] *Ibid*.

[13] Gilbert, p. 16.

[14] *Christian Science Monitor*, Feb. 10, 1970.

[15] *Miami Herald*, March 5, 1970, p. 10A.

[16] Weil *et al*., p. 156.

[17] *Ibid*., p. 173.

[18] Gilbert, p. 15.

[19] *Ibid*.

[20] *Ibid*., p. 14.

[21] *New York Times*, Oct. 21, 1974.

[22] *El Diario* (La Paz), July 30, 1976, p. 16; *El Mercurio* (Santiago de Chile), Feb. 6, 1977, p. 6.

[23] *Miami Herald*, July 30, 1974.

[24] Gilbert, p. 11.

[25] *Ibid*., p. 12.

[26] *Miami Herald*, March 5, 1970, p. 10A.

[27] Marvin Alisky, "Government-Press Relations in Peru," *Journalism Quarterly*, Vol. 53, No. 4 (Winter, 1976), p. 662.

[28] Interview with Nicanór Gonzales, international manager, programming, Telecentro, Lima, July 21, 1976.

[29] *Ibid*.

[30] Artega and Romero, p. 48.

[31] *Miami Herald*, Jan. 26, 27 and 28, 1972.

[32] Interview with Mario Castro Arenas, July 4, 1973; *Miami Herald*, April 7, 1972, p. 6C.

[33] Interview with Alejandro Miro9 Quesada, former director, *El Comercio*, July 23, 1976.

[34] *La Prensa* (Buenos Aires), July 30, 1973, p. 2.

[35] *La Prensa* (Buenos Aires), Aug. 21, 1973, p. 3.

[36] *Miami Herald*, April 12, 1974.

[37] *Miami Herald*, Dec. 24, 1971.

[38] *La Prensa* (Buenos Aires), July 30, 1973, p. 2.

[39] *Miami Herald*, Aug. 16, 1974.

[40] *Miami Herald*, June 1, 1974.

[41] *Washington Post*, June 19, 1974, p. 11.

[42] *Washington Post*, July 28, 1974.

[43] *Miami Herald*, July 30 and 31, 1974; *New York Times*, Aug. 11, 1974, p. 16.

[44] *Washington Post*, July 29, 1974; *Miami Herald*, Aug. 13, 1974.

[45] "Dark Day in Lima," *Index on Censorship*, Vol. 4, No. 1 (Spring, 1975), p. 79.

[46] Gilbert, p. 18.

[47] *Ibid*., p. 19.

[48] Interview, July 23, 1976.

[49] *Miami Herald*, Feb. 13 and 25, 1971.

[50] Interview with Dr. Arturo Salazár Larraín, president, Federación de Periodistas, Lima, July 22, 1976.

[51] Interview with Luis Jaime Cisneros, July 23, 1976.

[52] *New York Times*, Sept. 11, 1974.

[53]*New York Times*, Oct. 21, 1974.
[54]*Miami Herald*, Nov. 17, 1975.
[55]Gilbert, p. 21.
[56]*New York Times*, Aug. 17, 1974.
[57]*Miami Herald*, Sept. 14, 1977.
[58]*Miami Herald*, June 12, 1975.
[59]*New York Times*, Feb. 21, 1975.
[60]*Ibid.*
[61]*Index on Censorship*, Vol. 6, No. 3 (May-June, 1977), p. 69.
[62]*Miami Herald*, June 16, 1974.
[63]*Washington Post*, Nov. 22, 1974, p. 14.
[64]*New York Times*, Feb. 6, 1975.
[65]*Washington Post*, Feb. 9, 1975.
[66]*Miami Herald*, Feb. 14, 1975.
[67]*Miami Herald*, Oct. 11, 1976; *Index on Censorship*, Vol. 6, No. 2 (March-April, 1977), p. 68.
[68]*Washington Post*, June 19, 1974, p. 11.
[69]*Miami Herald*, Sept. 12, 1975.
[70]*Miami Herald*, Oct. 13, 1974.
[71]*Ibid.*
[72]*Miami Herald*, Aug. 16, 1974.
[73]*New York Times*, Nov. 21, 1974.
[74]*Miami Herald*, Aug. 18, 1975.
[75]*Miami Herald*, April 16, 1970, p. 4D.
[76]*Miami Herald*, Sept. 3, 1972, p. 4B.
[77]Report of the Committee on Freedom of the Press and Information, Inter-American Press Association, midyear meeting, 1976, Aruba, p. 28.
[78]*Miami Herald*, March 21, 1972, June 25, 1972, July 14, 1972.
[79]Interview with Christian Hamann, McCann-Erickson de Peru, July 22, 1976.
[80]*Journal of Commerce*, Oct. 16, 1974.
[81]*New York Times*, Jan. 6, 1975.
[82]*Christian Science Monitor*, June 3, 1976.
[83]Interview with Alejandro Miro Quesada, July 23, 1976.
[84]*Index on Censorship*, Vol. 6, No. 6 (November–December, 1977), p. 66.
[85]Report of the Committee on Freedom of the Press and Information, Inter-American Press Association, annual meeting, 1977, Santo Domingo.
[86]*New York Times*, March 22, 1977.
[87]*Christian Science Monitor*, March 13, 1970, p. 16.
[88]*New York Times*, Feb. 5, 1975.
[89]*New York Times*, Jan. 6, 1975.
[90]*Ibid.; Washington Post*, Nov. 11, 1976.
[91]Alisky, *Journalism Quarterly*, Vol. 53, No. 4, p. 665.
[92]*New York Times*, April 17, 1974.
[93]*Los Angeles Times*, Feb. 7, 1975.
[94]*Los Angeles Times*, July 21 and 24, 1975.
[95]Gilbert, p. 20.

NOTES FOR CHAPTER 7

[1]Robert N. Pierce, "Costa Rica's Contemporary Media Show High Popular Participation," *Journalism Quarterly*, Vol. 47, No. 3, p. 547.
[2]Interview with Enrique Santos, *El Tiempo*, June 28, 1973.
[3]*Miami Herald*, Oct. 30, 1955, p. 22A.

[4] Howard I. Blutstein *et al.*, *Area Handbook for Colombia* (Washington: U.S. Government Printing Office, 1977), p. 320.

[5] Thomas E. Weil *et al.*, *Area Handbook for Venezuela* (Washington: U.S. Government Printing Office, 1971), p. 271–72.

[6] Pierce, *Journalism Quarterly*, Vol. 47, No. 3, p. 546.

[7] *Miami Herald*, April 7, 1974.

[8] *Miami Herald*, May 25, 1973.

[9] *Miami Herald*, July 11, 1973.

[10] Interview, July 2, 1976.

[11] Interview, Sept. 9, 1976.

[12] Interview, Sept. 9, 1976.

[13] Interview, Sept. 9, 1976.

[14] "Media in Venezuela Today," Report by U.S. Information Service, Caracas, Sept. 15, 1973, p. 3.

[15] *Ibid.*, p. 4.

[16] John García, "Letter From Colombia," *Index on Censorship,* Vol. 6, No. 3 (May–June, 1977), p. 45.

[17] *Miami Herald*, April 24, 1976.

[18] Interview, July 7, 1976.

[19] Garcia, *Index on Censorship,* Vol. 6, No. 3, p. 45.

[20] *New York Times*, Jan. 28, 1973.

[21] *Miami Herald*, April 3, 1976.

[22] *New York Times*, May 3, 1973; *Miami Herald,* June 15, 1973.

[23] Interview, Sept. 8, 1976.

[24] Interview, July 1, 1976.

[25] Blutstein *et al.*, p. 332.

[26] "General Media Information," Report by U.S. Information Service, Bogota, 1976, p. 1.

[27] Instituto Nacional de Radio y Televisión, Resolution 1120 of 1967, Article 5.

[28] Interview, July 9, 1976.

[29] *World Communication: A 200-Country Survey of Press, Radio, Television and Film* (5th ed., New York: Unipub, 1975), p. 231.

[30] *Ibid.*

[31] *Revista de la Prensa* (Bogotá), January–February, 1977, p. 13; *World Communication* . . . , p. 323.

[32] *Washington Post*, July 21, 1974.

[33] George A. Flowers Jr., "Television in Costa Rica: A Response to Picture-Tube Imperialism?," unpublished research paper, University of Texas, 1977, p. 36.

[34] Quoted *ibid.*, p. 35.

[35] *Ibid.*

[36] *Ibid.*, pp. 41–44.

[37] Donald and Dorothy Stroetzel, "Singular Cruzada en Colombia Contra la Ignorancia," *Selecciones del Reader's Digest,* May, 1975, pp. 1–6.

[38] *Mass Communication* . . . , p. 231.

[39] *Miami Herald*, April 7, 1974.

[40] Republic of Venezuela, Law of Journalism, signed Aug. 4, 1972.

[41] Republic of Venezuela, Law of the Journalist, signed Dec. 18, 1975.

[42] Carlos Andrés Peréz, *Information for Freedom* (Caracas: Oficina Central de Informacion, 1976), p. 67.

[43] García, *Index on Censorship,* Vol. 6, No. 3, pp. 45–46.

[44] *Washington Post*, Oct. 23, 1976.

[45] Timothy Green, *The Universal Eye: The World of Television* (New York: Stein and Day, 1972), p. 56.

46 *Ibid.*, p. 57.

47 *Miami Herald*, Jan. 11, 1974.

48 Flowers, p. 22.

49 *Miami Herald*, May 23, 1974.

50 *Los Angeles Times*, Dec. 20, 1974.

51 Interviews with Claude Hippeau, Piete Van Bennekom and Martin McReynolds, July 6, 1976; interviews with Martin McReynolds in Buenos Aires, August, 1976; interviews with various UPI correspondents, July–September, 1976; telephone interview with H. L. Stevenson, May 3, 1978.

52 *Cromos*, July 9, 1976, pp. 90–92.

53 *Ibid.*

54 Republic of Venezuela, Law of Journalism, signed Aug. 23, 1972, Article 30.

55 Gabriel Ortíz, ed., *La Prensa Entre la Lealtad y el Miedo* (Bogotá: Asociación Latinoamericana de Periodistas para el Desarrollo, 1976), p. 32.

56 *Miami Herald*, July 22, 1971.

57 *Ibid.*

58 Talk at the Venezuelan Embassy in Lima, Dec. 10, 1974, quoted in Pérez, pp. 68–69.

59 *Ibid.*

60 *El Tiempo* (Bogotá), July 10, 1976, p. 11A.

61 *La Presencia* (La Paz, July 25, 1976. p. 3.

62 Interview, Sept. 9, 1976.

63 Blutstein *et al.*, p. 320; *Miami Herald*, Oct. 30, 1955, p. 22A.

64 Ortíz, p. 32.

65 *Ibid.*

66 *New York Times*, Nov. 8, 1975; *Miami Herald*, April 24, 1976.

67 *Christian Science Monitor*, April 21, 1977.

68 *New York Times*, Jan. 24, 1975.

69 *The Chronicle* (Cali, Colombia), Oct. 9, 1976, p. 1.

70 Weil *et al.*, pp. 270–71.

71 *Ibid.*, pp. 271–72.

72 Interview with Peter Bottome, director, Channel 2, Sept. 8, 1976.

73 *Miami Herald*, July 6, 1973.

74 Jaime M. Fonseca, *Communication Policies in Costa Rica* (Paris: UNESCO, 1977), p. 33.

75 Interview with Guido Fernández, Oct. 19, 1977.

76 *Miami Herald*, Dec. 27, 1976.

77 Weil *et al.*, p. 272.

78 Report of the Committee on Freedom of the Prfess and Information, Inter-American Press Association, midyear meeting, Aruba, p. 33.

79 *Ibid.*, p. 79.

80 Interview, Sept. 8, 1976.

81 Report of the Committee on Freedom of the Press and Information, p. 34.

82 *Punto*, Sept. 8, 1976, p. 5.

83 *New York Times*, Feb. 22, 1977.

84 *Miami Herald*, Aug. 3, 1972.

85 Report of the Committee on Freedom of the Press and Information, Inter-American Press Association, annual meeting, Santo Domingo, 1977.

86 Ortíz, pp. 33–34.

87 *Miami Herald*, May 7, 1967, and July 1, 1971.

88 Interview, June 30, 1976.

89 Ortíz, p. 97.

90 *New York Times*, Feb. 22 and 23, 1977.

[91]*Los Angeles Times*, Aug. 25, 1974; *Miami Herald*, Aug. 31, 1974.
[92]*Miami Herald*, April 24, 1976.

NOTES FOR CHAPTER 8

[1]Gabriel Ortíz, ed., *La Prensa Entre la Lealtad y el Miedo* (Bogotá: Asociación Latinoamericana de Periodistas para el Desarrollo, 1976), p. 93.
[2]*La Ensenanza del Periodismo en América Latina* (New York: Council on Higher Education in the American Republics, 1970), p. 23.
[3]Report of the Committee on Freedom of the Press and Information, Inter-American Press Association, annual meeting, 1977, Santo Domingo.
[4]For further details, see "The Absorbed Posture" in Chapter X.
[5]Interview with Nicolás Ulloa, Director, *Extra* (Guayaquil, Ecuador), July 16, 1976.
[6]*Gainesville* (Florida) *Sun*, April 24, 1977, p. 12A; *El Da* (La Plata, Argentina), Sept. 28, 1977.
[7]Robert N. Pierce, "Costa Rica's Contemporary Media Show High Popular Participation," *Journalism Quarterly*, Vol. 47, No. 3, p. 547.
[8]*New York Times*, April 3, 1976.
[9]Republic of Venezuela, Law of Journalism, signed Aug. 23, 1972, Article 30.
[10]Ortíz, p. 32.
[11]*Miami Herald*, July 22, 1971.
[12]Associated Press, *Miami Herald*, Nov. 11, 1977; *Washington Post*, Nov. 12, 1977.
[13]*IAPA News*, No. 237, December 1976–January 1977, p. 5.
[14]*IAPA Updater*, No. 15, April 3, 1978, p. 4.

NOTES ON CHAPTER 9

[1]Joseph T. Klapper, *The Effects of Mass Communication* (Glencoe, Illinois: The Free Press, 1960), p. 8.
[2]Robert N. Pierce, "Public Opinion and Press Opinion in Four Latin American Cities," *Journalism Quarterly*, Vol. 46, No. 1 (Spring, 1969), pp. 53–60.
[3]Rebecca Ann Ford, *"El Día* Editorials and Social Reform" (unpublished master's thesis, College of Journalism and Communications, University of Florida, 1975).
[4]Helen Miller Bailey and Abraham P. Nasatir, *Latin America:* The Development of Its Civilization (Englewood Cliffs, New Jersey: Prentice-Hall, Inc., 1960), p. 393.
[5]*Child of the Dark: The Diary of Carolina Maria de Jesus* (New York: New American Library, 1962).
[6]In particular, see *The Children of Sánchez: Autobiography of a Mexican Family* (New York: Vintage Books, 1961).

NOTES FOR CHAPTER 10

[1]Wilbur Schramm, *Mass Media and National Development* (Stanford, Calif.: Stanford University Press, 1964); John C. Merrill, *The Elite Press* (New York: Pitman Publishing Corp., 1968).
[2]*The Press in Authoritarian Countries* (Zurich: The International Press Institute, 1959), p. 8.
[3]*Ibid.*, p. 9.
[4]See "Factors Related to Freedom in National Press Systems," *Journalism Quarterly*,

Vol. 37, No. 1 (Winter, 1960), pp. 13–28, and "Freedom in the World's Press: A Fresh Appraisal with New Data," *Journalism Quarterly*, Vol. 42, No. 1 (Winter, 1965), pp. 3–14, 118–19.

[5] Nixon, *Journalism Quarterly*, Vol. 42, No. 1, p. 7.

[6] Arthur S. Banks and Robert B. Textor, *A Cross-Polity Survey* (Cambridge, Mass.: MIT Press, 1963).

[7] Ralph L. Lowenstein, "Press Freedom as a Barometer of Political Democracy," in Heinz-Dietrich Fischer and John C. Merrill, eds., *International and Intercultural Communication* (New York: Hastings House Publishers, 1976), pp. 136–47.

[8] *Ibid.*, pp. 138–39.

[9] Raymond D. Gastil, "The Comparative Survey of Freedom—VIII," *Freedom at Issue*, No. 44 (January–February, 1978), p. 4.

[10] *Ibid.*, p. 11.

[11] Interview, Aug. 25, 1976.

[12] *Miami Herald*, Jan. 29, 1978.

[13] Interview with Huascar Cajías, director, *La Presencia*, July 28, 1976.

NOTES FOR CHAPTER 11

[1] Howard J. Wiarda, ed., *Politics and Social Change in Latin America: The Distinct Tradition* (Amherst: University of Massachusetts Press, 1974), pp. 2–22.

[2] *Ibid.*, p. 18.

[3] Guillermo A. O'Donnell, *Modernization and Bureaucratic-Authoritarianism* (Berkeley, California: Institute of International Studies, 1973).

INDEX

Aeromexico, 106
Agence France Presse (AFP), 45
Alemán, Miguel, 100
"All Nudity Will Be Punished" (film), 37, 197
Allende, Salvador, 18, 55, 57-70 *passim,* 73, 76, 77, 78, 165, 183, 188, 189, 190, 203, 207, 213, 232
Alternativa magazine, 153, 176
Amado, Jorge, 34
Amazon basin, 51
American Broadcasting Company (ABC), 92, 93, 164
American Popular Revolutionary Alliance (APRA) of Peru, 121, 123, 129
American Society of Travel Agents, 41
Amnesty International, 202
Anderson, Jack, 60, 74
Anti-Semitism, 7, 18, 22, 203
Arana, Elsa, 140
Arcocha, Juan, 88
Arequipa (Peru), 128
Argentina, 3-22, 28, 60, 79, 102, 139, 167, 169, 176, 182, 184, 185, 187, 188, 190, 197, 200, 201, 202, 203, 208, 209, 210, 213, 224, 226, 229, 230, 231, 234, 237; advertising in, governmental, 187, 188; anti-Semitism in, 7, 18, 22, 203; balcony speeches in, 210; censorship in, 9-13 *passim;* economic regulation in, 18-20; inflation in, 190; labor unions in, 190; Ministry of Press and Broadcasting in, 11; motion pictures in, 12-13, 37, 197;

music industry in, 11; nationalism in, 9, 10-11; newspapers in, 4-10 *passim,* 12-22 *passim,* 182, 188, 226; propaganda by government of, 21-22; radio in, 14; Telam news agency in, 15-16, 19, 21, 188; television in, 15, 21, 237; terrorism in, 4-7, 201, 202, 208, 230
Argentine Anti-Communist Alliance (AAA), 4, 7, 202
Argentine Publishers' Association (ADEPA), 8, 202
Arns, Paulo Evaristo Cardinal, 42
Associated Press (AP), 10, 45, 89, 144, 163, 220
Autocensura (self-censorship), 195, 228
Avance, 86
"Aveu, L' " (film), 66
Avila Camacho, Manuel, 110
Azuela, Mariano, 96

Bahamas, 149, 165
Bahia (Brazil), 49
Banks, Arthur S., 219, 220
Barranquilla (Colombia), 155
Batista, Fulgencio, 80, 81, 85, 86, 118, 188
Batlle y Ordóñez, José, 209, 229, 231
Belaunde Terry, Fernando, 137
Belem (Brazil), 51
Belgium, 21
Beltrán, Pedro, 122, 123, 131, 135, 140
Bernstein, Carl, 215
Betancourt, Rómulo, 148

To: Bettye Martin Musham

Guest Speaker in the

Krannert Executive Forum,

February 19, 1993

We deeply appreciate your

participation in this important

Krannert School activity!

EJ Weidenaar, Dean.

K. Shuster
1987

Management education at Purdue University had its formal beginning in 1956 when the faculty and graduate council voted to establish a graduate curriculum leading to a Master of Science in Industrial Management degree, later renamed Master of Science in Industrial Administration (M.S.I.A.). The first degree program, a unique and innovative 11-month course of study designed to provide professional management training for students with undergraduate engineering degrees, became the backbone of the School of Industrial Management formed in 1958. The doctoral and Bachelor of Science in Industrial Management (B.S.I.M.) programs also were initiated in 1958.

Herman Krannert, founder of Inland Container Corporation, and his wife Ellnora established a generous endowment in 1962 for managerial studies at Purdue. The Krannert Graduate School of Management and its home, the Krannert Building, are named in their honor. The adjacent Krannert Center for Executive Education and Research also bears the industrialist's name. Dedicated in 1983, the Center was constructed with the aid of funds from the Krannert Charitable Trust.

Since its inception, the Krannert School has built upon its special strength — superior management education for students with quantitative and technical backgrounds. Beginning with just 29 master's students in 1957, over the years the management programs have grown in scope, depth, and size with the addition of two-year master's degree programs in management and human resource management, highly regarded doctoral and executive programs, and undergraduate curricula offering majors in accounting, management, and economics. Throughout, the School's goal has remained constant — to educate graduates of the highest caliber for the nation's businesses, industries, academic institutions, and government.

KRANNERT
ON MANAGEMENT

Published by

KRANNERT SCHOOL OF MANAGEMENT

PURDUE UNIVERSITY

ACKNOWLEDGEMENTS

The Krannert School of Management gratefully acknowl-
edges the R. R. Donnelley & Sons Company, Crawfordsville,
Indiana, and Follett College Stores Corporation, Chicago,
Illinois, for their generous support in the publication and
printing of this volume.

1966 Dedication

To my wife

ELLNORA D. KRANNERT

whose companionship has kept me from being that "lonely
man at the top," whose counsel has wisely guided many
of my management decisions, and whose partnership
helped build Inland Container Corporation, the Krannert
Graduate School of Industrial Administration, and our
other "centers of excellence."

1987 Dedication

To The Krannert School's Past And Future Alumni

Their accomplishments provide a lasting tribute to Herman
and Ellnora Krannert for the vision and the commitment
that led to the founding of the Krannert Graduate School
of Management.

Library of Congress Catalog Number 66-6475
Printed in United States of America

TABLE OF
CONTENTS

HERMAN C. KRANNERT was an uncommon individual. From an early age, when a Chicago streetcar accident took his father's life, until his death in 1972, he accepted ever-increasing levels of entrepreneurial challenge, which culminated in his founding Inland Container Corporation and leading that enterprise for 47 years.

Two years after his graduation in engineering from the University of Illinois, Mr. Krannert went to work for the Sefton Manufacturing Company, a Chicago paper box firm. He rose rapidly, and within three years he was named manager of Sefton's Anderson, Indiana, plant. Two significant events subsequently occurred: he met and married Ellnora Decker, his lifelong partner in every venture thereafter; and he resigned his Sefton position over a policy matter and accepted all the risks inherent in establishing his own firm.

With six loyal friends and former Sefton associates, and the constant encouragement and support of his wife, Herman Krannert founded Inland Container Corporation in 1925. Active in company affairs until the end, he was chairman of the board when he died on February 24, 1972, at the age of 84. Ellnora Krannert died two years later. Under Krannert's leadership, Inland Container had become the world's fourth-largest shipper of corrugated fiber products.

Foreword

This reprinting of KRANNERT ON MANAGEMENT is in celebration of the twenty-fifth anniversary of Purdue University's Krannert School of Management. In the latter years of Herman Krannert's life, he and his wife Ellnora devoted much of their time to philanthropic projects and educational programs for the establishment of "centers of excellence." The Krannerts developed this concept as a way of investing in society a portion of the benefits they had earned from our country's free enterprise system.

One of those "centers of excellence" is the Krannert Graduate School of Management, which was founded in 1962 and bears its benefactors' name. Thereafter for eight years, as a visiting professor on the School's staff, Mr. Krannert delivered a noteworthy lecture to students and faculty on Purdue University's West Lafayette campus. After 1968, illness prevented the continuation of the lecture series, but Mr. Krannert's fundamental and practical management philosophy had gained many admirers both on campus and in the business world. The first five lectures were published in 1966 in a volume entitled KRANNERT ON MANAGEMENT; the volume was reprinted with three subsequent lectures in 1974. Now, on the twenty-fifth anniversary of the Krannert School's founding, through the generosity of R. R. Donnelley & Sons Company and Follett College Stores Corporation, it is again our priviledge to share Mr. Krannert's wisdom.

Little could anyone in 1962 realize the results of the Krannerts' vision and generosity. When the School was founded, management education was on the verge of an incredible period of growth. At present, there are over 1,200 organizations offering undergraduate degrees and in excess of 600 offering graduate degrees in management education. Of these, only a handful have achieved national recognition as part of the intellectual leadership in the field. Thanks in part to the vision and generosity of Herman Krannert, the Krannert School of Management has joined this elite group of educational institutions.

Most institutions never know the joy of such an achievement. Krannert's students, alumni, and faculty do. When a school is first created, its reputation hinges on that of the university in which it is situated—in our case, Purdue University, a leading international, research-oriented institution. As it matures, a school's reputation is enhanced by that of its faculty—and we have an exceptional group of educators committed to their dual role as teachers and researchers. As a school matures further, its recognition increasingly rests on the accomplishments of its alumni. At this stage in the Krannert School's relatively brief evolution, its alumni are becoming our best advertisement. Their accomplishments say more than anything else about what the Krannert School has and will continue to contribute to our society—effective leadership in the world of affairs. It is our society's scarcest commodity.

Ronald E. Frank

Ronald E. Frank
Dean
Krannert School of Management
October 1987

Attitude

"You have heard a lot of talk about the 'organization man,' and how in business we need to adapt our personalities to some prevailing type. Let me say right now this is a lot of malarky. Industry needs people who are willing to be themselves. You have heard much about square pegs in round holes. I think every chief executive would like to have a number of strong square pegs who can prove that they are valuable enough in terms of getting things done *to warrant our chiseling out square holes for them.*"

On May 16, 1962, Herman C. Krannert began his annual lectures at Purdue University. It was the 50th anniversary of his own graduation from the University of Illinois. He had just been installed as a Visiting Professor at the Krannert Graduate School of Industrial Administration.

Attitude

IT is stimulating to see how the youth of our country is moving to acquire greater education, greater knowledge, and the ability to use that knowledge. I am here today in a dual role. First, I would say, to benefit from the things I may learn from you, and secondly, to attempt to give you the opportunity of learning from me the basic philosophies which have been tremendously helpful in the development of my own business career.

I am pleased to start my new career as professor in an exciting school. This is my first experience as a formally appointed professor. But, on the other hand, I want you to know that I have been a teacher for a long time, having graduated from the hard school of experience. In that school, when you made the wrong decision you paid for it, and that makes quite a lot of difference.

I want to correct one statement Dean Weiler* made in introducing me—that when we started our own business in 1925 we started with what we had, and then we looked to the banks. Actually, the banks have mostly been concerned because we never came to them and asked for a loan. We didn't believe in borrowing money, a thing which is, of

*E. T. Weiler was Dean of the Krannert Graduate School of Industrial Administration at Purdue University.

course, quite contrary to the present-day concept in both our family lives and in business.

We believed in standing on our own, getting credit where credit was needed from suppliers, and then paying for things as we went along. We've done that, and I think we have a very enviable balance sheet, though we are criticized many times because we are too liquid; we have too much cash for a company of our size. But it's a comfortable feeling!

Principles Are Important

When we started Inland Container Corporation in 1925, our only assets were the loyalty of a small group of six people who came with me from Anderson, Indiana, and our willingness to learn together in a rapidly changing and growing industry. I might say briefly, principles and opportunities have a great deal to do with what happens in the development and unfolding of your life.

I had been with the Sefton Company for 10 years, and one day I was called to Chicago by the President. We met in the Chicago Athletic Club, and he told me that my work had been so satisfactory that he was going to make me a Vice President of the company and a director the following day. He said, "But I want you to vote the way I tell you to." I said I wouldn't do it; I therefore resigned. So right then and there, within an hour, I was out of a job. But this company had three factions, and I knew I didn't have any stock; I didn't

12

Attitude

have any equity position. I had nothing but my-self, and I was not going to act as a dummy on a Board of Directors doing what someone else told me to do. I either was going to run the show or I was not; and I decided to quit.

So I called my wife that evening and told her I was out of a job. She said, "That's fine, you will find something to do." My wife's unqualified support has always given me inspiration and confidence.

I *did* find something to do, and it was a hard job. We started this company in Indianapolis, and, as I said, six of my associates came from Anderson with me. The occasion was rather interesting.

Mrs. Krannert and I had moved to Indian-apolis. We hadn't made any arrangements for any-body else to work for us yet; I was really explor-ing and surveying the situation, trying to rent a building and a lot of things. But these six men came down to see us on a Sunday morning, and they told me that they had resigned from their jobs over in Anderson. They were going to work for me. I didn't know how they were going to do that, because we didn't have any money; I didn't have any money to pay them any salaries; we didn't have any money to buy machinery. But they were going to work for me. They quit their jobs, and they had confidence that we were going to go places. That alone made it essential and necessary to move only in one direction—ahead.

It took a lot of courage and a lot of guts to meet a situation like that, where immediately you

13

Attitude

took on, in addition to yourself, six families to carry forward on a new enterprise in a very highly competitive industry. In order to try to stop us, one competitor set up an emergency fund of $100,000, which it gave to its salesmen in Indianapolis to keep us from getting any business. Now that, of course, became a sales promotion activity, which we used to *get* business. You've just got to turn things around. You've got to make opportunity as you go, and there was probably nothing that helped us more than the $100,000 which was put in the "kitty" by our competitor to keep us from getting any orders.

Circumstances Are Tools

After we got started in Indianapolis, we got the machinery, and I rented a building 1,000 feet long and 100 feet wide, and we got along to the point where we had been in production for not quite a year, when the treasurer of the Marmon Automobile Company came over to see us. They were renting us the building. They said they would like us to cancel our five-year lease because they had decided to go back into the automobile business, and they'd appreciate it if we could vacate the property we were renting. Well, we said that would be very difficult, but if at all possible we would do it. That was the first impact that Roosevelts had on our company, because they were going to call this new car the Roosevelt. So, we had to move out because Roosevelt was coming in.

14

Attitude

That presented problems; we had no place to move. There was no building available in Indianapolis that we thought suitable, so I talked to the Vice President of our bank, and he said, "Well, now. If you just buy a lot down the street here, we'll put up a building for you." So we scouted around, went to my father-in-law and to brother-in-law Howard Decker here in Lafayette and we raised enough money to buy the property. We got a loan from the Meyer-Kiser Bank to put up the building. We moved right along to get the building up and just as we had about concluded the building and paying for it out of this loan, Meyer-Kiser failed. We got all our money out except $3.75, so that we did pretty well in skirting around the edges. It shows how much opportunity, circumstances, and conditions really control your future and what you do.

Some of the companies in our industry acted as if they always had the final answers. But we realized from the beginning and had been aware that there is no final answer to any problem and that truth in business as well as in universities is never absolute. However, in the short run, we must act as though we have the answers; we must be positive; and we must motivate other people to act definitely and without fear.

But while we are acting with one set of answers, we must be seeking new answers, always aware that there is no final solution. As a chief executive of a rapidly growing company, I have had to emphasize both attitudes, the willingness to

15

Attitude

think and the willingness to act. I am sure that your professors have been trying to get you to adopt both of these attitudes, committing yourselves to a course of action and at the same time, questioning this very course.

I welcome the chance to work with new colleagues in developing your capacity to live effectively in the industrial scene in a fast-moving world. I am particularly pleased that most of you have had undergraduate engineering training, because the world which you are entering is dominated by scientists and engineers. With this background, the courage to choose new answers and to discard old ones—the courage to gamble on a certain amount of uncertainty—is reinforced by sure technical knowledge.

Profit Is Vital

I think, as a legitimate goal, *profit* should be set as the objective. It is the one thing that is the common denominator of measuring performance and success. As I reflect on the experiences I have had in a business environment, there are a number of things I should like, as a professor, to say to you.

You have been taught by your professors to respect profit-making as a goal. You may even have been annoyed by their emphasis on profit as a legitimate end in itself. I should like to take this occasion, if I can, to strengthen their argument.

The market is an extraordinarily clever device for pitting the creative people in one organization

Attitude

against the creative people in other organizations. The number of ways in which these organizations can compete is legion, and I am speaking from a lifetime of experience in a highly competitive industry. Because people are always seeking new ways of doing things in practical affairs, there is nothing certain except change. No solution is ever good enough to last for a long time. The search for new truth has been so effective that there really isn't any way in the American economy to fix the market so there won't be competition. The world is too restless and in this complex competitive game of moves and counter-moves, profit is the *evidence* of success. And many companies are not successful. When we talk about the profit system, we should realize that we are talking about a profit and loss system, with many organizations coming out at the short end.

Let me then, as a new professor, support your classroom professors in their emphasis on profit as an important goal for a business organization. It not only measures the present success of an organization; it also is the admission ticket to the future. The company which is not making a profit will not have the new capital for new machinery and equipment and for maintaining the kind of an organizational climate which permits you to survive. And believe me, every company which is operating profitably has as a chief executive, a professor in the sense which I have been using the term—able to motivate people to act courageously in the face of uncertainty—also to encourage people to re-

17

Attitude

examine the basis for their actions. Or to put it another way, to act at the same time you seek truth.

It Always Can Be Better

Your role is this. I suspect that you have already accepted profit as a primary goal of business activity and what is bothering you is how you can participate most effectively in our profit system. This is a hard question to answer, but still the method is easy. All you have to do is perform the job that has been assigned to you better than it has been done before—better today than yesterday.

This is a continuing job—you must learn to do the job from the man on the job. You should assist him to do the job better and simpler, and above all, you should make friends with the man on the job. Do not look down on him. Start right from the beginning to develop teamwork. No one man can do the job alone. When you finish this year's work, you will have insights into the ways the pieces of an organization fit together and what is expected of each of the pieces.

But let me warn you, in your *first* job, you aren't expected to be a generalist with responsibility for the whole organization. You should be sensitive to what is happening in your company, and in your industry and in the national economy. I would expect you to continue studying your industry as you work.

In your first job with a company you will no doubt be a specialist. You may be a salesman, a

18

Attitude

foreman, an industrial engineer—and your first assignment is to succeed as a "doer." I would like to tell you that there is no substitute for success in your first job, and there is no substitute for hard work. You must establish yourself with your associates as one who knows how to get results. While you are working on this particular job, we do not want you to lose your capacity to be objective and to question constantly your attitudes. Yet, at the same time, we do want you to show that you can act promptly and effectively.

Individualism

You have heard a lot of talk about the "organization man," and how in business we need to adapt our personalities to some prevailing type. Let me say right now this is a lot of malarky. Industry needs people who are willing to be themselves.

You have heard much about square pegs in round holes. I think every chief executive would like to have a number of strong square pegs who can prove that they are valuable enough in terms of getting things done to warrant our chiseling out square holes for them. Your own personality is all you really have to use; you can't use the other person's personality as effectively as your own. If you are willing to accept the goals of the organization, and if you are truly a responsible person, your services will be valued in any healthy business organization I know. An organization which cannot

19

Attitude

accommodate itself to square pegs will not succeed in our profit system.

This does not mean that you should be different purely for the sake of being different, but in all things which are really important, always be yourself. Businesses are effective only because executives who are actively involved treat their business activity as important enough to put their whole selves into it. You can be an artist in the realm of business, but only if your attitudes and actions reflect your own personality—not a carbon copy of some other person.

Use Your Total Personality

And so, to tie this all together, the professor in business and the professor in the university are not too different, and I am happy to try my hand at professing in a different environment. In the world of affairs which you will soon enter, there are many bright and capable people. Your career is really another phase of your education and an exciting phase because you will not only be learning, but applying the things you learn, and the profit your efforts achieve will measure their success.

As you enter the world of affairs, study it. Think about what everything means. Never be content with the usual explanation—always probe. Study ways to improve what you are doing. But while you are thinking and puzzling, always be prepared to act. There is a time for caution and

20

Attitude

there is a time for courage. Most of the time we need courage, and in this, don't be afraid to use your whole personality. This is your greatest asset. You must develop confidence and conviction in your own ability.

The profitable organizations are the flexible ones, the ones which can accommodate themselves to people who want to be creative and are willing to invest all of themselves in creating the new and more vigorous business organization. Indeed, as I look around me at the chief executives of the successful American companies, I am heartened that they are not the "organization men" you have been hearing about. They are highly individualized persons who, like their counterparts in the universities, are sometimes called "characters." Don't be fooled. They are the people who have the courage to put their own personalities into the creation of a business which can succeed in the pitiless competition which characterizes the American scene.

So, in summing it up, *think creatively; act courageously; be yourself;* and your services will be sought by your superiors and by your associates.

21

Attitude

Decisions

"I have heard people say that there is a lot of luck in life, and I would agree that there is. But luck consists largely of being ready for opportunity, and this is where your intelligence and your education can be useful. Unless you are constantly figuring the odds—the cost of losing if you are wrong, or the profits to be gained if you are right—and unless you have developed a "style of play" that will tell you when the rewards are worth the risks you won't recognize the opportunities when they do present themselves. You won't be lucky, because luck consists of being ready for opportunity."

On May 22, 1963, Herman C. Krannert played a "return engagement" before students and faculty of the Krannert Graduate School at Purdue. The school was making tremendous strides in its curriculum—both in economics and the administrative sciences. And, Mr. Krannert's Inland Container Corporation was still growing, too.

Decisions

TODAY I want to talk about what it means to be an effective person in a business enterprise. I want to talk about what education can and cannot do to make you more effective.

When I started in business in 1925, we didn't have any college-trained persons. It happened this way: I was offered an advancement by the company by which I was then employed because of my good performance with them for a ten-year period. I was to be manager of the three production plants of the company and, in addition, I was to be elected a director. However, the President of the firm requested, as a consideration, that I vote as he directed. This, to me, was contrary to good business principles and ethics. I believe a director should be free to exercise his own judgement. Inasmuch as I could not agree with the President, I resigned from the company. I telephoned my wife that evening and informed her of the action I had taken. She said I had taken the right step and that we would somehow make out. *My decision-making career had started.*

With very little money, but with many friends and a burning desire to succeed, we started the Inland Container Corporation in 1925. Shortly after

25

I resigned, six of my former associates called at our home and informed me that they too had resigned and would join me in our new company. This took real courage on their part, but it placed on me the necessity of succeeding. None of these six men was a college-trained person. These men who came with me from Anderson, Indiana, had the courage to cast their lot with a new enterprise and a new businessman, and their courage carried them a long way. Working together, we were able to develop a business which now has some 4,000 people in it, with annual sales of well over 120 million dollars, and it is the second largest corrugated box company in America. Courage and the willingness to act can take people a long way.

Information Isn't Enough

Now that we are a well established company we are recruiting college-trained people because these trained minds are readily available. Although I don't want to sound discouraging, I am not sure that when the score is finally tallied, the college-trained people will prove to be any more effective than the courageous men who came with me from Anderson.

I know this may sound like heresy to a group of students completing their master's degrees in industrial administration, but I am worried about the emphasis schools of business and industrial administration are placing on processing of information as a means of making decisions. These days, I

26

Decisions

hear a lot about what computers can do for us, how they can process enormous amounts of information and finally print out the right decision. I hear also about the wonders of corporate staffs and how they can digest information and prepare carefully worked-out alternatives as a basis for executive decisions.

Both of these ways of processing information are based on the proposition that, if a man has more information, he will make better decisions. Right now I want to challenge this. I am not sure this has been demonstrated. I am inclined to think that this excessive reliance on data processing and on staff work is another of those "cure-alls" which have been tried in the past and found wanting.

Certainty Is Never Complete

Let me explain: Every time you make a decision there is something unique about that decision. You can never be absolutely sure of the outcome; there is always some element of gamble. I would guess from watching lawyers and physicians and other professional men work that there is an element of risk-taking in the practice of every profession.

At the end of World War II, Inland Container had a successful business, converting paperboard into corrugated boxes to serve industry. Many of my associates were satisfied with our position. Our balance sheet was healthy and we had a number of offers from larger companies who wanted to pay cash for our business; and it looked as though we

27

could "play it safe" by either staying small or by selling out. But it was also clear to me that only by becoming an integrated company, with control over our raw material supplies, could we survive the competition of the period ahead in the 1950's and 1960's. And so we took the plunge—we used our cash and put our credit on the line—to go into partnership with the Mead Corporation. We organized a joint venture in which each partner had a 50 per cent interest. We started with one mill and supporting timberlands. Then, as we grew, with the increasing demand for our products and services, we expanded, using profits generated from the business, until today we operate three large mills with a production capacity of more than 2000 tons of kraft paperboard per day, supported by more than one million acres of timberland. We had no assurance at the time that this venture would succeed. We had to have faith and be prepared to take the risks of doing something new.

There's Risk In Every Job

All of the significant business decisions you will be called on to make in your career will involve a large element of risk-taking. This will be particularly true in the next ten years while you are learning your trade as an engineer-businessman. We are in the midst of tremendoous changes which I am convinced are going to affect the way we do business, and you are going to have to estimate what these changes will mean to you.

28

Decisions

You may think that risk-taking is something which is reserved for top management. Let me assure you it is a necessary ingredient for success at each stage in your career. Every time you delegate a job to a subordinate, you are taking a risk. Your boss will hold you responsible even though he knows you may have to work through other people to get the job done. You can delegate the authority, but you cannot delegate responsibility.

If you are going to be an effective engineer-businessman, you must be prepared to take calculated risks in situations where there are no experience tables, no ways to hedge. You must "stick out your neck" and go ahead with what you believe should be done, even though you can't be sure in advance that you have made the right decision.

I don't want you to think that business is just one painful decision after another. You can have a lot of fun in your chosen career. The businessmen who are right more times than they are wrong can make a profit. Profits are not only the life blood of business; they are the reward for real skill in risk-taking.

Frequently I wonder why so many people want to "play it safe." Why do so many middle managers, who should enjoy the challenge of business, spend their time "laying mattresses" in strategic places so that they will have a place to dive when the shooting starts? Possibly, from the beginning of time, we have tried to fool ourselves about the kind of world we live in. We have wanted to believe that there is some way to beat the game—to succeed

29

Decisions

without really trying—to have the profits without taking the risks. Maybe it is just *too painful* for us to admit that the world is full of accidents and chance results. We have wanted to believe that if we do "the right thing" we can somehow be 100 per cent sure that we will get the right answer.

Is Science Sufficient?

In the days when primitive man was primarily superstitious, he tried to eliminate risks by making sacrifices to the gods; today he is using science, believing that for every result there is an antecedent cause; and that if he just learns enough about the web of cause-and-effect relationships in the world, he can figure out with certainty what will happen. And if he knows with certainty what will happen, he can figure out what to do to make the right things happen.

In the Twentieth Century, dominated as it is by science, in place of offering sacrifices to the gods, we are careful to take our vitamins, to avoid cholesterol in our diets, to get enough but not too much exercise, or, in the field of corporate management, we are careful to spend enough on research and development or to spend enough on advertising. We all want to be "on the right side" of science. We don't want to admit that some things just happen—that even the most careful person can be killed by the random twitch of a drunk driver coming toward him on the highway.

30

Decisions

From where I sit, this excessive reliance on science is another "cure-all" and is bound to fail as was primitive man's reliance on his sacrifices. The plain fact is that, regardless of what you do, you will always live in a frightening world. Regardless of the amount of information you have, you will make some wrong decisions. Each decision is a bet on life's roulette wheel, and the best you can do is insist that the odds match the risks. If you wait for sure things, you will never do anything. There is no way to avoid taking risks.

It takes courage to live with a sure knowledge that there is nothing you can do to make the world an absolutely safe place. Whether it is the saber-tooth tiger about to pounce on primitive man or the Chinese Communists about to explode the hydrogen bomb, the world is full of uncertainty. This is man's fate—and what I can't figure out is why we insist on believing that some place there is a Shangri-La. Maybe, instead of looking for snug harbors, we should get our fun out of facing the risks of life.

Your Style of Play

Facing the risks of decision-making takes not only courage but a philosophy of life which will help you keep your bearings regardless of how well or how badly you are doing at the time. You must develop your own style of play.

If you are the kind of person who insists on being sure you will be right, you will never play

31

Decisions

for very large stakes. If you are the kind who wants to play for larger stakes, you will have to take larger risks. My own style of play is to be conservative on small things and take substantial risks on big things. But I can't tell you what style of play you should have. The important thing is to develop a style of play which fits your personality and then maintain it. There is always the danger, after a series of good decisions, that you will get soft and start taking foolish risks; or, after a series of poor decisions, that you will become too conservative and insist on playing it too safe.

At the risk of upsetting your professors, I am going to tell you my favorite way of making difficult decisions. I think about all the possible outcomes for the decision. I sometimes even write myself letters recommending various courses of action. I talk it over with my wife. I examine all the evidence I can, but I don't agonize over the problem. Once I have thought the problem through, I look over my left shoulder and there is the answer. And once I see the answer, there is no question about what to do; the way is clear.

Then it is time to act. There is a time for thinking and a time for acting. To be effective, one must know when to stop thinking and start acting. If you are going to be a successful leader, never question your decision once it is made. People will not follow a doubtful leader. But remember you can make only one decision on any one subject. Discipline yourself to such action.

32

Most people have enough intelligence to figure out what to do; they just don't have the courage and self-confidence to face the uncertainty. A leader gives them this courage and self-confidence. He releases the intelligence and energy of people to go ahead in their own way to get things done.

It may turn out that the decision you have made is wrong. This isn't too serious if you accept my premise that this is a risky world, that in every decision there is an element of the gamble. It doesn't reduce your effectiveness to make a 180 degree turn. If you have been wrong, don't waste your energy blaming yourself. To other people, you may want to say that the situation has changed and it is time for a new look at things. You may want to say to yourself that the original decision was a gamble and not all gambles succeed. The important thing is to keep your courage and your judgment, so that regardless of the outcome of any particular decision you are in a position to make an intelligent gamble the next time you are called upon to make a decision.

I have heard people say that there is a lot of luck in life, and I would agree that there is. But luck consists largely of being ready for opportunity, and this is where your intelligence and your education can be useful. Unless you are constantly figuring the odds—the cost of losing if you are wrong, or the profits to be gained if you are right—and unless you have developed a "style of play" that will tell you when the rewards are worth the risks, you

33

Decisions

won't recognize the opportunities when they do present themselves. You won't be lucky, because luck consists of being ready for opportunity. To be an effective person, you need more than an education, although an education can be very useful to you. You must be prepared to place your bets in a consistent and intelligent fashion on life's roulette wheel.

The Age Of Over-Think

It is because I believe so strongly in the need for risk-taking at all levels of management in an organization that I am not so sure your generation of highly educated managers is going to do a better job than my generation, which has relied more completely on intuition.

You have a greater potential than we ever had. You know more about modern technology; you know more about psychology; but I am not sure you are willing to live life as dangerously as it must be lived to take advantage of the opportunities which luck offers you. When I look at American industry with its heavy emphasis on corporate staff, I wonder if we are not trying to "over-think" and "over-analyze" some of the problems. Maybe we need more people who, after they have thought through a problem, will have the courage to act.

And so I shall conclude by agreeing with your professors that an education can help you think things through; but unless you are willing to assume the risks of making a decision in the face of

34

Decisions

uncertainty, your education won't do you any good and you're going to miss most of the fun of living.

The real test of an education is its capacity to make you a better risk-taker; to make you ready to take full advantage of circumstances as you find them, even though you can never be sure in advance that you will be right.

Decisions

Time

"Everyone is wrong some of the time if he does anything. The man who tries never to be wrong will over-study every situation and over-studying can be a serious waste of time. There are two parts to every decision—the thinking part and the willingness to act in the face of uncertainty. Every businessman has to think. There are many fascinating puzzles in business. But, as I said last year, thinking is not enough. You must be prepared to go ahead and do something."

On May 11, 1964, the development program of the Krannert Graduate School was making great strides. As the noted industrialist spoke in Purdue's Memorial Union, the audience could look across the street and see a new building taking shape.

Time

ODAY I want to talk to you about *Time*. When I was your age and had just finished my engineering studies at the University of Illinois, I thought I had enough time to do everything there was to do in the world. I thought I could run the best company, read all the good books, see all the beautiful paintings—in other words, do everything I really considered worth doing. Now I know that there isn't enough time for everything. I am sure that you all accept the fact that there is an equal amount of time for each of us—seven days per week, 24 hours per day, with each hour representing 60 precious minutes. But have you really, genuinely, down deep in your being, realized that time is your most limited resource? Looking back over the span of years which separates us, I want to talk to you about using your time wisely. I am going to ask you to accept on faith the proposition that there is only a certain amount of time for each of us and that it will run out all too soon.

You and your parents have invested a great deal in your education. Indeed, as I look across the street and see our new Graduate School building going up, I feel that I too am investing in your education and that I have a stake in how you use your time.

The Machine Called You

What you now have for sale is a very intricate and expensive piece of capital. For this purpose, you might even think of yourself as owning a very costly computer which you are going to rent to some business as a means of realizing a return on the investment which you have been making in yourself.

Up to now, other people have been managing your time. You have been told by your parents what to do, given assignments by your teachers, maybe even a few orders from your wives. Now that you are about to enter the business world, you yourself will have to take the responsibility for the effective management of your own time. I realize that you will soon be working for someone else and that you will have to accept the goals of your employer. But if you are going to be an effective member of any organization you cannot expect them to organize your time for you. You are the only person who can do this.

So, first, let me tell you about some of the ways people in industry waste their time. I should warn you that these are my own views, distilled from over 50 years of experience in business.

How Time Is Wasted

I think perhaps the most important waste of time is the *excessive socializing* which people seem to think is necessary in order to succeed in business. This takes many forms: the long coffee-break—the

40

Time

extended wet lunch-hour with business associates—the cocktail hour—the weekend parties. Many people seem to feel that in order to be successful with other people you must spend your time socializing. *I don't believe this.* You have to be sensitive to the needs of other people and forthright in dealing with them, but I don't believe you have to accept the compulsive social life which seems to characterize the industrial scene and the campus these days.

You might think that this fraternizing will insure the support of other people in the office. I can assure you that what really counts in any company worth belonging to is how well you do your work, and how well you do your thinking. Entertaining may delay your dismissal six months in case you are not doing your work well, but it will not help you succeed in American industry.

There is another activity which is closely related to socializing, and this we shall call the *attendance at meetings.* Many people seem to think that if they are seen at the proper places it will somehow help them. And so they attend company meetings, trade association meetings, community affairs meetings, and many others. I really think very little has ever been accomplished in any meeting—and this includes committee meetings. I am sure you are going to have to attend some meetings, and I am not recommending that you avoid them completely—but don't confuse accomplishment with attendance. If you value your time, don't squander it sitting in meetings, listening to other people thinking out loud or making speeches.

41

Time

No Profit In Politics

A third time-waster is *office politics*. When you go into your first job, you are going to be scared, or at least awed with the new environment and new faces. It was the same with me when I took my first major job after graduating from the University of Illinois. This after-college job started me on my career as a manufacturer of corrugated containers and, later, as a manufacturer of kraft container-board, an important adjunct to corrugated containers. I should have said that this was not my first job since, like many of you, I had shorter jobs during summer and winter vacations. To name one such job—I worked with a dairy, filling milk bottles, taking care of the horses, and then delivering the milk with a horse and wagon to homes, starting at one o'clock in the morning. In order to save enough money to go to college, I deferred entry for two years. I started working as a draftsman, at $6 per week, for a company which manufactured steel towers for aeromotors, windmills and transmission lines. When orders dropped off in the 1906-07 depression I got a job with a foundry and metal-working company that designed power drives and gears and similar equipment. Later, in order to continue working, I took a job with the Chicago Telephone Company as a switchboard installer, then as a draftsman, and later as the manager of one of their telephone exchanges.

During these two years, I had saved about $200 after having given my mother funds for

42

expenses. At college, I worked with the experiment station and the Dean of the college, assisting in the preparation of the bulletins, and in the fourth year I had developed so much work it was necessary for me to employ two assistants, so you see I had gained considerable experience in working with people. I learned that it would assist me if I tuned myself in on every job.

I used my past experience on my first major job to discipline myself to meet my job day by day, to meet my associate employees on a friendly and personal basis. I greeted everyone cheerfully and constructively from the President, General Manager, the Sales Manager, the Superintendent, the workmen on machines, and down to the janitor. I performed my work promptly and thoroughly; I anticipated assignments and planned my work. I avoided gossip and rumors as if they were the plague. Soon I was called to the front office and was given a job as superintendent of one the company's largest plants. This was accomplished without any support from family, relations in the company, friends or politics. Recognition and advancement came from performance.

As I have just said, you may think you can relieve your fears by getting involved in the rumors and all the little maneuvers which go on in any organization. And once you are involved you will be amazed at how much time it takes from your job. Not only that, but it introduces unnecessary fears into your life. You hear all kinds of rumors, most of them without basis in fact. Possibly the worst

43

Time

thing that could happen to you is to feel that you have succeeded through some political maneuver, because once you think you have succeeded through this route (and I doubt very seriously that many people ever do) you have an additional fear to face and that is that somebody else will succeed in reducing your importance through office politics. It is just too small an activity for a person to get involved in. If you stay clear of it you will be a stronger man all your life.

More Mental Doodles

Another very popular waste of time is *trying to second-guess your boss.* No matter what job you are in, you have been trained and hired to do your own thinking. Your boss is going to like you better if you decide what needs to be done and proceed to do it without trying to protect yourself from criticism. I think many of the reports which are written in industry these days are not written because they will contribute to the company's profit, but rather to make the writer look good, even when he is wrong. Well-written reports, justifying wrong decisions, have never accomplished anything. And I hope that you don't feel that you have to use your time to protect yourself from criticism in case you are wrong.

A fifth time waster is *attempting to cover all the events in the world* from the reports in the daily newspapers, current magazines, TV and radio. These events which include editorials, politics,

44

Time

sports, crime, gossip items, and so on, are covered by the press with almost instantaneous worldwide coverage. An attempt to review all such communications can develop habits which are time-wasting. I was impressed early in my business career with a sage comment by our bank president who cautioned against spending too much time reading newspapers and similar publications. He urged a severely disciplined schedule of time to be used for this purpose. It is well that you plan your reading to keep informed, but whenever you come to a vital fact that can be used, act and take steps to put it into effect. A planned use of your time for reading will prove one of the more profitable decisions that you can make.

The Folly Of Fretfulness

And, finally, there is the time we waste *worrying*. I have often wondered why people worry. Worry is so destructive that it makes a man tired before he starts his day's work. You can make only one important decision on any subject every two or three years. Once you have made it, there isn't anything you can do about it. Everyone who makes decisions must accept the risk of being wrong. That is what you are paid to do—so why worry? I have made some wrong decisions, and if I kept beating myself over the head for the wrong decisions I have made, I would not be in a position to make the right decisions, and the right decisions keep us in business.

45

Everyone is wrong some of the time if he does anything. The man who tries never to be wrong will over-study every situation and *over-studying* can be a serious waste of time. There are two parts to every decision—the thinking part and the willingness to act in the face of uncertainty. Every businessman has to think. There are many fascinating puzzles in business. But, as I said last year, thinking is not enough. You must be prepared to go ahead and *do something*. It is the combination of intelligence and courage that brings the rewards in business. You have to think, but if you don't have the courage to act after you have thought a problem through, you will never succeed. So, in a sense, the worst waste of all is intelligence not linked with the courage to act.

Utilizing The Clock

I could go on listing the different ways I see people wasting time, but I think this would be a negative thing to do. Besides, I want to talk to you now about what you can *accomplish* in the time you have ahead of you.

First let me suggest a practice which will be helpful to you. Many successful businessmen I have known have followed the practice of keeping a record of their expenditures, writing them down at the end of each day. (This, I think, has been assisted in many ways by the Internal Revenue Bureau and it is possibly a way in which they're helping us by indirection.) This is not because they lack money;

46

Time

they want to spend their money wisely. I heartily endorse this practice, and I think the effective manager will go one step further. At the end of each day, he will review—and in some cases actually write down—the way he has used his time, because he will want to spend his time as wisely as he spends his money.

When I was a boy, people generally thought that the men who worked the hardest would be the most successful. I want to tell you right here that *we should never confuse work with accomplishment*. When I hear a man talk about how hard he works and how he hasn't taken a vacation in five years and how he seldom sees his family, I am almost certain that this man will not succeed in the creative aspects of business. And as I see business from the vantage-point of 50 years of experience, most of the important things that have to be done are the result of creative acts.

The Priority List

No matter how small your job when you start in industry, you will have to establish some priorities. Certain things you will find are really important and other things less important. If you set out to do the things which are really important you will find that your job isn't nearly so complicated as some people make it. In fact, I am continually appalled at how complicated some people make their jobs.

The way to approach your problem is to break the job down into basic elements and do things one

47

Time

at a time. Then your job becomes simple. Assign parts of the job, wherever possible, to others who are more expert and experienced on certain phases of the work. The end result which you obtain will develop confidence in yourself and others who have supported you, and the result will be the product of the trained minds on your team.

Speaking of job priorities, I don't know why people persist in using 90 per cent of their efforts on projects which will give them 10 per cent of the potential rewards. Your real job is to figure out the important things to get done and then spend 90 per cent of your effort doing the things which will give you 90 per cent of the potential return. The other 10 per cent may never get done, and I don't think you should worry too much about this. In fact, sometimes I like to measure a man by the things he decides to leave undone. The man who insists on getting 100 per cent of his job done either doesn't have enough to do or doesn't have the kind of stuff it takes to succeed in business today.

No Know-It-Alls

I would like to stop right here and philosophize with you about the businessmen I have known. I am sure that your other professors have been teaching you that you should be especially competent in all aspects of business. You might be inclined to think that you should be a good salesman, a good production supervisor, good with people, and even a good accountant. And you will probably feel that, since

48

Time

you can't be good at all these things, you don't have what it takes to succeed.

I want to let you in on a secret: the people I have known in business have *never* been good at *everything*. They have been *very* good in a *number* of things, but they have been informed and they have kept themselves informed about their own line of business. They have surrounded themselves with men experienced in merchandising, manufacturing and accounting. They have combined men with practical knowledge with men who have had training in engineering and science. This team then uses the innovations that are being developed in chemistry, engineering, electronics, and other new technologies to create new and better products that can be produced at lower costs. This fast-moving world is highly competitive and industry is looking for men who can do things better and develop a profit. *The secret is to surround yourself with compent, dedicated men, gain their confidence, and move as a team to get results.* This germ of leadership will produce results for you and your company.

Your problem is to recognize your strengths and to spend your time exploiting them, and to hire other people to do the things which you do not do as well as they could.

Now let me go back to the statement I made that one should not confuse work and accomplishment. Accomplishing things in business is an art. I am convinced that in business everyone has his own style of play, just as every artist has his own mode of expression. And, when you take your first

49

job, you are going to run into some very interesting characters. Some of these people may not be very prepossessing when you first meet them. Take the foreman on the night shift. He may be a thoroughly unpleasant person, but if you watch him carefully you will see that he probably does some things remarkably well. I am just cautioning you not to underrate the people with whom you are going to be in contact. Even though some of them may hold lesser positions than the one you aspire to, you can learn a great deal from everybody you work with if you start with the proposition that work is an art form and not a routine putting-in of time.

Relationships With Others

Not only should you use your time effectively but you should make sure your relationships with people are valid. You don't have to like a person in order to work with him any more than you have to like an artist to appreciate his work. The chances are that as you proceed from position to position you will run into some pretty difficult personalities. You may even have one for a boss. Don't hold this against a business. Every human activity has people in it who leave much to be desired. But just remember, you don't have to like your boss in order to work with him, nor do you have to like all of your subordinates. If you are not prepared to make your boss look good even when you don't like him, I don't think you should go into American industry. And

50

I think you should be as prepared to see your subordinates succeed even when you don't like them.

The young man who comes to me to complain about the people around him always makes me wonder a little bit. The man who expects all his relationships, including his working relationships, to be perfect cannot possibly succeed in this world. All you should ask of a working relationship is that it give you a chance to do a job and, if possible, in your own way.

In the world I see ahead, it is particularly important that you be able to work well with all kinds of people. When I started Inland Container Corporation almost 40 years ago, the major types of capital were money and machines. Now, with the rapid changes in the way things are done and our dependence on professional management, our major assets consist of the people in our organization. In fact, if I were to add up the future salaries of our managers and put the discounted value of these salaries on our balance sheet, we would probably see that we have more invested in our managers than in our machines.

A New Kind Of Capital

Our job in industry is to make the most effective use of this *new capital*. I am convinced that you cannot order people to be creative. People are creative only when they are doing the things they want to do. Our job—and your job when you get into in-

51

dustry—is to create a situation in which people will want to do the things which will contribute to the profits of their companies.

Be sure that you get perspective—both short-term and long-term. Think positively and constructively. Enthusiastically advance and recommend things which will profit your company. Avoid criticism of others, but compliment them for things which they have done well.

I repeat, the *new capital* that American industry must be most concerned with in the 1960's and 1970's are PEOPLE and IDEAS. And I hope that, when you get into industry, you will realize how much your employer is depending on you to use your time effectively to be a truly creative person.

There are so many more things I would like to say, but right here *I* am faced with the question of time.

In my industry, I am one of the few owner-managers left. The professional managers have moved in. I suspect that, as a group, we owner-managers were a pretty rough lot. We competed with brass knuckles. Our successors are a gentle-manly lot who want to occupy fancy offices and be recognized in their work as professional people. This is all right because the work is important enough to be recognized as a profession. But the danger is that our professional managers will not drop the less-competent people from their payrolls because of their tender concern for the rights of the individual.

52

Time

I believe that every manager must be completely fair in the way he treats people, but it is easy to mistake weakness for fairness. Companies can easily pad their payrolls with people who do not know how to use their time effectively. Indeed, I am convinced that a great deal of the cost-price squeeze we have been hearing about during the last few years arises out of the professional manager's failure to eliminate the time-wasters. In a sense this is misplaced humanitarianism.

The most humane thing any manager can do—and I hope the new breed of professional managers will remember this—is to run a tight shop and supply quality products at competitive prices. The least humane thing professional managers can do is to spend their time protecting jobs for people who are not creative in the way they use their time.

Getting Big Things Done

As an executive in the next 40 years you are going to have to be increasingly concerned with the effective utilization of the new capital which is dominating American industry. As an executive you are going to have to teach people to use their time effectively to accomplish great things. When you stop to think of it, it is remarkable that any company, made up as it is of imperfect people, runs as well as it does. The real fun in American industry is getting big things done with imperfect people. If you wait to assemble a team of perfect people you will be left at the post.

53

Time

And so let me summarize: Most of you have at least 40 years of industrial life ahead of you. Let me warn you that this isn't a very long time, even though you think right now it is endless. Don't waste your time being afraid and doing all the things that people do to keep from taking responsibility, such as endless committee meetings and business cocktail hours. Let me tell you right now that this is just so much window-dressing. Your job is to get things done, not merely put in time. And you are going to run up against a lot of difficult people in industry who *do* get things done. Respect them for what they can do.

Your investment, your parents' investment, and my investment in you is too great for you to waste your time on small accomplishments.

REMEMBER—TIME IS OF THE ESSENCE!

Time

Entrepreneurship

"In some sense, every company, is the reflection of the chief executive's hopes and dreams. Scientific management, computers, mathematical models and all of the other gimmicks which are so fashionable these days will never, in my estimation, reduce the importance of the effective dreamer. Nor substitute for him."

On May 6, 1965, the new nine-story building for the Krannert Graduate School was dedicated. Mr. Krannert delivered his lecture before a convocation in Purdue's Loeb Theatre. A side feature of the dedication ceremonies was a symposium on modern entrepreneurship featuring leaders of fast-moving, technically-oriented companies on the American stage.

Entrepreneurship

TODAY I want to talk to you briefly about my hopes—and, I must admit, my fears—for the Krannert Graduate School of Industrial Administration.

As one of the "centers of excellence" which we have been establishing in the great universities of the Middle West, the school carries the challenge to excel.

My hope is that the school will lead the whole nation in the preparation of talented young entrepreneurs for the American economic system. The dictionary defines an entrepreneur as the person who assumes the risk and management of business. Entrepreneurship is a million dollar name for a kind of magic which turns capital and people into success. But, perhaps this word *ought* to carry a big price tag because the quality of entrepreneurship is in short supply.

As I look back on 50 years of business experience, I am convinced that it is the entrepreneur who has built American industry—with all of its might and its capacity to produce a high standard of living. I sincerely hope that this school will turn out entrepreneurs who will function as risk takers—whether as foremen, superintendents, sales engineers, plant managers, or as chief executive officers.

And, I would be less than candid if I didn't tell you that I have some fears. Too many people who have gone to graduate schools of business want to be *sure* before they act. Before they take on a new responsibility, or install a machine, or launch a new sales program, they spend weeks and weeks assembling information. They insist on having such complete data that they never get to the point where they do something.

Overdoing Staff Work

Now, I believe that staff work can be valuable—and that somebody must keep the books and prepare the reports. And, I hope that the faculty in our graduate school will always be in the forefront of research on how to assemble and use information to make the best decisions. But, I have some fears that we can have too much respect for staff work. There is a place for thinking and a place for acting. And a man who can only think, but doesn't have the courage to act, will probably not succeed in this fast-moving world of business. My main fear is that we will over-emphasize the role of the intellect. People have to be smart and well-trained to be risk-taking managers nowadays, but they have to be something more. And it is this something more that I want to underline.

Sometimes this something more is called character. Well, it's true that integrity and courage are necessary to be an entrepreneur. But there are many men of character who are not entrepreneurs. And

58

Entrepreneurship

so, if you will permit me to look back in my life, I would like to tell you what it means to be an entrepreneur and chief executive officer of a company.

I hesitate a little because you might say "what has this to do with education?" My answer to this is that, if our school is to educate entrepreneurs, we should know just what an entrepreneur does. I am sure you will understand if I do not include many of my activities which really belong in sales, production, or finance.

When I was building Inland Container Corporation, I did a great deal of the selling. I always talked not only with purchasing agents, but with the owners of the business and the boys in the shipping department and the production plant. I wasn't just selling a product, but a method of service to customers that would help them to reduce their own costs of operation. I also got out into my plant with my fellows. And when I wanted to know what was happening in the economy, I talked to the bankers. And I would say to you—never get so far from the guts of the business that you can't take over one of these operating jobs when necessary. You have to know how they function before you can manage them. You don't step from the campus into leadership. You are really just beginning your postgraduate education.

The Chief Executive's Job

But, apart from these stand-by jobs, what does a chief executive officer do? Is there a separate job for the man who carries the big risk-taking func-

59

tion in a business? And, if there is, what *is* it? If everybody in a company did his job superbly well, would the chief executive have anything left to do? The answer, as I am sure you will agree, is YES.

Perhaps my first and most important job has been to *weave the larger dreams* which hold the organization together. All of us have dreams of what we would like to get done. When I was working in Chicago for six dollars a week, my dream was to support my mother and get enough money saved to pay for part of my first year at the University of Illinois. Our corrugator operators, our sweepers, our salesmen in Inland Container all have career hopes. And the job of the chief executive officer is to tie all these hopes together into a strong rope of company goals which every man can grab for support and strength.

Let me elaborate from my own past. Back in 1932, business was hard to come by, but dreams were just as big as they are today. The only way that Inland and its people could continue to grow during the depression was to get into big volume container business. It wouldn't happen immediately, however. There would be a time when money was shorter as we tooled up for large volume customers. I decided that the risk had to be taken so I went out and signed up our first volume customer —Postum. When I brought the news back to my associates, I found that my faith in their faith was well justified. As a matter of fact, all of them offered to take a salary cut, if necessary, to tide us over.

60

Entrepreneurship

Nowadays, as I watch professional managers develop job descriptions, salary brackets, five-year sales projections, personnel-manning tables, and all of the other traveling baggage of scientific management, the more concerned I become. If we send men out from Purdue with their heads full of figures and facts, suitcases full of techniques and computer tape—but *without* deep respect for the ambitions of people in the soul and a lively dream-making ingredient in the spirit—we won't be developing entrepreneurs.

Napoleon stated that an army marches on its stomach. What this implies, of course, is that an army must be well fed—which is true. However, I would like to remind you that Napoleon is alleged to have also said that "every French soldier carries a marshal's baton in his knapsack." It takes loyalty and inspiration to make achievements. And, in the same way, the scientific management gadgets that are so popular these days will not of themselves produce the loyalty and determination which makes a company move forward. Every business marches on its dreams.

Let me be more specific. When the dreams are too detailed, they don't allow enough room for the individual imagination of the people who get things done. And if the imagination runs wild, there are people who will say that the goals are impossible and they won't join in supporting the program. Some place between these two extremes there is

61

Entrepreneurship

always a dream which will capture the imagination of the people in a company who want to work and to advance. The dream must be big enough to serve as an umbrella over the individual dreams of many people, and yet, specific enough to serve as the basis for rewarding successful performance.

Lest you think that dreaming at the top level is a soft, feet-on-the-desk job, let me tell you that there is *plenty* of hard work in this kind of industrial leadership.

I am always puzzling about how I can communicate my dreams to my people. Just telling them is not enough. They must feel the urgency of these goals. I want them to join me in tackling the future with enthusiasm. This means that I must be prepared to reward the ones who are succeeding and to penalize those who are failing. One of my hardest assignments is to penalize the "status quo" people. Many are real friends and I hate to see them disappointed. But people who are not reaching cannot be rewarded if the *organization* is to stretch.

The Long Shadow

I have frequently heard it said: "Have no small dreams for they have no magic to stir men's souls." As I think about 40 years of running my own company, I would say that this task of "effective dreaming" is my most important activity. It is one I cannot delegate. And I doubt that companies which entrust it to some long-range planning department will succeed.

62

Entrepreneurship

It is the unique role of every chief executive officer to cast the long shadow over his organization. In some degree, every company is the reflection of the chief executive's hopes and dreams. Scientific management, computers, mathematical models and all of the other gimmicks which are so fashionable these days will never, in my estimation, reduce the importance of the effective dreamer. Nor substitute for him.

Now, in the second place, the chief executive must be a *master teacher*. I have done a lot of thinking about what it is that makes for what we call a "solid" business. We know, of course, that good people are essential—but this is not enough. Something else is needed. And I have concluded that this something else is the unique fund of knowledge which the organization has accumulated. If all of Inland's managers were suddenly to be transferred to the moon so that we would have to replace all of our earthly crew with fresh talent which, for the sake of argument, are as smart as the old ones— we would still lose something very important for our organization. And what we would lose is the knowledge that we have accumulated over 40 years of facing problems together.

Pools of Knowledge

The knowledge I am talking about is made up of the unwritten practices of the machine operators in our plants, of the contacts of our sales engineers, of the technical findings of our research people,

63

Entrepreneurship

and so on. There is a separate pool of knowledge which could be identified as Inland Container. Indeed, I suspect that every business organization is a unique pool of knowledge.

No person, least of all the chief executive officer, can have all the information in his company's pool of knowledge. But it is he who must constantly be asking—Is it adequate? Is there enough knowledge to handle the problems of the future? How much information in the pool of knowledge is wrong information? How can he get people to be skeptical without being negative? How can he blend the knowledge of the men on the line with the knowledge highly-trained college graduates bring to the organization?

These are the problems of teaching I have been facing for 40 years. I am convinced that the companies with the most up-to-date and usable pools of knowledge can earn the larger profits and better satisfy the needs of customers. My challenge has been (and yours will be if you become a risk-taking manager) to use the world of activity to teach people the knowledge they must have to succeed.

Many times this means watching people make mistakes while they are learning—even though I know, or think I know, a better way to do it. I encourage people to make some mistakes because it is much healthier for the company than paralysis. It gives a man more confidence when he gets himself off dead center than if you give him a push. However, I can tell you that teaching takes a lot of

64

patience so I have real sympathy with the teachers in this audience.

The Practical Classroom

I feel that a substantial part of my life has been spent in another kind of classroom. Every business organization is partly an educational institution. The main subject which must be taught by the chief executive is what you faculty people might call history—but, in industry, it is known as experience. Some young people don't want to wait long enough to accumulate experience. They won't go very far without it, however, and they would miss most of the adventure of business if they did.

It is not enough for a company to develop a recruiting program and to hire training directors. Both of these certainly make a real contribution. But the chief executive officer must himself be vitally involved in the process of knowledge accumulation if his company is to grow and prosper.

Not only is a company a pool of knowledge, it is also a communications system. Unfortunately, communications systems tend to destroy themselves in a number of ways. People gossip, and this puts static in the system. Personal ambitions lead to the withholding of information. And people get to thinking that if they write long reports, they can get promoted, and this leads to the clogging of the pipeline with a lot of useless knowledge.

Left to itself, every organization runs down. It gets choked with its own words and destroys

65

Entrepreneurship

itself. And nobody but the chief executive officer can really *keep the communication channels open and clear*. As long as he keeps the big picture clearly in front of people and insists that they live up to the challenge of change, they will talk to each other about things which are significant.

My problem is to keep people talking—but not too much—about the right things. And let me say right now that the committee—which, as I see it, is another gadget of scientific management—is not the way to do it. Mostly, the committee is a way to waste time. It would be a great contribution to society if our Administrative Sciences Department could originate a better way of getting people to communicate with each other without fear. And a better way of generating ideas than the typical committee meeting.

The Factor Of Risk

I am now going to turn to the most important task of every entrepreneur-manager. However, you are going to have to think this through with me because it is a difficult thing to convey in words. I am talking about the chief executive's responsibility to *bear risks*.

When any man looks at the world today, he has every reason to be scared. Changes are forever sweeping through our economy. No technical process can be expected to last very long. New products replace old ones while the old ones are

66

Entrepreneurship

still new. Even the concept of private property is being threatened. The odds against any single project succeeding in a world so full of change are pretty slim.

And then I will throw in another complication —and that's the role of pure accident. It's a world of chance we live in as well as change. The best paper machine may blow up or the strongest overseas market may have a revolution. Putting all these things together, I tell you right here that the world is a risky place and the chance of succeeding on any project is not very high.

The chief executive officer of any company must be *honest* in appraising these risks. He can't fool himself about their magnitude. At the same time, he must face the fact that most of the people who work for him can't take risk in such big doses. If they are asked to, they worry so much about it that they get nothing else done. So the chief executive's job is to give more security to his people than he gets from the world. He is like a banker who gives his depositors easier access to money than he gets.

Let me state it another way: every business consists of many ventures. Some of them are going to succeed and some of them will fail. The business, as a whole, must have enough successes to finance its failures. And the people who do the job of producing, selling, and financing each of these ventures must know that, after they have done their best, the organization will reward them regardless of the immediate outcome of that particular ven-

67

Entrepreneurship

ture. It is the chief executive's job to choose that collection of ventures which, on the average, will succeed. It is his job to give the employees involved in each venture the assurance that, despite the uncertainties of the world, their contributions will be fairly appraised. In a sense, the chief executive officer is an anchor to the windward in a storm his organization is always facing.

Bearing The Load

The chief executive is always breaking high-risk ventures into lower-risk projects for his men. He is absorbing risk because this is the only way big things can be done by people who have less capacity to take risks than he has. Let me tell you, this is no easy job. And it is something I have never found a way to delegate. It goes on all the time. It is exhausting. The risk-taker is always at work, mentally at least—whether he's in the office, driving home from work, or on vacation.

And I want also to say that the man who is bearing risks has no time nor energy for doing the jobs of his subordinates. In fact, it is my observation that the manager who insists on doing his subordinate's work is really trying to escape this awesome task of assuming risk. In many cases, he is magnifying the worry about risk for the other fellow rather than diminishing it. The person who looks for the escape hatch on risk is really a non-entrepreneur. He robs people of their effectiveness. Instead of adding, he subtracts.

68

Entrepreneurship

Well, there you have my four major jobs as chief executive officer. Now, what's the big unsolved problem of the entrepreneur today? In mathematical terms, it's how to multiply himself. Once we had rather simple businesses and one man could do most of the leading. Nowadays business is complex and we need risk-taking managers at every level.

Unorthodoxy Triumphant

In this connection, I want to share a problem with you. Over the last 40 years, I have noticed that most improvements in our company occur despite the established pattern of things. We think that once a routine is working, we can rest. Bureaucracy and complacency take over. I have noticed that the improvements which occur are usually because someone has broken a rule or because we are facing a crisis and something has to be invented fast. This is not right. There should be a better way to infuse the spirit of entrepreneurship in a company than to wait for the next crisis to develop.

The chief executive officer must find ways to create an environment in which people dare to upset successful procedures if there's a chance to make them better. We need more people who will stick their necks out above the old level of performance, people who would rather play it smarter than to play it safe. This kind of spirit must penetrate an organization from the appentice to the president if the company is going to successfully meet the

69

Entrepreneurship

challenges of the market place. And I must confess to you that I can't tell you how to do this in every organization. It seems so natural for an organization to keep doing efficiently what has been done in the past, to trade on past successes. But, many times, the road to future success is to do something different. It is better to do the right thing inefficiently than to do the wrong thing efficiently.

Every Man A Leader

I think we have a lot to learn about how to encourage entrepreneurship at all levels in our business. Every man bosses something and every man leads somebody. He should be practicing entrepreneurship every day on his job. He should recognize ways to get results easier, quicker, and more profitably. I hope that the Krannert Graduate School is studying entrepreneurship as a *process* for solving problems.

So let me summarize—I have real hopes that the Krannert Graduate School will *excel* in educating young men for modern entrepreneurship. It will not be enough to develop better computer routines and better staff procedures. In the future, I am convinced, we will have to have more young men who are willing to *take responsibility—who can dream big dreams*—who are *master teachers* in the classroom of activity—who can generate effective *communications systems*—who can *absorb risks*—and who can *encourage others to be venturesome.*

70

Entrepreneurship

These are my hopes, President Hovde*. I invest these hopes with you as I give you these keys to our new building. Use the keys to unlock the doors to education in modern entrepreneurship— and to open the door of leadership opportunity for the young men of tomorrow.

*Dr. Fred Hovde was President of Purdue University. He presided at the dedication ceremonies for the new Krannert Graduate School building.

71

Entrepreneurship

Leadership

"You, as this new type of leader, must have what amounts to a split-personality. You must be bold and yet, in your dealings with people, a person of great humility. You must be courageous and yet able to listen to the tedious babblings of those who are fearful. You must be articulate, but able to remain silent while other people awkwardly express their views. This is a tremendous assignment. But you will need these skills to work with your raw material."

On May 20, 1966, when Mr. Krannert spoke to the Purdue students, his Inland Container Corporation had entered a new phase of leadership. The company was building a new paper mill in eastern Alabama as the result of an entrepreneurial decision two years earlier. It had just set records of $138 million in annual sales volume and 7.9 billion square feet of corrugated in annual production.

Leadership

FOR some time I have been puzzling about what I, an industrialist with more than half-a-century of business experience, should say to a group of young engineer-businessmen.

I am tempted—because I too was a graduate engineer about to enter business some 55 years ago —to tell you how to do it, or at least what not to do when you take your first job. But the more I thought about this the more I realized that you probably look on a man past 75 as representing a completely different generation; and no doubt you are inclined to think—what does he know about the world we are soon to enter? And so I am going to tell you what I think it takes to be a leader today and the problems you may face when you get there.

Let me start by saying that, as I look back on my career, I feel I have lived through at least *500 years* of change. And you may think that for me to tell you how to manage your career would be like Thomas Edison telling our space scientists how to make a soft landing on the moon.

And so I have decided to talk about the fundamental changes which I see happening in our society and what these changes are going to mean to you as managers. Will the style of leadership which

I used to build Inland Container Corporation work for you?

The Change In Breed

I believe a basic change has taken place in the raw materials for leadership. The men I worked with when I managed a corrugated box plant in Anderson, Indiana, and the men I brought with me to Indianapolis when I started in business for myself more than 40 years ago, were the salt of the earth. They were dedicated, loyal employees. They fully expected to serve many years of apprenticeship before they became managers.

Six of my associates, who later rose to high positions in Inland, had no college education. They educated themselves by paying diligent attention to the lessons that the business taught them and by studying at home after working hours.

But, in contrast to my day, many of the young men you will lead will come from very permissive family backgrounds. Their mothers will have driven them to school, picked them up on every rainy day. They will have served on hundreds of school committees and student governments. Somehow the whole family and school apparatus will have led them to believe that if they are effective, success will come to them quickly. They will expect, when they come into your business, to be treated like partners. In fact, some of them even go so far as to tell me that they expect to become president of my company in the near future.

76

Leadership

Nothing could better show the complete shift in attitudes from one generation to the next than to have a young man your age come in and tell me he expects to replace me in a very few years. None of the young men I hired in the early years of my business talked to me that way. They expected to be helpful to me for years and then, if they were lucky, they hoped to be picked for positions of responsibility. From my vantage point, it looks as though the world has been turned upside-down.

The Change In Loyalties

Let me deal with another change that has come about—and this is in loyalty. The men I hired expected to stay at Inland Container for their life-times. They accepted my orders and knew they would be rewarded. But this is no longer true. The young men you will lead are primarily loyal to their own aspirations. They will stay with you so long as they feel they have opportunities for development and advancement; and if they don't, they will leave. They are mobile and they don't mind moving from one company or one part of the country to another. Sometimes I think they are a little arrogant. But possibly they are just different.

And this is not all: Business nowadays uses many specialists—accountants, engineers, chemists and so on. Every one of these professional groups has its own society. And these specialists tend to be more loyal to their professions than they are to their companies. When things don't go in the

77

Leadership

company as they think they should, they use their professional contacts to change employers. In the old days, we did a very good job of running a business without these professional groups. Now, as things stand, every business must depend on these specialists.

And so I must conclude that your world is going to be quite different from the one I grew up in and that you must practice a new style of leadership to succeed.

In Defense Of Old Leadership

But before I leave this, I want to defend some of the old leaders, and I include myself in this group. When you stop to think of it, they did some really great things. They took over an undeveloped country and created whole new industries, which have in turn brought a standard of living unmatched anywhere else in the world. And, I must say, the leaders I know expressed themselves vigorously in the way they ran their businesses.

I think, for instance, of George W. Swift, Jr. of Bordentown, New Jersey. He had a machine shop and a group of engineers who spent their time developing new machines for the manufacture of paper products.

The first corrugator consisted mainly of two notched drums. Paper was run between these drums and flutes were formed in the paper much as on the old-time Buster Brown collars for children. This corrugated paper was then combined with two

78

sheets of heavy kraft paper to form what is known as containerboard. The first machine was such a secret that it was enclosed under lock and key in a room with a slot cut in the wall. A man with a hand saw was stationed on the outside to cut off the corrugated paper as it came through the slot at the rate of no more than 10 feet a minute.

As demand increased, George Swift developed a heavy knife that traveled on the machine and cut off the paper automatically. However, as we increased the speed of the machine—and we simply *had* to increase productivity—the frame of the knife tended to break. At one of my meetings with George Swift, we discussed the feasibility of a rotating cut-off and he took the risk of developing a model, from which Inland took the risk of placing an order for the first such machine. The rotary cut-off enabled us to increase speed to 100 feet a minute and today corrugators are running at 650 feet per minute.

Facing The Big Problems

There are many characteristics of these great innovators which I hope you will have. They were all willing to dream big dreams. They were all willing to take risks. If they believed they could get a new market by introducing a whole new technology, they did it. Every organization constantly faces threats to its very existence and somebody has to deal with these threats. And these risk-takers— whether they were Andrew Carnegie, Henry Ford,

79

Leadership

or Henry Kaiser—never flinched when it came to doing new things.

In contrast, the specialist never really wants to deal with the big problems. He is content to work out a cost-accounting system, a new scheduling program or a new manning table. He always wants to work within an established framework which he hopes will never be modified. Unfortunately, as I see it, the same is true for many of our professionally-trained managers, who restrict the scope of their interests rather than risk failure. They don't actually want to be concerned with the major problems the company is facing. Let me give you an example:

A question facing my own industry is—Will box fabrication be transferred to our customers' plants?

When I talk about this, very few of my people even want to consider the possibility. It is just *too* upsetting. And I am sure this example could be multiplied many times in industries all over the country. I have always puzzled about the unwillingness on the part of many of our managers to face their strategic problems. They are wonderful tacticians but they hesitate to face the unknown.

Our Tricky World

It may be, and here I have to speculate, that these men have been over-educated. They want too much evidence before they make a decision. And usually by the time they get all the facts their competitors have captured the market. I don't know why, in this area of strategic decision-making, modern society produces so many "Nervous Nellies." In any case, in my generation of businessmen we seldom flinched if we had to make a risky decision. We rather gloried in it. And, as a result, the people around us had few doubts and were willing to move with authority to deal with a new threat.

I think that this capacity to accept the world as non-guaranteed, tricky, full of accidents and unexpected events, is necessary at all levels of management. You will never have all the facts you need. Leadership means risk-taking and this is particularly true of a world which is changing as rapidly as ours. This great quality which my peers had of being willing to move in the face of uncertainty is something you are going to need in generous amounts if you are going to succeed.

Many Instead Of Few

But here is where the parallel ends. The new style of industrial leadership is going to be very different from the style of the past. Let me develop this by an analogy: Let's think of the master managers of the past as painting great murals, their employees standing by, mixing the paints, handing them the right brushes, admiring the painters' work and making sure they were well supported.

But now the situation is reversed. The murals of the future will be painted by hundreds of eager young men, each painting his portion as best he can.

81

Leadership

The new leadership is going to be largely concerned with making sure that each of these young men has the materials, the brushes, the paints and the pallettes necessary to do a good job. The efforts of the many will somehow blend together to replace the picture the old master painted by himself.

This is going to be a much more difficult job than we faced. You are going to need great patience to work with these aspiring young artists. Human beings are difficult. They are both wonderful and terrible, courageous and frightened, timid and brash, factual and deceitful, cooperative and destructive, innovative and bureaucratic. You are going to need a genuine understanding of the way your organization works. You must know how communication moves up the organizational ladder, as well as down.

In the future, the company must represent the creative inputs of many prospective leaders. And so I have come to the conclusion that you, as the leader of the future, will have to be a very complicated person. On the one hand, you must be bold— willing to face the world in all its complexities. You must see big designs and have all of the great qualities of business daring. But, on the other hand, you must be willing to sense the needs of the aspiring young men coming up in your organization and be primarily concerned with providing a framework in which these men can express their own individualities. You must invite their genuine participation in the setting of the company goals, even though your job is always to challenge and to raise their

82

sights. You must be deeply concerned with establishing a reward system which will encourage the "wild duck" and not the slick conformist. And you must constantly be immersed in the problem of supporting—emotionally as well as financially—the many who will manage the total enterprise.

Split Personality

You, as this new type of leader, must have what amounts to a split-personality. You must be bold and yet, in your dealings with people, a person of great humility. You must be courageous and yet able to listen to the tedious babblings of those who are fearful. You must be articulate, but able to remain silent while other people awkwardly express their views. This is a tremendous assignment. But you will need these skills to work with your raw material.

When I talk to people in universities I get the feeling that they think trained specialists can replace leadership. Underlying this view is the faith that knowledge by itself will solve all problems. I can understand why college professors, who are devoted to the search for knowledge, would believe this. And I can understand also why public opinion-makers, who are for the most part rebelling against the facts of organizational life, would like to instill this belief in you. Neither of these groups really knows what it is talking about.

Leadership

The specialists are just as near-sighted as the loyal servants of the past. They are unwilling to deal with the big problems and they are as human in their failings as any other group the world has ever known. They gossip. They destroy communication channels. They denigrate each other. The whole organization, without this active positive sense of leadership, will deteriorate rapidly. If anything, leadership is more necessary in these days of specialists than it was in the past.

There is another prevailing view which I would like to deal with briefly—and that is that brilliance can take the place of leadership—that the man with the so-called great thoughts can supply the specialists with all the stuff they need to build the enterprise. *This is wrong.* We need bright people in industry, as in every other walk of life. But being bright is not enough. The person who aspires to leadership must be both imaginative and *patient*. He must deal with human beings. *They* are his raw material.

A Few Pitfalls

Not only will tomorrow's leader have to contend with misconceptions, but he must face some special pitfalls which my generation did not encounter. As I said before, you are going to have to gain acceptance for a new idea before your subordinates will move ahead with authority toward a new goal. And there is always a danger you will mistake consensus for truth. I always knew in the forty

84

years I was building Inland Container that for the most part my colleagues would agree with me. They came out of a generation which tended to agree with the boss; and I always earned their support by taking the full responsibility for the success of the enterprise. But I never made the mistake of believing that just because they supported me I was right. I had to adopt a self-questioning attitude and thus be my own best critic. The cushioning effect of consensus should in no way make one less exacting of himself.

Another pitfall is the belief that it is better not to make a decision than to make a mistake. This is stultifying. If I hadn't made enough decisions to be wrong some of the time, Inland wouldn't be where it is today. It is best to be right about the big decisions, of course, but it is downright disastrous to let fear of being wrong keep you from ever sticking your neck out.

Still another pitfall is the idea that the leader has to know everything that is done in the organization. The leader doesn't have to know everything his subordinates know, but he should know enough about each specialty that he can test the validity of their knowledge. You, as the new leader, cannot be the impeccably dressed modern manager who refuses to meet with the labor organizer in the rough and tumble of negotiation. Or, if you have a production problem, you cannot refuse to get involved in the difficult and messy conflicts among human beings. You must know that your function is to support your productive people.

85

Leadership

Many times I have found that there is a kind of competition between the boss and his subordinates so that the boss will never want to admit that he doesn't know as much as his subordinates. This is wrong. You should be proud of the fact that you are able to hire people who know more than you do. In the past the boss was able to know just about every operation—but in this day of specialized knowledge and decentralized management, this is not feasible.

As one of tomorrow's leaders, you must know the limitations of your specialists and try not to over-use them. And at the same time you must respect them and never downgrade them. This is a very difficult role to play. This is an easy place to fail; it is truly a pitfall. You must learn to delegate but you must remember that you never delegate responsibility.

I could go on listing other pitfalls, but I suspect you are going to learn how to avoid them, as I did, by falling into a number of them and somehow scrambling out. As I have said, there are many, many worse things than making mistakes—so long as you really learn from them. Most managers in one sense are self-trained. Here at Krannert Graduate School we can give you a start, but your education will have to be continued on your own, largely by the process of stumbling, and picking yourself up, and trying again.

86

Leadership

I *do* have some advice, though, as you seek your first position in industry. Look for the opportunities and not for the rewards. The rewards will automatically follow if you meet your opportunities successfully. I know you will be tempted to move into the organizations where they have already embraced this new kind of leadership—with a personnel system which makes it possible for a young man who has proven himself to move into positions of responsibility early in life. But unfortunately these companies tend to be over-provided with management talent. Many of the space and electronic companies on the two coasts have already hired so much talent that your competition is going to be awfully rough.

On Choosing A Company

I would advise you to look around for the companies which are in the process of changing to this new style of leadership. Many of them have fine balance sheets and they have real gaps in their management structures; and you will find your best opportunities in these companies. The Midwest is full of organizations of this kind which are going to change tremendously during the next decade. Company after company will be switching from the old style of leadership to the new. And while these changes—in some cases drastic—are difficult, I think you should seek out these companies because there is only one way they can go. And if you are around when a company makes the successful tran-

Leadership

sition to the new kind of leadership, you will have opportunities which will dwarf anything you can find elsewhere.

And so I want to wish you luck in your new journey. I think you are going to have a terribly exciting time. The greater the difficulties, the greater the opportunities. Your palette is richer but your canvas is rougher. Good luck as you paint the masterpieces of the future.

Experience

"I have been telling you that during the initiation and experience stages you will need to conform in order to learn how the organization functions. I have also told you that you should understand the wisdom that has made the organization you are in successful. And now I am going to reverse myself to tell you that in the end, to succeed as a leader, you will need to be a creative nonconformist. In other words, you're going to use a predictable organization to accomplish novelty. This capacity to use order to achieve change is a rare ability."

On July 27, 1967 Herman C. Krannert returned to Purdue to deliver a commencement address to graduating students in the masters and doctoral programs of The Krannert Graduate School of Industrial Administration.

Experience

FOR many years I have wondered what I would say if I were asked to give a commencement address, and when Dean Weiler asked me to do it this year, in place of my usual spring lecture, I must say I was pleased.

I want to congratulate you on your achievement. Most of you have finished four years in an excellent engineering school, graduating in the upper third of your class; and now you have completed a year of what our faculty tells me is a very rigorous program in Industrial Administration. You will soon have your Master's Degree and you have reason to be proud of what you have done. If you keep on learning and, in addition, learn to use your knowledge, you will have a fine future.

Despite these achievements, as I look forward to the problems you are going to face, I think I must say to you: *You aren't really ready to practice the difficult art of management.* Formal education is not enough. And today I want to talk to you about this additional preparation you are going to have to have. In fact, I have wondered whether we shouldn't withhold your diploma until you have combined your education with the ten years of experience you will need to be certified in this most difficult of all professions—the profession of management.

Over-confidence?

As it is, some company is going to subsidize each of you for the next five years because, as of now, you are not worth what you are going to be paid.

I realize that your generation has a great deal of self-assurance. Some people even call it arrogance. But let me tell you right now that *you are going to need every bit of the confidence you have developed.* From now on, many many people are going to be chipping away at your confidence— and with some justification. You don't know as much as you think you know. So, perhaps it is just as well that you are starting out with a good supply of self-assurance—you may have a little left when you get to my age.

And now, I want to talk to you about the stages you are going to go through before you can expect to be a professional manager.

Stages in Career

Most business careers go through at least four definite stages and, if you will excuse me, I shall use my own life as an example:

1. EDUCATION:

I went through the same type of college as you, although I did not have a School of Industrial Ad-

92

Experience

ministration to attend. As a graduate engineer who had put himself through the University of Illinois, I thought I was ready to lick the world.

2. Initiation:

I was offered a job by the Sefton Box Company. It wasn't as big a job as I would have liked, but I soon realized that I didn't really know all the answers. They had invested in me—not I in them—and I had to go through an initiation period while they looked me over. Maybe it was my acceptance of this fact that induced Sefton to send me to Anderson, Indiana, as plant manager.

3. Experience & Self-Education:

During the next nine years, I gained experience in the industry and in the handling of people —people as employees and people as customers. I also studied on my own. The Sefton Company was developing a new material called corrugated board. What I learned from being associated with this gave me the basis for pioneering the corrugated box in my own company a little later on.

4. Major Responsibility:

Then finally, at the age of 38, I undertook the responsibility of starting and managing a whole enterprise, Inland Container Corporation.

And so today I want to talk with you about what you can expect to have happen at each of these stages—education, initiation, experience, self-education, and major responsibility.

Experience

With respect to education, let me just again congratulate you on the completion of your Master's Degree in Industrial Administration. I hope you will remain close to the Krannert Graduate School. Your professors have a real interest in you and in your continuing education. You may want, from time to time, to ask about what books to use to develop some new knowledge you need. Or you may want to come back to discuss problems with your professors. Just remember, we think of you as part of a growing army of engineer-managers who are going to have a real impact on America, and we don't want to lose track of you.

SECOND, INITIATION:

When you take your first job, you are going to be disappointed. You will be put in a menial first job. Perhaps you will be put on one of the work crews, or you may even be an assistant to some rough and tough foreman on the night shift, where the educational experience you have had will seem to count for nothing. And you will wonder after a short while why your company is wasting you this way.

Well, no matter how smart the recruit, all organizations require an initiation period.

Your fraternity sent you on humiliating missions; the Army will put you through boot training; if you are a doctor you will do routine tasks as an intern; and if you are a lawyer you will do time as a

94

Experience

legal clerk. In all these professional activities, the skills you have developed in college will not soon be used to their fullest. And you are going to wonder: is this period of initiation really necessary? I think there is a good reason why it is.

Every organization needs loyal people to accomplish the jobs it must do. And once you have gone through a difficult initiation period, the organization will be able to count on you not to throw up your hands because of some temporary disappointment.

Another reason is this. It is important, for every future change you may wish to make, to understand how things run at the company today —and why they are that way. After all, this is a successful outfit you will be joining and you can't get very far by overlooking the wisdom that is already in it. Instead, you need to really understand it and the only way to do so is to participate in it, to be one of the boys. You may think some of the forms and practices are for the birds, but I urge you to go along with them until you know first-hand why they exist and how they work.

No Time for Odd Balls

Let me give you some advice on this line that will be helpful during your initiation period. You may want, as a matter of pride, to be a little different from the other people with whom you're working. *But this is not the time to emphasize any differences.* Your first important task is to identify yourself with the group

95

Experience

you join—and I don't think you will compromise yourself if you emphasize the similarities rather than the differences. Later on you will be pleased that you have. To lead others, you must first win their acceptance and confidence.

To insist on pointing up superficial differences at initiation time is just not bright. As a "college boy"—and you should realize that this is how you will be known when you go into business—you may want to have your hair cut differently—or not at all—wear Ivy League clothes, speak academic English, or in some obvious ways separate yourselves from your co-workers. If this is your tendency, DON'T DO IT.

(As an aside, I might say that I have not been able to understand the new campus rebels who insist on being unwashed and unshaven, because it seems to me that this is such an insignificant way to rebel when there are so many interesting and useful ways to be different. Mostly, then, I feel sorry for these people because they apparently lack imagination.)

I am glad to see that none of you has had time for this. I hope, instead, during your initiation period, that you will think well enough of yourselves, regardless of the job you are doing, to be concerned with your appearance. It may not seem of major importance the way your shoes are shined, the way you scatter ashes when you smoke, the way you sit or stand. However, many men make the mistake of indicating through such small things that they don't think too much of themselves, and

96

Experience

you can't expect other people to think much of you unless you hold yourself in high regard.

But, let me move on to the third period in your career, an overlapping time of experience and self-education.

The Period of Residency

Once you have proved to your organization that you are one of them, they are likely to start giving you work assignments which are intended to develop your capacity as a manager. I think of this period as being like a "residency" in a medical career. Or we can think of it as resembling the first ten years in a young lawyer's professional life, when he is neither a legal clerk nor a partner. In fact, I can think of no profession which doesn't require an apprenticeship period. There are many skills you will need to develop and many things you will need to find out about yourself during this period.

You will want to know whether you can keep your faith in people when they seem to be letting you down. We would all like to believe that people are always honest and decent, hard working and loyal. The fact is that people are a mixture of good and bad. In some situations they're heroic and gallant and in others they're petty and disappointing.

Quite frankly, the problem of every manager is to keep his faith in people. The only way you will ever get the best out of your people is to believe in them, recognizing at the same time that they may

97

Experience

disappoint you. And let me tell you, this goes for your bosses as well as your subordinates. You may tend, after you have been in the business for a short time, to get an exalted view of your boss; and, then, one day he will disappoint you. If you then lose faith in him and find it difficult to work with him because he is only human, you will demonstrate that you are not ready for management.

People Aren't Consistent

And the same thing is going to be true of your subordinates. Put them in a tough situation and they may rise to the occasion magnificently—and the next day, in the middle of some mundane activity, you will find them skimping on the job, gossiping, and behaving in a second-rate fashion. And if, at this stage, you lose faith in them, you will not be a good manager. In other words, you must learn to take people as they are—part saint and part scoundrel—and fit them together into an organization which works.

You will want to know, during this "experience" period, whether you can be cautious about the small things and at the same time carry the burden of uncertainty on the issues which really count. If the people you work with are going to get anything done, you are going to have to give them courage to do new things. This may involve the way you operate a new piece of equipment or the way you organize your sales force. But unless you are willing to shoot for what you think is the best, even though

98

Experience

the new try might turn out to be not so good as the traditional way, you will not be lifting the sights of your people. Your job is to make other people brave enough to innovate and to carry their uncertainty for them when they have a tendency to worry.

Another thing you will want to test, as an industrial "intern,' is how good you can be at controlling the costs in whatever job you may hold. You will find out that there is no corporate Dad to write for money. You have to live on a budget and you will be judged by the profit you deliver. You will find that the margin of profit depends a lot on what you have to spend and you won't be able to control costs completely by machine. It's mostly a matter of getting people—including yourself—to work most effectively.

The Invisible Organization

And during this period you will want to learn also whether you can live *effectively* in the organization. Will you be able to sense the "INVISIBLE ORGANIZATION"—the structure which makes things run and which may include the President's secretary and the storekeeper, as well as the Vice Presidents and the Majority Stockholder. Every company has an invisible communications track, made up of people, their personalities, their actions and reactions—and it's quite important to know how it works. Can you use the "INVISIBLE ORGANIZATION" without becoming so committed to it that

99

Experience

you become just another party boy or a link in the gossip chain?

Please understand, I am not telling you that you should ignore the organizational chart. You will want to work within channels most of the time, but if you are going to succeed, you must be sensitive to the way people really communicate with each other in organizations. Some managers really believe they can get things done through a series of orders. They actually think the organization chart functions the way it is supposed to, and when they find it doesn't, they are disappointed. Indeed, part of your job is to keep the "INVISIBLE ORGANIZATION" working for you without at the same time letting it compromise you to the point where people say you are just another politician.

Margins for Mistakes

Another thing you will want to find out for yourself is how well you can tolerate error in your bosses and your subordinates. Mistakes are always being made and you will have to discipline yourself to accept them—and to correct them, when you can —without spoiling your healthy relationships with your colleagues.

If you're so anxious to succeed that you think that every mistake is intended to hurt you, you'll not be able to survive as an effective member of an organization. I think you will come to realize that organizational life is full of mistakes, but it has been my observation that most of the things which

100

people get annoyed about are unintentional slips and do not involve bad motivation.

And you will have to learn whether you can actually communicate with your colleagues. Communication is a difficult thing. You must learn to listen carefully, because only if you listen carefully will people listen to you. You will want also to be a forthright, positive person that people will listen to because they know you will not dissemble; and yet you must not be so predictable that they can safely take bets on what your next word or act will be. Some people are so predictable that they're dull; others are so unpredictable that they are unstable. Can you find the right balance between these two extremes?

In other words, what I am suggesting during this "residency" period is that you will learn through experience what it means to be an effective member of an organization. Some of you will learn this pretty quickly and some of you may never learn it. I am hoping, though, that most of you will learn, because organizational skills are essential for you if you are going to be managers.

You may wonder why I have been emphasizing the importance of learning to work with people during your "residency" period. It is because I assume you will automatically learn whatever you need to know about the production scheduling systems or selling practices of your industry. You have already demonstrated you can acquire knowledge quickly and effectively through your success in our School. So I assume that this is not going to be a

Experience

problem for you. And I am convinced that management consists largely of managing people, and this is what takes experience to do well.

Teaching Yourself

During this "residency," you are also going to have to find out whether you can continue your education. You have already proved that you can learn from books if you're preparing for a class. You have proved that you are good pupils; but are you good students? And there *is* a difference. Can you be an exacting teacher for yourself? Can you give yourself a limited assignment, such as reading a new book, and complete it on schedule? Are you willing to give yourself the examination of being able to talk intelligently about it? Do you have the capacity to write the text you should be learning from as you face the job you are doing? Will you welcome chances to go back to Purdue, or some other institution, to continue your formal education as a means of opening new areas of interest and learning to work with new kinds of people?

In short, how effective are you going to be as your own teacher? The world is changing so rapidly that unless you have this capacity the education you are getting now will be worth very little in five years. You must update it. And I can tell you about some bad habits which will keep you from doing this.

102

Experience

One of these bad habits is spending too much time reading "so what" stories and news accounts. I know people who bury their heads in newspapers and magazines from the time they start home on a commuter train until the end of the evening, and then start with the same bill-of-fare the next morning on their way to work. I know others who spend all evening in front of the TV set. I would agree that you should keep up-to-date on what is happening, but I find it takes a limited amount of reading and viewing time to do this and you can use the rest of your time for planned programs of study.

I think also that you should read some books and I hope you will keep the books you read so that you can look back at them at the end of the year. The books can cover a wide range of fields and still be relevant to the practice of management. In any case, I hope you will constantly push yourselves to learn from books and other sources.

And there are many other ways you can waste your time—too many cocktail parties, too much mowing of the lawn, too great a commitment to family togetherness, too many politically-important golf matches, too many community activities. (Not that all of these things, in moderation, are bad; but they can easily become all-absorbing of your energies.)

103

Experience

The Planned Pause

I think it is vitally important that during your "experience" period you should have planned pauses in your life, either during vacations, weekends, early in the morning, or when you have time to yourself. These should be periods when you can reflect on what you have been seeing and reading.

Some of you may want to return to a university environment to talk over what you are learning with some of your professors. In any case, particularly after I started my own business, I always tried to get away for two extended vacations a year. It was during these so-called vacations that I did much of my business planning and much of the thinking which led to new policies for our company. One, for instance, was the planning of Inland's first paper mill, which was one of the first to be opened after the war. And I commend this. During these reflective pauses in your life I hope you will extract the meaning from what you have seen and read so that it really becomes part of you and not just a mass of information that you hope some day to process.

And so, to summarize what I have been saying: during this period of "residency," you are going to have to pay a price for your own development. And I hope that most of you will be willing to pay this price. You are setting out to learn the most difficult profession in America—the profession of managing. And there are no shortcuts.

104

Experience

I am sure you must wonder why it takes years of experience to develop this ability to deal with people effectively. You may wonder why, with your fine education, you can't become a company president within the next five years. And I guess my answer to you is that you must learn first to deal with people, to command their imagination and their loyalty. And this takes much time—and lots of people—and a willingness to be immersed in the life of the organization.

And now to the climax you have been waiting for, I imagine—your taking over of a major responsibility. I keep wondering as I look at you how you are going to act after you have developed the capacity to manage. Will you have the discipline, the courage, the physical strength, and, above all, the imagination to take on the responsibilities of a leader in an organization?

I have been telling you that during the initiation and experience stages you will need to conform in order to learn how the organization functions. I have also told you that you should understand the wisdom that has made the organization you are in successful. And now I am going to reverse myself to tell you that in the end, to succeed as a leader, you will need to be a creative non-conformist. In other words, you're going to use a predictable organization to accomplish novelty. This capacity to use order to achieve change is a rare ability. Will you have it?

105

Experience

At this stage, if you have this ability, you will want major responsibility, and not because you are going to get paid more for it. You may hesitate to believe this, but I really don't think I have ever done anything in my life because of the money I was going to get from it. Don't bargain too hard for money. Bargain for the chance to carry real responsibility, and the money will follow automatically.

When I started my business some forty years ago I didn't do it solely for financial gain. I did it because I needed to do it. And, I think that every man who's a manager must have the will to manage. Once you have proved that you can carry real responsibility, you will have so many opportunities to use this demonstrated capacity in different endeavors that your company is going to reward you handsomely in order to keep you.

When you get to this stage of your life you will understand the organization so well that you will know how to use its regulations without being so completely a part of it that it does your thinking for you. In other words, you will be a non-conformist, using an organization of largely conforming people to pursue new and different goals. And this is a gaint-size task. This will make you a top manager and not just a member of middle management.

You will have the ability to understand and feel the way an organization functions and still be somewhat independent of it in your own thinking.

106

Experience

This is the supreme challenge a manager faces. This is why true managers are so scarce. And this is why so few people now go all the way to the top in industry. It requires an unusual combination of abilities.

The Excitement of Change

Once you get to this stage you will be involved in the most exciting activity the world has ever known —the profitable management of change. Each decade in the last sixty years is marked by as much change as formerly occurred in a century. So, in a sense, you have already lived two hundred years. Your job will be to lead organizations successfully towards profitable new goals, to make the bets on the new technologies, to learn how to handle the new wave of graduates coming from the colleges —in other words, to make history happen. I can think of nothing that will be as exciting as this.

And so today I welcome you to the world of activity, to a world that is more exacting and more demanding than your teachers have ever been. This is *really* a commencement and I repeat what I said before—you know so little of what you need to succeed that you had better start learning fast and keep at it for the rest of your life, or you will be left at the starting gate. Good luck to you in your exciting activities in the years to come.

Experience

Profit

"In the history of the world the struggle for power has produced more casualties on the battlefield of life than the struggle for profit or the drive for money. Given the frailties of mankind, I think the drive for profit is the least damaging and the most humanitarian of all the **effective** ways to get things done."

On July 11, 1968 Herman C. Krannert returned to Purdue to deliver a Founders' Day address to students in the Master's and Doctoral Programs of The Krannert Graduate School of Industrial Administration.

Profit

IT is a pleasure for me to come back to the Purdue campus to deliver another of my annual lectures. In the seven years I have been doing this, Dean Weiler tells me that over one thousand engineers and scientists have received their Master's Degree from our School. And it is gratifying to see how much progress has been made in the building of the facilities and the developing of your program. Even though I realize how sophisticated and advanced many of the subjects are that you are taking, I still think that the basic problems in business have not changed during the sixty years I have been in business. And, therefore, I hope you will understand when I talk to you about something fundamental, which is very close to my heart—and that is the role of profit in business.

Profit Defined:

Before I go further I want to define profit: According to Webster, profit is "The excess of returns over expenditures in a transaction or series of transactions. Specifically, the excess of the selling price of the goods over their costs." This sounds very simple, but let me tell you that it is not easy to face

111

Profit

competition year after year and still earn a profit. And as I listen to the speeches businessmen are giving these days, I hear more about the social responsibilities of businessmen than I do about their profit-making responsibilities. Properly defined, I don't think there is any difference. And I would not want you to assume that I'm against your participating in community activities. Indeed, I hope you involve yourselves energetically in the creating of a better society; but I hope also that you will never apologize for making a profit. Today I shall argue that if you do pursue profit relentlessly you will be making a contribution to the growth and development of the American economy. Of course, when I talk about profit I am not referring to the "quick buck" artist, but rather to the responsible businessman who is thinking about profit in the longrun.*

Before I develop this argument, however, I would like to talk about the philosophical meaning of profit. When a man can make profit it means that the returns from the activity are greater than the costs. In this sense, almost any activity can be judged by the profitability. As you know, Mrs. Krannert and I have been involved in the develop-

---

*Today, with the complexity of business and the encroachment of Government into business, it is highly important that the ground rules are closely defined—not only by Government Agencies, but by (1) the most competent business legal counsel, and (2) specialized accounting counsel—but more of this in a later speech.

112

Profit

ment of a number of new projects such as this School. During the last year we have been building a new Center for the Performing Arts at the University of Illinois and whenever we embark on one of these projects we ask ourselves whether—in a larger sense—the activity is profitable. We feel sure that the Center for the Performing Arts will prove to be a profitable venture. It will bring culture and pleasure to the students of Illinois and to the people in the surrounding communities.

The new art museum in Indianapolis, in the process of being built and in which we are vitally, and financially, interested, will also be a profitable undertaking, as will the Krannert Pavilion in the new Indiana University Hospital located at the Medical Center in Indianapolis. All these projects and many others in which we have an interest will add to the culture in the Midwest. And, indeed, as I look at you today and think of the many exciting things you will be doing in industry, I am inclined to think that the Krannert Graduate School is a profitable operation. And when Dean Weiler tells me the salaries you are commanding, I realize that the business community also approves of our project. And this is the main test.

So I am going to argue that the search for profit, whether in business or in community affairs, is a rational man's way of deciding whether or not something is worth doing. If you can't make profit from an activity—again, using profit in the larger

113

sense—you may be sure that the activity is not worth doing. In fact, if you persist in doing something which is not profitable, you will be irrational, whimsical and irresponsible. Actually, every businessman owes it to his associates, his workers, and his stockholders to make a profit. He really doesn't have the right to use their resources to make things for which people are unwilling to pay a price high enough so that a profit is earned. Or, looking at it another way, if a businessman is consistently losing money, he cannot justify keeping the men and machines together to produce whatever product he is selling.

Profit: The Admission Price to the Future

Profits are particularly important in a dynamic economy such as ours. New products and new processes are always challenging old ones; and it is a truism that very few products are profitable for a very long time. Therefore, I am going to argue that profits are the *admission price to the future*. In fact, it has been said that profits are usually earned on products which are already in the process of becoming obsolete.

I remember when we had just finished our first paperboard mill in Macon, Georgia—a sixteen million dollar project in 1946—our manager was showing it to me very proudly. He said it was the lowest-cost and most modern mill in the industry,

114

and, although it shocked him, I told him right then
—"Your mill is already obsolete and it is going to
become more obsolete each year. You had better
make profit on it now so that you will have the
money to add improvements as competition forces
the industry to modernize." And as I look back on
the twenty-two years since we built our first mill,
I must say that I was right. You must continue to
improve and develop new products. Some companies state that they have ten per cent or more turn-
over of products each year. Unless you can make a
profit on the products and factories you have now,
you won't have the credit or the markets which will
give you the opportunity to build new and modern
facilities. You will be powerless to face the future.
*Profit is the springboard which propels you into the
future.* Without profit you will just drop off the
edge of the pool into the water and drown.

You hear a great deal these days about the
need for long-range planning. And I agree that
every businessman must be thinking about how he
is going to adjust to the future. Indeed, it has been
my practice to spend long vacations thinking about
changes in my industry and the way we, as a company, would adjust to them. This thinking period,
uninterrupted by conferences or telephone calls,
permits the executive to plan constructively. Many
companies, like International Business Machines,
have reserved rooms which they call "Think
Rooms" which give the top executives and planners

115

uninterrupted time to plan for profit. These "Think Rooms" complement rooms reserved for conferences, or "Talk Rooms." But don't ever let your long-range planning blur the drive for profit out of your present facilities. Unless you can make a profit from the facilities and the organization you have, there is no point in doing long-range planning. There is just no easy way to get from HERE to THERE.

Profit: A Legitimate Goal

And so I am going to try to make my case as strong as I can and say that making a profit is an *imperative* which you cannot ignore if you are going to be successful in business. But I want to say also that you should always be concerned with doing a quality job for your customers. You will never get very far in our American economic system by selling shoddy merchandise. Quality and service must be built in if your markets are going to be there in the future. Customers have long memories. Nor can you make profit by undermining the morale of your workers, because they also have long memories. And so I am going to repeat—*profit, in a longrun sense, is a completely legitimate goal for you to pursue as a businessman.* I hope you will all be profit-minded.

Competition is so rough these days that to survive you will have to build what I call "plus factors" into your products. That is, you must give

116

Profit

quality, good service, and dependable deliveries. You must know your costs and you must have the confidence and salesmanship to ask a price which includes a profit. Very few businessmen can squeeze enough fat out of their costs to make the kind of profit which will give them a ticket to the future. Profit of the kind we are talking about is based on relationships with customers and suppliers which give you some room to move around. You are not just another competitor. You are something special. And this is based on fair play. As I look at my sixty years in business, I can make no case for the person who thinks he can make a profit by cheating. It just doesn't work that way. There are many who try, but they don't last; and I want you to be the kind of businessman who lasts.

Profit: A Management Tool

Now I want to change my emphasis and talk about profit as a management tool. We sometimes forget that business is a human activity. It involves the emotions of men and women. Very little has ever been accomplished by people who are merely obeying orders. If you are going to succeed you are going to need more than a man's "brain-power;" you are going to need his "heart-power" as well. And the task you are going to face in the organization of any business activity is to enlist the creative powers of people and not just their routine performance.

117

Profit

You will want people working for you who think of different ways to make a profit—while they are shaving, driving to work, having lunch. You will want them to think and breathe "profit" and not just treat profit-making as an interesting activity. You will want people who are genuinely committed to making a profit.

Let me share with you some strategies I have used to test the people working with me to see whether they are really committed. When a man comes to me with a new project which he wants very much to see initiated, I say "NO." And if he goes away and doesn't come back I know he wasn't committed. In fact, I carry it further than that: I say "NO" three times and if he comes back for the fourth time and is still convinced he is right, I am inclined to say "YES," providing he controls his expense. You would be surprised how many "Nervous Nellies" fall by the wayside. But the managers who are really convinced they are right, despite my objections, are the ones who will get the job done. They are the ones with the courage and strength to face many pitfalls in any new project. I know that this sounds like an odd way to make a decision; but let me tell you right here that it works. I can't emphasize too strongly the importance of "heart-power." It is probably the most important ingredient in business. Unless you get this kind of commitment from your people, you are not really going to succeed. And the real question is how can we use

118

Profit

profit as a management tool to get this kind of creative enthusiasm. Let me give you three rules:

1. Make sure that the goals you give each man at every level of the organization are clear and forthright so that he really understands the target.

2. Then give him independence or, in a sense, "distance" from his boss so he feels he is responsible and not just a "yes" man.

3. Have a definite reward system and generously reward the people who get the job done and eliminate those who don't.

Profit: A Source of Independence

How are these three rules related to the drive for profit? Profit is a clear target. If you give a man ten different goals he never knows which is most important. When profit is used it is a single figure; it blends the multiple goals involved in each activity. One man can pay less attention to the production line and more to selling and succeed. Another man can emphasize production and play down accounting and still succeed. The profit figure tells you on balance whether one person's mix of activities is better than another's. It reduces many goals to a common denominator.

119

I have always thought in this connection that it is important to have an accounting system which measures profit at many different centers in a business. Sometimes, I must admit, this is difficult and we have to accept some compromises. But every manager should be able to look at a figure which measures, even in a rough fashion, the contribution he is making to the profit of a business. Possibly the computer will finally give these figures. If it can produce a profit figure—or something which serves as a profit figure for every level of business—just think what this can mean. Even complex businesses can be managed as a whole series of interrelated smaller businesses, each with its own monthly, or even weekly, profit and loss statements. My own view is that we are just on the edge of some startling developments in accounting which are going to make profit measurements more important than they have ever been in the past.

Secondly, profit figures in a business can make a man independent of his immediate superior. I can remember as a young man, when I became a plant manager in the Sefton Box Company, I wanted to do things very differently from the way they had been done. I was careful at first, as I hope you will be, to follow the rules; but after I had been there a while I had confidence that so long as I was producing profits I could do things the way I wanted to do them. It gave me some "distance" from my boss because the profit figures showed I was doing a good

120

Profit

job. And I want the people working for me to have that same kind of independence and opportunity.

Profit: A Protection Against Bureaucracy

Thirdly, if you use profits as a measuring device you will be able to appraise your subordinates more objectively. I have found that supervisors frequently are afraid to appraise their subordinates. They seem to fear either praising a man or criticizing him. And one of the things you are going to have to learn is how to reward and penalize. If you don't do this you will find that your business will be run as a comfortable club with everyone getting promoted on the basis of seniority. And in the long-run your business will not survive. I realize that you aren't going to be perfect on this count—nobody is. But if you have some profit measurements to use which both you and your subordinates can look at together, you will be much more able to do this very difficult job. Profit measurements are essential to keep a business from becoming bureaucratic.

I want to enlarge on this because as I look back on my years in business I realize again that all human organizations tend to deteriorate and become bureaucratic—that is, they are run by rules and seniority. But this is a lazy way to operate and it leads to all kinds of subtle abuses. (This way of operating seems at first sight to be humanitarian because nobody is being hurt or judged too harshly.) Your subordinates will try to figure out what you want in advance and then tell you what they think you want to hear. They will find effective ways to compliment you, figuring that any kind of political activity will earn them some preference. Or they may join your country club and make sure that they get to have a drink with you. They will try to succeed without accomplishment, and this is the real corruption of any bureaucratic organization, whether in Government or business.

I could go even further and point out that business always involves risk-taking, and at every level. And nobody is going to take the risk of violating even one of the minor rules in an organization unless there is a clearly defined profit payoff from the successful taking of risks.

Profit: An Encouragement to Risk-Takers

One of the biggest jobs you are going to have as a businessman is to hold together a team of risk-taking, innovative, creative people. And if you take the easy way out, which is to manage a business bureaucratically, you lose these risk-taking people. They will go to places where they can demonstrate their courage and imagination and be recognized. It is true that in a profit-oriented organization life won't be as smooth and you may have around you

122

some guys with rough edges. But this is what you want so long as their performance can be measured by their contribution to profit.

Profit: Consistent with Community Responsibilities of Businessmen

I would hope also that you would be active in community activities, serve on hospital boards, Community Fund drives, service clubs—and all of the other welfare projects which make up the fabric of a community. You will find these activities rewarding and, indeed, I don't see how you can be responsible businessmen without taking your full measure of responsibility for the community you are living in. But what I am arguing is that you shouldn't think of your life as divided into two parts—the useful part while serving your community and the selfish part while earning a profit. Both kinds of activity are important. Both are useful and necessary.

To return to profit-making—may I point out here that the struggle for power in politics or an executive suite is not as dignified an activity as the struggle for profit. Too often the person struggling for political power will do so by selling his integrity and not his demonstrated capacity to do something. In fact, in the history of the world the struggle for power has produced more casualties on the battlefield of life than the struggle for profit or the drive

123

Profit

for money. Given the frailties of mankind, I think the drive for profit is the least damaging and the most humanitarian of all the *effective* ways to get things done.

Profit: A Source of Managerial Mobility

And let me point out also that if you can demonstrate that you can earn a profit there is always a market for your services. You will never be dependent on any one organization. And this, too, will add to your sense of confidence and well-being. I realized this years ago when I had a disagreement with the company I was working for. The fact that that I had earned a profit made it possible for me to successfully seek and obtain the manpower and the credit I needed to start a new business.

I think we face a new danger these days—that of awarding jobs to people on the basis of their educational credentials. If we do this we shall be like the old Chinese dynasties which awarded jobs on the basis of the ability of people to memorize the great sayings of the past. And there is some danger of becoming a credentials-oriented economy in which everybody expects to be appointed to positions on the basis of their educational achievements. This won't work. An economy which does this may produce some good poets, but not good plumbing, or good boxes.

124

Profit

With profit as a goal, we keep our society open not only to the people who can think, but those who can act as well. We don't have to be concerned about a man's beginnings or his alma mater. If he can do the job and produce profits, we can use him. The gray-flannel-suit boys with their MBA's or other fancy-looking credentials will not be able to take over American business unless they can perform. Please understand, I am not downgrading education. Education will make it possible for a businessman to analyze his problems more effectively and to lay out successful courses of action. I am confident your education will help you, but it will not guarantee success. In the end, it will be performance and not the degrees after your name that will count.

In my day there were many flamboyant, dramatic people who helped to create the industry I am in. Their calling card was the profitability of their activities and they needed nothing else. They demonstrated that they could do a job. As you go into the world I hope you are going to represent this Krannert tradition and not rest on your laurels as a man with a Master's Degree. I hope they will say of you that you know how to hold an organization together to create a profit. And if they can say this of you, it will mean that you are making a social contribution as well.

125

Profit

Conclusions:

In the summing up, then, may I repeat: profit, defined in a longrun sense, as a goal of business behavior, is more humanitarian and more sustaining than many of the vague noble-sounding goals that men like to talk about. Profit gives a clear measurement of performance as a means of organizing a business and does *not* create a society of "yes men." It frees people to be themselves, giving them a way to prove they are right.

Many of you are about to take your first job and I want to state my position bluntly—you have two general assignments when you enter the business world. The first is to help your employer make a profit, and the second is to get involved in a meaningful way with community activities. Both of these activities are important; and I don't want you to think that just because earning a profit involves money it is socially less important than helping to solve some of our awesome social problems. Only profitable companies can really help solve the problems of America as we face the future.

So my advice to you is to figure out what will make profit—in a longrun sense—for your employer. And then apply yourselves in such a way that he will see that you are really making a contribution to what must be his major problem—

126

Profit

namely, the establishing of a strong financial base which he can use to attack the future and maintain a healthy society. Both of these activities are exciting and rewarding. GOOD LUCK TO YOU AS YOU TACKLE THE NEW WORLD OF BUSINESS.

Profit

Management

". . . I cannot emphasize too strongly that you, as the generalist, the business-man, the politician, the administrator, whoever you are, have to MAKE UP YOUR OWN MIND. You cannot run a business by committee. You can—and you must —use the expertise of your specialists, but you must have the guts to make the final decisions and to implement those decisions. Remember, only you—not the committee, the lawyer, the tax accountant or the industrial engineer—are to blame if your decision is wrong. In the end, it is you, the generalist, who is respon-sible. Indeed, when you think of it, all of the generalists combined really run the world—not the experts."

On July 29, 1968 Herman C. Krannert returned to the Krannert Graduate School of Industrial Administration at Purdue University to deliver what was to become his last address to a graduating class in the professional master's program.

Management

 T ODAY is a particularly happy occasion for me—
and I hope, for you. This is the eighth year for
this series of lectures which I look forward to each
year. Moreover, I am aware of the fact that you
are but two weeks away from your graduation,
poised and ready to spring into the exciting world
of business. So this Founders' Day address really
takes on a double significance for me, and I am
deeply honored to have this privilege. What follows
in my remarks may shock you or disappoint you
or excite you. Whatever the case, I hope it will
stimulate your thinking about your future, perhaps
from a different point of view than you have considered until now.

A Statement of the Problem

Today I want to talk to you about a problem which
must be of real concern to you.

Should you be—

>A specialist working in a staff job, or
>A line manager responsible for the opera-
>tion of a business?

So that we can clearly differentiate between the
two, let us consider these obvious differences: the
line manager—or the generalist—is responsible for
the success of any operation. He has *authority* and

131

responsibility for making a profit. In short, his job is to get things done, whether it is making a profit or running a hospital, a university or a city.

On the other hand, the staff person—or specialist—has responsibility for his expertise only. He can advise, guide, assist, counsel and help line people, but he is not responsible for the end result of a business operation.

To put it another way, line managers—or generalists—execute plans, while staff members—or specialists—assist when needed by helping to develop plans.

Your career choice is further complicated by recruiting talk. Frequently, such talk describes staff jobs as offering comfortable hours, beautiful home offices, contact with top managers and the promise that you are going to be a key man immediately upon joining the company.

At the same time, a recruiter looking for a potential line manager will talk to you about the need for being *completely* familiar with his industry and that, more often than not, his training program requires that you start as an assistant foreman on the third shift. And that hardly sounds glamorous to you—or to me, for that matter.

As I look at you today, I suspect your career choice is even further complicated because you have been exposed to many specialists among this faculty. One is an expert in finance; another in industrial management; still another in production. And this must make you wonder whether you, too, shouldn't become a specialist of some kind.

132

Management

I Employ Specialists

Let me say that I have high regard for specialists—or department managers. I have many in my business—lawyers, accountants, labor negotiators, industrial engineers. And, of course, we are constantly turning to experts outside the business. We would never think of making an important move without expert counsel from the outside. In fact, I have such high regard for these people that I asked my lawyer[1] and my accountant[2] to give me statements on the appropriate relationship between an expert and a businessman. This lecture reflects many of their ideas.

Specialists Should Not Run Anything

To be really blunt about the matter, let me say categorically that I do not believe a specialist should ever run anything—be it a business, a hospital, a university, or even a governmental agency. I have some real doubts that a specialist should have the last word on a health problem, or a general on a military problem. *The good of the whole cannot be left to the specialist who has, of necessity, concentrated intensely on but a part of it.*

The Role of the Generalist

Instead I am going to suggest that there is a tremendous role for the generalist—the business man-

---

1. *Robert S. Ashby—Barnes, Hickam, Pantzer & Boyd*
2. *Raymond A. Hoffman—Price Waterhouse & Company*

Management

ager who listens to the experts, takes full account of what is advanced, but then makes up his own mind and makes a decision. For instance, if your health is involved, only *you* can decide whether walking ten miles a day to develop a heart that will last five years longer is worthwhile. As a citizen, only you can decide whether you want—as a taxpayer and a businessman—to spend an extra 20 billion dollars on a defense system in order to be 3 per cent more nearly certain that you will not be attacked by the enemy. It is the generalist, the businessman—citizen—administrator, who must make the final decision.

Experts See the World Through Their Specialties

Therefore, I will argue that you, as a young businessman, should not prepare to be a specialist. I know when I say this that I am going to disagree with some of your other advisors, but I think at my age, and with my experience, I have the right to disagree with them.

Let me explain further: the experts—on taxes, finances, and law—tend to see the world through the lens of their specialties. Many times the tax lawyer—and I must say that in these days you must always consult your tax lawyer on everything—is prone to see an Internal Revenue Service auditor in back of every woodpile. He is not entirely wrong, of course, but you can't have your life dominated by exclusive attention to taxes.

I'm sure you all remember the story about the three blind men holding different parts of the ele-

Management

phant, and not one of them being able to imagine the elephant in his entirety. I would hesitate to say that specialists are blind, but I might say that they tend to overemphasize the importance of their specialties.

I should imagine that your college professors tend to see the answer to all business problems in terms of their own specialties. I am sure that a social. psychologist always sees the problems of business as a need for better team work. But whatever the answer to the problem—be it need for better financing, better control systems, better team work— it will be the generalist and not the expert who must make the decision.

Self-perpetuating

There are other biases of the experts which bother me. For example, each specialty develops a social club, where each specialist seeks the admiration of his fellow specialists. I am reminded a little of stamp collectors who want nothing more than to have fellow stamp collectors oooohing and aaaahing about some rare specimen. I certainly would not apply this to all lawyers, but I have known many whose sole aim in life was to be a lawyers' lawyer. I believe this is particularly true of college professors who are ranked on the basis of the articles they have written on their specialty. It is difficult to keep in mind one's part in the whole scheme of things when one is so heavily involved in a mutual-admiration society which is not too concerned with practical applications.

135

Management

Over-spending

In any business environment this has very serious implications. A specialist inside the business tends to become a spendthrift. For example, I have never seen the head of an aviation department who didn't want a bigger plane or a better plane or more planes regardless of the amount of flying done by the executives. It is not that specialists really want to be extravagant, but any expenditure on their specialty seems justified to them even without effecting cost reductions. The same thing is true of computer experts; they always want bigger computers. And in hospitals the radiologist will want the best possible X-ray equipment, even though he may use it but once or twice a year.

This tendency of specialists to spend in their own areas makes them a soft touch for other specialists who come to them insisting that they need better equipment or more company resources. It becomes "you rub my back and I'll rub yours."

Possibly the reason many hospitals and universities are so badly run is because they tend to be run by doctors and professors.

I hasten to add that I have a great deal of sympathy for the administrator's role in a university. It resembles the manager's role in industry. Both must stay on top of the demands made by the experts they hire, and they must always make the final decisions on expenditures, even though the experts claim they are the ones who can do it better.

136

Management

I have another objection to an over-reliance on specialists—or departmental managers. Usually they want too much knowledge before they are willing to make a decision. We all know that the lawyers and accountants do not practice an exact science and that the most we can hope to get from a good lawyer is a probability statement. When they give us advice they tell us what they think is most likely to happen if we follow a certain course of action. For that matter, the same thing is true of doctors. All they can really say is what they think is likely to happen; and yet, if you let them, they will put you through the most comprehensive set of examinations just to reinforce their original diagnosis.

Because these experts are selling their knowledge they usually want to be more certain than it is possible to be. And this tends to be particularly true inside businesses. The staff people are proud of their thoroughness and, if you allow it, they will study a problem to death before they give you the benefit of their judgment. So I think most decisions have to be made on the basis of a "best guess," and to insist that this be calculated to the second decimal point before quoting a price is to paralyze the whole organization. (Some historians feel that there were so many French experts debating strategy during World War II, instead of making some hard decisions, that they were an occupied country before they quit talking.) Sometimes information just isn't that important and you must have the guts to go ahead and make a decision.

137

Management

Understand, I am not saying that we should ignore the experts; but there are times, after listening to their advice, that the best thing you can do is look over your left shoulder and come up with a decision, saying—"That's final; I am not even going to consider it again."

In any case, I hope you won't do as many business men do and allow your staff people to over-study a problem. Over-justifying a new plant expenditure to the point where you never get around to doing the things you should do is the worst possible strategy.

I am reminded of that famous quote that says that if you have to see all the way to the end of any journey you will never take the first step. And this can be tragic for a business, a hospital, a university, or any other activity. Sometimes a bad decision is better than a good decision made six months too late.

Are Staff People Superfluous?

Does this mean that I am against the use of advisors or specialists in business? Are the staff people in the home office really superfluous? The answer is a clear *NO*. They *are* useful and I am in favor of making the right use of our staff people. I could not have built my business without a strong financial man at my right hand, or a good industrial engineering department; and certainly my lawyer's advice and help have been invaluable. There are ways to use these people, and I would like to tell you how you should use both your inside and out-

138

Management

side advisors when you get into a position of responsibility.

Choose Advisors Carefully

First let me give you some rules which I have followed all my life: Choose your advisors carefully and, most of all, make sure of their basic honesty. No matter how bright and able a man is, if he is willing to bend his advice to fit the answer he thinks you want, he is no good. He is nothing more than a "yes man." At the same time, you would not want a man who would try to manipulate you through the advice he gives you and who would bend his advice in such a way as to get control of you. This boils down to a question of integrity. Just because a man is a good lawyer, a good tax accountant, or a good industrial engineer doesn't make him a completely honest man.

Testing Advisors

I have various ways of testing my advisors. Frequently, after they have given me advice, I say: "O.K., I am going to do just the opposite. What will be the consequences?" If they are so committed to their original answers that they are unwilling to think about the consequences of an opposite course of action, I begin to feel they are trying to use me to accomplish their ends. Understand, I want them to tell me what they think the probable result will be from an opposite course of action. But I don't want them to threaten me into following their advice—no matter what. This is a test of their willingness to be objective and honest in appraising an entirely different course of action.

139

Management

Keep Staff Informed

Second, keep your staff people fully informed. Take them into your confidence so they know what your problems are and what you are trying to achieve. Don't keep them in the dark until you want some advice. You really can't over-inform them about the problems you are facing. And, at the same time, try to create a situation in which they can honestly say what they think should be done, even though they might think you don't want to hear what they are going to say.

Reward Honesty

In other words, if you expect them to be honest they have a right to expect you, as a businessman, to be honest in your appraisal of them. The executive who wants a "yes man" and who creates an environment in which only a "yes man" can survive obviously does himself a disservice. In such an environment he makes his decisions without accurate knowledge of the consequences and without the best advice available. The executive, while he encourages frank statements from his specialists, is never afraid to probe the basis of their conclusions or to encourage a Socratic exchange which may lead to different opinion on the part of the expert or a different interpretation of the risk on the part of the executive. If "yes men" thrive in your organization you drive out the people you really need. If you want valuable advice, make it possible for people with views different from yours to function.

140

Management

Don't Pit Your Experts Against Each Other

Third, don't pit your lawyers, tax accountants, or any outside advisors against each other. I know businessmen who try always to have two lawyers comment on every subject. And it doesn't take the lawyers long to learn this. So they do one of two things: they become overly-competitive with each other and begin to take extreme positions, or they try to cover their tracks so well you never know what they mean. People who are too competitive with each other will not keep your values in mind. They will be so anxious either to win or not to be criticized that they won't give you good service.

In Negotiation

If you use staff people to negotiate for you—and I would strongly recommend that you do—give them all the available information so that they can adequately represent you. Let me explain why I think it is wise to let them negotiate large-purchase contracts or labor union settlements. You will find that they can negotiate and then retreat to your office to talk over what should be done next. If you are doing the negotiating you will have to make a decision on the spot, which isn't usually the wise thing to do.

Initial Draft Important

Make sure that your negotiator starts with an initial draft of a contract or a settlement which is both fair and equitable and contains all of the clauses you want in the settlement. This will give him the confidence he needs to negotiate as stubbornly as

141

Management

he will need to in order to succeed. It also increases the probability that the clauses you want in the contract will be there when you finish. If there is a deadlock, your negotiator can come to you and the two of you can work out a solution which will solve the deadlock without requiring you to make a premature decision or compromise.

Lawyers Are Advocates

Remember, too, that lawyers tend to become advocates. Some of them thrive on controversy, and they become so absorbed in their advocacy that they lose their objectivity. As the businessman, you have to call the shots. You have to "run" your lawyer instead of his "running" you. And when you are confronted with what will appear to be impossible situations, change your tactics. Take a different approach. Reverse your field, if necessary— even over the strong protest of your counsel. The talents which prompt a man to choose the law for his profession are very different from the talents which prompt a businessman to choose business. The businessman must determine the objectives and, when circumstances dictate, he must also alter them.

Make Up Your Own Mind

Fourth, I cannot emphasize too strongly that you, as the generalist, the businessman, the politician, the administrator, whoever you are, have to *make up your own mind*. You can not run a business by committee. You can—and you must—use the expertise of your specialists, but then you must have

142

Management

the guts to make the final decisions and to implement those decisions. Remember, only you—not the committee, the lawyer, the tax accountant or the industrial engineer—are to blame if your decision is wrong. In the end, it is you, the generalist, who is responsible. Indeed, when you think of it, all of the generalists combined really run the world— not the experts.

Horrible Example

As a horrible example of what happens when you don't make your own decisions, we have only to recall the late John Kennedy's reliance on the Central Intelligence Agency and the military experts to tell him how the Bay of Pigs Invasion should work out. And now nobody remembers who the C.I.A. head was at that time, or the Chief of Staff. They remember only that the decision was disastrous and that it was made by the President of the United States.

Original Question

So I come back to you, the student. What does all this mean for you and for your career? Again, I think the question really is: DO YOU WANT TO BE AN EXPERT AND SPEND ALL YOUR LIFE BEING KNOWN AS AN EXPERT? OR, DO YOU WANT TO BE THE BOSS WHO RUNS THE ORGANIZATION OR SOME PART OF IT AND IS COMPENSATED ACCORDINGLY?

If you choose the job of being a generalist, of being a manager and, therefore, the man who uses the experts and is not used by them, you must

143

Management

expect to have some almost impossible problems to deal with. You will seldom have the sense of satisfaction that an accountant has when he finishes off the books for the year, or the lawyer has when he turns out a good brief on a case. So you will probably be involved in many compromise solutions of the kind that nobody will really like or understand. And half the time your victories will be the kind you won't want to talk about; they will have been just too messy.

Compromise

To use an example outside my field, the manufacturer of automobiles must make a compromise between safety and beauty. And the people who want beauty in a car won't like it and the people who want absolute safety will condemn you. Yet, somebody has to decide what compromise between these two values is best to present to the American public. When you make "messy" decisions of this type, you won't get the same sense of satisfaction that you would get from developing a new program for the computer or a new market analysis of a product. Nor will you be surrounded by admiring fellow experts who can get their egos massaged at professional meetings by being elected third vice-presidents or getting medals for having made the most significant contribution to the professional literature.

If you succeed, people won't like you very well. And while success isn't everything, FAILURE ISN'T ANYTHING AT ALL. Likewise, if you fail at this

144

Management

hazardous business of reaching compromise solutions, you aren't going to be liked. Furthermore, your job will really never be finished. You will go home every night at 6:30 or 7:00, and, if you have lots of courage, you won't take any work home, knowing you must get to work early in the morning. But inevitably you will be thinking about your problems—when you are driving—shaving. Indeed most of the time. You will never have the satisfaction of knowing that your work is completely done and that you can close the books and say they balance. But, with all the compromises and lack of any clear-cut feeling of victory, YOU STILL HAVE TO WIN.

These Are Some Satisfactions

There are some real satisfactions to be gained from being a generalist. There is a score card which is kept on you (I talked about that in my last speech here) and that is the making of profit. For the businessman who is a responsible member of the community, who is careful to live within the spirit of the law and who is concerned about the long-run welfare of our society, there is a real satisfaction in making a profit. Because he knows that making a profit is the measure of his contribution to solving the complex problems facing our society, he welcomes this yardstick. A profit performance demonstrates his ability to use the knowledge inherent in the minds of his experts, but not to be used by them.

145

Management

High Excitement

At the end of your career you will be able to say: I have run the company; I have created an organization; I have managed a city—and the city is better than it would have been had people like myself walked away from the job and left it to the experts.

If you choose to be a generalist—and I hope you will take the risk of starting your business career as the assistant foreman on the third shift knowing full well that this is not to be your life's work—you will come to experience a special high excitement and reward of advancement. Putting a whole project together and seeing it go is an indescribable thrill of accomplishment.

This is the job of a generalist—and he is the man who hires and uses the specialists—not the reverse.

Management